Africa in Chaos

George B. N. Ayittey

St. Martin's Griffin
New York

ISBN 0-312-21787-0

Library of Congress Cataloging-in-Publication Data

Ayittey, George B. N., 1945-
    Africa in chaos / by George B.N. Ayittey.
        p. cm.
    Includes bibliographical references (p.) and index.
    ISBN 0-312-16400-9 (cloth)
    ISBN 0-312-21787-0 (paper)
    1. Africa—Economic conditions—1960- 2. Africa—Economic policy.
3. Africa—Social conditions—1960- 4. Africa—Politics and
government—1960-I. Title.
HC800.A981997
330.967'032—dc21
                                                    97-11236
                                                      CIP

First published in hardcover in the United States of America in 1998
First St. Martin's paperback edition: February 1999

PERMISSIONS

Quotations in chapter 5 from pages 151 and 165 of D. K. Fieldhouse, *Black Africa, 1945-80,* 1986, reprinted by permission of Routledge.

Quotations in chapter 5 from pages 161, 162, and 167 of *Politics and Society in Contemporary Africa* by Naomi Chazan, Robert Mortimer, John Ravenhill, and Donald Rothchild, reprinted by permission of Lynne Riener Publishers.

Quotations from *West Africa* magazine in chapters 5, 8, and 9 are reproduced by permission of *West Africa* magazine.

Quotations from *The Washington Post* in chapters 6 and 7 reproduced by permission of *The Washington Post.*

Quotation in chapter 7 from *The Wall Street Journal,* 22 October 1996, p. A22, reproduced by permission of *The Wall Street Journal.*

Quotations in chapter 8 from pages 95, 97, 98, 166, and 201 of *The Road to Hell: The Ravaging Effects of Foreign Aid and International Charity* by Michael Maren reprinted by the permission of Michael Maren and The Free Press.

Quotations in chapter 8 from *TV Guide,* 24 May 1986, p. 3, reproduced by permission of *TV Guide.*

Quotation in chapter 8 from *The Washington Times,* 3 March 1996, p. B2, reproduced by permission of *The Washington Times.*

DEDICATION

Algeria: Berber singer, Lounes Matoub, gunned down on 26 June 1998 at a roadblock on the road to his village in Beni Douala for his outspoken criticisms of the government and Islamic groups. The Armed Islamic Group claimed responsibility.

Burkina Faso: Professor Guillaume Sessouma and Doin Redan, assassinated by security forces.

Burundi: Meldior Ndadaye, the civilian president baynotted to death in 1993 by the Tutsi-dominated military.

Ethiopia: Assefa Maru, an unrelenting advocate of freedom of association and individual rights, shot in cold blood by security forces in May, 1997; Alebatchew Goji, beaten and tortured to death while in police custody in July 1994. Mustafa Idris, who mysteriously disappeared in 1994.

Gabon: Nang-Veca Bryce, journalist at Radio Liberte, beaten and tortured in detention in 1994. Francois D'Assisses Obiang-Ebe and Antoine Mba Ndong, both killed by security forces in 1994.

The Gambia: J.B. Ayitey, a Ghanaian teacher who was abducted by three gunmen from his home at Brikama on the night of June 2, 1996 and sentenced to death by firing squad.

Ghana: Tommy Thompson, the intrepid publisher of Free Press. Paul Ansah, a fearless crusader of freedom and a columnist for The Ghanaian Chronicle. Ahunu Honger, Yaw, and the two other Kume Preko martyrs brutally killed on May 12, 1995.

Guinea: Alseny Limam Kourouma, tortured to death in police custody in August, 1993.

Lesotho: Selometsi Baholo, killed by security forces in Jan 1994.
Liberia: Brian Garnham, the British manager of Vilab, a biomed-
              ical research laboratory and colony for chimpanzees)
              brutally killed by the Armed Forces of Liberia in Jan
              1993.
Mauritania: Cheik Saad Bouh Kamara, president of Mauritanian
              Human Rights Association. The over 500 black Mauri-
              tanians, largely Halpulaar and Soninke, who were killed
              in military custody during 1990 and 1991.
Mozambique: Andre Filipe, a RENAMO guard beaten to death while
              in police custody in July 1994.
Nigeria: Chief Moshood Abiola, the winner of the 1993 presi-
              dential elections, who died in jail. Professor Claude
              Ake, a seasoned and gallant critic of military dictator-
              ships; Kudirat Abiola, savagely gunned down by gov-
              ernment-hired assailants, while her husband, Chief
              Moshood Abiola, was in jail; Tai Solaren, an ardent
              campaigner for people's rights; Ken Saro-Wiwa, and the
              eight Ogoni leaders, brutally hanged in November
              1995; Tunde Oladepo, a senior editor of The Guardian,
              who was gunned down in his Ogun State home in front
              of his wife and children on Feb 27, 1998.
Kenya: Jaramogi Ajuma Oginga Odinga, a stalwart in the search
              for democracy and justice. Dr. Frederick Shikuku Has-
              inde, killed on June 26, 1994, just 24 hours before he
              was declared the winner of the by-election in the
              Mathare constituency, north east of Nairobi. He was the
              first candidate in Kenyan history to win a seat posthu-
              mously. The 10 witnesses to Robert Ouko's case who
              died in mysterious circumstances, strange illnesses, or
              road accidents: Hezekiah Oyugi, Nehemiah Obati,
              James Otieno Gor, Agallo Obonyo, Ahido Agallo,
              Joseph Otieno Yogo, Pius Omolo, Sergeant Martin
              Ochwada, Vitalis George Okok, Eric James Onyango,
              Justice Fidahussein Abdullah. Dr. Ouko was murdered
              on Feb 13, 1990 and his body burned after exposing
              corruption in high government circles. Mohammed

	Amin, the TV photographer who captured those moving pictures of the Ethiopian famine.
Rwanda:	Agathe Unwingiliymana, the Hutu Prime Minister who was murdered in April 1994. Straton Byahagamba, correspondent of Radio Vatican, stabbed to death at him home by Hutu death squads in October 1993. Callixte Calisa, a journalist for the Rwandan TV shot dead in Kigali in Nov 1993; and the over 800,000 Tutsis savagely slaughtered over a 3-month period in 1994.
Somalia:	The foreign journalists, peacekeepers and U.S. Rangers killed in 1993.
South Africa:	Oliver Tambo, former president of the ANC. Chris Hani, Joe Modise, brutally assassinated in 1993. People should not be killed because of their political views, no matter how offensive they might be.
Sudan:	Abdel Meneim Rahma, opposition activist tortured to death in police custody. Khojali Osman, the world renowned musician, brutally knifed to death by a militant Islamist at the instigation of the military regime of Lt.Gen. Omar El-Bashir in November, 1994.
Tanzania:	Christopher Mtikila, leader of the Democratic Party, arrested in 1993 for "threatening" the President. Stan Katabalo, a journalist who was killed by senior politicians involved in a scandal he was exposing.
Togo:	Gaston Edeh, deputy of CAR; Tchao Idrissou, labor leader, killed by security forces in 1994. Laurent Kokou Agbemavo, a lawyer, opposition MP Gaston Edeh, M. Agbakpem, an accountant at the French Bank of West Africa; Kpakpo Atcha, director of security at Lome Airport who were all brutally gunned down in 1994 and 1995.
Uganda:	Hussein Musa Njuki, founder and editor of Assalam newspaper, who was killed by security agents on August 28, 1995 for his outspoken criticism of human rights violations and the suppression of democracy. Andrew Lutaakome Kayiira, a political activist who was killed in 1987. Charles Owor, the District Administra-

tor of Nebbi, who was ambushed and killed by NRA soldiers on March 13, 1993. Peter Forbes, a Canadian researcher and his colleague, John Ongom, who were murdered by government security men. Monsignor Fredrik Drandua, Catholic Bishop of Arua, who escaped an assassination attempt in 1994.

Zaire: Pierre Kabeya, a journalist abducted and shot to death in June 1994. Adolphe Kavula of the newspaper, Nsemo, beaten semiconscious by security forces, died in November 1994.

Zimbabwe: Sydney Malunga, Christopher Ushewokunze (Minister of Industry and Commerce), Johnson Ndlovu (an opposition MP) all killed in mysterious "road accidents" in 1994.

Contents

CHAPTER 9

Introduction
African Governments and OAU/ECA Proposals
Black American Proposals
Western Proposals
Radical Alternatives
Debt-Free Zone—A Digression
How the West Can Help African Reform

CHAPTER 10

Summary
Africa's Intellectuals
Intellectual Mandate for the Twenty-first Century
The Ten Commandments for African Intellectuals
Caveat Emptor

ACKNOWLEDGMENTS

On account of its extraordinary diversity—54 countries, 4 racial groups, and more than 2,000 ethnic communities—writing a book on Africa is a formidable undertaking. Any such book is bound to raise the ire of some group, not to mention that of the corrupt and repressive African governments. Were that not enough, there are the various "African constituencies" and "friends of Africa" in the West to contend with: African-Americans, African exiles, companies that do business in Africa, and aid and development agencies that run various programs in Africa. All these groups have some particular "interest" in how Africa is portrayed, as if she is being entered into some "beauty contest."

Black Americans, desirous of rediscovering their African roots, are the most vociferous of the groups. A "negative" portrayal of Africa, some blacks allege, feeds the racist myth that nothing good can come out of Africa. The Western media in particular has often been the target of frontal attacks, for allegedly perpetuating ethnocentric misconceptions about Africa by reporting only coups, civil wars, refugees, brutalities, and corruption—ignoring the "positive" events that occur daily on the continent.

This issue has become so sensitive that a mere indiscreet statement about Africa could unleash such a furor that it could obliterate the message a book seeks to deliver. Such a fate appears to have viciously struck Keith Richburg, a black American and the foreign correspondent for *The Washington Post,* who wrote *Out of America: A Black Man Confronts Africa* (Basic Books, New York: 1997).

I attended a launch and panel discussion of his book at the Freedom Forum in Rosslyn (Virginia) on 4 March 1997. The panelists were Melvin Foote, executive director of Constituency For Africa, a Washington-based non-profit organization, and Rich Mkhondo, the Washington bureau chief for independent newspapers in South Africa, including the Johannesburg daily, *The Star.* The moderator was Gwen Ifill, an NBC news correspondent, and the audience was about 40 percent black.

Richburg had written earlier about the 1994 Rwandan genocide in a *Washington Post Magazine* article. After witnessing the savage brutalities and the horrific massacres in Rwanda, Richburg had become thoroughly disgusted with man's inhumanity to man. And he made his feelings known: He was angry and disillusioned. He had taken up an assignment in Africa to learn more about the continent of his slave ancestors. How could he relate to or explain to Americans back home the hundreds of thousands of human bodies—victims of the genocide—floating down rivers in Rwanda, polluting drinking water supplies?

He was emotionally tormented. To remain "faithful to his race," he must advance a sufficiently credible explanation for the slaughter. He could not find any; this time, there were no "white devils" around to blame. Could it be that black Africans were capable of this horrific slaughter? His experiences in Rwanda and Somalia, nations that also had descended into savage anarchy, were so galling that he was forced to reconsider his own identity and the issues of slave trade as well as the meaning of Afrocentricism.

He concluded that he was glad to be an "American" and the designation "African-American" was meaningless—devoid of content. Perhaps the slave traders did him a favor by shipping his ancestors out of Africa in slave ships for America. This unguarded and intemperate statement so rankled a large segment of the African-American community that a group of black activists stormed the Freedom Forum, with daggers drawn and fangs bared, ready for combat.

When the floor was opened for questions, one could virtually feel the tension. The questions were predictable: Which whites paid him to write the book? What was his agenda? Where was the "balance" in his book? Wasn't he reinforcing his own childhood "Tarzan" image of Africa? Horrors! None of these questions had anything to do with the gist of his book—a continent's descent into hell. It is at times like these when a writer on African issues needs his "friends" and "supporters" the most.

I went through a similar searing ordeal. Like Richburg, I was also emotionally tormented by the horrific spectacles in Rwanda, forcing me to reexamine not my African identity, which I cannot change, but the entire issue of colonialism and independence. Independence was supposed to bring Africans "freedom," "peace," and "prosperity," right? What happened? These questions raced through my mind as I watched television footage of the Rwandan massacres. Of all the pictures and images, two left a gaping gash in my African psyche.

The first was televised footage of a mass burial of the victims of the 1994 Rwandan genocide that had claimed at least 800,000 lives. The bodies of hundreds of thousands of slaughtered Tutsis had floated down the Kagera River into Lake Kivu. The human carcasses were collected for mass burial in Goma, Zaire. A bulldozer had dug a deep trench and a front-end loader had scooped up a heap of dead bodies. As it lurched forward to dump its load, a hand twitched. "It's alive, it's alive!" someone screamed. Relief aid workers frantically pulled the body of a woman out of the heap, but attempts to revive her failed and she died.

I turned off the television. I could not stand it. "It must come to this?" I kept asking myself. Corpses of dead Africans being bulldozed into a mass grave in full glare of Western TV cameras? Whatever happened to "freedom from colonial rule?" I couldn't bear the thought. Out of disgust, I could say that one television scene probably did more to smash my African dignity and pride than 200 years of colonialism, but non-African blacks would probably misinterpret that statement.

The second image was an award-winning photograph by a Western journalist that showed a severely emaciated child crouching frailly on a dirt road. His eyes were glazed and his mouth open, gasping for air. A swarm of flies hovered around his face and lower lips. In the background, maintaining their distance, was a cackle of vultures, patiently waiting for the child to die.

In all these tribulations and torment, various people, both Americans and Africans, foundations, institutes, and agencies have provided me with support and encouragement. I owe each one of them a huge debt of gratitude. Deserving foremost mention is David B. Kennedy, president of the Earhart Foundation in Ann Arbor, Michigan, which provided me with funding to support field trips to Africa and research. Dr. Larry Diamond, a Senior Fellow at the Hoover Institution, Stanford University, has been extremely supportive. During my tenure at American University, I have been fortunate to receive critical reviews and encouragement from Professors Robert Lerman, Alan Isaac, Walter Parks, Robert Feinberg, and Jon Wisman, and excellent secretarial support from Lyndle Lindow, Sheila Budnyj, Sharon Childs-Patrick, Tanecia Prue, and many others in the Economics Department. The Board of Directors of The Free Africa Foundation, its staff, scholars and associates must also be mentioned, as well as Roger Ream of Fund For American Studies, and Ed Feulner of the Heritage Foundation, Ian Vasquez and Ed Crane, president of the Cato Institute.

There are many others (Americans, Canadians, South Africans, and those of other nationalities) to whom I still owe a debt of gratitude: Pierre Beaulieu, Paula Caffey, Lynne Criner, Learned Dees (NED), Tony Ellison (FAF–RSA), Robert Fox, John Fund *(The Wall Street Journal)*, Georgie Ann Geyer (nationally-syndicated columnist), Cliff Gosney, C. Paul Hilliard, Bert Holtje (my book agent), Emily Hunter, Tom Lasner, George Lister, Elis Majd, Sandy Matheson, Robert McMurray, Linda Menghetti, Ralph Moss, Audna Nicholson, Ralph Phillips, Gregory Simpkins, John Sullivan, Joe Szlavik, Jude Wanniski, and others.

Edgar Ridley, the author of *An African Answer: The Key to Global Productivity,* deserves particular mention. My numerous exchanges and discussions with him proved invaluable. They helped me to sharpen my focus and rigorize my analyses.

Last but not least have been the numerous Ghanaians and Africans who have shown unflappable support for my work and writings— especially those who came to my defense when I was being ripped apart on the internet. One of them was Oki Kwoshi Dzivenu, who posted this message at *Okyeame,* a Ghanaian forum on the Internet on 9 March 1997:

> Some people persist with the erroneous and arrogant attitude that any son or daughter of Ghana who points out what is wrong with the country and gives pointers as to how we can go about building a better country is automatically a traitor. These "Ghana-owners" think that anyone with a dissenting view ought to be insulted, vilified and called all sorts of gutter-names and discredited for anything they're associated with except the article or point of view they originally professed.

> It is very frightening that some of these "Ghana-owners" are young and "educated" folks. Imagine the culture of intolerance that will ensue if they carry this attitude into positions of power back home?

> May God continue to bless and look after what Edward Said called "energetic dissenters" like you. Otherwise we'll be doomed into a perpetual cycle of "Yessa massa," "Yessa massa"!!!

> Your biggest fan,

> Oki Dzivenu,
> Molecular Biophysics,
> University of Oxford,
> Oxford, UK.

Other Ghanaians and Africans are Dr. Emmanuel Ablo, Dominic Adu-Gyamfi, Opanyin Adu-Gyamfi, Boakye Agyarko, Felix Amankona-Diawuoh, Kobina Annan, Stanley Ansong, Dr. Isaac Amuah, Eugene Baffoe-Bonnie, Dr. Kofi Baidoo, Jerry Simpson, Kwadwo Boahene, Dr. Agyenim Boateng, Kofi Coomson *(The Ghanaian Chronicle)*, Dr. Emma Etuk, Kwaku Danso, Lily Danso, Seth Dogbe, Alex Gyedu, Charles Hamidu, Mohamed Idris, Yakubu Imdru, Karanta Kalley (WEFA), Remingius Kintu, Professor Willie Lamouse-Smith, Osbert Lartey *(The Ghanaian Chronicle)*, Dr. Charles Mensa, Fabian Makani, Steve Mallory *(The African Observer)*, Michael Molley ("Rambo"), Walusako Mwalilino, Ben. Kwaku Newmann, Sulaymang Nyang, Ablorh Odjijah, Hawa Yakubu Ogede, Helen Okpokuwuruk, John Orleans-Lindsay, Reverend G. B. K. Owusu, Mr. George Owusu, Eben Quarcoo *(Free Press)*, Michael Sackey, William and Adwoa Steel, Mamadou Traore, Tommy Thompson *(Free Press)*, Lynda Bdy Ukemenam, Professor Ernest Uwazie, Verna Warren, Marjorie Winful, Frantz Wulff-Tagoe, Dr. Kojo Yelpaala, and many others.

A special mention must be made of Meron Agonafer, an Ethiopian and administrative assistant at The Free Africa Foundation. Her diligence, steadfast support and research assistance were very much appreciated.

In the final analysis, however, the views expressed in this book are my own and any errors or misstatements are my sole responsibility.

George B. N. Ayittey, Ph.D.
Washington, D.C.—4 November 1997.

Prologue

When I was in high school in Ghana, the stock of our school's equipment, books, and materials was insufferably pathetic. We 32 students in the class had one textbook to share. Desks were fantasies we daydreamed about. The hard, sun-baked, lateritic ground was our seat. The class was conducted under a tree to which was nailed a piece of warped chalkboard.

Since an occasional downpour always resulted in a school cancellation, we were more interested in learning every step of the rain dance than the day's lesson. When that failed, one of us would climb the tree and sprinkle a few drops of water from a container. Very often this ruse would precipitate a class dismissal until the teacher finally noticed that it only seemed to "rain" around his desk—a rickety table with one leg missing, which was stolen as a prank. Once he looked up and there I was, nervously perched with the incriminating evidence.

Pure, unadulterated mischief was our credo in those early years. My younger sister, Sherry, who was in the same class, outperformed me academically. She often placed ninth in the class while I struggled at the twenty-eighth position. Of course, I was never found wanting of a battery of self-serving rationalizations. "The teacher liked her," "My dad gave her more pocket money," "You can't learn much with only one textbook to share with thirty-one others," and "A class under a tree is ridiculous" were some typical excuses. But then there occurred an event that completely changed my life.

One evening, an uncle named Paul came to visit us at home. Uncle Paul was an affable but stern type. He shepherded an older brother, Caleb (who is now deceased), and me into a room to teach us spelling. The grumbling and foot-dragging were not muted. To overcome that reluctance, he promised the equivalent of 25 cents to the one who could spell "Mississippi" and "hippopotamus" the next day. Back then, in the 1950s, that would buy two meaty candy bars or a whole meal of fried plantains and bean stew.

The following day Caleb failed the spelling test. He had lost his exercise book, he lamented. Upon being called, I stumbled a couple of times but successfully managed to spell the words. Much to my astonishment, Uncle Paul, true to his word, gave me the 25 cents.

Subsequently at school, my position in class improved steadily and dramatically: from twenty-eighth to second, surpassing Sherry. Within two years I was jumped into a class ahead of her. I went to the University of Ghana and upon graduation secured two scholarships to pursue graduate studies in either Canada or the United States. I chose Canada because the United States, in the latter part of the 1960s, was plagued by race riots in Detroit and other American cities. In 1981 I completed my Ph.D. studies in Economics at the University of Manitoba (Canada) with an overall grade point average of 4.00.

By American standards, that achievement would not be considered stupendous. After all, it did not qualify for a Rhodes or Fulbright Scholarship. In retrospect, it was made possible because someone, who was not even a certified teacher, cared enough to devote a little of his time and attention to offer an incentive, as little as 25 cents, to an incorrigible tyke. That reward, incidentally, was offered by a private individual, not by the government of Ghana.

Over the years, I have often wondered how my life would have turned out if Uncle Paul had withheld that 25 cents. My unsteady faith in the educational process probably would have been terminally shattered and my progress in life perniciously restricted for lack of adequate education. It is purely a matter of speculation at this juncture, but there would have been one certainty: This book would certainly not have emerged.

I often consider myself to be living proof that incentives do work. A little incentive can help surmount hurdles, such as having to share one textbook with thirty-one other pupils in the blazing tropical sun in Africa. Given the necessary incentives and rewards, Africans too can excel just like any other people. *The Economist* concurred: "What Africa does not lack are ordinary people who respond to the sort of incentives that ordinary people in most other countries take for granted" (4 March 1989, 14).

By Western standards, African peasants may seem to be limited by illiteracy, using "primitive and backward" tools and techniques. But the right incentives can unleash their productive and innovative energies to feed Africa and even have surpluses for export. That they are capable is borne out of the fact that, in the 1950s and 1960s, these peasants were doing exactly that: feeding Africa and exporting food.

In the same vein, given a carefully crafted system of incentives and a conducive intellectual environment, the black African mind can develop. The notion that Africans are intellectually inferior is offensive mythology. The illiterate Ashanti peasants were able to use their raw native intelligence to construct a wooden loom with which they continue to weave one of the world's most beautiful hand-woven cloths, the *kente*. If the black African intellect can produce the *kente,* it also can be developed to produce more Nobel laureates, more writers, more novelists, more poets, and, above all, more economists to devise solutions to Africa's economic infirmities. What are needed are sets of inducements, conscious efforts at encouragement, a multitude of "25-cent" incentives, and a congenial intellectual environment. But rather incongruously, what African governments often mete out is precisely the converse. When their subjects try on their own to excel or to devise solutions to their countries' problems, they are not rewarded with praise, pecuniary awards, or even 25 cents. Instead, they are brutalized with arrest, detention, or death. It is this intellectual barbarism, perhaps more than anything else, that lies at the heart of the African crisis.

CHAPTER 1

Introduction: The Lost Continent

Mobutu and his cronies have turned Zaire into little more than a bankrupt kleptocracy. They bear more allegiance to their own bank balances than to their country's future. And what makes the tragedy of Mobutu's Zaire so much worse is that it is so unnecessary. The country should be prosperous. It has fertile lands, enormous mineral resources and a talented population. Instead, it is poor, even by African standards.

> —David Rieff, *The Washington Post*
> (16 November 1996, C1)

Nigeria, the comatose giant of Africa, may go down in history as the biggest country ever to go directly from colonial subjugation to complete collapse, without an intervening period of successful self-rule. So much promise, so much waste; such a disappointment. Such a shame. Makes you sick.

> —Linus U. J. Thomas-Ogboji,
> *African News Weekly* (26 May 1995, 6).

Africa is four times the geographical size of the United States and, with its approximately 770 million people, has more than thrice that of the United States. It is a continent with immense untapped mineral wealth. Africa has "40 percent of the world's potential hydroelectric power supply; the bulk of the world's diamonds and chromium; 30 percent of the uranium in the non-communist world; 50 percent of the world's gold; 90 percent of its cobalt; 50 percent of its phosphates; 40 percent of its platinum; 7.5 percent of its coal; 8 percent of its known petroleum reserves; 12 percent of its natural gas; 3 per cent of its iron ore; and millions upon millions of acres of untilled farmland. There is not another continent blessed with such abundance and diversity" (Lamb, 1983, 20). Angola, for example, "contains an estimated 11 percent of the world's known reserves of diamonds. Its diamonds are stunning: at an average price of about $140 a carat, with some reaching $350, they are second in quality only to Namibia's, and more than 12 times more valuable than Australia's" (*The Economist,* 14 September 1996, 68).

In addition, Africa has 64 percent of the world's manganese, 13 percent of its copper, and vast bauxite, nickel, and lead resources. It also accounts for 70 percent of cocoa, 60 percent of coffee, 50 percent of palm oil, and 20 percent of the total petroleum traded in the world market, excluding the United States and Russia. The tourism potential of Africa is enormous. Unrivaled wildlife, scenic grandeur, and pristine ecology constitute Africa's third great natural resource after agriculture and mineral wealth.

Yet, paradoxically, a continent with such abundance and potential is inexorably mired in steaming squalor, misery, deprivation, and chaos. It is in the throes of a seemingly incurable crisis. Eating has become a luxury for many Africans, and hunger stares them squarely in the face. "We cannot afford even a meal a day," said Andre Miku, a retired mechanic in Kinshasa, Congo. "We try to keep at least the children fed" (*The Washington Post,* 14 September 1998, A16). In Nigeria,

> Many homes cannot afford one meal a day, talk less of the ideal three square meals. Millions of Nigerian children are out of school because their parents cannot afford tuition fees or books. Many families do not have shelter. Nigerians are now clothed like destitutes. There is constant fuel scarcity. The healthcare system is a shambles. Communications are nothing to write home about. Power supply is ridiculously epileptic. The roads are in terrible condition. Intra and inter-city transportation is a nightmare. Robbers, and assassins are on the loose. Prostitution has become a pastime. Able-bodied Nigerians are roaming the streets jobless" (*Post Express,* 14 May 1998, 2).

Nigeria's own head of state, Gen. Abdusallam Abubakar, himself admitted the serious economic deterioration for the country as a whole:

"Every human-welfare and development index measuring the well-being of our people is on the decline. Currently, we are the world's 13th-poorest nation. Given our resource endowments, this sorry state is a serious indictment" (*The Economist,* 29 August 1998, 45).

When Africa gained its independence from colonial rule in the 1960s, the euphoria that swept across the continent was infectious. It was best evinced by the late Dr. Kwame Nkrumah, the first black president of Ghana. "We shall achieve in a decade what it took others a century . . . and we shall not rest content until we demolish these miserable colonial structures and erect in their place a veritable paradise," he declared exuberantly (Nkrumah, 1957, 34).

The nationalists who won freedom for their respective countries were hailed as heroes, swept into office with huge parliamentary majorities, and deified. Currencies bore their portraits and statues were built to honor them. Criticizing them became sacrilegious and, very quickly, the freedom and development promised by Nkrumah and other African nationalists transmogrified into a melodramatic nightmare. In many countries these nationalist leaders soon turned out to be crocodile liberators, Swiss bank socialists, quack revolutionaries, and grasping kleptocrats.[1] After independence true freedom never came to much of Africa.[2] Nor did development.

For many Africans, the "paradise" promised them turned out be a starvation diet, unemployment, and a gun to the head. Disaffection and alienation set in. A spate of coups quickly swept across Africa in the early 1960s. The first occurred in the Belgian Congo on September 15, 1960, barely three months after independence. In West Africa the first coup occurred in Togo on January 13, 1963. Between 1963 and February 1966 there were 14 significant cases of military intervention in government. By 1968 there had been 64 attempted and successful interventions across Africa (Decalo, 1976, 6).

The first generation of coup leaders in the 1960s was professional soldiers who brooked zero tolerance for corruption, inefficiency, government waste, and mismanagement. They threw out the elite *bazongas* (raiders of the public treasury), cleaned up the government house,

---

1. Socialism, as elsewhere, became an ideology for the systematic exploitation and oppression of the people—even in Cuba. The 28 July 1997 issue of *Forbes* magazine ranked the wealth of royalty and dictators ruling in the Third World. A shocking entry at No. 10 was Cuban President Fidel Castro with a personal fortune estimated at $1.7 billion. [The Sultan of Brunei headed the list with $38 billion in wealth.]

2. This was the subject of my book, *Africa Betrayed*—by its leaders.

instilled discipline in the civil service, and returned to their barracks. They were hailed as "saviors" and idolized by the people.[3]

The second generation of military rulers, who assumed control in the 1970s, emerged from the dregs: They were more corrupt, incompetent, and brutal than the civilian administrations they replaced. They ruined one African economy after another with brutal efficiency and looted African treasuries with military discipline. Africans watched helplessly as they experienced yet another betrayal. This second batch of "military coconutheads," as Africans call them, came from the bottom of the pit and left wanton destruction and carnage in their wake.

In 1978 Edem Kodjo, then Secretary General of the Organization of African Unity (OAU), echoed the sentiments of many Africans when he solemnly lamented before the African heads of state gathered for an OAU summit that, "Our ancient continent is now on the brink of disaster, hurtling towards the abyss of confrontation, caught in the grip of violence, sinking into the dark night of bloodshed and death" (Lamb 1983, xi).

Since then, things have gotten progressively worse. By the beginning of the 1990s, it was clear something had gone terribly wrong in Africa. The continent was wracked by a never-ending cycle of civil wars, carnage, chaos, and instability. Economies had collapsed. Poverty, in both absolute and relative terms, had *increased*. Malnutrition was rife. In addition, censorship, persecution, detention, arbitrary seizures of property, corruption, capital flight, and tyranny continuously plagued the continent.

Infrastructure had decayed and crumbled in much of Africa. Roads, schools, and telecommunications systems were in shambles. Empty bookstore shelves greeted visitors to university campuses. Many school buildings showed obvious signs of decay and disintegration. Most buildings had not even seen a coat of paint since the colonialists departed. The quality of education had deteriorated sharply. Nigeria's 38-school university system, for example, was in ruins. Students could not get books. Nor could professors do research. Ahmadu Bello University is one such facility in a dilapidated state. Dormitories are overcrowded, laboratories lack chemicals to perform experiments, and some buildings are collapsing.

---

3. The public adulation, however, went to the heads of some these "saviors." For example, General Moussa Traore of Mali came to power in a 1968 military coup that overthrew a left-wing government that had pursued policies of nationalization and embraced Soviet ideology. But Traore introduced no institutions to build national unity. In fact, he retained the one-party state system and won unopposed presidential elections in 1979, 1984, and 1989 for successive five-year terms.

When the vice-chancellor of a major Nigerian university wanted to resign, he called a press conference. As Linus U. J. Thomas-Ogboji, a Nigerian scholar based in Asheville, described it: "His reasons for abandoning the job are a pathetic commentary on the putrid demise of a once-promising nation: admission and grades were being sold openly; dormitories for adolescent females had become brothels; threats of death and mayhem by gangs were rife on a campus that had gone without electricity or running water for years" (*African News Weekly,* 26 May 1995, 6).

A similar decrepit situation was described by a Ghanaian university student, Foster Koduea: "The University of Ghana, Legon, established in the [1950s] with very comfortable accommodations, beautiful buildings and surroundings, is now in a deplorable state. A room meant for two students is now used by six students and a room which is supposed to be used by three or four students is now inhabited by eight to ten students. At Legon Hall most of the rooms are very congested and hardly is there room for free passage. Lecture halls are congested" (*Focus,* 13–20 February 1995, 4).

In most places in Africa, telephones do not work; they "bite back." Electricity and water supplies are sporadic. What are called roads are often passageways truncated by crevasses large enough to swallow a truck. Hospitals lack food and medical supplies. Doctors even have difficulty finding paper on which to write prescriptions. Often patients are requested to bring their own blankets and bandages. Communicable diseases such as yellow fever, malaria, and cholera—once believed vanquished—have reappeared with a vengeance.

In the cities, many banged-up and unrepaired vehicles move sideways in a crab-like manner. Even government buildings have reached advanced stages of dilapidation. Broken windowpanes abound while offices reek of mold, rust, and dust. Civil servants, and even diplomats, go for months without pay. One Nigerian civil servant at the Ministry of Works in Lagos, George Adeleye, "died from exhaustion while waiting for hours to collect monthly wages of 1,500 *naira* ($20)" (*African News Weekly,* 16–22 September 1996, 26). "He complained that he had not eaten for two days as he was without money," said one of his colleagues.

For four months, November 1988 to February 1989, Sierra Leone's high commissioners and ambassadors accredited to overseas countries received no budgetary allocations. Electricity and water supplies to its embassy in Washington, D.C. were disconnected for nonpayment of utilities. In March 1989 teachers in primary and secondary schools boycotted classes in protest against salary arrearages, which in some cases, went back as far as October 1988 (*West Africa,* 20–26 March 1989, 436). Ironically, Sierra Leone is well endowed with minerals such as diamonds, gold, rutile, iron ore, chrome, and illemite as well as piassava and coffee. As Robert Kaplan (1994), an American journalist put it:

> Sierra Leone is a microcosm of what is occurring, albeit in a more tempered and gradual manner, throughout West Africa and much of the underdeveloped world: the withering away of central governments, the rise of tribal and regional domains, the unchecked spread of disease, and the growing pervasiveness of war. West Africa is reverting to the Africa of the Victorian atlas. It now consists of a series of coastal trading posts, such as Freetown and Conakry, and the interior that, owing to violence, volatility, and disease, is again "unexplored." (48)

Indices of Africa's development performance have not only been dismal but have also lagged persistently behind those of other Third World regions. Economic growth rates in Africa in the 1970s averaged only 4 to 5 percent while Latin America recorded a 6 to 7 percent growth rate. Average per capita gross national product (GNP) in 1981 was $770 for Africa, $973 for Asia, and $2,044 for Latin America. From 1986 to 1993 the continent's real GNP per capita declined 0.7 percent, while the average for the Third World increased by 2.7 percent. For all of black Africa, real income per capita dropped by 14.6 percent from its level in 1965, making most black Africans worse off than they were at independence.

High taxes, rampant inflation, runaway government expenditures, unstable currencies, and high-level corruption have stunted Africa's economic growth potential. "Africa's deepening crisis is characterized by weak agricultural growth, a decline in industrial output, poor export performance, climbing debt, and deteriorating social indicators, institutions, and environment" (World Bank 1989, 2).

Agriculture, which employs the bulk of Africa's population, has performed abysmally. Since 1970 agricultural output has been growing at less than 1.5 percent—less than the rate of population growth. Consequently, food production per capita declined by 7 percent in the 1960s, by 15 percent in the 1970s, and by 8 percent in the 1980s. Over the postcolonial period 1961 to 1995, "per capita food production in Africa dropped by 12 percent, whereas it advanced by leaps and bounds in developing countries in Asia" (*The Economist,* 7 September 1996). Zaire, now the Democratic Republic of the Congo, exported food when it was the Belgian Congo. Today, it cannot feed itself, nor can postcolonial

Zambia, Sierra Leone, and Tanzania. In 1990, about 40 percent of black Africa's food was imported, despite the assertion by the Food and Agriculture Organization of the United Nations that the Congo Basin alone could produce enough food to feed all of black Africa. The situation has deteriorated so rapidly in Nigeria that many people eat only once a day.

Increasingly, Africa has become unattractive to foreign investors and even to the donor community which suffers "donor fatigue" after so many failures. Net foreign direct investment in black Africa dropped dramatically from $1.22 billion in 1982 to $498 million in 1987. From 1989 to mid-1994, over half of British manufacturing companies with African subsidiaries divested from those operations. In mid-1989 there were 90 British companies with 336 equity stakes in Anglophone African manufacturing enterprises. By mid-1994 only 65 companies with 233 equity stakes remained (*African Business,* May 1995, 16). The French also have become disillusioned: "French direct investment in sub-Saharan Africa ran at $1 billion a year in 1981-1983; by 1988 that had translated into a net outflow of more than $800 million" (*The Economist,* 21 July 1990, 82). Between 1990 and 1995 the net yearly flow of foreign direct investment into developing countries quadrupled, to over $90 billion; Africa's share of this fell to only 2.4 percent.[4] According to the World Bank, in 1995 a record $231 billion in foreign investment flowed into the Third World. Singapore by itself attracted $5.8 billion, while Africa's share was a paltry 1 percent, or $2 billion—less than the sum invested in Chile alone (*The Economist,* 9 November 1996, 95). "Even that meagre proportion has been disputed by some analysts who believe the true figure to be less than $1 billion," said *The African Observer* (11–24 April 1996, 20).

To maintain income and investment, African governments borrowed heavily in the 1970s. Total African foreign debt has risen 24-fold since 1970 to a staggering $400 billion in 1996, which was equal to its yearly GNP, making the region the most heavily indebted in the world. (Latin America's debt amounted to approximately 60 percent of its GNP.) Currently debt service obligations absorb about 40 percent of export revenue, but only about half of the outstanding debts are actually being paid. On the other half, arrearages are continually being rescheduled.

The exceptions to this horrid picture of economic atrophy are pitifully few: Botswana, Mauritius, and possibly Uganda. One could

---

4. The percentages in the five previous years, beginning with 1990, were: 3.5, 5.2, 3.2, 2.6, and 3.7 percent.

focus on these success stories, hoping that other African countries would emulate their policies. This approach has the additional advantage that it presents a positive image of Africa. The World Bank and other Western organizations are veterans in this trade, peddling one African country after another as a success story, only to abandon it in search of another in the twinkle of an eye. But the World Bank's obsession with "success stories" blurs its vision for Africa.

On 21 June 1997 *The Washington Post* carried a story, "Africa: A Grim Picture," which painted a sobering vision of the continent. The vice presidents of the World Bank's African region, Callisto Madivo and Jean-Louis Sarbib, took offense: "The picture ignores the other side of the Africa story. Togo, Lesotho, and Uganda have averaged more than 10 percent growth in the past two years" (*The Washington Post,* 11 July 1997, A22).

It is a shame that the World Bank does not get the larger picture. Furthermore, when large African countries, such as Algeria, Angola, Kenya, Nigeria, Sudan, and Zaire, were either imploding or on the brink of explosion, the Bank was trotting out Togo, Lesotho and Uganda as "success stories." This is not much consolation in the wake of the destabilization of so many other nations. Now most Africans view World Bank labels of "success stories" with rabid cynicism and even as a morbid premonition. It may be recalled that the Bank declared Cameroon, Kenya and Zaire as "success stories" in the 1980s. Then in March 1994, the labels were applied to Burkina Faso, Gambia, Ghana, Nigeria, Tanzania, and Zimbabwe. What happened to all these African "success stories"?

Robert Kaplan was quite worried: "Ghana is being touted by the U.S. State Department as a West African success story, even as 67 villages were destroyed in tribal warfare there last February between Kokombas and Nanumbas. The results were 13,000 refugees and 1,000 corpses buried by Ghanaian security forces. Labeling of places as 'success stories' prior to their dissolution promotes public cynicism toward a place like Africa. Kenya was once a 'success story,' remember? Now its capital, Nairobi, is known as 'Nairobbery,' due to surging violent crime [and ethnic strife]" (*The Washington Post,* 17 April 1994, C2).

The focus on the few success stories is a futile exercise in grand delusion. Jon Qwelane, a columnist for the *Johannesburg Star* said : "Sure enough, Botswana and Namibia have been shining exceptions to the general rule since each attained its independence. But on a continent of some 52 independent nations, two exceptions are not exactly indicative of a very healthy state of affairs." (24 May 1997, 10) Moreover, it is a dishonest attempt to conceal the fact that an overwhelming majority of

African countries have performed dismally in the postcolonial era. Problems cannot be solved when their existence is either denied or concealed. It would be far more useful to evaluate *why* the majority of African countries are imploding and performing poorly economically.

Since the beginning of the 1980s—described by most analysts as "the lost decade"—one African country after another has collapsed, scattering refugees in all directions: Ethiopia (1985), Angola (1986), Mozambique (1987), Sudan (1991), Liberia (1992), Somalia (1993), and Rwanda (1994). In March 1994 the United Nations Development Program (UNDP) grimly predicted that nine more African countries were on the brink of complete social disintegration: Algeria, Burundi, Egypt, Liberia, Mozambique, Nigeria, Sierra Leone, Sudan, and Zaire. In November 1996 the threat of imminent starvation of 1.2 million Hutu refugees in eastern Zaire compelled the international community to prepare a military intervention force to be led by Canada. Its objectives were twofold: to feed the starving refugees and to establish an "aid corridor" to facilitate the return of Hutu refugees to Rwanda.

Few would quibble with the objectives of that humanitarian mission. To stand by idly and watch thousands die daily from starvation and disease would be immoral and cruel. But to barge into an African crisis situation without any understanding of the complexities of the issues involved and without any clue as to what the long-term solution should be, knowing full well that the mission will be abandoned should the going get tough, is even crueler. Time and again in recent years the international community has mounted eleventh-hour humanitarian missions into Africa. And time and again these missions have been abandoned at the least sign of complication or trouble. A memorable example was the Somalia debacle, which cost the international community $3.5 billion and the lives of 18 U.S. Rangers and scores of U.N. Pakistani soldiers, leading eventually to the 1994 pull-out by the United Nations. These "stop-and-go" Band-Aid solutions compound Africa's crises by covering up festering wounds.

Long-term, durable solutions to Africa's innumerable problems require an understanding of their root causes. That, in turn, requires making two fundamental distinctions: first, between African leaders and the African people, and second, between traditional Africa and modern Africa. Western administrators often use the generic term "Africans" to refer to African leaders, as in the expression, "Africans are reforming their economies." But this usage is misleading. It carries the implication that *all* Africans are involved in this process when in actual fact it is the *leaders* who claim to be "reforming their economies."

Furthermore, lumping the leaders and the people together prevents many from criticizing the policies of African leaders for fear of being labeled "racist" if one were white or "traitor" if one were black. Most African leaders are despots and failures. But leadership failure is not synonymous with failure of Africans as a people. And criticizing African leaders does not mean one hates black people.

TWO AFRICAS CLASHING

The second distinction is even more important. There are two Africas that are constantly clashing. The first is traditional or indigenous Africa that historically has been castigated as backward and primitive. Yet it works—albeit at a low level of efficiency. Otherwise, it would not have been able to sustain its people throughout the centuries. Today it is struggling to survive. The second Africa is the modern one, which is lost. Most of Africa's problems emanate from its modern sector. They spill over onto the traditional, causing disruptions and dislocations and claiming innocent victims. Most Westerners generally have difficulty dealing with and reconciling these two Africas, as American teacher Ronald Pahl (1995) pointed out:

> [One] image of Africa in the popular press and on television is focused on sensational, mostly negative, events that are often colored with 19th century and colonial European bias. These largely negative images of Africa are in sharp contrast to peaceful rural images of Africa that many visitors to that continent retain. Missing from these lurid news reports are the central issues of human beings of all colors and their attempts to build stable societies around them. . . . [The other] Africa—strange viruses, brutal dictators, and "savage" wars. Are we reading Joseph Conrad's *Heart of Darkness* or this morning's newspaper? From our U.S. vantage point late in the 20th century, we may find it difficult to tell the two apart. (12)

Most Western teachers and analysts erroneously assume that the two Africas operate by the same principles and logic. Traditional or rural Africa is the home of the real people of Africa—the peasant majority, who produce the real wealth of Africa: agricultural produce, cash crops (cocoa, coffee, tea, etc.), timber, minerals, sculpture, and other artifacts. They lack formal education, but with their raw native intelligence and skills, some of them have been able to produce great works of art. The sculptures of Yoruba, Ibo bronzes, the beads of the Masai and Fang masks, Zulu headrests, and Sotho snuff containers "are masterpieces by any standard" and "did so much, via Picasso, Derain, Braque and Matisse and Gris and others, to change the face of 20th-century European art" (*The Economist,* 7 October 1995, 97). "Rockefellers and Rothschilds were early connoiseurs of Shona sculpture. Prince Charles has become a collector" (*Newsweek,* 14 September 1987, 80).

African natives have always been free enterprisers, going about their daily economic activities on their own volition. They do not queue before their rulers' palaces or huts for permission to engage in trade, fishing, or agriculture. They produce surpluses that are sold on free village markets, where prices are determined by bargaining, not dictates from the tribal government. Their traditional societies are generally peaceful and stable. They live not only in harmony with others but also with their natural environment, including wildlife. They run their societies with their own unique political and economic institutions.[5]

A careful study of their "primitive" societies reveals an astonishing degree of functionality: participatory forms of democracy, rule of customary law, and accountability. Their system of government was so open that some allowed participation by foreign merchants. No modern country, even the United States, can boast of such an open government. Africa's traditional rulers were no despots, despite their characterization as such by European colonialists in order to justify various pacification campaigns. According to the Ghanaian scholar, Daniel Boamah-Wiafe (1993), "The power of the ruler is derived from the people and held in their trust by kings and chiefs. The traditional African ruler did not rule alone. Established customs and traditions, or unwritten constitutions, exist in almost every African community which impose on the ruler the obligation of appointing advisors to whom the authority of the people is delegated. . . . Customs and traditions also set limits to the authority of the king, his cabinet and advisors" (169).

The ruler was surrounded by various councils, bodies, and institutions to prevent abuses of power and corruption. Furthermore, the ruler was held accountable for his actions at all times and could be removed at any time if he was corrupt or failed to govern according to the will of the people. "Under most traditional African constitutions, bad or ineffective rulers were more readily removed from office than most modern constitutions allow. Divine kingship does not absolve a ruler

---

5. For a comprehensive discussion of these institutions, see Ayittey (1991).

from removal if he fails to live up to his responsibilities or constitutional duties. Important decisions were made only after necessary discussions and consultations had been made. Akan kings had no right to make peace or war, make laws, or be directly involved in important negotiations such as treaties without the consent of their elders and/or elected representatives" (Boamah-Wiafe, 1993, 169).

Modern Africa, by contrast, is the abode of the elites, the parasitic minority group. This sector is a meretricious burlesque, operating by an assortment of imported or borrowed institutions. The end product is an internally contradictory system that bears no affinity to either the indigenous system or the colonial state. It is a monstrosity that was created by the ruling elites themselves after independence by copying and grafting here and there from foreign systems they little understood. Over time it evolved into the present-day bizarre politico-economic system that admits of no rule of law, no accountability, no democracy of any form, and even no sanity. Here common sense has been murdered and arrogant idiocy rampages with impunity. All key institutions of government—the military, judiciary, civil service, banking and the government itself—have been debauched. For example, government as understood by most Western analysts does not exist in many African countries.

In most places in Africa, government is perceived by the ruling elites as a vehicle to be used to rob and terrorize the people. What one observes in many African countries is an "artificial government"—"government by deception," run by a phalanx of degreed bandits sporting Ray-Ban sun glasses and bazookas. They are not only out of touch with the people but perennially locked in combat with them. Said the *African Observer* of Africa's armies: "They prey on the rural populations to line their own empty pockets. They raid livestock, loot homes, divert humanitarian aid and extract false taxes. The more organized of the military units are moving into commerce and fight to control resources such as diamonds, ivory, timber or drugs,' says Alex de Wall, coordinator of the human rights organization, African Rights. Even the ferociously centralized former Ethiopian army of Mengistu Haile Mariam saw officers selling arms and ammunition in the last years of the war" (17-30 October 1996, 31).

Soldiers, whose basic function is to defend the territorial integrity of their nations, have transformed themselves into uniformed bandits, preying on the very people they are supposed to defend. In August 1988 two Belgian members of parliament, Paul Staes and Jef Ulburghs, cataloged the military's horrifying human rights abuses in Zaire. According to their report, the Zairian Green Berets killed several peasants and merchants in the Northern Kivu (Eastern Zaire) region during the summer of 1988. In addition, the army went on a rampage, plundering and looting the area and the Kibali-Ituri region. The two Belgians provided details of rape involving three schoolgirls by six soldiers in the town of Lumee. Reports indicated that two other schoolgirls were raped by soldiers in Goma and Bulera-Vuhovi. A group of women organized a demonstration in Kinshasa to protest against these heinous crimes and appeal to President Mobutu to bring the culprits to justice. About "88 of the women who participated in a women's demonstration on April 19 in Kinshasa were themselves raped" (*New African,* September 1988, 22).

When factional fighting flared up in Liberia in 1990, the Economic Community of West African States (ECOWAS) dispatched the ECOWAS Ceasefire Monitoring Group (ECOMOG) into Liberia to maintain peace, order, and democracy. But very quickly, some of the so-called peacekeeping troops themselves began to take part in the looting. The Nigerian peacekeeping force, for example, was dismissed by many Liberians and diplomats as "just another looting militia" (*The Washington Post,* 14 April 1996, A24). In fact, "Nigerian ships regularly called at Liberia's ports to carry off booty, including an entire iron-ore processing plant in Buchanan that was dismantled in 1994. Diplomats reported that peacekeeping troops were also selling arms to rival factions in southeastern Liberia" (*The Washington Post,* 23 April 1996, A12).

They even joined in the factional fighting. "General Philip Kamah, chief of staff of the Armed Forces of Liberia, said on BBC Radio that Guinean peacekeepers had joined rival factions—the United Liberation Movement of Liberia for Democracy and the National Patriotic Front of Liberia (NPFL)—in the shelling" (*The Washington Post,* 14 April 1996, A24).

Since part of the mission of the ECOMOG soldiers was to establish democracy, one would have thought that they practiced democracy in their own countries. But alas, of the 15 countries that make up the ECOWAS, only two, Senegal and The Gambia, were democratic in 1990. In 1996 the number was still a pathetic four: Benin, Cape Verde Islands, Mali and Senegal. A coup in The Gambia on July 22, 1994 terminated its democratic experiment.

Tell the police you think a government minister is embezzling taxpayers' money and it is *you* they will arrest. "An Accra [Ghana] weekly, *The Vanguard,* has disclosed that 106.6 billion *cedis* ($174.75 million) is missing from the disbursement of the 1993 Budget.... The police have invited the editor of *The Vanguard* to help in the investigation of the alleged missing state funds" (*Ghana Drum,* March 1993, 15).

Nigeria's military rulers, in place to shepherd the country through a transition to democratic rule, have instead made the transition process itself permanent. Since 1980 Nigeria's ever-competent military vagabonds have been trying to return the country to democratic rule. In November 1995 the regime set out to hang human rights activist Ken Saro-Wiwa on trumped-up charges of treason and murder. It took five attempts to execute the dastardly deed because of equipment malfunction. An irate Kwesi Obeng of University of Science and Technology in Kumasi, Ghana, wrote "to register his protest and revulsion at the way African leaders have been disgracing the black race. Just look at the way Ken Saro-Wiwa and Co. were hanged like pigs without the benefit of an appeal" (*The Ghanaian Chronicle,* 18–22 January 1996, 4).

On 5 March 1995 Nigeria's radical lawyer and human rights activist Gani Fawehinmi launched the National Conscience Party (NCP) in defiance of General Sani Abacha's ban on the formation of political parties. Thousands of NCP members and supporters then staged a mass rally in Lagos, chanted anti-Abacha slogans, and handed out leaflets denouncing the state of the nation. The leaflets cited among other things, the lack of food, transportation, health facilities, electricity, and free press. Trigger-happy soldiers immediately sprang into action, arresting some of the protesters. Police had to borrow Fawehinmi's vehicles to convey the accused to court.

In neighboring Niger, after General Ibrahim Bare seized power in a 27 January 1996 coup, he decided to contest the presidential elections he was holding for the country on 6 July 1996. When early results showed that he was losing,

> Mainassara sacked and replaced the Independent National Electoral Commission (CENI) with his own appointees, placed his opponents under guard in their own houses. The other contenders' home phone lines were also cut off. A ban on public gatherings in Niamey was announced on the evening of July 9. Security forces were deployed at candidates' homes and some political party offices. The floodlit Palais des Sports where results were centralized was guarded by an armored car and heavy machine guns mounted on pickup trucks. Two radio stations were stopped from broadcasting and all of the country's international phone lines were suspended. (*African News Weekly,* 15–21 July 1996, 2).

When it comes to beating up and shooting unarmed civilians, Africa's security forces can do so with efficient relish. But how really courageous are the security boys? According to *Ghana Drum* (February 1995):

> Soldiers on guard duties at Ghana Broadcasting Corporation no longer guard an observation post behind the TV studio because of a ghost who slaps officers who go on duty there at night.
>
> In September 1994, an officer on guard at that sentry came running to the head of security in the middle of the night complaining of an invisible hand which had on two occasions pulled his helmet from his head, pushed him and he fell headlong onto the green grass. The senior officer who was unmoved by the soldier's story, chided him for being a coward and superstitious. He, therefore, decided to prove [the soldier] wrong by manning the post himself.
>
> Within an hour, the senior officer fled to the office telling a similar tale, this time the ghost allegedly smacked him four times on the face. (33)

Was this a case of divine intervention? And Ghana's police? Recently when the late chief of Jamasi was being buried, the lights in the town suddenly went off. According to *Weekly Spectator* (15 June 1996): "Pandemonium broke out when even the Police took to their heels. The Police joined the people in the flight for safety for fear of falling victim to the Ashanti tradition that people are beheaded during the burial of chiefs so they can serve the chief in the next world. When interviewed, a police spokesman denied that the Police fled and said they only took cover to review their strategy for any eventuality" (3).

In Kenya, members of the group Release Political Prisoners (RPP) have been campaigning vigorously for prisoners, whom they claim are being held for political offenses. On 19 July 1996 they held a demonstration in Nairobi and distributed pamphlets accusing the government of involvement in the 24 March 1996 murder in Nairobi of RPP chairman Karimi Nduthu. Twenty-one members of the group were immediately arrested and jailed without bail for "holding an illegal meeting, inciting violence and being in possession of a seditious publication" (*African News Weekly*, 29 July–4 August 1996, 4).

When armed Kenyan policemen came up against a group of bank robbers in Nairobi, however, they took to their heels. "When you see armed policemen running away, then things are hot," said Peter Asiaya, a customer at the time of the bank robbery. "I saw one police man running away from the scene holding a pistol facing downwards" (*The African Observer,* 15–28 November 1994, 19).

A tribal chief in a rural farming community in Lesotho complained bitterly: "We have two problems: rats and the government" (*International Health and Development,* March/April 1989, 30). These official rodents have almost everything backward. "Development" to them means "mansions," *"pajeros,"* Swiss bank accounts, and an ever-expanding list of mistresses. The growth of the economy is inversely related to the size of their potbellies and cheeks. Foreign investment? They have that backward too. To them, "foreign investment" means investing their booty in a *foreign* country. "According to one United Nations estimate, $200 billion or 90 percent of the sub-Saharan part of the continent's gross domestic product (much of it illicitly earned), was shipped to foreign banks in 1991 alone" (*The New York Times,* 4 February 1996, 4).

Ever notice that in Africa it is the oppressors who are chanting "Revolution!" "People's Power!"? Even Mobutu Sese Seko of Zaire (now the Democratic Republic of The Congo) called his party *"Mouvement Populaire de la Revolution"* (Popular Movement of the Revolution). Zaire's economy had collapsed. In 1994 economic growth was minus 7.4 percent and inflation clocked at 23,769 percent (*The Washington Times,* 24 January 1997, A13). Infrastructure had disintegrated and basic essential services had ceased. Civil servants, even diplomats, had not been paid for months. Sitting atop this ruin was Africa's most notorious kleptocrat, who styled himself "the Guide" and a "revolutionary."

A "revolution" is a major, cataclysmic event that brings about an overthrow of the *ancien regime* or a complete change in the order of doing things. It makes a clean break with the existing way of doing things and establishes a *new* way. In politics, for example, a "revolution" occurs when the subjugated class rises up to overthrow the oppressors—as occurred with the American and French revolutions. No such "revolution" has occurred in Zaire, Ghana, or many African countries in the postcolonial era.

In the Sudan, Lieutenant-General Omar el-Bashir proclaimed an "Islamic Revolution" that would deliver the Sudanese from abject poverty and squalor by tapping the country's oil and mineral riches to create a model economy. But Sudanese complain of rampant inflation (about 70 percent), high unemployment, corruption, and endless conflicts. "They talk and talk about Islam. The Prophet Mohammad never had a big house like theirs. We the people are left on the street waiting for something to eat," said a Sudanese trader bitterly (*The Washington Times,* 27 July 1995, A19). Meanwhile, the ruling *mullahs* (elders who are consulted on various social and religious matters) continue with the plunder. Islamic strongman Sheik Hassan Turabi, the de facto ruler of Sudan, is "one of the country's richest men, with controlling interests in hotels, shipping and import-export businesses, and his agents have cornered the local arms bazaar and a gold souk" (*The Washington Times,* 19 September 1995, A11). According to *The Atlantic Monthly* (August 1994), "Five years after the revolution in Sudan, the Islamists have brought about almost the exact opposite of what, to judge from their prior writings, they intended. The civil war rages, the secret police operate without restriction, the press is censored, the military reigns, and political opponents languish in ghost houses when they are not simply killed. Like so many would-be reformers in other places and other times, the professors [of Islamic revolution] proposed enlightenment but delivered a nightmare" (29).

Standing before a mosaic designed by a murdered priest in Yaounde, Cameroon—Nigeria's neighbor—on 15 September 1995, Pope John Paul II asked African clergymen to strike back at corruption and hopelessness that leave the continent in "unspeakable suffering." The pope likened Africa to a man left beaten and near death and said "This very sad situation also has internal causes such as tribalism, nepotism, racism, religious intolerance and the thirst for power taken to the extreme by totalitarian governments" (*The Washington Times,* 16 September 1995, A8).

In a 150-page document, known as the Apostolic Exhortation that was published in Cameroon after his celebrated open-air mass, the Pope blasted corruption and repression by African governments. "Africa's economic problems, the pope says, were compounded by the dishonesty of corrupt governments leaders who diverted public funds to their own pockets. This is plain theft, whatever the legal camouflage may be" (*The Washington Post,* 16 September 1995, A24).

What keeps Africans poor is their powerlessness to rid themselves of predatory governments or force existing ones to adopt the right policies in a peaceful way. More treacherously, those highly educated Africans—the lawyers, professors, and intellectuals—who ought to be the watchdogs have themselves joined the official gangsters and rodents. As a last resort, the people may rise up to overthrow the cabal of looters with destructive consequences. But then again, the next batch of rats will prove no better.

What modern Africa needs, perhaps more than anything else, is a commonsense revolution. Nigerian scholar Felix Oti lamented that: "We have come to be regarded as empty vessels that make a lot of noise. . . . There is a difference between academic intelligence and common sense. The latter is the motor that effectively and successfully drives the application of the former. Unfortunately, the average Nigerian intellectual, though overwhelmed with the former, fails to exhibit enough of the latter to be taken seriously. The very same squabble is just a replica of what is, and has been, going on in the Mother continent—the inability to put heads together and form a united front; the root cause of Africa's many problems" (*African News Weekly,* 21 April 1995, 22).

Most of Africa's self-appointed leaders do not use their heads. Their primordial instinct is to perpetuate themselves in power, loot the national treasury, and brutally squelch all dissent. The intellectuals who should know better also refuse to use their heads. But an even greater tragedy is that many of those foreign governments and organizations that purport to "care for the African people" and set out to help them do not use their heads either. U.S. Ambassador to Chad Laurent Pope admitted that "half of the $300 million in assistance that the US AID has provided Chad since fiscal 1982 has been wasted. We never build or fix anything, to speak of, and our programs have little direct contact with poor people" (*The Washington Times,* 27 July 1995, A4).

In northern Kenya, Norwegian aid officials built a fish-freezing plant near a lake for the Turkana tribesmen in the 1970s. Problem was, the Turkana are pastoral people who survive by raising cattle, goats, and camels. Worse, after the plant was built, it was discovered that freezing fish in the daily 100-degree temperatures would take more electricity than was available in the entire Turkana district. Next, "the part of the lake where most of the fish had been caught dried up, and the Turkana who had taken up fishing found themselves totally dependent on handouts from their would-be benefactors" (Whitaker, 1988, 75). Back in the 1980s, the World Bank lent Tanzania more than $10 million to finance the expansion of the country's cashew industry. By 1982 the processing plants created had "a capacity three times the country's annual cashew crop and [was] vastly more expensive than factories in India offering similar services" (Whitaker, 1988, 76).

Swedish Foreign Minister Lena Hjelm-Wallem bragged that her country was for many years very "close to South Africans in their struggle against apartheid." Sweden also disbursed about $400 million to South Africans during their years of struggle (*The Washington Post,* 18 October 1996, A48). But how much assistance did Sweden—or for that matter,

Western governments—give to other Africans elsewhere struggling to liberate themselves from tyranny?

In October 1994 the World Bank crowed about the "second miracle of the decade in South Africa," regarding that country's progress on the road to a market-oriented economy. The secrets of South Africa's success? "According to Stephen Demming, director of the World Bank's Africa office, 'We said specifically we cannot give to the South African apartheid regime the primacy we usually accord to government.' [The World Bank] said no project in South Africa would proceed unless all political parties consented, and one mission was called back to Washington after the ANC objected" (*The Wall Street Journal,* 6 October 1994, A15).

Did the bank ever consider applying the same standard elsewhere in Africa: giving less primacy to corrupt and brutal governments? Or proceeding with projects only after consultation with other political parties? Of course not. South Africa was "different" because blacks gunned down by the white racists went to hell whereas blacks gunned down by African tyrants went to heaven. Applying this strange standard, the World Bank sent a mission to Rwanda in September 1993. The mission ignored all indications of an impending implosion and issued a glowing report in April 1994— exactly the same month Rwanda was engulfed in conflagration.

In this game of doublespeak on African policy, however, the French are perhaps the worst. French policy in Africa goes beyond mere folly into criminality. Jean-François Medard, a world-renowned professor of African affairs at the Institute of Political Studies at the University of Bordeaux, told *Newsweek* (21 November 1994) that "French policy in Africa is erratic and criminal" since his country's government "operates, not on principle, but on cynicism" (30).

France has had an appalling record of supporting and coddling brutal African dictators. In the case of Rwanda, France was sending arms, helicopters, even 700 of its own soldiers between 1990 and 1993 to help the Hutu government of Juvenal Habyarimana fight off the Tutsi rebels of the Rwanda Patriotic Front. And when the Hutu government soldiers were routed, France created a "safety zone" for the murderers—not for the victims of genocide—because the French were more interested in maintaining their cultural dominance in Rwanda. The Tutsi rebels were invading from Uganda—an English-speaking country, where they lost their French-language skills after decades in exile.

When the Hutus fled Rwanda, after massacring nearly a million Tutsis in 1994, they settled in refugee camps in Goma (Zaire), and

Tanzania. The United Nations embarked on a humanitarian mission to feed the refugees. Guess who the United Nations employed as soldiers to guard the delivery of, and to distribute, the food aid: "All are tall and light-skinned. So are UN workers supervising the unloading. These are townspeople, dressed in smart jeans and sporting flashy watches. All are Tutsis" (*The Economist*, 19 October 1996, 45).

At that time, the Zairean state itself was fiction—on the verge of complete collapse, pillaged by an idiotic buffoon. When the humanitarian crisis erupted in eastern Zaire in November 1996, President Mobutu was convalescing comfortably from prostate cancer surgery in Nice, France, on a fat bed of loot he had plundered from his country. Although his personal fortune in Swiss bank accounts was estimated to be as high as $10 billion, he could not pay his own soldiers, much less contribute a penny to the international intervention force that Canada was to lead to help save his own country. Nor did he have the sense to use just $1 billion of his fortune to establish a modern prostate cancer research hospital in Zaire. How could the U.N. tribunal pursue Rwandan war criminals while France was saving the chief bandit and super-war criminal who had brought untold hardship and suffering to the Zairean people?

O, common sense, how scarce thou art! It appears nobody is using their head when it comes to Africa. Western governments and donors are at liberty to throw away their money in Africa. But they should not ask the suffering people of Africa to pay for their folly.

PLAN OF THE BOOK

The purpose of this book is to examine why Africa has been imploding and remains intractably mired in poverty. Writing a book on Africa is always an extremely difficult undertaking. Not that the issues and problems defy solutions; quite often the solutions are simple and as clear as daylight. But so many extraneous factors intrude that rational and dispassionate discussions are scuttled. A book on Africa must cross racial, cultural, ideological, geographical, ethnic, religious, and class lines. Leftist radicals tend to see a "racist conspiracy plot" in every African misfortune. The colonial bogeyman has been the favorite of African governments and intellectuals. "Political correctness" prevents whites from criticizing inane policies of African leaders, while black Americans often blindly defend these leaders in the name of "racial solidarity." As a result, there is much confusion about what Africa must do to overcome its woes.

Then there is the additional difficulty of covering 54 countries: 6 North African and 48 sub-Saharan. Generalizations can be risky and therefore I have tried to show that many African countries face common problems, such as corruption, inefficient bureaucracies, inflation, and runaway government expenditures. Providing documentation for each country would easily overwhelm the reader. A few might suffice but then they tend to be repetitive of the problem. The reader's indulgence is entreated.

Although this book is about economic development, I have tried to write it in a non-technical language. I have also relied extensively on quotations from African sources: magazines, newspapers, and people. The primary purpose for doing so is to give the reader a feel of what Africans themselves, not just this writer, are saying about their own conditions and what they think the solutions should be, since, ultimately, it is they who must solve Africa's problems. They may not speak perfect English but it is important to hear what they have to say.

The key to Africa's long-term economic survival and prosperity lies in investment, both domestic and foreign. Investment, however, does not take place in a vacuum but in an "environment." Investors, both domestic and foreign, have not found Africa attractive. The business climate that prevails over much of Africa is inimical to investment and to development as well. This environment is characterized by weak currencies; inflation; myriads of state controls; political instability; corruption; rampaging civil wars; capital flight; absence of rule of law, accountability, and good governance; and a host of other problems. These "environmental defects," for want of a better expression, are man-made or artificial and can be remedied through legislative and political action. They must be distinguished from what may be called the "structural obstacles" to development, such as low savings, low rates of literacy, lack of capital, and inadequate health care, among others. Real development cannot occur until the "environmental defects" are rectified. The environmental defects create crises whereas the structural obstacles retard economic development. Quite often African policy makers and Western donor agencies fail to make this distinction and prescribe remedies that prove ineffective. This crucial distinction is the subject matter of chapter 2. For example, the problem of corruption cannot be effectively solved when the head of state himself is the chief bandit. There is nothing inherent in indigenous African culture that predisposes Africans to corruption, but it has become a serious malady as a result of the peculiar economic and political systems established by African leaders. Since these systems are fused, economic measures alone cannot eradicate or reduce corruption.

Back in the 1950s and 1960s, development economists paid little attention to the "development environment"; they took this to be "a given constant" and focused on structural obstacles. "All other things being equal," more inflow of capital into a developing country was expected to generate a higher rate of economic growth. Over time, however, the environment deteriorated so rapidly in Africa that few would dispute the assertion that sinking $1 billion into Nigeria would hardly make any difference to its rate of economic progress. "A poll of businessmen judged Nigeria the most corrupt country in the world, a place where you can buy anything, including the police" (*The Economist*, 8 June 1996, 46). Corruption, political chaos, repression, civil war, and capital flight must all be rooted out in order to establish an "enabling environment" in Africa. This ought to be the first order of priority.

Little progress, however, has been made on this score because there is little agreement on the *causes* of Africa's crises. A hot and emotionally charged debate still rages between externalists and internalists. Externalists believe the causes are external in origin and include colonial legacies, Western imperialism, the slave trade, an unjust international economic system, and exploitation by oligopolistic multinational corporations, among others. Internalists, on the other hand, emphasize such internal causes as incompetent leadership and the establishment of defective political and economic systems in postcolonial Africa—systems that bear little or no relationship to Africa's own indigenous systems.

This book takes the internalist stance, arguing that since the causes are primarily internal, the solutions lie within Africa itself. These solutions can be found in Africa's own indigenous systems—in its own backyard, so to speak. Philosophically, Africans bear the ultimate responsibility for solving their own problems. But its leaders have failed to craft what may be called "African solutions to African problems."

Chapter 3 discusses Africa's indigenous political and economic systems. Traditional African rulers were chosen and held accountable at all times. The rule of law prevailed and the rulers could be removed at any time. African chiefs were surrounded by councils upon councils to prevent abuse of power and despotism. By contrast, modern heads of state in postcolonial Africa are presidents-for-life and military bandits who are not held accountable for their misdeeds.

Indigenous Africa's economic system was characterized by private ownership of the means of production, free enterprise, and free trade. Free village markets existed in Africa centuries before Europeans set foot on the continent. Economic activity in these village markets—in West

Africa, for example—was dominated by women, and prices were determined by bargaining. They were not fixed by African chiefs and violators were not arrested and jailed. Pervasive state controls and state enterprises were the exception rather than the rule in traditional Africa.

Modern Africa's leaders and elites, however, spurned their own indigenous heritage, went abroad, and copied all sorts of esoteric systems for transplantation into Africa. These borrowed systems—for example, the one-party state system—never worked in Africa and created enormous problems. This is perhaps the single and most spectacular failure of African leaders and elites: Their failure to return Africa to its roots and build on its own native institutions. Chapter 4 discusses why African leaders and elites acted that way. It examines the motivations, beliefs, and lifestyles that facilitated the ruination of Africa.

After renouncing their heritage, the elites proceeded to establish economic and political systems in which all power was concentrated in the hands of the state. After independence, African nationalist leaders did not dismantle the authoritarian colonial state. Rather, they strengthened and expanded its scope. Subsequently, they abused and misused the powers of the state to achieve their own selfish ends. Gradually a "mafia state" evolved—a state that has been hijacked by vampire elites, hustlers, and gangsters, who operated with their own notorious ethic of self-aggrandizement and self-perpetuation in power. The institutions of government were debauched, the country became the personal property of the ruling elites, and the meaning of such terms as "development" was perverted. Chapter 5 examines the modus operandi of the predatory state and its tactics of survival.

The centralization of power transformed the state into a prize for which all sorts of groups compete. This competition can be ferocious, and it often degenerates into civil war because, in Africa, political power is the passport to great personal fortune. The richest persons in Africa are heads of state and ministers. So the "educated" African will fight for the presidency, even though it might be hazardous to his health—literally. According to *Africa Insider* (August 1995), "Kghoma Ali Malima, leader of Tanzania's main opposition group, recently died of a heart attack at his son's home in London just months before landmark multiparty elections. Tanzanian journalists compared his death to that of Stephen Kambona, a would-be candidate who collapsed and died in Washington in 1994. Both men lacked a history of illness or heart problems" (6).

Once captured, the instruments of state power are used by the ruling elites to advance their own selfish ethnic or professional interests and to exclude everyone else—the politics of exclusion and discontent. Consider Nigeria, for example, where a cabal of Hausa-Fulani has monopolized political power since independence in 1960. All oil revenue is appropriated by the federal government, which allocates only 3 percent to the oil-producing states in the east. Obviously, producing states are unhappy about this. This is a sure-fire recipe for an upheaval; those excluded from the gravy train will either seek to overthrow the current beneficiaries or to secede as the Igbos attempted to do in 1967.

Thus one word, power, explains why Africa is collapsing and breaking apart: the struggle for it, the seizure of it, and concentration of it in the hands of one individual or group, and the subsequent refusal to relinquish or share it. In fact, most of Africa's problems emanate from this policy of exclusion, made possible by two defective systems imposed on Africa after independence by its leaders and elites: sultanism and statism. Both systems are marked by extreme concentration of political and economic powers in the hands of the state—and, ultimately, one individual. These systems, as chapter 3 makes clear, cannot be defended upon the basis of "African tradition."

The activities of the predatory state have created enormous problems: corruption, embezzlement, capital flight, repression, and others. These problems, as chapter 6 argues, feed on one another and eventually suck the country into a vortex of violence and implosion. For the long haul, Africa has no choice but to reform its abominable political and economic systems by establishing democratic systems of government and market economies. The object of such reform is dispersal of power; that is, the taking of both political and economic power out of the hands of the state and giving it back to the people, where it belongs. Naturally, the African record on reform has been dismal, since the ruling elites have not been willing to implement meaningful reform that would reduce their power. They take one step forward and three steps back. Chapter 7 examines the acrobatics on reform.

As difficult as resolving Africa's crises have been, the sad fact is that Western governments and organizations have not been helpful in this exercise. Quite often they have compounded Africa's crises—not by deliberate design but by default or sheer ignorance. Chapter 8 examines Western culpability. Chapter 9 offers alternative solutions to Africa's crises, including radical ones that policy makers are reluctant to discuss for diplomatic reasons. The final chapter looks ahead and places the responsibility for saving Africa, as well as for leading the continent into the twenty-first century, squarely on the shoulders of Africa's intellectuals.

CHAPTER 2

Africa's Crises and Underdevelopment

The trouble with Nigeria is simply and squarely a failure of leadership. There is nothing basically wrong with the Nigerian character. There is nothing wrong with the Nigerian land or climate or water or air or anything else. The Nigerian problem is the unwillingness or inability of its leaders to rise to the responsibility, to the challenge of personal example which are the hallmarks of true leadership. . . . We have lost the twentieth century; are we bent on seeing that our children also lose the twenty-first? God forbid!
—Chinua Achebe (1985, 3).

Many a time we have wondered if the so-called African leaders sometimes lack the capacity to think and understand the ramifications of their actions. After all the bloodshed in Rwanda you would think we have learnt a lesson but no! Idiocy of our power-hungry leaders seems to triumph over pragmatism and common sense. The rationale for the current fighting defies any logic. . . . The world must be getting tired of us, given our self-inflicted tragedies galore. We seem to lack any sense of urgency to handle problems in an expedient manner devoid of bloodshed. Lord Have Mercy!
—Editorial, *Ghana Drum* (November, 1996).

CRISIS VERSUS LACK OF DEVELOPMENT

An understanding of Africa's woes requires a distinction between "underdevelopment" and "crisis." Since their causes are different, prescribed solutions for one may not be suitable for the other. Technically speaking, "development" means an improvement in living conditions for the average person. This means not only increased income but also better access to education, health care, and nutrition. To determine the average person's income, economists take the gross national product (GNP)— the total value of all goods and services produced in a country in any given year—and divide this by the population. The result—called GNP per capita—gives an idea of what each person would receive if the national pie (GNP) were divided equally among the population. It is not perfect, but it is a rough and ready measure of evaluating economic welfare. If the GNP per capita increases from, say, $350 to $400 in a year, the average person can be said to be slightly better off.

An improvement in living conditions requires an increase in GNP per capita. A straightforward increase in GNP is called economic growth. For example, if a country's GNP was $100 billion a year ago and is now $102 billion, the country has experienced a 2 percent rate of economic growth. But if the country's population grew by 3 percent, then the average person's standard of living fell by 1 percent. In other words, the national pie increased by 2 percent but the number of people who have to share it grew by 3 percent. Therefore, economic growth is a necessary but not sufficient condition for an improvement in living conditions. For the latter to exist, the rate of economic growth must exceed the rate of population growth.

Development, thus, is defined as a sustained annual increase in GNP per capita of at least 5 percent or more, provided prices are not rising rapidly, unemployment and distribution of income are not worsening, and so on. Some of these caveats are self-explanatory. For example, a country may succeed in raising its income per capita to $10,000. But what if in the process the environment became so polluted that its people start dying at the age of 30? Other caveats might be added but these should not detain us here. For our purposes, "development" will be taken to mean a sustained increase in GNP per capita of at least 5 percent per annum.

As we saw in chapter 1, income per capita for most African countries has dropped so precipitously that they are worse off economically than they were at independence. The most spectacular example is that of Nigeria, the income per capita of which dropped from about $1,200 in 1983 to about $250 in 1995. Why did African economies fail to achieve a rate of growth greater than population growth rate of 3 percent in the postcolonial period of 1960 to 1995?

Back in the 1950s and 1960s, development experts espoused a host of theories that identified various obstacles to development: lack of capital, a low level of technological development, illiteracy, and so on. Development literature stressed capital formation; that is, capital accumulation or investment, as the key building block in the basic model of development. So heavy was the emphasis on investment that this approach was derisively referred to as capital fundamentalism. The process of capital accumulation was constrained, however, by the operation of a vicious circle. Investment, which is financed out of savings, was low in Africa because savings were low. But savings come out of people's income. And since Africans are poor (that is, their incomes are low), then their savings would be low and, hence, investment as well.

The circle could be broken in a number of ways: (1) by an infusion of foreign aid, which may be regarded as the savings of foreigners that have been made available to Africans; (2) by attracting foreign investment, which would supplement inadequate domestic investment; and (3) by exporting more goods and services, which would enable an African country to earn more foreign exchange or income to speed up its rate of capital formation. Correspondingly, measures may be taken to raise domestic savings and investment.

Other vicious circles were soon identified. Illiteracy spawned ignorance of family planning and use of contraceptives. The results were large families. Inability to feed the children caused serious cases of malnutrition and poor health. That in turn lowered the productivity of African workers. Low productivity meant low income and inability to afford education, thus resulting in continued illiteracy..

These vicious circles, it was argued, were buttressed by factors beyond the control of Africa—the "external obstacles" that made capital accumulation exceedingly difficult. The first of these was dependence on a single export cash crop, such as coffee, cocoa, or rubber, which made African economies highly vulnerable to gyrations in world commodity markets. Unfavorable terms of trade were another: The prices African countries received for their export produce were fixed unfairly by oligopolistic multinational corporations in a hostile international economic environment. And these prices have been declining while those of manufactured imports have been soaring. Deteriorating terms of trade made it impossible for a developing country to earn more by exporting more.

The situation has been further aggravated by a "debt overhang." In 1996, Africa's total foreign debt stood at more than $400 billion. For most African countries, the service ratio was about 40 percent: That is, 40 cents out of every dollar earned on exports had to be spent to service the debt, leaving little to import essential spare parts, textbooks, and medical drugs, let alone capital equipment.

Most of these "structural obstacles," however, have progressively lost their operational significance or validity. Development is the sum total of economic activities, and these do not take place in a vacuum but in an "environment" that is created by the institutions and policies of government. Prior to 1990, most development experts assumed this "environment" to be constant and focused on the structural obstacles, such as lack of capital, and how to relieve this constraint.

Since the 1960s, however, this "environment" has deteriorated so sharply that it can no longer be assumed to be constant. In fact, it stunts growth. For some countries such as Liberia, Somalia, and Zaire (Congo), an infusion of billions of dollars of foreign aid or investment would be a waste. Another example is Nigeria, whose foreign debt stood at $35 billion in 1995. But most Nigerians would assert that, even if this debt were wiped out clean, the country, given prevailing conditions, would accumulate another huge foreign debt in no time.

The antidevelopment environment that prevails in most African countries is characterized by political tyranny, instability, chaos, senseless civil wars, horrible carnage, corruption, and capital flight. These, for want of a better expression, may be called environmental obstacles. These man-made obstacles must be distinguished from structural obstacles, such as lack of capital. For example, the amount of capital that is siphoned out of Africa by the elites (capital flight) *exceeds* the amount that comes in by way of foreign aid and investment. (See chapter 7.) In this case, it would be more judicious to remove the environmental factor that aggravates the capital shortage problem than to seek the infusion of more capital into Africa.

The environmental factors are crisis producing. By definition, a crisis is a serious adverse condition that requires immediate attention. There is an element of urgency. A crisis cannot persist for long without a major social upheaval or economic explosion. It would be preposterous to expect economic development in a country in which political structures have collapsed and savage banditry, carnage, and chaos flourish. Nor does it make much sense to talk of "economic development" when a civil war is raging, with bridges, roads, and power stations being blown up. Perhaps an analogy would be appropriate here.

Consider the development process as embarking on a journey in a vehicle, leaving Point A (state of under-development) and going to Point B (developed state). The road is strewn with obstacles. Development literature has identified a host of obstacles: low income, low investment, low savings, illiteracy, high population growth rates, and so on. The interplay of these factors produced the notorious "vicious circle of poverty" discussed earlier.

The vehicle for this journey may be private or state owned. In virtually all African countries, a state vehicle was taken in the 1960s, but this state vehicle has now broken down. It is a motley collection of obsolete, discarded parts scrounged from foreign junkyards and operates on borrowed ideology. The carburetor was a gift from Norway and the battery was donated by Austria. The tires came from Britain and China and are mismatched. A headlight is broken and the electrical system malfunctions. Turn the ignition switch and the windshield wipers fall off. The engine sputters and belches thick smoke that pollutes the entire country. There are no brakes or shock absorbers (no checks and balances). The fan belt is ripped, which means its cooling system is inoperative.

Clutching the wheel of the state vehicle is a reckless and unskilled egomaniac who proclaims himself "driver-for-life" and insists that he, and he alone, must be the driver till kingdom come since the vehicle is his own personal property. Aboard are his ministers, cronies, tribesmen, mistresses, sycophants, and other patronage junkies, who, in turn, have brought along their relatives, tribesmen, and friends. A goat, stolen from the people, has been tied to the rear bumper for a future feast.

As Makau Wa Mutua, a Kenyan lawyer and project director of Harvard University Law School's Human Rights Program, lamented, "Since independence in Africa, government has been seen as the personal fiefdom a leader uses to accumulate wealth for himself, his family, his clan. He cannot be subjected to criticism by anyone, and everything he says is final. The apex of this notion of owning government is the idea of a life president like Hastings Banda [former president of Malawi]. Once they replaced the colonial rulers, they wanted to become just like them. They wanted to be all-powerful and omnipresent. We just replaced white faces with black faces" (*The Washington Post*, 9 September 1991, A20). In Togo, "Mr. Gnassingbe Eyadema—hailed by the grovelling media as the "Great Helmsman"—ran Togo as a personal fief. His Kabye people, who make up no more than 15 percent of the population, scooped the best government jobs; the army was nearly two-thirds Kabye as well. But three times as many Togolese belong to the southern Ewe and Mina peoples, who loathe the president" (*The Economist*, 5 September 1992, 47).

Somewhere along the journey, the smoke-belching, dilapidated state vehicle broke down: dead battery, radiator overheated with the coolant boiling over, and tires flat. This is a crisis situation, which must be resolved *before* continuing on the journey. But instead of fixing the state vehicle, Somali and Liberian warlords battle ferociously to determine who should be the driver, while Africa's politicians and intellectuals argue furiously and endlessly over who would be a better driver. Meanwhile, Western governments and donor agencies busy themselves with removing the structural obstacles on the road. Since independence, few have occupied themselves with the *condition* of the vehicle.

Changing the driver through democratic elections or coups d'état would not make any difference to the journey (development). Removing the obstacles on the road (building schools to improve literacy rates or sinking bore holes for drinking water, for example) would not make any difference either. Adding super high-octane jet fuel, brand new shock absorbers, or emission control devices to cut down on the pollution would be futile. That state vehicle is going nowhere fast. In fact, if it moves at all, it will land in an economic ditch. It has to be junked or completely overhauled.

Therefore, questions of "accelerating" development (getting to Point B faster) must be deferred *until the vehicle is fixed* (reformed). That cannot be done until the cause of the vehicle breakdown—that is, the cause of the African crisis—is determined, which, in turn, requires an understanding of how the vehicle operates and knowledge of its component systems. The state vehicle in Africa is composed of two defective systems: statism and sultanism (personal or one-man rule), which will be discussed in chapter 4. Until these defective systems are rectified, the development journey will be extremely slow, interrupted by constant breakdowns.

WHY AFRICA'S CRISES HAVE PERSISTED

Africa's crises have remained intractable not so much because of a dearth of solutions but rather because of the flawed approaches its leaders took to solve them. Scientifically, effective resolution of a problem requires taking five basic steps. The first is to expose the problem, which normally is done through the media (newspapers, magazines, radio, TV) and public fora (conferences, seminars, workshops, and speeches). That is the business of intellectuals, journalists, editors, and writers. The second is to diagnose the causes of the problem. The third is to prescribe a solution. The fourth is to implement the solution, and the fifth is to monitor it to see if it is working. If not, the dosage may be increased or an entirely new remedy tried.

The diagnosis may be considered the crucial step. A faulty analysis of the causes may lead to a wrong prescription, which may treat only the

symptoms and not the fundamental causes, or worse, m
ailment. To avert such possible malpractice, a diagnosis
to critical public review and debate to determine its valid
that important causative factors have not been overlool

Regrettably, in most African countries the process c
rarely went beyond step two (the diagnosis stage). If step two was reached,
a faulty diagnosis was invariably performed, leading to the prescription
of a wrong solution. Worse, that solution was itself implemented poorly
or not at all in many cases. Corruption scandals fall into this category.
In 1993, for example, Ghana's auditor general released a report that
detailed a catalog of corruption and embezzlement by high government
officials, costing a staggering 401 billion *cedis* (about $400 million) over
a ten-year period (1983-1992). But not one single bandit was indicted.

For six years, 1988 to 1994, Nigeria's military rulers squandered
$12.4 billion in oil revenue, estimated by the Pius Okigbo Commission
to be a third of the nation's foreign debt. A Petroleum Trust Fund set
up by former head of state General Ibrahim Babangida "lost" $600
million. No one was prosecuted. Most Nigerians collapsed into hysterical
laughter when they heard their late head of state, General Sani Abacha,
had launched "a war on corruption," because they knew that "several of
his cronies, active or retired, are millionaires and no military men
involved in the banking scandal [that cost the country $180 million]
have been touched. 'When the soldiers have eaten enough, he retires
them,' said a civil-rights lawyer" (*The Economist,* 8 June 1996, 48).

Exposure

"He who conceals his disease cannot expect to be cured," says an
Ethiopian proverb. Yet, for much of the postcolonial period, exposing a
problem in Africa has almost always been impossible because of censorship, brutal suppression of dissent, and state ownership or control of the
media. Corrupt and incompetent governments denied or concealed their
embarrassing failings (abuse of power, looting, and atrocities) until the
problems blew up in their faces. But by then it was too late to solve them.
As Adam Feinstein, editor of the monthly publication of the International Press Institute, put it: "The press is always a first scapegoat of
governments. They can't blame themselves, so they have to blame
somebody else" (*The Washington Post,* 6 April 1995, A15).

The freedom that is most critical to the existence of all other human
freedoms is that of expression—the freedom to express one's thoughts,

wishes, and criticisms by words and actions without fear of reprisal. For Africa to find solutions to its problems, Africans must have this freedom. They cannot solve their problems in a "culture of silence," characterized by intimidation, censorship, and intolerance of alternative viewpoints. To expose corruption, human rights violations, economic mismanagement, and abuse of political power, freedom of expression is crucial.

Only in an atmosphere supporting the free exchange of ideas can the people find internal, self-reliant, native, and efficient solutions. The absence of intellectual freedom prevents the search for and development of internal solutions. This, in turn, has two pernicious ramifications. First, it perpetuates the offensive notion that Africans are incapable of devising their own solutions to their problems. Second, it forces the adoption of externally generated solutions, which do not always work.

In Africa's own supposedly primitive and backward indigenous system, freedom of expression was recognized and respected. At council meetings and village assemblies, ordinary tribesmen participated in the decision-making process by voicing their opinions freely. Further, they took part in debating the various positions until a consensus was reached. Former president of Ghana Dr. Kofi Abrefa Busia (1967) observed, "The traditions of free speech and interchange of views do not support any claim that the denial of free speech or the suppression of opposition is rooted in traditional African political systems" (29).

Traditional African rulers did not arrest, detain, or "liquidate" those who disagreed with them. In fact, one of them, Chief Osagyefo Kuntukununku, stressed the need for freedom of expression to reach consensus: "Future governments would do well to encourage a dialogue between themselves and the populace, confront contrary views with well reasoned arguments rather than intimidation and detention. Suppression of dissent and the denial of the right to express contrary views can only encourage sycophancy and opportunism. There must be a free press to enhance dialogue, efficiency and accountability and to champion the cause of victims of governmental vindictiveness and arbitrariness" (*West Africa,* 27 August–2 September 1990, 2372).

In modern Africa, private newspapers that were courageous enough to expose the problems were shut down and their editors either jailed or murdered. For example:

> Although Zimbabwe is on paper a multi-party democracy, open debate—
> let alone outright political dissent—has been increasingly discouraged. At
> the University of Zimbabwe, students and staff have been swatted by riot
> police with teargas and clubs for complaining about corruption, a growing

scourge. . . . [And] three senior journalists at the weekly *Financial Gazette*, the country's leading free voice, have been charged with "criminal defamation." . . . [And] a new law enables the government to sack outspoken board members of any independent charitable organization and replace them with government-blessed appointees" (*The Economist*, 19 August 1995, 38).

The supreme irony of the vilification and repression campaign is that quite often it is counterproductive. It is a truism that persecution of a person by a brutally repressive regime never achieves its intended objective. Rather, it transforms the victim into a hero, because what is bad in the eyes of the devil must be good. Countless examples can be given: Lech Walesa, Nelson Mandela, Kwame Nkrumah, Kenneth Kaunda, and Wole Soyinka were all persecuted by repressive governments, but they subsequently became presidents of their respective countries. The military government of Ghana never learned from this. One K. Danso-Boafo wrote: "By preventing the Movement for Freedom and Justice (MFJ) from using the premises of the Teachers' Hall for a symposium, and holding and questioning its deputy national secretary Mr. Kwesi Pratt, [Ghana's] PNDC functionaries are making 'political martyrs' out of the MFJ and its leadership—something any astute politician would want to avoid. The political history of Africa is replete with such political miscalculations" (*West Africa*, 3–9 June 1991, 892).

On 12 May 1994, persons believed to be agents of the PNDC sneaked into the premises of *Free Press* and littered it with human excrement. The result? The circulation of the crusading *Free Press* soared and it became Ghana's most popular paper.

Intolerance of alternative viewpoints is a disease that afflicts the ruling elites of Africa. Until supposedly educated Africans learn to accept intellectual diversity among themselves, they are doomed as a race.

The Diagnosis: Externalists Versus Internalists

Even when a problem was finally exposed in Africa, the second and crucial step of diagnosis was usually mishandled. On the causes of Africa's crisis, there have been two schools of thought: the *externalists* and the *internalists*.

The externalists believe that Africa's woes are due to external factors. Disciples of the externalist school include most African leaders, scholars, and intellectual radicals. For decades the externalist position held sway, attributing the causes of almost every African problem to such external factors as Western colonialism and imperialism, the pernicious effects of the slave trade, racist conspiracy plots, exploitation by avaricious multinational corporations, an unjust international economic system, inadequate flows of foreign aid, and deteriorating terms of trade. "Marginalization" has now become the new complaint of African leaders. The West's abandonment of Africa for Eastern Europe, they warn, will vastly impede their efforts to alleviate crushing poverty and squalor.

When the African crisis first emerged in the late 1970s, the causes and diagnoses most frequently offered by African intellectuals and government officials were external. Debates and public scrutiny were not permitted. In his book *The Africans* (1986), African scholar and historian Professor Ali Mazrui examined the African crisis, claiming that almost everything that went wrong in Africa was the fault of Western colonialism and imperialism. "The West harmed Africa's indigenous technological development in a number of ways" (164). He attributed Africa's collapsing infrastructure (roads, railways, and utilities) to the "shallowness of Western institutions," "the lopsided nature of colonial acculturation," and "the moral contradictions of Western political tutelage" (202). In fact, "the political decay is partly a consequence of colonial institutions without cultural roots in Africa" (199). Therefore, self-congratulatory Western assertions of contributing to Africa's modernization are shallow: "The West has contributed far less to Africa than Africa has contributed to the industrial civilization of the West" (164). Decay in law enforcement and mismanagement of funds were all the fault of Western colonialism too. "The pervasive atmosphere in much of the land is one of rust and dust, stagnation and decay, especially within those institutions which were originally bequeathed by the West" (210). They signal "the slow death of an alien civilization" (204) and Africa's rebellion "against westernization masquerading as modernity" (211). Western institutions are doomed "to grind to a standstill in Africa" or decay. "Where Islam is already established, the decay of western civilization is good for Islam since it helps to neutralize a major threat" (19).[1]

---

1. Mazrui, of course, was guilty of the same ethnocentric charges he leveled against Westerners. Islam was not indigenous to Africa. Mazrui devoted several pages to the iniquities of the Western slave trade. "A substantial part of Africa's population was dragged off, kicking and screaming and shipped to the new plantations of the Americas" (100). Curiously, Mazrui never mentioned the atrocities of the East African slave trade that brought suffering or death to at least 2 million black Africans in the nineteenth century. The East African slave trade was largely controlled by Arabs. Mazrui, a Muslim, devoted only one sentence in his entire book to this Arab slave trade (160).

Many African leaders also subscribed to and espoused the view that the causes of Africa's crises were externally generated. In fact, since independence in the 1960s, almost every African malaise was ascribed to the operation or conspiracy of extrinsic agents. The leadership was above reproach and could never be faulted.

A problem with the educational system was, of course, the fault of colonialism. An electricity failure was unquestionably due to an imperialist plot. Commodity shortages were easily explained: the nefarious activities of neo-colonial saboteurs. Even bribery and corruption, according to Mazrui, was the fault of colonialism and the "coming of new institutions such as Western-style banks, with their new rules and new values" (241). President Mobutu offered a more dramatic elucidation. Asked who introduced corruption into Zaire, he retorted: "European businessmen were the ones who said, 'I sell you this thing for $1,000, but $200 will be for your [Swiss bank] account'" (*New African*, July 1988, 25).

In his address to the third Congress of the Democratic Union of Malian People recently, President Moussa Traore observed that,

> The world economy is passing through a period characterised by monetary disorder and slow trade exchanges. The worsening crisis is affecting all countries, particularly developing countries. . . .
>
> Due to the difficult situation, which is compounded by the serious drought, socio-economic life has been affected by serious imbalances that have jeopardised our country's development growth. Debt servicing, characterised mainly by state-to-state debts is a heavy burden on the state budget. The drop in the price of cotton which accounts for much of the country's foreign earnings, has led to a great reduction in export earnings. (*West Africa*, 16 May 1988, 876)

High-ranking African government officials, needless to say, toed their leaders' lines. According to C. M. Nyirabu, governor of the Bank of Tanzania in 1985, "Africa's ills are the result of severe exogenous shocks, such as steep oil-price escalations in the last decade, persistent drought, prolonged recession in the industrial countries and their resort to increased protectionism, continued policies of strict monetarism, and reduction in real terms of external assistance" (Lancaster and Williamson, 1986). David Phri, the governor of the Bank of Zambia in 1986, was quite explicit: "The hostile world economic environment has been the dominant factor in the problems now confronting developing African countries" (Helleiner, 1986, 93).

The United Nations Economic Commission for Africa (ECA) echoes the same "external" dirge. In July 1989 it launched its document, "The African Alternative Framework to Structural Adjustment Programmes for Socio-Economic Recovery and Transformation." In a review, *West Africa* magazine (17-23 July 1989) noted that "The framework is not just another plan. . . . By starting with a structural analysis of Africa's economy, it is able to identify the real impediments to development. In the process, it formulates a critique of the legacy of colonialism, the borders which render 14 countries landlocked, bequeathed 13 with a land area of less than 50,000 hectares each, and have left 23 with a current population of less than 5 million each. It addresses engendered dependence on commodity exports, infrastructural inadequacy, and the dominance of commerce over production (1160).

The constant wailing over colonial legacies was at best disingenuous and attributing much of Africa's crisis to external factors alone was intellectually deficient. In fact, they became standard excuses that many African leaders conveniently employed to conceal their own failures and incompetence. Finally in March 1986, at the Special United Nations Conference on Africa, the African delegates themselves, in a refreshing breath of candor, admitted that "past policy mistakes," especially the neglect of agriculture, had contributed to the African crisis. An earlier report by the Organization of African Unity (OAU), which served as the core of the African sermon at the United Nations, urged African nations "to take measures to strengthen incentive schemes, review public investment policies, [and] improve economic management, including greater discipline and efficiency in the use of resources." Most notably, the OAU Report pledged that "the positive role of the private sector is to be encouraged."

Even a year before that, the African Development Bank and the Economic Commission for Africa produced reports that were adopted at the OAU meeting in July 1985. A review of these reports by *West Africa* was quite revealing:

> The African region is described as suffering from a long-standing crisis rooted in low productivity, limited capacity for adjustment, government policies which have long over-emphasized intervention and control and overlooked incentives, and an international economy characterised by weak demand for Africa's exports, high interest rates, and stagnating resource flows.
>
> But while external factors have played a determining role in present difficulties, the report says that African policymakers are accepting that

internal policy failures are also to blame and that there must be change. *The overall direction of change is seen to be towards more market freedom, more emphasis on producer incentives, as well as reform of the public sector to ensure greater profitability.* (*West Africa*, 21 April 1986, 817) (Emphasis added.)

That was back in 1985. Since then, the OAU or African governments have made little effort to draw up internal solutions. As it turned out, the "admission" of the role of internal factors lacked sincerity and a commitment to address them. It was more of a ruse to extract greater foreign assistance. But such tricks are not helpful in solving a crisis. If internal factors played a role, they ought to be tackled.

The Colonial Legacies

Of all the external factors used to explain Africa's crisis, perhaps the most frequently used has been that of the legacy of European colonialism. The same litany of baneful colonial legacies has been trotted out again and again since independence in the 1960s. African intellectuals have not realized that African government officials often use these legacies as excuses to conceal their own mismanagement and incompetence. It is true that colonialism did not bequeath much to Africa. When Tanzania gained its independence in 1961, it only had 16 university graduates to run the country. Zambia was a little luckier: It had 100 university graduates, 1,500 dropouts with full secondary education, and 6,000 with two years at secondary schools in a country of 4 million.[2] What the Portuguese in Guinea-Bissau left after 300 years of colonial rule was pitiful: "14 university graduates, an illiteracy rate of 97 percent and 267 miles of paved roads in an area twice the size of New Jersey. There was only one modern plant in Guinea-Bissau in 1974—it produced beer for the Portuguese troops—and as a final gesture before leaving, the Portuguese destroyed the national archives" (Lamb, 1983, 5).

But in many African countries, the leadership could not maintain, let alone augment, the little that was inherited from colonialism. In fact, they destroyed it. The inherited infrastructure—roads, bridges, schools,

---

2. Rather foolishly, both Tanzania and Zambia after independence opted for state planning and development—an economic system that made heavy demands on skilled bureaucrats, the very inputs they lacked.

universities, hospitals, telephones, and even the civil service machinery—
are now in shambles. For example, when Zaire obtained its independence
in 1960, it had 31,000 miles of macadamized roads. Today less than
3,500 miles remain usable. In Ghana, where the "colonial" roads are
strewn with yawning potholes, officials insist that it is the vehicle owners
who must obtain "road-worthiness certificates" for their vehicles and not
the roads that must be made "vehicle worthy."

In the 1950s Makerere University in Kampala, Uganda, used to be
proudly called "the Harvard of Africa." Today it is in a state of
dilapidation. Universities in Ghana, Nigeria, and other African countries
are in similar states of decrepitude. The University of Ghana, for
instance, has not seen a new coat of paint since the colonialists departed
in the 1950s. Bridges built by the colonialists are now falling apart for
want of repairs. Railways and other infrastructural facilities are in various
stages of decay. Who is to blame for all this? The colonialists or
incompetent African leaders?

It is true that the past must be studied to provide guidance for the
future. But a mind deeply obsessed with the past is captured by it. Such
a captive mind is incapable of cogent analysis of present and future issues.
Nor can it take advantage of auspicious opportunities that are currently
available. World conditions are certainly not what they were 50 or 100
years ago. There are new technologies, new commodities, new tastes, new
attitudes, and new opportunities. But all these remain invisible to the
mind that is deeply engrossed in colonialism. When a new market
opportunity arises, many African presidents captured by the past analyzed it with woefully outmoded mental constructs.

There has been a constant whimpering over Africa's artificial
colonial borders as the source of many of the crises plaguing the
continent. Says Denis Sassou-Nguesso, former president of the Republic
of Congo and former chairman of the OAU, "Africans were placed
within colonial boundaries. Today, the agitation, the periodic outbursts
of rage, the procession of displaced populations, and the trail of refugees,
reminds us how arbitrary these national borders really are. . . . World
powers pressure African nations to work toward democracy and economic reform, but they seem unconcerned about helping us to solve the
crisis of displaced people: a crisis which stems from artificial colonial
boundaries" (*The Washington Times,* 5 December 1996, A17).

This, however, could not be further from the truth. While it is true
that several ethnic groups, such as the Somali and Ewe of Ghana, found
themselves sliced up and allotted to different countries, the people of

Africa traditionally have paid little attention to borders. They move when the need arises, border or no border, as attested to by the movement of refugees. The best reflection of this traditional reality would be one black African nation south of the Sahara, in which people of various tribes could move freely without harassment from the border police, or at least the political equivalent of a free trade zone, in which people and goods could move freely.

Somalia proves that the artificial borders are not the real cause of the crises. Although it is ethnically homogenous, it collapsed. And when the Republic of Somaliland seceded, it broke away along *colonial* lines. During the colonial era, the Italians occupied the northern part of Somalia and the British the southern part. As Richard Dowden, Africa correspondent for *The Economist,* noted, "Almost no protagonists in Africa's current wars are calling for changes to boundaries and none of these wars would be solved by them. In these wars, rebels are fighting for power—or a slice of power—at the center; that is, in the capital, where the trappings of a unified state are" (*Prospect,* July 1996, 61). And, "By creating artificial countries, the argument goes, yesterday's map-makers are responsible for today's Africa's wars. It sounds plausible, but it is not true. There is not a significant movement in Africa today that wants secession or a change in borders. No ethnic group divided by a frontier is demanding reunification; on the contrary, most such groups have learnt to exploit their situation commercially and politically" (*The Economist,* 25 January 1997, 17).

Furthermore, the practicality of redrawing boundaries to conform to ethnicity is questionable. There are more than 2,000 ethnic groups in Africa; nationalism given full vent might result in more than a thousand little "Djiboutis," each with its own currency, flag, national airline with a one-plane fleet, and a Swiss bank account for the president. Moreover, why the lament over artificial colonial borders when the OAU recognizes the "territorial integrity of each member nation" in its charter? Only African governments—the same members of the OAU—pay much attention to borders for the collection of import "duties" by official and unofficial personnel.

Travel today in independent Africa has been rendered far more difficult than even during the colonial days. Travelers have to contend with not only numerous border checkpoints but also roadblocks within a country itself. It is no secret that these roadblocks serve only as points where uniformed vagabonds extort money from innocent passengers. In an irate letter to *West Africa* (17–23 July 1989, 1184), Mr. R. A. Dawson, headmaster of St. Bartholomew's Boarding School, Zaria, Nigeria, wrote:

In June 1989, I arrived at the Murtala International Airport, Ikeja, on a
Ghana Airways flight No. GH502. After clearing customs and immigration, I boarded an airport taxi for Iddo motor park where I hoped to find
another vehicle to the north where I reside and work.

At Illupeju roadblock, our taxi was stopped by three policemen who
checked my luggage and papers, an act outside their jurisdiction. Then to
the astonishment of the driver and myself, police corporal No. 64539 took
all the money I had on me. When I protested, he threatened to shoot me
dead, and later defended his action by claiming that I was an armed robber
caught in the act because as a Ghanaian I had no right to decent
employment in Nigeria. (1184)

This occurred in a sub-region where the leaders pompously affirm
the ECOWAS protocol of free movement.

The New and Angry Generation of African Internalists

Internalists are those who believe Africa's woes are due more to internal
than external factors. This school of thought maintains that while it is
true that colonialism and Western imperialism did not leave Africa in
good shape, Africa's condition has been made immeasurably worse by
internal factors: misguided leadership, systemic corruption, capital flight,
economic mismanagement, senseless civil wars, political tyranny, flagrant violations of human rights, and military vandalism.

Internalists argue that the attribution of Africa's crises solely to external
forces is intellectually deficient for several reasons. First, pragmatism and
scientific scholarship demand, at the very least, an unerring scrutiny of *all*
causative factors, both external and internal. Common sense dictates looking
both ways before crossing a street, or risk being hit by a truck. Africa is in
bandages because its leaders looked only one way—at the external.

Second, external factors are beyond the control or manipulation of
most African countries on an individual basis. Even if possible, any effort
to alter the external environment is likely to be protracted, taking
decades. For example, the basic structure of the international economic
system has not changed much in the past 50 years, although there have
been improvements in payment mechanisms, transportation of goods,
and information delivery systems. This international economic system
is likely to remain for a long time to come.

Third, internal factors are mostly man-made or artificial and are
therefore more amenable to change or correction by African governments

than the external factors. No matter how much colonialism is abhorred, that artifact of history cannot be undone or rewritten; it must be seen as a given.

In the internalist school of thought may be found Nobel laureate Wole Soyinka, Kwesi Armah, the author of *The Beautiful Ones Are Not Yet Born*, the present author, and the silent peasant majority. When soldiers seized power in Africa, they almost always cited corruption, economic mismanagement, and high cost of living as justification. And the average person on the streets does not blame colonialism and American imperialism for his hardships.

Because of censorship, repression, intolerance of diversity of opinion, and persecution—even in the broader African intellectual community—the number of internalists in the public arena is small. Incompetent African leaders naturally reject the internalist position and place blame on external factors. The state-controlled media carries their position. They are aided, directly and indirectly, by vocal leftist radicals who denounce internalists as "Uncle Toms," accusing them of "letting the white man off the hook" and "providing ammunition to the racists." This is a reflection of the insidious intolerance of intellectual diversity among black elites that we noted earlier.

Internalists are fighting back against this invective. A growing number of African intellectuals are now deemphasizing historical and external factors and looking inside Africa itself for the true causes of the crises and solutions. Said Akobeng Eric, a Ghanaian, in a letter to the *Free Press* (29 March–11 April 1996): "A big obstacle to economic growth in Africa is the tendency to put all blame, failures and shortcomings on outside forces. Progress might have been achieved if we had always tried first to remove the mote in our own eyes" (2).

A strange thing happened at an international conference on Africa's Imperative Agenda, held in Nairobi in January 1995. The conference document, prepared by Philip Ndegwa, former chairman of Kenya's Central Bank, and Reginald Green, of the Institute of Development Studies at the University of Sussex, stated in stark terms: "Africa is now a continent which cannot feed itself, meet its external financial obligations or the bill for its essential imports, protect its increasing population, prevent environmental degradation, or exert any meaningful influence in the international decision-making process. . . . A substantial number of African countries are now in danger of national disintegration, including some which, as recently as the late 1980s, were held up as success stories" (*Africa Recovery*, June 1995, 8). It is striking that the document devoted only 3 of its 18 sections to the external dimension of

Africa's multiple crises and focused more on Africa's own responsibility and initiatives.

Internalist influence was also evident at the "Africa 2000" Conference organized by the Hofstra Cultural Center of Hofstra University in Hempstead, New York on 12 October 1995. In its "Call for Papers" flyer, part of the instructions read: "All papers should focus on, or at least prominently discuss, the immediate future faced by Africa. Thus papers dealing with historical events, for example, would not be appropriate, unless the thrust of the discussion related the historical context to an understanding of the present or immediate future." Traditionally, conferences on Africa have featured speaker upon speaker who perorated passionately about the iniquities of colonialism, the slave trade and Western imperialism. The Hofstra conference sounded a call for a paradigm shift, making it clear that papers dealing with such historical factors would not be welcome.

On 12 August 1995 various Nigerian groups and organizations held the Nigerian National Leadership Forum in Nashville, Tennessee, to find out exactly what the "problem" was with Nigeria. As *African News Weekly* (26 August 1995) reported:

> Professor David Murauko, the chairman of the forum, was sure he knew what Nigeria's biggest problem is. Tribalism. After all, this is what motivated him to organize the conference. So he opened his presentation by asking the audience what they felt was Nigeria's greatest problem.
>
> One participant got up and said Nigeria's greatest problem was corruption. Another person said Nigeria's biggest problem was poor economic conditions, explaining that if everyone had something to eat, no one would be complaining. Another person said lack of democracy; another said lack of rule of law; and yet another said personalized politics. (2)

No one at the forum blamed colonialism, imperialism, slavery, exploitation by an unjust international economic system, or other external factors. The report continued: "One participant summed it up this way: Asking people to define Nigeria's problem is like sending twelve blind men to feel an elephant and then describe it. They would all have different but accurate descriptions of the animal depending on what part they touched"(2).

Metaphorically speaking, the "elephant" is the alien, all-powerful, gargantuan, predatory state that was established by African leaders and elites after independence.[3] This "elephant" has been the source of most of Africa's "environmental problems." Invested with tremendous powers to which there have been no countervailing checks and balances, the marauding state pillages, rapes, and loots, trampling upon human rights, and leaving human debris and carcasses in its wake. This abominable political monstrosity was created by African leaders themselves and, therefore, cannot be blamed on colonialism.

Bad and Corrupt Leadership

The leadership in much of Africa has not only been a hopeless failure but also a disgrace to black people. President Mobutu Sese Seko of Zaire was a prime example. Zaire should be a prosperous country; it is blessed with vast mineral deposits and rich agricultural lands in the fertile Congo basin. But arrant misrule and plunder have reduced it to tatters.

More and more Africans now blame their leaders for the mess they find themselves in. Said Chinua Achebe (1985):

> The fear that should nightly haunt our leaders (but does not) is that they may already have betrayed irretrievably Nigeria's high destiny. The countless billions that a generous Providence poured into our national coffers in the last ten years (1972–1982) would have been enough to launch this nation into the middle-rank of developed nations and transformed the lives of our poor and needy. But what have we done with it? Stolen and salted away by people in power and their accomplices. Squandered in uncontrollable importation of all kinds of useless consumer merchandise from every corner of the globe. Embezzled through inflated contracts to an increasing army of party loyalists who have neither the desire nor the competence to execute their contracts. (3)

Said John Hayford in *New African* (April 1994): "Africa's biggest problem today lies with the leadership. They are so removed from the people that they are looked upon as foreigners. They are driven by self-interest, so excessive that their peoples' interests are forgotten—hardly

---

3. The word "alien" is chosen deliberately because of the basic antinomy of the modern systems with indigenous African institutions. This is important in order to avoid sterile ideological debates that inevitably result from the assessment of systems. The standard being used to evaluate them is *African*, not foreign.

different from the colonial masters" (7). A Ghanaian university student, Kwesi Obeng, added this view: "In all hue and cry, what is both infuriating and irritating is the speed with which African countries together with their leaders are quick to blame all that go wrong on the continent on our supposed 'Enemy'—the West. This sad culture is what has propelled me to protest with all the venom that I can muster. . . . Why can't we accept our responsibilities as a race (black race), face the music for our deeds and always tend to pass the buck?" (*The Ghanaian Chronicle,* 21 January 1996, 4).

More tragic has been the failure of Africa's intellectuals. One Nigerian scholar, Linus U. J. Thomas-Ogboji, excoriated members of his own profession:

> We Nigerian [intellectuals] bear the mark of Cain. Ours is the incredible stigma of the man who whimpers and averts his gaze while thugs rape his wife and daughters. We have acquiesced in the unmitigated horror that smothers Nigeria. Many of us bite our tongues because we nurse secret hopes of a chance at the feeding trough. A few, with expectations of reward, even go so far as to defend the Nigerian army. But most of us are just plain scared, paralyzed by fear and chagrin. . . . Is it fear of death that holds us emasculated? There comes a time to die and in death gain redemption. . . . When a people give up the desire for freedom, they are better off dead. (*African News Weekly,* 26 May 1995, 6).

By attributing Africa's ills to external factors, many of Africa's intellectuals, wittingly in expectation of reward or unwittingly, absolved the leadership of responsibility. Additionally, the stress on external factors presupposed that the solutions had to come from external sources; hence the repeated appeals to the international community. Unfortunately, this approach has proven disastrous. Foreign solutions have not worked well in Africa because they do not fit into its unique sociocultural milieu. The continent is a graveyard littered with a multitude of failed imported schemes and systems. Name a foreign system and a collapsed replica can be found—from basilicas to congresses and even combine harvesters.

THE REAL CAUSES OF AFRICA'S CRISES

The environmental defects identified—political instability, chaos, corruption, and the like—are interdependent. For example, abuse of political power may be inextricably bound up with incompetent leadership. Further, many of them are merely symptomatic of two fundamental ailments: the defective political system of sultanism and the defective economic systems of statism.

Sultanism or personal rule is the monopolization of political power by one individual, the grotesque forms being president-for-life and military dictatorship. By statism is meant state hegemony in the economy and the direction of economic activity or development by the state through such devices as price controls, legislative acts, regulations, state ownership of the means of production, and operation of state enterprises. The statist behemoth, with wide-ranging powers, is backed by a coercive military and judicial force. The combination of sultanism and statism results in the concentration of enormous powers in the hands of the state and ultimately in one individual:

> With the passage of PNDC Law 42, which gives all Legislative, Executive, Judicial as well as Administrative powers to one man, Chairman of the PNDC, Ghana as a whole has virtually become a large poultry farm with the Chairman of the PNDC as the sole poultry farmer. What the 14 million souls in Ghana will eat or drink, when the 14 million souls have to sleep and when they have to wake up, what they say and where they have to say it, how the 14 million souls in Ghana may die and what happens to their dead bodies all appear by virtue of PNDC Law 42 to be the prerogative of the Chairman of the PNDC alone. (*Free Press*, 10 April 1997, 2)[4]

Ideology is not particularly relevant in the analysis of Africa's crisis. Regardless of their professed ideologies, most African regimes have been statist. The economic and political systems established in postcolonial Africa were neither colonial nor indigenously African. The colonial state structure benefited the European powers, while the current systems benefit the ruling elites, a tiny minority—an "elite apartheid." In country after country in Africa, the story has been the same: the monopolization

---

4. The writer, Mr. Obeng Manu continued by railing against the collaboration of lawyers: "To be frank, I admire the ingenuity and craftiness of the lawyers who drafted the PNDC Law 42 but I cannot at the same time keep feeling that such a masterpiece is equally an indictment on the legal profession and an eternal, monumental shame on the present and future generations of lawyers."

of both economic and political power by a tiny group (racial, ethnic, or professional), which uses its governing authority to extract resources from the peasantry and spend them to enrich itself. All others, the majority, are excluded.

Under South Africa's abominable system of apartheid, whites captured political and economic power while blacks were excluded from participation in government and the spoils system. But similar systems of political and economic apartheid pervaded the rest of Africa. In Sudan and Mauritania, Arabs held power and blacks were excluded (Arab apartheid); in Rwanda and Burundi, the Hutus and Tutsis alternatively usurped power; in Nigeria the Hausa-Fulani ran the government (tribal apartheid); Togo, Zaire, and Uganda were overtaken by the military (stratocracy); and Angola, Côte d'Ivoire, Mozambique, Kenya, and Tanzania were run by one political party (one-party state). Regardless of the circumstances, each system practiced the politics of exclusion.

A white South African émigré in Michigan, Lindi Jordan, had some sharp words for her fellow white South Africans who kept deluding themselves that their system of apartheid was different: "Welcome to Africa, South Africa. Like a Black African government of an elite minority holding all economic and political power, whites under apartheid ran a bloated and inefficient civil service with a brutal and corrupt security apparatus to suppress the majority. It is an absurd vanity of white South Africans to regard themselves as different from the rest of Africa. You ARE Africa and Africa is YOU" (*Juluka*, December 1996/January 1997, 9).

The politics of exclusion has been the source of Africa's chronic political instability, civil strife, wars, and chaos. Where the ruling elites had the foresight and wisdom to agree to and implement real democratic reform and power sharing, they saved not only themselves but their countries as well: Examples include Benin, Malawi, Mali, and South Africa. But where benighted rulers and hardliners refused to share or relinquish power, those excluded had no choice but to seek to overthrow the system or to secede. Either course of action resulted in violence, carnage, and destruction, as evidenced by Burundi, Ethiopia, Liberia, Rwanda, Somalia, and Zaire.

To maintain their grip on power, recalcitrant despots often resort to trickery and manipulation of the democratic process. Indeed, a careful study of the numerous civil wars that have ravaged Africa in the postcolonial period is quite revealing. The destruction of an African country, regardless of the professed ideology of its government, *always* begins with some dispute over the electoral process. Blockage of the democratic process or the refusal to hold elections plunged Angola, Chad, Ethiopia, Mozambique, Somalia, and Sudan into civil war. Hardliner manipulation of the electoral process destroyed Rwanda (1993), Sierra Leone (1992), and Zaire (1990). Subversion of the electoral process in Liberia (1985) eventually set off a civil war in 1989. The same type of subversion instigated civil strife in Cameroon (1991), Congo (1992), Kenya (1992), Togo (1992), and Lesotho (1998). Finally, the military's annulment of electoral results by the military started Algeria's civil war (1992) and plunged Nigeria into political turmoil (1993). All this destruction stemmed from the adamant refusal of one individual or the ruling elites to relinquish or share political power.

The 1993 Somalia Crisis

Somalia's descent into barbaric lawlessness did not occur overnight and could have long been predicted. Although the Somalis are ethnically homogenous, their plight under and after colonial rule bore testimony to the capriciousness of colonial boundaries. They were split five ways, finding themselves in British Somaliland, Italian Somaliland, Ethiopia (in the Ogaden), Kenya, and Djibouti. The nation of Somalia was formed and granted independence in July 1960 when the British Protectorate and the Italian Trust were joined, while the rest of the Somali people were left in Ethiopia, Djibouti, and Kenya.

The civilian administration that assumed power after independence became hopelessly corrupt and incompetent. On 21 October 1969 it was overthrown in a bloodless coup by Major-General Mohamed Siad Barre, who adopted the socialist model and the designation "Jalle" ("Comrade"). Government was centralized under a "Supreme Revolutionary Council," and Somalia turned to the Soviet Union for tutelage during the period 1970 to 1977.

The break with Moscow came when the Soviets refused to support Barre's grand scheme of uniting the Somali in one "Greater Somaliland." Both Somalia and Ethiopia were Soviet allies in the Horn of Africa, and the Soviets were unwilling to support military incursions into Ethiopia. Although Barre seized the Ogaden in southern Ethiopia in a successful military campaign in 1977, he was routed and expelled by Ethiopian forces with help from Moscow in March 1978.

Barre then turned to the United States. The Carter administration promised to help if Somalia would cut its ties to Moscow. It did so, and

on 22 August 1980, Somalia and the United States signed an agreement
permitting the United States the use of military facilities at the port of
Berbera. In exchange, Washington agreed to provide Barre with $20
million in credits for purchase of military equipment, $5 million in
budgetary support, and $20 million in general credits. But this alliance
switch did not save the country, which was already beyond redemption.

Earlier, in July 1976, the Revolutionary Council had been disbanded
and replaced with the Revolutionary Socialist Party, the sole legal party.
The Italian Socialist Party gave considerable backing and support to the
Barre regime. According to Italian journalist Wolfgang Achtner, "The
[Italian] Socialists flooded Somalia with millions of dollars of aid. Siad
Barre obtained arms, military advisers and trainers for his armed forces"
(*The Washington Post,* 24 January 1993, C3). American journalist
Michael Maren (1997) wrote:

> For ten years before the 1992 famine, Somalia was the largest recipient of
> aid in sub-Saharan Africa, in some years the third largest in the world
> behind perennial leaders Egypt and Israel. But most of Somalia's 6 million
> people never saw a penny. Much of what wasn't filtered out to pay the
> expenses of the relief agency was lost in the corrupt maze of the Somali
> government's nepotistic bureaucracy. . . . Aid money went to Somali
> bureaucrats whose primary skill was in earning money by dealing with
> foreign charities. And when money did drip down to the people it was
> used in ways designed by a government desperately trying to cling to its
> diminishing power. (24)

Socialist policies failed to engineer economic development.
Although Somalia did become a major world supplier of bananas, by
1979 the economy was in shambles. The International Monetary Fund
(IMF), summoned in 1980, called for market-oriented economic policies, devaluation of the Somali shilling, and sale of unprofitable state
enterprises. After eight years of government policy zigzags and posturing,
a frustrated IMF pulled out in June 1988, declaring Somalia ineligible
for further borrowing.

Over the period 1965 to 1987, living standards remained stagnant.
Despite receiving substantial amounts of foreign aid, GNP per capita
grew at a miserable 0.3 percent per annum, earning Somalia the title "the
Graveyard of Aid" (*New African Yearbook,* 1991–1992, 303). Over $800
million poured in from the United States during this time, and Italy
alone spent more than $1 billion to sponsor 114 projects between 1981

and 1990. Corruption soared and foreign aid just replaced capital outflows. In 1984, for example, $15 million flowed out of Somalia. Misguided socialist policies did not help food production either. Food production per capita declined by 2.7 percent over the period 1975 to 1980 and a further 1.3 percent from 1980 to 1985. By 1987 consumer prices had risen 1,000 percent over the 1980 level.

As Barre's regime became increasingly corrupt and unpopular, it resorted to brutal force to crush all opposition. Torture, mass executions, pillage, and carnage were the regime's signatures. So paranoid was Barre's military regime that it declared war on its own people. In May 1988 it dropped bombs on its own citizens after they demonstrated against Barre's 20-year despotic rule. Hundreds of thousands of innocent people were summarily put to death or imprisoned. Many politicians, businessmen, religious leaders, and young students simply vanished or were butchered. For example, on 16 July 1989, in the early hours of the *Iid Al Adha* day, a Muslim holy day, government forces swooped down and arrested six prominent imams after the morning prayers. Whole sections of the crowd of worshippers were gunned down. Innocent people were rounded up in the hundreds, and many were murdered and buried on the Jasira beach. Over 1,000 died that day.

In March 1990 Africa Watch, a New York based human rights organization, charged Barre's regime with "responsibility for the deaths of 50,000 to 60,000 civilians since hostilities broke out between the government and rebels from the Somali National Movement." Africa Watch also noted that "Entire regions have been devastated by a military engaged in combat against its own people, resembling a foreign occupation force that recognizes no constraints on its power to kill, rape or loot" (*Africa Report*, March/April 1990, 10).

Two rebel movements—the United Somali Congress (USC) and the Somali National Movement (SNM)—set out to overthrow Siad Barre. In January 1991, the same month the Persian Gulf War erupted, they succeeded in driving him out of power. His ouster caused a power vacuum, and internecine rivalry erupted between the rebel groups. The USC controlled the south, including the capital, Mogadishu, while the SNM controlled the north. In March of that year, the north seceded to form the Republic of Somaliland. Then factionalism emerged within the ranks of the USC.

One faction was led by interim President Mahdi Mohamed and the other by General Mohamed Farah Aideed. Mogadishu became a divided city as the two battled for the presidency. Aideed controlled most of the southern sector while Mahdi's stronghold was the Kaaraan district and other northern areas. This turn of events shocked many Africans. The country, in the process of removing Barre, had already been devastated—reduced to an ash heap of charred buildings and burned-out vehicles, with decomposing bodies littering the streets. Yet "educated" barbarians were waging a fierce battle to determine who would be president, totally unconcerned about the plight of their people.

For much of 1992, most of Somalia lay in ruins—effectively destroyed. It had no government, no police force, no basic essential services. Armed thugs and bandits roamed the country, pillaging and plundering, and murderous warlords battled savagely for control of Mogadishu. The carnage, worsened by a drought, claimed over 300,000 lives, and horrific spectacles of emaciated bodies of famine victims were daily visited upon Western television viewers.

During 1993 an international humanitarian mission was launched jointly by the United States and United Nations to end the hunger and violence. Although the goal of the mission was long achieved, the United Nations found itself dragged into the Somalis' battles, resulting in the deaths of dozens of U.N. peacekeepers and hundreds of Somalis killed by U.S. and U.N. forces. In June 1993, 24 Pakistani soldiers serving under U.N. command were ambushed and killed by bandits loyal to General Mohamed Aideed. When 18 United States Rangers were killed in October 1993 during a firefight with General Aideed's forces, it became apparent to U.S. policy makers that establishing a functioning society in Somalia was more complex than first conceived. The United States and subsequently the United Nations pulled out of Somalia in 1994.

Somalia would have been saved if the late Siad Barre had agreed to democratic reform and power sharing, as did the whites later in South Africa. The subsequent destruction could have been halted if the warlords had been amenable to reason.

The 1994 Burundi-Rwanda Crisis

The Rwanda-Burundi crises were a replay of Somalia's, except that a recalcitrant despot played the ethnic card to keep his grip on power. The colonialists had played that card too but tyrannical African heads of state in the postcolonial period refined this stratagem to an art form.

Both Rwanda and Burundi are populated by two ethnic groups—the minority Tutsis, who constitute less than 15 percent of the populations in both countries, and the majority Hutus. The tall Tutsis (also called Watutsis) are pastoralists who originally migrated southward from Ethiopia and established their sovereignty over the native Hutus, who are smaller in stature and mostly farmers. The Tutsis enforced overlordship and segregation through superior wealth (measured in cattle), superior military organization, and control over the allocation of land. The Hutu peasantry was held to an inferior status and forced to labor for the Tutsis as servants and tillers.

The master-client relationship was accentuated at first by German colonialists (1890-1916) and then by Belgian administrators (1916-1962). The Tutsis were accorded authority and power over the country, given administrative jobs and a monopoly in the educational system set up by Catholic missionaries. The Hutu peasantry, held in centuries of serfdom and subjugation by the minority Tutsis, became increasingly resentful during colonial rule. On 25 July 1959, they rose in rebellion and overthrew their Tutsi overlords, killing an estimated 100,000 Tutsis. A shocked Belgian colonial government hurriedly and belatedly introduced political reform. A 1961 U.N.-supervised referendum adopted a republican constitution, and parliamentary elections brought the Hutu majority party, *Parmehutu,* to power. Independence was attained on 1 July 1962, but thereafter the Tutsis have launched sporadic guerrilla operations to regain their old hegemony. One such expedition in 1963 by Tutsi guerrillas, unwisely backed by China, resulted in the massacre of more than 20,000 Hutus.

The Hutu-controlled government grew increasingly despotic and corrupt. The mysterious 1985 murder of Dian Fossey, the American naturalist who devoted her life to saving the mountain gorillas in the Volcano National Park, briefly drew world attention to Rwanda. In 1990 another rebel Tutsi group, demanding democratic pluralism, led an invasion into Rwanda from neighboring Uganda. There had been allegations that Tutsi rebels have been trained by Uganda's military and that Uganda's military dictator, Yoweri Museveni, was a Tutsi. Fighting and killings erupted intermittently in and around the capital, Kigali, despite the presence of 2,500 U.N. peacekeeping troops drawn from 24 countries. All these Tutsi insurrections failed to win political power and efforts to reach an accord between Tutsi rebels and the Hutu-dominated government led to an impasse in 1993.

Burundi was the sister German colony to Rwanda, administered jointly by the Germans as Ruanda-Urundi. The German, and subsequent Belgian, colonial policy of indirect rule through chiefs, which gave strong powers to Tutsi overlords, exacerbated social tensions in Burundi just as in Rwanda. The assassination of Louis Rwagasore, a Tutsi and a nationalist leader, on 13 October 1961, by a European, just months before independence in 1962, opened up deep divisions and suspicions within the Tutsi elite, which led to their defeat in the 1964 parliamentary elections. But the then head of state, Mwami Mwambutsa, refused to name a Hutu prime minister, whereupon the Hutu military and political elite staged an abortive coup in October 1965. A brutal purge of Hutus from the army and the bureaucracy followed, leading to a Hutu uprising in April 1972 that resulted in the deaths of about 1,000 Tutsis. The ruling Tutsi aristocracy decided to eliminate the "Hutu threat" by killing every Hutu with education, a government job, or money. Within three months, more than 200,000 Hutus had been slain.

The Tutsi minority maintained its monopoly on political power and instituted a bizarre passbook system—akin to the ignominious South African apartheid pass system—to exclude the majority Hutus from key government and army positions. Then in August 1988, following an abortive coup attempt, the Tutsi-run military government under Pierre Buyoya massacred an estimated 20,000 Hutus. U.N. officials at refugee camps near the border with Rwanda told of soldiers chasing, machine-gunning, and bayoneting fleeing Hutus. The scale and barbarity of the atrocities shocked many Western aid officials.

The carnage was repeated in 1993, following Burundi's first multi-party elections, which were won by the Hutus. A Hutu civilian president, Meldior Ndadaye, was sworn in as president. Within three months, the Tutsi-dominated military overthrew the civilian government and bayo-neted its president to death, instigating a horrific tribal massacre that claimed over 100,000 lives and sent more than 500,000 refugees streaming into Rwanda, Tanzania, and Zaire.

On 4 April 1994, President Habyarimana of Rwanda traveled with Burundi's president, Cyprien Ntaryamira, to Dar es Salaam, Tanzania, where they and other African leaders met in an attempt to end years of ethnic warfare in their countries. On their return from Tanzania, on 6 April, the two presidents were killed in an apparent rocket attack on their plane. "The rockets were fired from the immediate vicinity of the Kigali airport, an area controlled by the Rwandan army" (*The Washington Post,* 17 April 1994, C2). It was unclear who fired the rockets but Alison DesForges of Human Rights Watch/Africa speculated that, "The assailants could have been extremists within the Rwandan Army who wanted to remove Habryarimana before the transitional government took power. They could have been soldiers linked to the internal opposition, impatient with the delays in implementing the peace accords. Whatever the circumstances, it provided extremists within the ruling group with the long-sought pretext for wiping out their opponents. Within an hour of the announcement of Habyarimana's death, the elite presidential guard launched a search-and-destroy mission" (*The Washington Post*, 17 April 1994, C2).

Hutu hard-liners then turned on Hutu moderates, who favored negotiations. In the beginning, these groups in the army, cabinet, and civil service battled one another. Rwanda's interim prime minister, Agathe Uwilingiyimana, three cabinet ministers (all Hutus and of the same tribe as the soldiers), 17 Jesuit priests, and at least 10 Belgian peacekeeping soldiers were brutally killed. "At first the killing wasn't purely ethnic. It was also political," said Desire Habiyambire, a Hutu moderate who fled Rwanda with his three children "after his name was circulated on a hit list" (*Time*, 16 May 1994, 58). "I am caught in the middle," he added. "Extremism is my enemy. If I meet a Hutu extremist, he will kill me. If I meet a Tutsi extremist, he too will kill me."

Taking advantage of the confusion, people began settling old tribal scores. The melee quickly degenerated into a free-for-all. "Everyone is fighting against his own brother," said Philippe Gaillard, chief of the Rwanda office of the International Committee of the Red Cross (*The Washington Post*, 14 April 1994, A1). About 700,000 Tutsis were slain in the orgy of violence. With the presidential guard and army destroyed, the small Tutsi rebel battalion sailed into the capital, Kigali, meeting little resistance. Fearing reprisals, about 1.1 million Hutu refugees fled across the border into Zaire.

Once again, this carnage would have been avoided had both the Tutsis of Burundi and the Hutus of Rwanda been willing to share political power.

The 1995 Liberian Crisis

Ever since Liberia was founded in 1847 by freed U.S. slaves, its history has been characterized by truculent perfidy. The freed U.S. slaves, known as Americo-Liberians, established an overlordship over the indigenes that was similar to white settler colonialism in other parts of Africa. They even imposed forced labor, akin to slavery, on the indigenous peoples. The sale of such African slaves to Spanish colonialists on the Atlantic Ocean island of Fernando Po in 1930 so outraged Britain and the United States as to cause them to sever diplomatic relations with Liberia for five years.

Americo-Liberians rarely mixed or shared power with the local population. Resentment boiled.

When on 12 April 1980 a group of enlisted men under the command of Sergeant Samuel Doe, a member of the Krahn tribe, stormed Liberia's executive mansion and overthrew the regime of William Tolbert, native Liberians roared with euphoria. But it quickly evaporated. Liberians who had initially welcomed the coup recoiled in horror when Doe, an illiterate, proceeded to institute a brutal reign of terror and his own brand of tribal apartheid. All top positions in his government, the army, and his presidential guards were filled with members of his own tribe.

The coup itself was accompanied by acts of savage brutality. Tolbert was murdered as he lay in bed. The soldiers disemboweled the dead leader and gouged out one of his eyes with a bayonet. His mutilated body was displayed for two days at the John F. Kennedy Hospital morgue and then buried with 27 others in a mass grave. The soldiers then went on an orgy of massacres and barbaric reprisals, killing an estimated 200 people. In a chilling spectacle that was televised nationwide, high government officials of the deposed regime were summarily tried and executed by a drunken firing squad. Their half-naked corpses were then dangled from a row of telephone poles on the beach.

Under pressure from the United States, Doe held elections in 1985, but they were massively rigged to produce himself as the winner. In December 1989 Charles Taylor, a descendant of the Americo-Liberians, set out with about 150 ragtag rebel soldiers of the National Patriotic Front of Liberia (NPFL) to oust General Doe from power. Other tribes, including the Gio and Mano tribes of eastern Liberia, who were victims of Doe's brutal tyranny, joined in, as did half of even Doe's own soldiers, who deserted.

But the objective of the uprising quickly changed. Bitter feuding emerged, even before Doe was captured and killed in September 1990, between Taylor and his commander, Prince Yormie Johnson, with each claiming the presidency. To prevent further deterioration of the situation, the Economic Community of West African States (ECOWAS) rushed in a peacekeeping force, the Economic Community Ceasefire Monitoring Group (ECOMOG) in August. It set up an Interim Government of National Unity (IGNU) under Amos Sawyer. Seeing his presidential ambitions thwarted, Taylor declared war on the ECOMOG. Remnants of Doe's army sensed an opportunity, regrouped into the United Liberation Movement (ULIMO), and joined the ECOMOG to fight Taylor. The ULIMO subsequently split into a Krahn faction led by Roosevelt Johnson (ULIMO-J), and another faction led by the Muslim Alhaji

Kromah of the Mandingo tribe (ULIMO-K). Other factions emerged, and very quickly the situation degenerated into a mad tribal grab for power.

All sides committed atrocities during the war: the mass destruction of villages and rape of married women by Liberian Peace Council fighters in Grand Bassa county; the slaughter of at least 547 people at Carter Camp, near Harbel, by the Armed Forces of Liberia militia on 6 June 1993; the hacking to death of about 60 people, mostly women and children, in the small town of Yosi in May 1995. Roadblocks were mounted everywhere for extortion. Every movable item was looted, even U.N. vehicles.

The war's insanity unnerved even its own prosecutors. In July 1994 Tom Woewiyu, former defense spokesman for the NPFL, called a press conference to denounce his leader, Charles Taylor. "Over the years, everybody seemed to have given the NPFL the opportunities to accomplish its goals through politics, but Mr. Taylor has constantly obstructed that, insisting that he must be President of this country by force; not even by election, or else, the war will not stop. NPFL is not the problem. The problem is our leader, Mr. Charles Taylor. He is opposed to any peace in the country" (*The African Observer*, September 1994, 34).

Thirty percent of Taylor's estimated 10,000 soldiers were child warriors under the age of 15. They were inducted by a mixture of coercion and enticement. Said a 12-year-old boy named Emmanuel: "I was asked to fight ULIMO because they beat my mother and father. Besides, there was no food, and if I joined I could get food for my family, at least a bag of rice" (*The African Observer*, September 1994, 34). To make the soldiers more belligerent, they were fed marijuana, cocaine, and mixture of cane juice and gunpowder, which can cause brain damage. "Charles Taylor takes pride in walking around with other people's 8-year-olds dragging an AK-47 behind him while his children are in private schools in Geneva and other parts of the world," Tom Woewiyu revealed.

The human and economic toll of Liberia's seven-year civil war was enormous. More than 150,000 people perished and over a third of Liberia's 2.3 million people fled to neighboring countries. The war also spilled over into neighboring Sierra Leone, eventually toppling the regime of General Joseph Momoh. Gambian soldiers returning from a stint in Liberia ousted the democratically elected government of Sir Dawda Jawara.

The 1996 Eastern Zaire Crisis

The crisis in eastern Zaire resulted from the confluence of the effects of four concurrent unresolved political conflicts in Burundi, Rwanda, Zaire, and

Uganda. Each country has an ethnic Tutsi population. Tribal solidarity mandates defense assistance to kinsmen under attack in any of the four countries. Although the world sees the crisis as emanating from tribal conflict, in reality it is more of a protracted struggle for political power that uses ethnicity as a tool. Why else would Hutu militiamen slaughter their own kinsmen who were making preparations to return to Rwanda?

It may be recalled that in 1959 the Hutus rose in rebellion in Rwanda and Burundi and massacred thousands of Tutsis, with survivors fleeing to Uganda. From there they launched sporadic invasions, the most serious being that in 1993, which resulted in the 1994 carnage. France was "sending arms, helicopters, even 700 of its own soldiers in 1990-93 to help the Hutu government of Juvenal Habyarimana fight off the Tutsi rebels of the Rwanda Patriotic Front" (*The Economist,* 23 July 1994, 21). Said Gerard Prunier of the Paris-based National Center for Scientific Research, "By offering military and diplomatic support to the regime and not employing their troops to stop the killings, the French unwittingly gave a green light to the mass murder. The Hutu regime began to think it could do anything. President Francois Mitterrand believed he was simply employing the old strategy of shoring up a local Francophone strongman against Anglophone 'wrongdoers'" (*The Wall Street Journal,* 24 January 1997, A14).

When the Hutu government soldiers were routed, France created a "safety zone" inside Rwanda to protect fleeing Hutus. France feared that the invading Tutsis from Uganda, an English-speaking country, had lost all trappings of French culture after their long exile. The Hutus eventually fled Rwanda and were shepherded into French-speaking Zaire.

In November 1996 the Hutu refugees in eastern Zaire faced imminent death from starvation and diseases such as cholera, dysentery, and malaria. Canada proposed to lead an international military intervention force, with as many as 10,000 troops, to deliver vital relief supplies and medicine. Canada was to commit up to 1,500 of its soldiers and the United States, after dispatching a 40-member team to Central Africa to assess the supply and security situation needs, was to contribute 4,000 soldiers.

The glaring deficiency of the mission was the utter abdication of African leadership on this issue. The Organization of African Unity, which has persistently railed against foreign meddling in Africa's internal affairs, was nowhere to be found.

During his five-nation African tour in October 1996, Secretary of State Warren Christopher proposed a new United States–supported crisis-response force of 10,000 to 25,000 troops. This African Crisis Response Force (ACRF) would be deployed to intervene in serious cases of insurrection, genocide, or civil strife to avert a Rwanda-like conflagration in crisis-laden African countries, such as Burundi, where an estimated 150,000 Burundians have perished in ethnic warfare since 1993. Only two African countries, Mali and Ethiopia, agreed to supply troops for such a force—naturally. The standing joke in the African community is that the rest of the African governments declined because they needed their soldiers at home to suppress and brutalize their own people.

France aided and abetted African leadership abdication, and even explicitly defended such inaction whenever it suited its general anti-Anglophone posture in Africa. It slammed the African Crisis Response Force idea proposed by the United States as a "trespass on traditional French territory." On 9 October 1996 France's Minister for Foreign Cooperation, Jacques Godfrain, charged that Christopher's trip was politically-motivated to pander to black voters in the forthcoming November elections and to African governments whose support the United States needed to deny Boutros Boutros-Ghali a second term as United Nations Secretary-General. Ironically, in 1994, at the Biarritz Summit of Francophone African states, France had proposed exactly such a force—a continental peacekeeping force manned by African soldiers and trained, equipped, and financed by France, other European countries, and the United States—to absolve the West of any need to get embroiled in Africa's wars. "The time has come for Africans themselves to resolve their conflicts and organize their own security," the late French President, Francois Mitterrand, had then declared.

The Collapse of Zaire

The fictional state of Zaire, before it imploded in October 1996, was long in an advanced stage of decay due to 32 years of misrule by former president Mobutu Sese Seko. Government structures had collapsed, infrastructure crumbled, paved roads had been reduced to cratered cartways. Civil servants and soldiers went for months without pay. Zairean diplomatic missions abroad were not spared; they were constantly plagued by termination of phone and electricity services for nonpayment of bills. In Denmark, in 1992 the Zairean ambassador was found sleeping under a railroad trestle after being evicted by his landlord. In Zaire itself, entire provinces, notably Shaba and Kivu, were in a state of rebellion, asserting their independence from Kinshasa.

Hyperinflation raged at 23,000 percent a year. The Zairean currency was worthless. A new bank note of 5 million *zaire* was introduced in January 1993 and used to pay Mobutu's soldiers. When shopkeepers refused to accept the notes (deemed worth only about $2), soldiers went on a rampage, looting and destroying property. Among the targets was a warehouse belonging to the United States Agency for International Development (US AID), where 50 vehicles and $3 million worth of equipment was stolen or destroyed. During the rampage, the French ambassador was shot to death while watching the violence from his office window. Mobutu called out his Presidential Division soldiers to quell the rampage, and human rights groups estimated that before it was over, 266 people died in hospitals and 300 others had been killed.

To maintain his grip on power, Mobutu, just like the other Africa despots, played the same divide and conquer tactic with deft skill. The only difference was that Zaire was a much bigger country, with about 400 tribes. In addition, his control over the military was unyielding. In 1992 the Zairean army numbered around 100,000 personnel. The largest sector was the regular army, known as the Zairean Armed Forces (FAZ), which numbered 81,000—60,000 of whom were under arms. To prevent the military from overthrowing him, Mobutu ran down the regular army to 20,000 men and formed a succession of strike forces to use against internal threats. He presided over six specialized security forces, hand-picked for loyalty, including the 10,000-strong Civil Guard, headed by General Kpama Baramoto, Mobutu's brother-in-law. But it was the Special Presidential Division (DSP), numbering 15,000 under arms that represented the strong arm of Mobutu's rule. Both the Civil Guard and the Special Presidential Division were answerable to the president, while the Zairean Armed Forces were under the control of the ministry of defense. Senior officers were largely from Mobutu's Equateur region and Gbande tribe. Fragmented military and security organs, each watching the other, could not overthrow him. Similarly, Mobutu allowed the country's infrastructure to crumble for political reasons rather than due to sheer neglect. With roads impassable and communication systems in shambles, it was next to impossible for political opponents to organize against him.

On 24 September 1991, Zairean soldiers, angry at not being paid, rioted and looted businesses and private homes. The stolen goods, including television sets, video recorders, bicycles, sewing machines and cars, were brazenly sold at an open market at an army barracks (Camp

Kokolo). "Camp Kokolo is proof not only that the military is completely out of control but that the senior officers are afraid of their own soldiers," said Albert Moleka, a member of the opposition party Young Republicans (*The New York Times*, 4 November 1991, A6).

The October 1996 crisis in eastern Zaire was triggered by a series of events occurring simultaneously. First, Zaire's ill-disciplined and unpaid soldiers, noted more for their brutalities than for defense of the country, had resorted to pillage as their livelihood. In Kivu and Lower Zaire, the business communities decided to pay soldiers' salaries to prevent further incidents of looting. However, eventually fed up with brazen extortion, businesses closed their doors. The arrival of Rwandan Hutu refugees in Kivu and Lower Zaire provided the soldiers with new sources of revenue. They sold weapons to former Rwandan government officials and Hutu militiamen who had fled Rwanda. Relief supplies were plundered. When relief workers stood vigilant, Zairean soldiers increasingly ransacked villages in Kivu, populated by rebellious and fiercely independent ethnic Tutsis called the Banyamulenge, who had lived in Zaire since the eighteenth century. Their independent stance had increasingly rankled Mobutu, who revoked their Zairean citizenship in 1981. In August 1996 the governor of Kivu Province ordered them expelled from Zaire—a decision that was subsequently rescinded.

Second, Hutu militiamen who had acquired weapons from Zairean soldiers joined them in the plunder of Banyamulenge villages. Zairean Tutsis saw another pogrom coming, armed themselves, and sought help from their kinsmen across the border in Rwanda, Burundi, and Uganda.

Third, according to Rwanda's powerful defense minister Paul Kagame, who led the Tutsi rebellion that toppled Habryimana's Hutu government in Rwanda in 1994, "the impetus for the war was the Hutu refugee camps. Hutu militiamen used the camps as bases from which they launched raids into Rwanda and were preparing a full-scale invasion of Rwanda" (*The Washington Post*, 9 July 1997, A18). Attempts by Rwandan officials to persuade the United Nations and Western powers to demilitarize the refugee camps and separate the Hutu troops from the real refugees got nowhere. "They were insensitive. We told them [the U.N. and Western countries] that either they do something about the camps or they face the consequences," Kagame complained (*The Washington Post*, 9 July 1997, A18).

The Rwandan army then began training the Banyamulenge while Rwandan agents started making contacts with other Zairean rebel forces opposed to Mobutu. On 18 October 1996 long-time opponents of the Mobutu regime joined forces with the Tutsis in an Alliance of Democratic Forces for the Liberation of Congo-Zaire (ADFL). The Alliance (ADFL) was made up of the following groups: (1) The People's Democratic Alliance (*Alliance Democratique des Peuples*—ADP) led by Deogratias Bugera; (2) The National Resistance Council for Democracy (*Conseil National de Resistance pour la Democratie*—CNRD) which was created in 1993 by Andre Kisase Ngandu of the MNC/Lumumba, the original group behind this movement for the liberation of Congo (Zaire)[5]; (3) The Revolutionary Movement for the Liberation of Zaire (RMLZ) (*Mouvement Revolutionnaire pour la Liberation du Zaire*— MRLZ) of Masasu Nindaga; and (4) The People's Revolutionary Party (*Parti de la Revolution Populaire*—PRP) of Laurent Desire Kabila.

Laurent Kabila was a Marxist revolutionary who existed in obscurity for three decades. In the 1960s, he was a disciple of Pierre Mulele, a Chinese-inspired Marxist, who together with Kabila launched the failed Simba rebellion in Shaba for independence. That struggle briefly attracted the attention and support of the legendary Ernesto "Che" Guevara, who flew in a contingent of Cuban fighters. But "Che" became bitterly disappointed in Kabila, who "seemed reluctant to visit the front and drove around Dar es Salaam in a Mercedes Benz" (*The African Observer*, 5-11 June 1997, 13). Kabila subsequently founded the People's Revolutionary Party. It based itself near Uvira but remained politically inactive.

---

5. MNC/Lumumba stands for *Mouvement National Congolais/Lumumba* (National Congolese Movement/Lumumba), whose president Dr. Albert Lumumba Onawelho lived in exile in London. In 1993, Mr. Andre Kisase Ngandu, along with Mr. Henri Mangala, went to London to seek from Dr. Onawelho instructions for his MNC's fighters who had already been carrying out raids in eastern Congo (Zaire) since 1991. Upon their return to Africa they created the National Resistance Council for Democracy (NRCD) (*Conseil National de Resistance pour la Democratie*, CNRD) as the armed wing of MNC/Lumumba and teamed up with the *Front de Liberation National du Congo* (FLNC), which was run by ex-Kantagese *gendarmes*. These were Zaireans who failed in their bid for autonomy for mineral-rich Katanga province in the 1960s and 1970s and subsequently fled to Angola. They returned—together with the children of the original separatists—to join the uprising against Mobutu.

On 1 November 1996 the Alliance conferred the position of spokesman on Kabila. Rebel commanders explained that "Kabila, 56, who had been fighting against Mobutu since 1963, was convenient choice. He had good relations with Rwanda, Uganda and an important rebel faction, the Banyamulenge of South Kivu Province, a group of Congolese Tutsis who constituted some of the rebels' most successful forces. But he himself was a Luba, not a Tutsi, and thus more palatable to Congo's 400 other tribes" (*The Washington Post,* 6 July 1997, A17).

The Alliance's opportunity came in early October when the Rwandans received word of a plan by the Hutus in Zaire to attack the Banyamulenge, who live near Uvira and Bukavu, south of Goma. Rwandan agents also learned of a plan to invade Rwanda with 100,000 Hutus, including 40,000 Hutu militiamen. The Tutsis in both Rwanda and Zaire prepared for war.

After repeated pillaging by Zairean soldiers, the Banyamulenge struck back and seized on 24 October their first major town, Uvira, at the northern end of Lake Tanganyika. After routing Mobutu's soldiers, the rebels targeted the Hutu refugee camps in Goma, Mugunga, and Bukavu. A rebel bombardment of Mugunga, the largest refugee center with rockets, mortars, and heavy artillery for six hours on 14 November, set off an exodus of Rwandan Hutu refugees from Mugunga and other camps. About 700,000 Hutu refugees returned to Rwanda, the remainder fled west and south into Burundi.

Kabila arrived in Goma from Bukavu just a few days after the fall of Uvira, Bukavu, and Goma. He then made his first statement as spokesman for the Alliance. Two days later he was already presenting himself as the Alliance's President without the agreement of the other members of the ADFL (*The Washington Post,* 6 July 1997, A17). General Andre Kisase Ngandu reminded Kabila that he was not the Alliance's President but simply its spokesman and should desist from representing himself to the international press as the President of the Alliance. Kabila refused, accusing him General Ngandu of wanting to overthrow him (Kabila).

Retreating Zairean soldiers, humiliated by Tutsi rebels, laid Kisangani to waste, sending waves of villagers scampering into the surrounding rain forest. Zairean soldiers also crossed into Uganda to retaliate against President Yoweri Museveni, a Tutsi, who had been supporting the rebels. Skirmishes erupted at the town of Kasetse on the Uganda/Zaire border. Elsewhere in eastern Zaire, Mobutu's defeated soldiers resorted to plunder. Again, as in Kivu, some local businessmen and relief agencies tried to appease the marauding troops by providing them with food and gasoline—the same extortionist demands that were made by the "technicals" (bandits who roamed freely in Mogadishu in open trucks with machine guns mounted on the cargo rack) of Somalia and the warlords of Liberia.

At that point the rebel soldiers had achieved their goal of driving the marauding Zairean soldiers out of the east. Zairean soldiers barely put up a fight. In Kalemie, Goma, Bukavu, and Uvira, hundreds of them defected in droves with their weapons to the rebels' side. The rest simply fled, looting and pillaging on the way. But the swiftness with which the rebels accomplished that mission and the reception they received from the populace, who everywhere hailed them as liberators, as well as the lack of resistance offered by Mobutu's soldiers, convinced the rebels that the rest of Zaire was theirs for the taking.

The primary objective of both Uganda and Rwanda was to clean up the border area and create a buffer zone along their borders with Zaire. Although that objective had been accomplished and the Hutu refugee camps emptied, Paul Kagame felt that "doing it halfway would be very dangerous. We found the best way was to take it to the end" (*The Washington Post,* 9 July 1997, A18). Angola's government, which sent soldiers to help the rebels, also wanted to continue the campaign and topple Mobutu because he had helped Angola's UNITA rebel movement, which was headed by Jonas Savimbi. Then came Kabila's declaration that the removal of Mobutu from power was now the ultimate goal.

During this time President Mobutu was in France recuperating from prostate cancer when the crisis in eastern Zaire erupted. He returned on 17 December 1996 to a tumultuous reception in Kinshasa, amid wild expectations that he was the only person who could keep the country together and resolve the crisis. He appointed a new armed forces chief to reverse the humiliation suffered by his troops at the hands of the rebels. He reshuffled his government to launch a counter-offensive against the rebels. But three weeks later he returned to France for more cancer therapy. "Catcalls greeted his motorcade the day he left. And shortly afterward, when new bank notes went into circulation and sparked fears of inflation, Kinshasa's grapevine gave the money a vicious name. 'Prostate money,' they called it: Just like cancer, the new bills can kill" (*The Washington Post,* 24 January 1997, A25).

The government counter-offensive began on 20 January 1997 with air strikes aimed at the rebel-held towns of Bukavu, Shabunda, and

Walikale. Undeterred, the rebels continued their relentless advance on several fronts. After capturing Bunia and Beni on the Rwandan border, the rebels moved north. Young men cheerfully volunteered to join the rebels and more African countries (Angola, Eritrea, Tanzania, Zambia, and even Zimbabwe) joined in the support of the rebel cause, as Mobutu's regime had become a canker on the continent.

By the time Mobutu returned from France on 7 February 1997 a third of the country was under the control of the rebels, who were advancing relentlessly toward Kisangani, Zaire's third largest city with a population of 300,000. Mobutu flew in French, Russian, and Serbian mercenaries, paying each $2,500 a month while his own soldiers received the equivalent of $1 a month. The defense of Kisangani was to no avail. Its fall marked a crucial turning point in the war. It represented the worst military setback for Mobutu and a strategic triumph for the rebels. The capital of Upper Zaire province and the army's northeastern headquarters, Kisangani boasted two airports, from which bombing raids were launched against rebel-held towns in the east, and a key commercial route on the Zaire River.

A flurry of diplomatic initiatives, launched by the United Nations and the Organization of African Unity (OAU) to end the civil war, failed abysmally. Two peace conferences held by the OAU in Nairobi and a follow-up March 26 Summit at Lome, Togo, got nowhere. Nor did private efforts by President Mandela aboard a South African frigate.

By 14 April 1997 half of Zaire was in rebel hands, as they continued their steady march on Kinshasa. Faced with deserting soldiers, Mobutu surrendered. On 16 May 1997 a government spokesman declared that Mobutu "has ceased all intervention in the affairs of the state" and had left for his northern jungle palace at Gbadolite, from where he left the country into exile aboard an aging Russian cargo plane. The next day, Kabila's rebels sailed into Kinshasa and took power. On 22 May 1997 Laurent Kabila was sworn in as the new head of state of the Democratic Republic of the Congo—Zaire's new name. The Zairean story should have had a happy ending but tragically it turned out to be yet another postscript to Africa's truculent tale of betrayal. The removal of an African despot does not necessarily usher in a period of stability and prosperity.

As desirable as the ouster of Mobutu was, the international community should not enthusiastically embrace people who shoot their way to power in Africa. Such active and open support for a rebel insurgency poses a serious setback to the democratization process in

Africa. It sends a dangerous signal and delivers a destabilizing jolt to a continent already reeling from wanton brutality, chaos, and carnage. Other insurgencies would be encouraged. In this vein, a communiqué issued on 9 May 1997 by political parties in Zaire's parliament is noteworthy. It observed that peaceful demands for democratic change had failed to produce results and, "given that the only language understood by those in power is the language of arms," it expressed support for armed struggle to establish democracy (*The Washington Times,* 11 May 1997, A13). But then, Africa's experience with rebel leaders has been the most ghastly and disconcerting. The record of rebel insurgencies or liberation movements in postcolonial Africa hardly inspires confidence and hope.

Most of the rebel leaders, who set out to remove tyrants from power, turned out to be crocodile liberators, who left wanton carnage and human debris in their wake. And hitched to their movement was a cacophonous assortment of quack revolutionaries, vampire elites, political entrepreneurs and intellectual hyenas. Even before they accomplish their liberation mission, rebel movements often splinter into factions along tribal lines and turn their guns on themselves. Ghanaians have this expression which Ethiopians, Liberians, Somalis, and Zaireans can relate to: *"Obiaara baa saa"*—"Everybody who comes, the same."

The honeymoon for a new African leader is usually six months but for Kabila it was distinctly brief. Within a couple of months, it became apparent to Zaireans (now Congolese) that they had simply traded one despot for another. Mini-skirts were banned by Kabila's government, as well as any political activity. In April 1997 he seized and nationalized Sizarail, the Zairean railroad company owned by South African and Belgian interests. Then he began speaking of establishing a "social market" and collective farms, raising the specter of "Swiss bank socialism" all over again. Most grievous was his failure to include Etienne Tshisekedi in his transitional government. Tshisekedi had been Zaire's most popular opposition leader with his support bases in Kinshasa and Kisangani. He had been Mobutu's ferocious foe since 1980. Kabila's misguided attempt to marginalize Tshisekedi and cut out his supporters provoked riots and demonstrations. Tshisekedi urged his supporters "to resist the new regime." A protest march by his supporters in Kinshasa on 24 May 1997 turned violent, prompting a rebel soldier to fire into the air to disperse the crowd. Subsequent protest marches led to the arrest and detention of Tshisekedi and his family by Kabila's regime. The

Tshisekedis were picked up at midnight and released after ten hours, after being warned to stay out of politics. "They told me I have lots of influence over the press, and I must muzzle the press. They told me to abandon politics" (*The Washington Times,* 8 July 1997, A15). On 9 July 1997 opposition politicians called for the creation of a Popular Army to resist Kabila's government. Jacques Matanda ma Mboyo, a former Kabila ally, said in Paris that the new president has established a "neo-Mobutism" (*The Washington Times,* 10 July 1997, A10).

The most serious threat to Congo's stability, however, came from Kabila's own ADFL, a fractious alliance of four political parties. Even before Kabila took office, a serious rift within the alliance had resulted in the 6 January 1997 assassination of General Andre Kisase Ngandu, who, it may be recalled, asked Kabila in October 1996 not to represent himself as the president of the ADFL. According to *Washington Post* correspondent James Rupert, "Rebel officers who opposed [Kabila's] policy were done away with. One, Andre Kisase Ngandu, a senior commander, was gunned down by Rwandan Tutsi troops near Goma on 6 January, a senior non-Tutsi rebel officer and other sources said" (*The Washington Post,* 6 July 1997, A17).

The prominent role played in the insurgency by Zaire's minority ethnic Tutsis—the Banyamulenge, who number less than 1 million of Zaire's 43 million people—was deeply resented by the Baluba, the Babembe, and the Bahunde—strong and fiercely independent tribes of eastern Zaire—as well as others, such as the ex-Katangan *gendarmes.* Tension between them and Tutsi soldiers erupted into a gun-fight in Goma in April 1997. Tutsis feature prominently in key positions in Kabila's administration and the military, leading his critics to charge that Congo is being ruled by a Rwandan occupation force.

Indeed, in an interview with *Washington Post* correspondent James Pomfret, Paul Kagame disclosed for the first time that "the Rwandan government planned and directed the rebellion that ousted the long-time dictator and that Rwandan troops and officers led the rebel forces" (*The Washington Post,* 9 July 1997, A1). By Kagame's accounts, the war, which began in eastern Zaire near the borders of Rwanda and Uganda, was planned primarily by Rwanda, and the plan to remove Mobutu also originated in Kigali. Questions about Kabila's role in the insurgency are bound to rise.

Elsewhere in Africa, no sooner had Kabila taken office than fighting erupted in three more African countries: Congo (Brazzaville), The

Central African Republic, and Sierra Leone. Africa's civil wars, respecting no artificial colonial borders, often spill over from one country to the next, while the OAU pontificates hysterically over the sanctity of the borders. Already the "Kabila effect" is threatening to destabilize Kenya. Chanting "Moi-butu, Moi-butu!" and *"Mwizi,"* a Swahili word for "thief," angry protesters poured into the streets of Nairobi on 7 July 1997, demanding constitutional reforms before that year's elections. The reaction of the Moi regime was swift and vicious. "Police shot at students, grabbed passengers from buses and raided an Anglican cathedral in downtown Nairobi, lobbing tear gas canisters and setting upon members of the congregation" (*The Washington Post,* 11 July 1997, A29). Eleven people were killed, but the protesters were not deterred.

They demanded a constitutional change that would allow a coalition government. The constitutional prohibition against coalition governments allowed Moi to retain power in 1992 despite winning only 38 percent of the vote. In addition, they sought the following: (1) the repeal of the Public Order Act, which requires a permit for any gathering of nine or more Kenyans; (2) the repeal of the Chief Authority Act, which officials invoke to break up political and civic education meetings held in private homes; (3) a non-partisan Electoral Commission; and (4) equal access to the airwaves; radio and television licenses are issued to only those who promise not to broadcast news or make political commentaries.

Meanwhile in Sierra Leone, a group of soldiers revolted, claiming that their pay was inadequate, and overthrew the civilian government of Alhaji Tejan Kabbah on 25 May 1997. They demanded $46 million before restoring the Kabbah back to power. Gani Fawehimni, human rights activist and Nigerian lawyer, described the coup leaders as "armed buffoons whose sole aim of taking power was to destroy democracy, impose anarchy, perpetuate barrack gangsterism, and loot the treasury" (*The African Observer,* 29 May–4 June 1997, 3).

Sierra Leoneans have a proverb which goes like this: "The moon shines brightly but it is still dark in some places." A village elder might use this proverb in the following situation. Suppose a village family scrounged under their mattresses, pots, and pans for enough of their life savings to send a child to school, who returns to the village a monumental disaster. He cannot do anything right and messes up colossally. Finally the elder might look steely at him, shakes his head and says, "O the moon shines brightly but it is still dark in some places."

When rebel leader Charles Taylor in neighboring Liberia started his guerrilla campaign to oust the brutal military dictator, the late General Samuel Doe, from power in 1989, a previously unknown rebel group, the Revolutionary United Front (RUF), was also agitating for democracy in Sierra Leone, then laboring under the military dictatorship of General Joseph Momoh. RUF operated in the countryside, waging a low-intensity guerrilla campaign under the leadership of Foday Sankoh. Sierra Leone's ill-equipped and undisciplined national army, like their counterparts in Zaire, proved no match against the rebels. In fact, they resorted to opportunistic plunder. They were soldiers in the daytime, but at night, they shed their military uniforms, donned rebel attire and pillaged villages. Sierra Leoneans coined the term "sobels" (soldier-rebels) to describe them.

It was at this time that the ferocious mayhem in Liberia forced ECOWAS to dispatch ECOMOG peacekeeping troops with a mandate to restore peace, establish an interim government, and prepare the country for democratic rule. The ECOMOG troops were drawn from five West African countries: The Gambia, Guinea, Sierra Leone, Ghana, and Nigeria. Out of the five, only The Gambia—at that time in 1990— had a democratic government; the rest were ruled by military dictatorships. Imagine these governments going to restore peace and establish democracy in Liberia.

It soon became apparent that ECOMOG was not neutral in the Liberian conflict. West Africa's military dictators who sent troops were sympathetic to their own kind—General Doe. In fact, General Doe was a personal friend of Nigeria's former military dictator, General Ibrahim Babangida. Frustrated at his bid to remove General Doe from power and assume the presidency, Liberia's rebel leader Taylor demanded the withdrawal of ECOMOG forces to no avail. Taylor decided to take revenge by helping RUF, operating in neighboring Sierra Leone, which had dispatched soldiers as part of the ECOMOG force. In response, Momoh's government formed a joint commission with Nigeria to promote economic and social integration, as well as to reach a mutual defense pact. In 1991, in co-operation with Guinea, Nigeria sent troops and equipment to Sierra Leone to ward off threats from Taylor's forces.

After 1990, however, the civil war in Sierra Leone intensified. Its economy was teetering on the brink of collapse. General Momoh's regime was increasingly being rocked by scandals. A major one hit the headlines when it was discovered in 1991 that no work had been done on about 32 government contracts that had a price tag of 1 billion *leones* (about $2 million), although 500 million *leones* had been paid out to the contractors. Just as in Zaire, corruption had so inexorably drained government coffers that it could not even pay its own soldiers it had sent off to the countryside to fight RUF rebels. A group of soldiers, returning from the war front and led by Captain Valentine Strasser, overthrew the General Momoh's regime. However, the change of government did not improve its fortunes in its campaign against RUF rebels.

In 1993, the new Strasser regime hired the services of Executive Outcomes, a private South African military outfit, to train Sierra Leone's battered military. Within a few years the war situation changed dramatically. Rebel gains in the countryside had been reversed and peace restored. Elections were held in 1996. But success had its cost. Guess whom the newly trained soldiers subsequently turned their guns on? On 25 May 1997 they overthrew the civilian president Alhaji Tejan Kabbah and formed an alliance with RUF! The moon shines brightly . . .

General Sani Abacha, head of Nigeria's military government, leader of the ECOMOG forces trying to restore peace to strife-torn Liberia, and signatory to a defense pact with Sierra Leone, refused to allow this to happen. On 2 June he dispatched a contingent of 2,000 Nigerian soldiers to Sierra Leone to force the coup leaders to return power to Kabbah. At the titanic battle between "armed buffoons" and coconut-heads, the Nigerian soldiers had the worst of it and 300 of them were taken prisoner. The supreme irony was that General Abacha himself overthrew a civilian government in 1994 and jailed the civilian, Chief Moshood Abiola, who had won the 1993 presidential elections. Here was a military general charging ahead to restore a civilian president to power in another country while his own civilian president was languishing in jail. Nobel laureate and Nigerian playwright Wole Soyinka (1996) has not been impressed: "It is a fair assessment of the IQ of Abacha that he actually imagines that his transparent ploy for self-perpetuation would fool the market woman, the roadside mechanic, the student, factory worker, or religious leader of whatever persuasion. Even the village idiot must marvel at such banal attempts to rival a disgraced predecessor" (10).

The OAU, met in June in Harare, Zimbabwe, and issued a communiqué clearing the way for a Nigerian military invasion of Sierra Leone. The *Mail & Guardian* (6 June 1997) of South Africa was irate:

> The OAU decision is like seconding the Mafia to raid dope smokers at a high school. Nigeria's corrupt and brutal military regime has had an enormous destabilizing role in West Africa. If the OAU is really serious

about standing up to the forces that impede democracy on the continent—as that great democrat and now OAU chairman Robert Mugabe claims it is—it should be assembling an intervention force to go into Nigeria and overthrow Sani Abacha who illegally came to power in a coup in 1993. But there is not a whisper even about economic sanctions against Abacha. That is because restoring democracy is not what this trade union of criminals—as Ugandan President Yoweri Museveni described them so succinctly last week—is seeking to achieve. (4)

Indeed, a "trade union of criminals" flocks together. Said *Ghana Drum* (June 1997) in an editorial: "The coup leaders in Sierra Leone are doing the same thing other soldiers in other countries did or are doing. They overthrow constitutionally elected governments promising changes that never come. Get civilian sycophants to help write new constitutions in their favor. Indemnify themselves. Hold and win 'elections' as civilians and continue to rule. What a shame! Call them despots, egomaniacs, bullies, and what have you but despot after despot, idiot after idiot we keep marching on to our economic abyss. What a tragedy!" (2).

RESOLVING AFRICA'S CRISES

A serious study of Africa's interminable and innumerable crises reveals that they all share a similar evolution. Each crisis begins when an "educated" buffoon, civilian or military, assumes power through an election or a coup d'état. He then proceeds to entrench himself in office by amassing power and surreptitiously debauching all key government institutions: the military, the civil service, the judiciary, and the banking system. With all powers in his hands, he transforms the state into his personal property—to benefit himself, his cronies, and tribesmen, who all then proceed to plunder the treasury. All others who do not belong to this privileged class are excluded, as the politics of exclusion is practiced.

The tyrant employs a variety of tactics to decimate opposition to his rule: co-optation, bribery, infiltration, intimidation, and "divide and conquer." Opposition leaders compound their weakness by their constant bickering. Out of frustration, a rebel group emerges from the excluded class and mounts a guerrilla campaign to oust the despot and his cohorts from power or to secede, as in the Biafran secession in 1967. In the course of the insurgency, the guerrilla movement splits into several factions, often along tribal lines. If the campaign to overthrow the regime is unsuccessful, the war drags on for years, even decades, as in Angola, Mozambique, and Sudan. If the head of state is ousted or killed, a power vacuum emerges and factional leaders battle ferociously to fill the void, as in Somalia and Liberia.

Chaos and carnage ensue. Infrastructure is destroyed. Food production and delivery are disrupted. Thousands are dislocated and flee, becoming internal refugees and placing severe strains on the social systems of the resident population. Food supplies run out. Starvation looms.

The Western media bombards the international community with horrific pictures of rail-thin famine victims. Unable to bear the horror, the international community is stirred to mount eleventh-hour humanitarian rescue missions. Food, tents, blankets, portable toilets, high-protein biscuits, and other relief supplies are airlifted to the refugees.

Factional leaders, who initially welcomed the humanitarian mission to feed refugees, turn against the mission and refuse to cooperate with it because its presence accords some legitimacy and recognition to the hated regime. Factional leaders then demand that relief organizations deal with them and not the regime. The demands soon turn into extortion. At some point, relief supplies are attacked and aid workers are taken hostage or killed. The mission loses public support and is terminated; relief workers are pulled out and the starving refugees are left to fend for themselves. That is, until another African country blows up and the whole macabre ritual is repeated. Nothing—absolutely nothing, it seems—have been learned.

More maddening is that the solution to all these crises lies internally—in each African country. It entails the modernization of an indigenous African political tradition—the village assembly. When a crisis erupted in an African village, the chief and his council of elders would summon a *village meeting*—similar to New England's town hall meetings. There, the issue would be debated by the people until a *consensus* was reached. Once a decision was made, everyone in the village, including the chief, would be required to abide by it.

This indigenous tradition was revived, modernized as a "sovereign national coference," and used to resolve political crises and make peaceful transition to democratic rule in Benin, Cape Verde Islands, Malawi, Mali, Zambia and South Africa. By contrast, the national conference convened by Mobutu in 1992 was not sovereign. The conference was packed with delegates from the more than 200 political parties that Mobutu created himself, leading Zaireans to scorn multi-partyism as "multi-Mobutuism." Nor were the decisions of the conference binding upon Mobutu. In fact, he repeatedly sabotaged the conference.

Kabila was expected to rectify this but failed to do so. Instead he fixed September 1999 as the date for multiparty elections. It is not Kabila nor Mobutu who must fix the date for multiparty elections, as Mobutu did in 1996, but rather a sovereign national conference. The destiny of an African nation does not lie in the hands of one person.

Two factors underlie Africa's never-ending political violence and civil wars: the absence of mechanisms for (1) peaceful transfer of political power, and (2) for the peaceful resolution of conflicts. As we argued, carnage and chaos often result from a mad grab for power centralized at the capital. Those grappling for power lose sight of the ideal and become too heavily involved in achieving this short-term goal instead of looking to the future, which requires focusing on long-term goals. Long-term solutions would involve the decentralization or diffusion of power and the adoption of power-sharing arrangements; namely, democratic pluralism. There are far too many oppressive dictatorships in Africa. The democratic reform process, which gathered momentum after the collapse of communism in 1989, has stalled. In 1990, only 4 of the 54 African countries were democratic. Although this number had grown to 14 in 1996 (Botswana, Benin, Cape Verde Islands, Central African Republic, Madagascar, Malawi, Mali, Mauritius, Namibia, São Tome & Principe, Senegal, Seychelles, Sierra Leone, South Africa, and Zambia), political tyranny is still the order of the day.

Wily autocrats quickly learned new tricks to beat back the democratic challenge by inflating voter rolls, manipulating the electoral rules, and holding fraudulent elections to keep themselves in power, as in Algeria, Angola, Cameroon, Ghana, Kenya, and Zimbabwe. Nigeria, for example, is in a perpetual state of transition to democratic rule under the watchful eyes of its ever-competent military bandits. Benin, Cape Verde Islands, Malawi, Mali, South Africa, and Zambia held democratic elections and peacefully changed governments. There were no refugee crises in these countries. In the rest, the only way to remove an incompetent, corrupt, and oppressive regime from power, is by waging a destructive civil war.

Second, there has been a near-total absence of mechanisms or institutions for peaceful resolution of conflicts, internally and continentally. Disputes arise in all societies. Two people may claim the same plot of land. Five political parties may claim the presidency of a country. A society that does not have the means or structures for resolving disputes simply self-destructs. In prehistoric times, Neanderthals resolved their disputes with clubs. Naturally, the one wielding the biggest club always won. The modern equivalent of this barbaric form of dispute resolution is resorting to the bazooka. The one with the largest arsenal, of course, wins the dispute, with the country thoroughly destroyed.

There are *civilized* ways of resolving social, economic, and political disputes. Society establishes a structure, forum, mechanism, or institution to settle them. These mechanisms are of two general types. The first is the direct, face-to-face dialogue, or negotiation, which may be formal or informal. The informal kind occurs when a disputant invites the other over, say, to his home for dinner, to talk over their disagreement. No third parties are involved and the deliberations are strictly private. However, when two parties enter into formal dialogue, third parties or the press may be present.

Of course, African leaders are aware of dialogue and are quick to recommend it to others. When the Liberian crisis flared up, members of the Economic Community of West Africa, led by Nigeria and Ghana, urged the warlords to dialogue. Ghana even held at least four peace conferences in Accra for the warlords. But the military regimes in Ghana and Nigeria refused to sit down to dialogue with their opponents. Nigeria's military ruler, General Sani Abacha for example, decided that the best way to dialogue with Chief Moshood Abiola was to keep him in jail.

Dialogue or negotiation is not possible if one or both parties is not interested in talking. A dialogue can redress a grievance only if *both* parties are willing to sit down to talk, *both* show good faith in the deliberations, and *both* are willing to abide by the results. If any of these conditions cannot be satisfied, then the alternative is to present the dispute to some other body to adjudicate.

Thus, the second general type of dispute settlement technique is to engage the services of a third party. The parties may take their dispute to a court or submit it to arbitration by a panel or commission. But for any of these modalities to work, the independence and impartiality of the third party must be assured and the disputants must agree to abide by the rulings.

For the court system to work in resolving disputes, it must not only act impartially but also be seen as impartial and independent; that is, free from intimidation or control from any quarter. A supreme or district court that is packed with government lackeys, as in Kenya, Ghana, or Togo, is not impartial. Establishing an impartial court is only half the story. A court ruling must be accepted by both parties; if one side is not willing to accept the ruling, then the whole exercise would be a monumental waste of time and resources. This can be overcome by empowering the court to enforce its ruling. For example, if one party disregards the court's ruling, he could be arrested, fined, or jailed for being in contempt of court. If the erring party is the president of the country, he could be impeached for the same offense.

Binding arbitration is another form of third-party dispute resolution. A panel or commission of respected personalities, such as retired judges, professors, army generals, or traditional leaders, deliberate on the dispute and render a judgement, which is binding on both parties. Both must agree to the constitution of the panel and its terms before it begins deliberation.

Each modality has its own advantages and demerits. Face-to-face dialogue can be quicker, since the disputants face each other and each can adjust or modulate his position as the horse-trading proceeds. But the two parties must have the capacity to be flexible. Dialogue is not likely to succeed when bitter enmity exists between the two parties or when disputants enter with hardened positions. The court system has the advantages of legal backing and the possibility of appeal. A district magistrate court's ruling can be appealed to a higher court, but that can take time and cost money. Binding arbitration can be quicker but it allows no appeals.

Whatever the modality, successful resolution of disputes must have three key features. First, the forum must be recognized by all as the place to take disputes to. Second, the adjudication process must be transparent; that is, judges must be impartial and the process open, with no backroom deals struck. Third, the rulings must be accepted by all. If not, an appeal must be allowed, but a limit should be placed by establishing a final court of appeal.

In much of Africa, these structures are woefully lacking. Thus, a trivial political dispute can easily escalate into a full-blown civil war that sends refugees streaming in all directions. A typical example was the February 1994 deadly ethnic conflict in northern Ghana between the Konkomba, the Nanumba, the Dagomba, and the Gonja, which claimed over 2,000 lives. The conflict was started by a simple dispute over the price of a fowl. This dispute flared up into a general conflict because there was no local institution for resolving disputes.

Tension had long been simmering among the ethnic groups. At issue was the Konkomba claim to paramountcy and a traditional council. They contended that they had their own land, their own political district, and their own culture and language. Their "land" comprised the entire Oti Basin, stretching from the northern tip of the Northern Region to the northern part of the Volta Region, which they claimed to have inhabited as far back as the seventeenth century. As such, they claimed to be entitled to a paramountcy to be sited at Saboba.

According to the Ya-Na, king of the Dagbon, "the Konkombas do not own any land in Dagbon. Rather they cohabit on Dagbon land with Dagbamba and will never be given the land they were seeking." "I can assure you that much as I am resolved never to cede a square inch of Dagbon land, I am equally determined that all persons on Dagbon land should enjoy the protection of the law and should be free to pursue their legitimate business unhindered by any person or authority" (*Ghana Drum*, April 1994, 21).

Since the dispute could not be solved at the local level, the case had to be referred to Accra, the seat of government. But it took time to get the facts of the case to Accra. Even then, Accra was notoriously slow in responding. It might send government delegations or promise a commission of inquiry while people were being killed. Worse, Accra took sides in the dispute.

As many as 18 National Democratic Congress members of parliament from the Northern Region sided with the Nanumba-Dagbon. Most reprehensible were allegations by Dr. Mohammed Ibn Chambas, MP for Bimbilla in the Nanumba District, that the Konkombas started the violence, with the backing of the government of Togo. An NDC minister without portfolio added fuel to the fire by calling upon the government to "teach the Konkombas a lesson they deserve." In cases such as this, African governments fail to act with scrupulous neutrality and thereby aggravate the conflict.

If impartial and formal mechanisms for the peaceful resolution of disputes do not exist or are not supported by the government, then people with grievances will seek alternative, unorthodox means, such as protest marches (peaceful or violent), civil disobedience, strikes (work stoppage and obstruction), sabotage of government machinery, riots, coups d'état, revolutions (to overthrow a tyrannical government), terror or intimidation campaigns and civil strife or war. None of these, of course, is palatable. Each is disruptive, costly, and destructive. African governments are right in disapproving of such courses of action. But then, most of them refuse to open up legal channels for redress of grievances or peaceful resolution of disputes and claims. And if a dispute cannot be solved within a country, then recourse must be made to regional or continental bodies. Here the prospect is even more hopeless because that scandalous Organization of African Unity, whose mandate is conflict resolution, has yet to resolve one.

Back in 1993, Ghana's state-owned paper, *The Mirror* (June 26, 1993), wrote a scathing editorial on the OAU Summit of that year:

> The socio-political situation of Africa continues to grow from bad to worse as millions of lives are being lost with the passage of each day. The OAU seems to have lost its grip on affairs on the continent. Looking at the number of hot spots, one wonders if the wishes and aspirations of the founding fathers of the organization, still continue to be a dream.
>
> Although other speakers at the meeting criticized the industrialized countries for tending to regard Africa as a hopeless disaster continent, *they did not fail to admit that many of the continent's problems were due to mismanagement by the leaders.*
>
> The time has come for African leaders to re-examine themselves and find out whether they are prepared to face and overcome the challenges facing the continent to make it what the founding fathers had meant it to be. The future of Africa lies in the hands of her sons and daughters and we must do everything in our power to save our continent. The time is now or never! (2). (Emphasis added).

All this, however, fell on deaf ears. Commenting on the 1996 OAU Summit held in Cameroon, even the state-owned daily, *The Cameroon Tribune* (5 July 1996) could not resist taking a swipe: "At 32, neither the OAU nor most of its members actually behave at that age, in terms of conflict resolution, democratic practices and acceptable governance." (4)

African children, holding their own parallel mini-summit in Cameroon, were also bitter. Said Christopher Kello, 17-year-old from Uganda, a nation that has been ravaged by civil war for most of its post-colonial history: "You are the leaders, you are the adults creating problems for us." He said the children noted with regret that African leaders spend vast sums of money on arms. "We wish that money to be used for economic activities, education, peace and more children's summit. Africa is full of mess," he admonished (*The African Observer,* 7-15 July 1996, 3).

The absence of mechanisms for conflict resolution means that a minor political conflict can escalate into a full-blown civil conflagration and rage for years until foreign powers intervene to impose a settlement or mediation, as in Angola, Ethiopia, and Somalia. Unfortunately, foreign intervention does not always work, as recent experience in Somalia attests. It must be stated categorically that it is not the responsibility of the international community to feed Africa or solve every African crisis. The international community can help, but the initiative has to come from Africa itself.[6] Ultimately, it is Africans who must craft their own durable African (home-grown) solutions to their African problems.[7] Additionally, apart from upholding the principle of self-reliance, African solutions are far less expensive than foreign ones. The international rescue mission into Somalia, for example, cost the international community $3.5 billion without even ending the carnage and the collapse of the country.

Home-grown solutions can be found in Africa's own indigenous systems, almost everywhere castigated as backward and primitive. A hierarchical system of jurisprudence existed in most traditional African societies. Casely Hayford, a native of the Gold Coast and fervent anti-colonialist, (1911) wrote this about Ashanti courts:

---

6. The present author espoused this idea in a series of articles in U.S. newspapers. *The Los Angeles Times* published an op-ed entitled, "Africa's Salvation Lies Within Itself" on 14 April 1994, generating substantial editorial comment. *The Reporter-Herald* in Loveland, Colorado, published one such comment on 25 April 1994: "This idea has most recently been espoused by George B.N. Ayittey. He suggests, as have other thoughtful commentators, that the solution to Africa's self-destructive behavior lies in itself and the ultimate responsibility of saving Africa lies with its leaders." That editorial was also carried by the *Daily Record* newspaper in Canon City, Colorado on 28 April 1994.

7. I first coined this expression in a *Wall Street Journal* editorial on 7 October 1993, regarding Somalia: "Somalia is an African problem, requiring an African solution." The expression was adopted by U.S. Secretary of State Warren Christopher during his 7 October 1996 five-nation trip to Africa. He preached "African solutions for African problems" and exhorted African leaders to create an African Crisis Response Force, which could be sent to intervene in imminent crisis situations to prevent a Rwanda-like massacre. I had earlier espoused this idea in a television interview on 19 May 1994, on the PBS program *McNeil/Lehrer NewsHour* when Rwanda blew up in 1994. I argued that what was needed was an "African invasion force," with a mandate to do combat, if necessary, to bring peace and order to that country. Did African leaders embrace this idea? Only two (Mali and Ethiopia) agreed to supply troops.

At a "palaver," which is the word for a suit before the Court, the King sits with his Councillors; and the Court is an open one, which any member of the community may attend. There is no secrecy about the proceedings. The complainant states his case as fully as he can, and he is given a patient hearing. In the course of his statement questions are freely asked him by the Councillors, and doubtful points elucidated. The same process is gone through with the defendant, and with the witnesses called by either party. The Council then retires to deliberate upon the facts, and its verdict is given by the King's Linguist (251).

For the Fanti of Ghana, James Christensen, an English writer who visited the Gold Coast, wrote in 1952:

[Since time immemorial] the Fanti have had a rather complex system of courts and hearings. Presiding at any dispute or trial may be a group of elders, a chief and elders, or a panel of chiefs, depending on the nature of the case. A dispute, after submission to a group of elders for arbitration, may be further referred to a higher authority, such as a sub-chief or the paramount chief of a state. The latter, known as the *omanhene,* was the ultimate authority. The plaintiff and defendant generally present their own case to the court, call witnesses and cross-examine those who give testimony for the opposition. During a hearing, proverbs are quoted by the litigants. Proverbs may be regarded as the verbalization of social norms or "laws" which govern interpersonal relations.

Many proverbs may be regarded as legal maxims since they are utilized most frequently in disputes. For example, a request for the postponement of a case may be supported by the statement, "it takes time to make a dress for the hunchback." Another proverb often quoted to indicate prior ownership in a land dispute is, "The bathroom was wet before the rain fell." (236)

Kwame Arhin of the University of Ghana studied the hierarchy of Akan courts. The first was the extended family court known as *badwa,* with its members known as *badwafo,* which consisted of heads of the households of the family groups, heads of other family groups with certain relationships from intermarriage or occupying the same *brono* (ward), and respected heads of other family groups. The *badwa,* an arbitration gathering, settled internal disputes between members of the family groups. These included, for example, theft; certain kinds of abuse, such as slander and tale bearing; cases regarding property and pawning;

loans, surety, and recovery of debt; rights to land and inheritance of property; quarrels between married couples and adultery; and petty squabbles that did not affect the village as a whole. These disputes were referred to as *afisem*. "The settlement of a household case aimed at reconciling the parties and ensuring good relations within and between the family groups. *Mpata*, a reconciliation fee, normally in the form of a drink, accompanied by an apology, was given to the offended. Both parties then swore by the elders present that they would thereafter live at peace with each other" (Arhin, 1985, 18).

The *badwafo* relied on the respect due to the family elders and other elders and the force of public opinion for compliance of any judgment reached. Those who refused to comply with decisions would be disowned by their close relatives.

Disputes between members of different family groups that could not be settled by a joint *badwa* of the family groups concerned were referred to the *Odikro*'s *nhyiamu* (village chief's court). This court also settled cases that involved rules made by the council. There were village *afisem*, which concerned such issues as clearing paths leading to the main farming areas and the performance of ceremonies in connection with village shrines. "The settlement of disputes at the *odikro*'s court differed from that at the family group level in that the former was supported by the physical force at the disposal of the village as a whole. Offenders found at fault could be compelled to comply with the decisions of the court. In cases of refusal to comply, or if a party was dissatisfied with the court's decision, the oath of the *ohene* (king) was sworn, and the case transferred to the divisional court. The case then ceased to be an *afisem* of the village and became a matter for the division" (Arhin, 1985, 22).

The divisional, or *ohene*'s court, was a court of original jurisdiction as well as an appeal court; it could hear cases which originated in the division and appeal cases brought up from the *odikro*'s court. At the apex of the hierarchy was the *omanhene*'s court, the final court of appeal.

Public offenses, some of which carried the death penalty, were tried at any level of jurisdiction and decisions could be appealed. Such offenses, called *akyiwadee* (taboos) by the Akan, included murder *(awudie)*, homicide, and suicide; certain sexual offenses, such as incest, sexual intercourse with a woman during her menstrual period, with a half sister by one father, and with a woman in the bush; assaults on the ruler; theft of royal regalia or material symbols of the state and the property of the state shrine, such as a sword, a stool, a quantity of gold dust or nuggets;

and treason, which included breaking the oath of allegiance to a ruler or the cowardice of a warlord in battle.

The trial of public offenders in Akan courts proceeded as follows:

> The parties made preliminary payments, *dwomtadie,* a kind of earnest money. Witnesses were named and sent into concealment, and, after the parties had made full statements in court and been questioned by the court, were brought to testify under oath. They were then questioned by the parties to the dispute and the court panel, after which the court retired to consider its verdict, which was delivered by an *okyeame,* a spokesman of the ruler, who acted as interpreter. The court was concerned with reconciling the men to one another but above all with pacifying the spirits disturbed when a breach of the taboos was committed through the offense under adjudication, or through the swearing of an oath, and doing justice to the wronged party. The hearing and resolution of public offenses entailed repairing the damage done to society as a result of the alienation of the spirits due to the offense. (Arhin, 1985, 26)

Within the tribe, mechanisms and procedures existed by which disputes could be settled. Unfortunately, no such systems existed for the resolution of intertribal disputes, except a few ad hoc measures or attempts at diplomacy. This was why the Konkomba and Nanumba disputes flared up into tribal war.

After independence, African nationalists and elites abjured their own native institutions and rushed to blindly copy foreign systems they did not understand. Had they looked in their own backyard, they would have found the solutions to many of Africa's recurrent crises there.

CHAPTER 3

The Indigenous and the Modern Systems: A Comparative Analysis

> We have to go back to our traditional ways of solving our
> problems, traditional ways of working together. Otherwise,
> Boosaaso [a port in war-torn Somalia] would not have peace.
> —General Mohamed Abshir, Boosaaso's de facto
> administrator in *The Washington Post*,
> 3 March 1996, A29.

AFRICA'S HERITAGE OF PARTICIPATORY DEMOCRACY AND CONFEDERATION

It is an enduring myth, not only among Westerners but also, shamefully, among African leaders, that Africa had no viable institutions of its own before the European colonialists arrived. The primary source of this myth is the confusion between the *existence* of an institution and *different forms* of the same institution. For example, a mall and a bazaar are different forms of the same institution: the market. The fact that malls do not exist in African villages does not mean the market as an institution is unknown in Africa. Neither does the absence of hamburger in the diet of Africans mean that they do not eat.

It can be stated categorically that the European colonialists introduced no new institutions into Africa—only different and more efficient forms of already existing institutions. The institution of money is one example. The Europeans introduced paper currency, while Africans had been using a variety of commodity money, such as gold dust, cowrie shells, and salt. Thus, the Europeans did not invent the institution of money in Africa although the paper currency they introduced may have been more efficient than salt in purchasing a cow, for example. In the same vein, the Europeans did not invent the institution of marriage, democracy, or even imperialism; there were empires, kingdoms, and states in Africa before the advent of colonialism.

Native African Governments

Despite awesome diversity, there were striking similarities among the ways Africans governed themselves. There existed two main distinct types of indigenous political organization, with further differentiation within each. The first type, tribal groupings, existed as separate political entities and governed themselves independently. Of these tribes, some were led by chiefs and others were not. Tribes with chiefs and their attendant administrative and judicial institutions were referred to as chiefdoms or states. Tribes that dispensed with chiefs but governed themselves peacefully were called stateless societies.

In the second type, imperial rule, some conquered tribes came under the hegemony of others, as in kingdoms and empires. This type also included two discernible political subcultures. The first, the most common, type of indirect rule afforded the vassal states extensive local independence or autonomy, as in the Asante and Zande empires of the nineteenth century. The second type of imperial rule required the vassal states to assimilate into an allegedly superior foreign culture. Notable examples included the Mandinka, Fulani, Hausa, or, in general, the Islamic empires in the eighteenth and nineteenth centuries in West Africa. This was rule by assimilation.

In virtually all the African tribes, political organization of both types began at the village level. The village was made up of various extended families or lineages. Each had its head, chosen according to its own rules. In general, there were as many as four basic units of government in African societies governed themselves. The first was the chief, the central authority. The second was the inner or privy council, which advised the chief. The third was the council of elders. If there were ten lineages in a village, for example, their heads would form a ten-member council of elders. The fourth institution was the village assembly of commoners, also called the village meeting.

What follows is a brief description of governance in chiefdoms. More extensive discussions can be found in Ayittey (1991) and Boamah-Wiafe (1993).

Chiefdoms

African societies that ruled themselves had all four units of government: a chief, an inner council, a council of elders, and a village assembly. Tribes that had chiefs included the Fanti of Ghana, the Yoruba of Nigeria, the Mossi of Burkina Faso, the Swazi, and the Zulu of South Africa. In most cases, the chief was a male. He was the political, social, judicial, and religious head of the tribe. As such, he had wide-ranging powers.

The chief usually was assisted in governance by a small group of confidential advisers called the inner, or privy, council. Membership was not limited but was drawn mainly from the inner circle of the chief's relatives and personal friends, who might include influential members of the community. The inner council served as the first test for legislation. The chief would privately and informally discuss with the inner council all matters relating to the administration of the tribe. He might consult his advisers severally or jointly to form an opinion before bringing an issue to the people.

After the chief had raised an issue with his inner council, he might take it to the council of elders. This was a much wider and more formal body comprising all the hereditary headmen of the wards or lineages; in essence, the council of elders represented the commoners.

In matters of serious consequence, the chief had to summon all members of the council of elders. Such matters included additional tributes, market tolls, proposed new laws, declarations of war, and serious quarrels. The chief presided over this council and sought its opinion. Essentially, the council of elders had two functions: to advise and assist the chief in the administration of the tribe and to prevent the chief from abusing his power by voicing its dissatisfactions, criticizing the chief, and keeping him under necessary control.

Under normal governance, the chief would inform the council of elders of the subject to be dealt with, and those wishing to do so would then debate it. Routine matters were resolved by acclamation. Complex matters would be debated until the council reached unanimity. Decisions so reached were sure of acceptance by the rest of the tribe since the councilors were influential members of the community.

Generally, the chief would remain silent and watch the councilors debate. His role was to weigh all viewpoints, not to impose his decision on the council; doing so would defeat the purpose of the council's debates. The chief did not rule; he only led and assessed the council's opinions. If the council could not reach unanimity on a contested issue, the chief would call a village assembly to put the issue before the people for debate. Thus the people served as the ultimate judge or final authority on disputed issues.

Village meetings began with the chief explaining the purpose of the meeting. He would not announce any decision reached in council meetings; he would merely state the facts involved and order discussions to begin. His advisers would open the debate and would be followed by headmen or elders. Then anyone else wishing to speak or ask questions might do so. These deliberations continued until a consensus was reached. In such a process of consensus building, minority positions are not only heard but also taken into account. In a majority-rule process, on the other hand, a minority position can be ignored. Consensus is far more difficult to reach on many issues, and that was one reason why African political tradition is noted for the length of time, sometimes days and even weeks, it took to reach a consensus. But once reached, there was unity of purpose since *all* participated in the decision-making process. Note that consensus, by its very nature, is the antithesis of autocracy. One cannot impose one's will in a system that is traditionally structured to reach decisions by consensus. Thus despotism does not inhere in the African political tradition.

Freedom of expression was an important element of village assemblies. Anyone—even those who were not members of the tribe—could express his views freely. Sensible proposals or ideas often were applauded, and inappropriate ones were vocally opposed. Dissent was open and free, with due respect to the chief. Many African tribes—especially the Igbo, Yoruba, Ga, Asante, and Abesheini—fiercely defended the right to free speech. Chiefs did not incarcerate those who held different opinions because the collective survival of the tribe, not the chief's individual survival, was at stake.

Checks Against the Powers of the Chief

In theory, the African chief wielded vast powers—which led many observers to characterize him as autocratic. But in day-to-day administration and legislation, the chief rarely made policy. He only led—an important distinction. Chiefs and kings were not above the law and had to obey customary laws and taboos. That is, the rule of customary law prevailed. In some tribes, the king was not to venture out of his palace into town except under the cover of darkness. The king was never to speak to his people directly, except through a spokesperson (*okyeame* as in the case of the Akan). The Akan chief or king was forbidden to meet with any foreigner except in the presence of a member of the council of elders.

Some of these injunctions in traditional Africa were intended to enhance the sanctity of the office. But there were others that were clearly designed to check despotic tendencies and misuse of power. The African chief was surrounded by various bodies and institutions to prevent an abuse of power and corruption. A chief with despotic tendencies was first reminded of the oath he took upon assumption of power. For example, when the Krontihene of the Ashanti (Ghana) is installed, he is admonished thus: "Do not go after women. Do not become a drunkard. When we give you advice, listen to it. Do not gamble. We do not want you to disclose the origin of your subjects. We do not want you to abuse us. We do not want you to be miserly; we do not want one who disregards advice; we do not want you to regard us as fools; we do not want *autocratic* ways; we do not want bullying; we do not like beating. Take the Stool. We bless the Stool and give it to you" (Busia, 1951, 12). (Emphasis added).

Any violations could result in immediate destoolment (removal from office). In many African tribes, it was also the duty of the queen-mother to scold and rebuke the chief for transgressions. If she failed in this duty, she herself could be destooled. The next check was the inner or privy council of advisers. If a chief persisted in his despotic ways, the advisers might abandon him. If this check failed, the third line of defense was the council of elders, which could destool the chief. If the council of elders failed to do so, the people would "vote with their feet" (migrate) and abandon the despotic chief. The African chief was appointed to rule for life. He did not appoint himself. But he could be removed at any time—not after, say, four years—if he was corrupt or failed to govern according to the will of the people—and so he can be even in modern times.

Consider the fate of Nana Ekwam VIII, chief of Gomoa Ekwamk-rom of Ghana. The elders of the town convened a meeting and summoned the chief to account for a sum of 780,000 *cedis* (about $600)—being 572,000 *cedis* from land sales and 258,529 *cedis* the chief is alleged to have withdrawn from the town's bank account. As *The Mirror* (6 January 1996) reported,

> The chief stood up and replied that he had nothing to pay to the town and denied making any previous promise to pay. The *Obaahema* [queen-mother] of the town, Okomfo Asaba, then stood up to address the meeting

and drew the attention of the chief to their last meeting in October, 1995 where he made the pledge.

Nana Ekwam shouted the old woman down and called her a liar. He said he was not at that meeting because he was attending to a sick aunt. Almost immediately, a voice from the gathering asked "which aunt" and the chief replied "your mother."

The meeting from then on degenerated into verbal exchanges but matters came to a hilt when the chief delivered his bombshell of the Akan profanity: "All of you, your mothers' genitals." There was a brief silence and the chief walked out of the meeting in anger. But before he could turn in the direction of his palace a group of young men, numbering over 20, knocked him down and removed his cloth and sandals. (1)

In Akan culture, the chief's bare feet never touch the ground. The removal of his sandals, therefore, constituted destoolment.

Native African Empires and Kingdoms

While independent tribes governed themselves with or without chiefs, other tribes were subject to imperial rule by their conquerors. Differences in imperial rule generally lay in the degree of autonomy conquerors granted to the subjugated tribes. At one end of the spectrum were the Islamic empires such as the Mandinka, which made conscious efforts to supplant existing cultures by forcing subjugated tribes to assimilate into an allegedly superior culture. At the other end were the Asante and the Zande, who adopted a policy of indirect rule by according the traditional rulers of the subjugated tribes extensive autonomy.

The internal structure of the Asante empire was one of confederacy. A confederation is a rather loose form of political association in which the constituent states retain significant autonomy from the central authority. In a unitary state, virtually all powers are concentrated in the center. Apparently confederation was quite widespread on the former Gold Coast in the nineteenth century. Beyond the Gold Coast, there existed other kingdoms and empires with remarkably similar political structures. Strong centralized rule was exceptional in sub-Saharan (black) Africa; poor communications made it difficult to prevent states from breaking away.

Only a few African kingdoms and empires, such as sixteenth-century Benin and nineteenth-century Zulu, were able to impose a strong centralized rule. In the Hausa states, however, there was a trend, often promoted by the influence of Islam, toward greater power at the center, with closer control over official positions and the establishment of servile standing armies. But empires that attempted to achieve centralization by military force crumbled as rapidly as they were built. For example, the Oyo empire collapsed in the first half of the nineteenth century, the Akwamu in the Gold Coast in the eighteenth century, and the Zulu empire in the latter part of the nineteenth century.

The tendency of many tribes to decentralize government by delegating authority and responsibilities to local entities and by instituting a complex system of checks and balances to curb autocracy evidenced their fear of tyranny. In central Africa, delegation of the king's authority usually amounted to delegation of almost all authority save religious—and on a few occasions, even religious authority was delegated (Bohannan, 1964, 192).

Monarchical divinity is often confused with either absolutism or tyranny. In the African scheme of kingship, despotism could not be reconciled with the traditional role of the king. The Asante king appeared absolute, yet he had to procure the consent of the chiefs to bring about group action. The Zulu king could make no decisions of national importance without the *ibandla*, the highest council of state (Olivier, 1969). Similarly, in the kingdom of Swaziland the authority of the Swazi king, *Ngwenyama*—chosen by the *Ndovukazi* (queen-mother)—was checked by the *Liqoqo* (inner council) and the *Libandla* (general council).

If a ruler committed a very grave offense, he was dethroned. The Asante people destooled three kings: Osei Kwame in 1799 for, among other reasons, absenting himself from Kumasi and failing to perform his religious duties during the Adae festivals; Karikari in 1874 for extravagance, among other failings; and Mensa Bonsu in 1883 for excessively taxing the Asante people. Many other destoolments occurred among the Akan and Ga peoples as well as other tribes. Each tribe had its own procedures for divestiture. While the Serer tribe of Senegal adopted a distinctive drumbeat to signal the end of a king's reign, the Yoruba of Nigeria demanded the king's suicide by a symbolic gift of parrot's eggs.

Native African Governance: An Assessment

Once again, the African "village meeting under a big tree" and the European "parliament" were simply different forms of the same institution of democracy. What Africans had was participatory democracy. The Europeans introduced parliamentary democracy. A unique characteristic of Africa's indigenous system of government was that it was open and inclusive. No one was locked out of the decision-making process. One did not have to belong to one political party or family to participate in the process; even foreigners were allowed to participate. For example, in the sixteenth century, King Alfonso of the Kingdom of Kongo had Portuguese advisers; among them were Alvare Lopez, Muel Pacheco, and Francisco Barbudo. They represented the Portuguese segment of the resident population and even acquired a seat on the electoral college.

Further, the chief did not declare the village to be a one-party state, nor did he impose an alien ideology on his people. At village meetings, the people expressed their views freely, which was vital for consensus to be reached. No one was arrested or detained for disagreeing with the chief.

Second, larger political entities—empires and kingdoms—were governed upon the confederacy principle or marked by extensive devolution of authority. Local communities enjoyed the substantial autonomy to run their own affairs, which partly explains why over 2,000 distinct tribes remain in Africa today.

SULTANISM: PERSONAL RULE

After independence, African leaders and elites did not establish political systems that bore any resemblance to indigenous systems. It is true that they inherited an authoritarian colonial state at independence. However, they could have dismantled it and returned Africa to its roots. They did neither. Instead, African leaders *strengthened* the unitary colonial state apparatus and *expanded* its scope enormously—especially the military. Even repressive colonial measures used to quell black aspirations for freedom were retained. For example, within a year of Ghana's independence in 1957, Nkrumah introduced the Preventive Detention Bill of July 1958, which gave the government sweeping powers "to imprison, without trial, any person suspected of activities prejudicial to the state's security." Nkrumah, who himself had been jailed by the colonialists, proscribed opposition activities and arrested some of its leaders. In Zambia, the state of emergency, used to crush black aspirations for freedom, was continued by President Kenneth Kaunda for 20 years and used by him to arrest and jail many of his opponents. In Zimbabwe, President Robert Mugabe similarly kept the state of emergency in effect for over ten years, as well as the price and exchange controls former white supremacist leader Ian Smith had introduced to fight off sanctions after his Unilateral Declaration of Independence from Britain.

In the 1960s, African nationalists, such as Kwame Nkrumah, Julius Nyerere, Kenneth Kaunda, and Hastings Banda, who won independence for their countries were all hailed as heroes, swept into power with huge parliamentary majorities, and deified. Statues were built for them; monuments, stadiums, and streets named after them. Currencies bore their portraits. They heaped vainglorious epithets upon themselves: *Osagyefo*, the Guide, the Messiah, the Redeemer, the Teacher. They brooked no criticism. Criticizing them was sacrilegious. Newspapers that did so were banned and their editors jailed. The leaders used their parliamentary majorities to subvert their constitutions, outlaw opposition parties, and declare their countries "one-party states" and themselves presidents-for-life. They dismissed the concept of "democracy" as alien, claiming that multiparty democracy was "a Western thing," "a luxury Africa could not afford," and so on. Others claimed that "Africa had no democratic culture," and "too many feuding tribes make democracy a risky venture." For example, Presidents Paul Biya of Cameroon and Daniel arap Moi of Kenya vehemently opposed multiparty democracy on grounds that it would degenerate into destructive tribal politics. In Ghana, Nkrumah (1968) denounced it as an "imperialist dogma"(8). Said President Mobutu Sese Seko of Zaire: "Democracy is not for Africa. There was only one African chief and he ruled for life. Here in Zaire we must make unity" (*The Wall Street Journal*, 14 October 1985, 1).

Admittedly, the dilemmas faced by African leaders after independence may have precipitated the rush toward personal rule. First, artificial colonial boundaries did not coincide with ethnic groupings, and, therefore, few African countries constitute nation-states. As Richard Sandbrook (1993) explained: "A nation, on the one hand, is a social group that develops solidarity on the basis of shared customs and institutions; on the other hand, a state is a political organization laying claim to power in a particular territory. Where nation and state are coterminous, ethnic loyalty (nationalism) fuses with state loyalty (patriotism). The state acquires legitimacy and internal cohesion permitting it to override personal and sectional preoccupations with a vision of a greater good" (49).

In Africa, however, these conditions are rarely met. Although Swaziland, Lesotho, and Somalia qualify, most of the states are multinational (or poly-ethnic). A citizen's loyalty may not extend beyond his own ethnic group, making state legitimacy very fragile. A unifying leader, like a Gandhi or a Tito, may then emerge to provide that article of cohesion and thereby check resurgent ethnicity. But to be successful, he must rule with absolute impartiality, placing the interests of the state above his own and those of his ethnic group—a criteria that most postcolonial African leaders have failed to meet.

Second, predominantly peasant societies were left in Africa after colonialism and peasants are notoriously difficult to organize on a national class basis. In addition, social stratifications between capitalists and workers had not crystallized. Thus, tribalism was more relevant to African political life than ideology or class warfare. This set the stage, as Sandbrook (1993) has noted, "for a strongman to play the central integrating role. He overcomes political schisms and builds his personal rule by distributing material benefits, capitalizing on personal loyalties and coercing recalcitrants. Appeals on a class or patriotic basis are unsuccessful" (64).

However, these dilemmas, regardless of their validity, played into the hands of the nationalists and provided them with the cover to advance their own selfish political ambitions. They proceeded to set up autocratic, one-party state systems that bore no affinity to their own indigenous systems. In country after country, heads of state filled important positions in key institutions (such as the civil service, the military, and the judiciary) and surrounded themselves with members of their own ethnic group: the late Samuel Doe of Liberia with the Krahn; Moi of Kenya with the Kalenjin; Biya of Cameroon with the Beti; Eyadema of Togo with the Kabye; Rawlings of Ghana with the Ewe; and so on. As Peter Wanyande (1988) noted: "In African one-party states, the rulers have tended to use their power and the institutions they control not only to promote their own individual and group interest as rulers—and in some cases sectional as opposed to national interests—but also to manipulate and undermine the rights and freedoms of the rest of society" (74).

Personal rule has prevailed in most African countries over much of the postcolonial period. Richard Sandbrook (1993) gave a composite portrait of the typical African tyrant and how he rules: "The strongman, usually the president, occupies the centre of the political life. Front and centre stage, he is the centrifugal force around which all else revolves. Not only the ceremonial head of state, the president is also the chief political, military and cultural figure: head of government, commander-in-chief of the armed forces, head of the governing party (if there is one) and even chancellor of the local university. His aim is typically to identify his person with the 'nation'" (90).

He is present everywhere: his picture is hung on public walls, billboards, government offices, and even private homes. His portrait also embellishes stamps, coins, paper currency, and even stationery of state corporations. Schools, hospitals and stadiums are named after him, and the state-controlled media herald his every word and action, no matter how misguided.

None of this fits Africa's own indigenous political heritage. The most heinous departure has been military dictatorships. Many scholars, including Africans, have acquiesced to brutal military regimes in Africa by citing Africa's warrior tradition. But an exhaustive study of indigenous African political systems does not reveal soldiers or men in uniform serving as chiefs or heads of village governments. The heads were always civilian.

The traditional function of warriors or soldiers was to defend the village and the tribe against rival tribes or slave raiders. In such defensive encounters the soldiers proved their valor and earned their people's respect. Warrior tribes did exist, and a warrior could become chief, but if he did, the government could hardly be characterized as a military government in the sense that soldiers occupied all positions of power.

Many tribes did not have standing armies. Professional military classes were small and standing armies rare. In the face of an imminent external threat, the chief would summon young men of a certain age and present them to the king for war. In most states, the people were the army and the monarchs had no independent full-time forces of their own. After a war, the army was disbanded. Thus the historical and cultural evidence does not lend support to military rule as uniquely African. If anything, the colonialists introduced standing armies into Africa. Therefore, military rule is as alien as colonial rule.

THE INDIGENOUS ECONOMIC INSTITUTIONS

Africa's indigenous economic system is probably the area least understood. The myth of "hunters and gatherers" persists, giving the impression that Africa had no economic institutions or culture before contact with the Europeans. Inexorably tied to the land, Africans supposedly eked out livings from primitive agriculture. Trade and exchange were supposedly unknown, since self-sufficiency and subsistence farming were the operative commands. Books on precolonial Africa dwelt excessively on the "backwardness" of African technology. But Africa did have economic institutions.

West Africa was particularly noted for its indigenous economic development. As Elliott P. Skinner (1964) put it:

> The peoples of [precolonial West Africa] had economies which made
> agricultural produce available in amounts large enough to be sold in rural

and urban markets; craft specialization often organized along the line of craft guilds, whose members manufactured goods to be sold in these markets; different kinds of currencies which were nearly always convertible one to another and, later, to European denominations of values; and elaborate trading systems, external as well as internal. Goods produced in even the smallest West African societies were circulated in local market centres, and ultimately by porters, caravans, and boats, to the large Sudanese emporiums from which they could be shipped to Mediterranean areas in exchange for foreign products. (205)

Africans engaged in a wide variety of economic activities. Although mostly primary—agricultural, pastoralism, hunting, fishing, and wood-working—there were also crafts and other industries such as cloth weaving, pottery, brass works, and the mining and smelting of iron, gold, silver, copper, and tin.

Agriculture was the primary occupation of Africans, and the basic unit of production was the extended family. Each family constituted itself into a working unit or labor force and acted as an operative economic entity that produced goods and distributed the fruits of labor as its members saw fit, allowing for individual discretion and reward. Within the family, there was specialization of labor and sexual division of occupation. Different crops were raised by different members, and certain tasks were reserved for women. For example, the cultivation of food crops (domestic staples) was almost everywhere a female occupation. The majority of Africa's peasant farmers today are women. In Ethiopia, however, women raised goats in addition to farming.

What a person grew on the land was his own free decision to make. The produce was private property. Even among the Kalahari Bushmen, "all that a woman gathered belonged to her alone, and of course was shared with her family" (Marshall, 1973, 113). How much a person shared with his kinsmen and how much he kept for himself was an individual choice. There were rarely mandated, proportional distribution of produce among the extended family. As M. J. Field (1940, 62) observed of the Ga people of Ghana, "in farming every married man has his own farm though all help each in clearing, so problems of division of produce do not arise."

In much of indigenous Africa, all the means of production were owned by the natives, not by their rulers, the chiefs, or by tribal governments. Feudalism was not commonplace in Africa, except in Abyssinia (Ethiopia). That means, in popular language, that all the means of production were privately owned. The hunting spears, fishing nets, cattle, pots, huts, farm produce, fish, textile looms, gold jewelry shops, and various tools and products were all privately owned. As Robert F. Gray (1962) observed of the Sonjo of Kenya: "Generally speaking, property is privately owned among the Sonjo. The only important exception is the building plots upon which houses are built. These are owned communally. The other forms of property are owned by individuals. Thus, a piece of property such as a field, a beehive, or a goat, at any given time can be traced in ownership to an individual. According to Sonjo law, a man has ultimate ownership rights in his own property and in all property possessed by his patrilineal descendants for as long as he lives. When he dies, these rights are inherited by his heirs" (45-46).

Ownership of land, however, was an issue over which there was a great deal of confusion among development experts. In the early days, unoccupied land belonged to no one. Anyone could use natural waters and pastures. But as soon as a man sunk a well or built a dam, he could exercise exclusive rights over the water it contained (Schapera, 1953, 17). "The man who first came with his followers to settle in a previously unoccupied area was usually termed the 'owner of the land' and his heir would continue to receive respect for his primacy" (Colson, 1953, 204). Among the Tonga, who occupy the plateau of southern Zambia, the owner was called *ulanyika* and *tendaana* among the Dagaaba on northern Ghana.

On the inherited land, family members exercised only usufructural rights. A son had the right of use but could not sell the land. Ownership and control remained within the lineage. Lineage control over the land was exercised by the elders and in some small tribes by the chief. Communal ownership is really a misleading description of this system, for it implies open access by all in the village to any piece of land, which was certainly not the case. Clearly, if what obtained was communal tenure, then shifting cultivation would be possible only when the whole community moved to another location. As Bohannan and Bohannan (1968) contend, "Communal tenure is an illusion that results from viewing the systematic exploitation by kinship groups of their environment through the distorting lens of western market-oriented and contract-dominated institutions of property and ownership" (88). The more accurate description is family or lineage ownership. All those who trace their ancestry to a certain individual are entitled to use his original plot of land. The individual farmer would make his own determination what to cultivate on that land.

Africans engaged in a variety of industrial activities in the precolonial era. For example, in Benin, "the glass industry made extraordinary strides" (Diop, 1987, 136). In Nigeria, "the cloth industry was an ancient craft" (Olaniyan, 1985, 104). Kano attained historical prominence in the fourteenth century with its fine indigo-dyed cloth that was traded for goods from North Africa. Even before the discovery of cotton, other materials had been used for cloth. The Igbo, for example, made cloth from the fibrous bark of trees. The Asante also were famous for their cotton and barkcloth *(kente* and *adwumfo).*

Economists define capital as anything that is not wanted for its own sake but aids in the production of further goods. Thus, Robinson Crusoe's fishing net was a capital good; similarly tractors, industrial machines, and scythes. By popular usage, however, capital has come to mean funds or money needed to operate or start a business. In indigenous Africa, capital funds were generally scarce. There were banks in colonial Africa, but the natives lacked the collateral to obtain credit. To secure initial start-up capital for fishing and commercial operations, they turned to two traditional sources of finance. One was the "family pot." Each extended family had a fund into which members made contributions according to their means. While members were not coerced to contribute, failure to do so effectively extinguished one's access to the pot.

The fund was used for both consumption and investment. For example, it was used to cover funeral expenses, weddings, the educational costs of the more gifted among them, extension of the family house, or as capital. Among the Ewe seine fishermen of Ghana, the family pot was called *agbadoho.* Members borrowed from this pot to purchase their fishing nets and paid back the loans.

The second source of finance was a revolving credit scheme that was widespread across Africa. It was called *susu* in Ghana, *esusu* in Yoruba, *tontines* or *chilembe* in Cameroon and *stokfel* in South Africa.[1] Typically, a group of say ten people would contribute perhaps $100 into a fund. When the fund reached a certain amount, say $1,000, it was handed over to the members in turn. To be operational, such a scheme required a liberal dose of trust among members and somehow the natives managed

---

1. The *stokfel* (or *stockvels*), however, was more than a rural credit scheme. It was an institution of mutual aid that provided support in case a member suffered a bereavement or went to jail. The support was invariably extended to the member's family (Iliffe, 1987, 136).

to make it work. In fact, for many businesses in the indigenous and informal sector, the loan club was the primary source of capital.[2]

One could also borrow money by pledging farms, a practice common in Ghana and Nigeria (Hill, 1987, 90). If borrowing was not possible, one could form a partnership with a person with capital. "A common arrangement involved three partners who shared the returns from a venture equally. In trading ventures, one partner supplied the capital, one transported the goods and braved the hazards of the trail, and the other organized the partnership, which in some cases involved little more than getting the capitalist in touch with someone who had the stamina and courage to make the trip" (Miracle, 1971, 400n).

Profit was never an alien concept to Africa. Throughout its history, there have been numerous entrepreneurs. The aim of traders and numerous brokers or middlemen was profit and wealth. In the brokerage business, the middlemen kept a fixed proportion of the proceeds. For example, among the Egba and Ijebu brokers of palm oil in Nigeria in the 1850s, a quarter of the price went to the broker and three-quarters to

---

2. Three observations regarding the *tontines* may be instructive. First, they are not unique to Africa alone. Similar schemes exist in other parts of the Third World. These are called *hui* in China and Vietnam; *keh* in Korea; *tandas* in Mexico; *pasanaku* in Bolivia; *san* in the Dominican Republic; "syndicate" in Belize; *gamaiyah* in Egypt; *hagbad* in Somalia; *xitique* in Mozambique; *arisan* in Indonesia; *paluwagan* in the Philippines; *chit* fund in India and Sri Lanka; *pia huey* in Thailand; and *ko* in Japan. Second, if the same *susu* scheme of the African natives were organized in the United States, it would be called a credit union. A credit union is simply an association of individuals who pool their savings together to lend only to themselves (the members). Third, these indigenous saving clubs still exist; "In Cameroon, a survey of 360 businesses showed that more than half started with help from the *tontines* or *chilembe*" (*South*, February 1989, 25). Also, "A sample of 398 village households in rural Niger in 1986 indicated that informal credit accounted for 84 percent of total loans and was equal to 17 percent of agricultural income. Informal *tontines* (rotating savings and credit associations) predominate. Out of a sample of 56 *tontines* in 22 villages, some had only 4 members, others more than 40. The average member contribution ranged from 100 CFA francs (25 cents) to CFA 25,000 ($70). The total size of all 56 *tontines*, as measured by member contributions per meeting, was the equivalent of $72,000. This suggests a promising base for deposit mobilization in rural Niger" (World Bank, World Development Report, 1989, 113).

African suppliers (Newbury, 1971, 101). Profit calculations were always on the mind of African traders. For example, "The Nupe saw to it that the prices of goods corresponded closely to variations in supply and demand, above all, to seasonal fluctuations. They also made sure that distance between the area of production and market, and the additional labour and loss of time involved in transport, entered into the calculation of price and profit" (Skinner, 1964, 218).

Profit made was private property; it was for the traders to keep, not for the chiefs or rulers to expropriate. On the Gold Coast in the seventeenth century, there existed men of wealth, such as the Akrosang Brothers and Edward Barter of Cape Coast, Aban and John Kabes of Komenda, John Kurankye of Annomabo, Asomani and Peter Passop of Akwamu and Accra, and John Konny of Ahanta (Daaku, 1971, 170). Chiefs did not sequestrate their wealth for equal distribution to all tribesmen.

The natives chose what they did with their profit. The traditional practice was to share the profit. Under the *abusa* scheme devised by the cocoa farmers of Ghana at the beginning of this century, net proceeds were divided into three parts: a third went to the owner of the farm, another third went to hired laborers and the remaining third was set aside for farm maintenance and expansion. Under the less common *abunu* system, profits were shared equally between the owner and the workers. Variants of these profit-sharing schemes were extended beyond agriculture to commerce and fishing.

Property Rights

Looting and arbitrary seizures of property by undisciplined soldiers was not a feature of traditional African society. Even the chief could not dispossess someone of his property without a full council hearing. When disputes pertaining to property arose, a chief's court adjudicated the matter. On precolonial African law and custom, Frances Kendall and Leon Louw (1987) observed that: "There were no powers of arbitary expropriation, and land and huts could be expropriated only under extreme conditions after a full public hearing" (18).

This view is corroborated by Digby Koyama (1980):

> Only in cases of, for example, the commission of a grave offence against the community, abandonment of the land, or when the chief required the land for himself or for another chief, was this right exercised. There could therefore be "despotic acts" giving evidence of an unbridled exercise of

power, but there was always the safeguard that the powers were not exercised recklessly. Public opinion would always be taken into account. There were also always the councillors whose advice was as a rule taken into account by the chief. *In practice, therefore, the rights of the individual were never nullified* (69). (Emphasis added).

Free Market, Free Trade Tradition

Some goods produced by the natives were traded or sold in markets. Market development was inevitable even if self-sufficiency was the preferred form of making a living, for it was physically impossible for one homestead to produce everything it needed on the farm. By necessity, a surplus had to be produced to exchange for what could not be produced. In earlier times, such exchanges were done by canvassing from hut to hut, a time-consuming process. A market was simply a place where exchanges could be made more easily. Where exchanges occurred regularly, a marketplace would naturally develop. The institution of a marketplace, then, evolved naturally. As Skinner (1964) remarked: "Markets were ubiquitous in West Africa. There were a few regions where aboriginal markets were absent—in parts of Liberia, southwestern Ivory Coast, and in certain portions of the plateau regions of Nigeria. Nevertheless, even here people engaged in trade, and benefited from the markets of contiguous areas. The markets served as local exchange points or nodes, and trade was the vascular system unifying all of West Africa, moving products to and from local markets, larger market centers, and still larger centers" (215).

There were two types of markets and trade: the small village market and the large markets that served as long-distance interregional trade centers. Rural markets often were sited at bush clearings or at the intersection of caravan routes. As Polly Hill (1987) asserted: "Rural periodic markets are such ancient institutions in many parts of West Africa and the literature on African markets is vast" (54).

Many of the precolonial rural markets of West Africa provided for the needs of local producers, consumers, and traders and also served as foci for long-distance traders. Some rural markets operated daily, depending on the volume of trade. In Nigeria, "Every village and town had markets which were attended in the morning or evening and in some cases, throughout the day. These markets were held either daily or periodically. The daily markets were local exchange points where producers, traders and consumers met to sell and buy. The periodic markets were organized on a cyclical basis of every three, four, five, and sixteen days to feed the daily markets. Every community had a market cycle which enabled traders and buyers to attend different markets on different days" (Falola, 1985, 105).

The local markets had two important characteristics. The first was their cyclical periodicity (Skinner, 1964). Market days would be rotated among a cluster of villages. For example, Yoruba, Dahomey, and Guro markets operated on five-day cycles. Igbo rural markets were on a four-day, or multiple of four-day, cycle while Mossi markets ran on a three-day or 21-day cycle (215).

The second characteristic of rural markets was the segregation of vendors or merchants according to the products they sold. Tomato sellers, for example, were all seated in one section of the market. The object was to promote competition. As Falola (1985) observed, segregation "made it convenient for buyers to locate the regular section of each commodity, to choose from a wide variety of goods, and to buy at a fair price since the traders had to compete with one another at the same time" (106).

Market Regulations and Controls

Generally, economic activity in African markets was not controlled by political authorities. Existing rules and regulations were aimed more at the preservation of law and order, the collection of market tolls, the use of standard weights and measures and the supervision of the slaughter of cattle. For example, apart from these events there were few regulations of the Igbo market but to avoid confrontations, there was a strict rule against carrying machetes or large knives in the market. Traders generally sat with others of their village-groups. There was no strict rule as to where they should remain, and there apparently were no price controls.

In the Mossi markets:

> There are no official restrictions on the kinds of goods which may or may not be sold. In pre-European times slaves and eunuchs were the common stock-in-trade of the major markets and of some of the smaller ones as well. The only active supervision that existed and still exists concerns the butchering of meat. Every person who sells meat in the market must exhibit the skin of the butchered animal in a public place so that there will be no question as to the ownership of the animal. If the meat in question is the remains of a cow killed and half-eaten by a lion, then the village or district chief must be notified before the meat enters the market (Skinner, 1962, 171)

Kojo Yelpaala (1983) also found that, in Dagaaba markets, "There was the freedom to buy and sell any commodity within the market environment (*daa*). Free and voluntary interaction between buyers and sellers produced a market-determined price. When this condition was violated, the transactions were said to result in *fao* (robbery), in the sense that the buyer or seller might extort a price lower or higher price than the market-determined price, thereby reducing social welfare" (370).

The Importance of Markets

The village market performed vital economic, social, and political functions that were well understood by the chiefs and the people. The marketplace was the central nervous system of the community. In fact, as Skinner (1962) observed of the Mossi of Ghana, " . . . whenever and wherever there is a large gathering of Mossi there is a market. . . . The rural market is the center of Mossi social life, and friends as well as enemies meet within its confines. What Mangin wrote some 40 years ago is still true: 'Every self-respecting Mossi—man or woman, child or elder—must go to market at least once in a while were it only to look . . . and to be looked at, if he can put on some handsome clothes.' Except for the Moslems who are now experimenting with a form of Purdah, there are few persons who do not go to market" (168). Among the Akan of Ghana, Daniel F. McCall (1962) noted that the marketplace was not only "the source of food and clothing for the family, it is the place where the wife and mother spends most of her waking day" (65).

In the 1850s, an American missionary, T. J. Bowen, provided a vivid description of the importance of Yoruba markets:

> The most attractive object next to the curious old town itself—and it is always old—is the market. This is not a building, but a large area, shaded with trees, and surrounded and sometimes sprinkled over with little open sheds, consisting of a very low thatched roof surmounted on rude posts. Here the women sit and chat all day, from early morning till 9 o'clock at night, to sell their various merchandise. . . . The principal marketing hour, and the proper time to see all the wonders, is the evening. At half an hour before sunset, all sorts of people, men, women, girls, travelers lately arrived in the caravans, farmers from the fields, and artisans from their houses, are pouring in from all directions to buy and sell, and talk. At the distance of half a mile their united voices roar like the waves of the sea. (Bascom, 1984, 25)

In East Africa, studies by Gulliver (1962) also showed that markets were extremely important to the Arusha because markets provided them their "main opportunity for personal contact with the Masai in the conscious efforts to learn and imitate all they could of Masai culture" (46).

The rural market served many purposes:

- It provided peasants with the opportunity to exchange goods or occasional agricultural surpluses and to purchase what they could not produce themselves.
- It provided an indispensable avenue for social intercourse: to meet people, to gossip, or to discuss and keep abreast of local affairs. Dancers, singers, musicians, and other artists often went to the markets to display their skills. Work parties and weddings often took place at the markets.
- It served as a center of interethnic contact and channels of communication (White, 1987, 41). It was at the market that important information about foreign cultures, medicine, product improvements, and new technologies was exchanged. As such, the market acted as an integrative force, a place for cultural and normative exchange.
- It often served as the meeting place for important political events such as *durbars* and village assemblies convened by the traditional rulers.
- It served as an important area for communication and dissemi-nation of information. Among the Mossi of Ghana, "the market is the main communication center of Mossi society and news of happenings in the region can be heard there. If a person is in an area one can be sure that the people in the market will know about him, or that he will sooner or later visit the market" (Skinner, 1962).
- Most marketplaces were associated with religious activities. Mar-kets were consecrated with shrines associated with them. The consecration emanated primarily out of the need for peace and calm at the marketplace. It was believed "such consecration would guarantee that supernatural sanctions would back up the political authorities in their maintenance of peace in the market-place" (Bohannan, 1964, 215).

Clearly, the marketplace was the heart of indigenous African society, the center not only of economic activity but also of political, social, judicial, and communication activities. Perhaps the easiest way to annihilate an ethnic group was to destroy its markets. Such a destruction would assail the core of the society and the extended family itself. The importance of markets in traditional African society has not diminished even today. As *West Africa* magazine (3–9 April, 1989) reported:

> Sixty years ago Cotonou was a cluster of villages surrounded by lagoons. Today, it is the economic capital of Benin with a population of 170,000. Its nerve centre is the Dantokpa Market. Animated from early morning to late at night, scores of small retailers line its voms, or streets. Mobylette repair shops, dressmakers, millers preparing corn flour and cabinet-makers carving red wood ply their trades next to traditional healers patiently waiting for clients. Vendors of pimento, peppers, spices and vegetables with piquant odors stand behind their stalls, while itinerant peddlers are everywhere selling dried fish, potato-fritters and corn flour.
>
> Near the old port are the stands selling textiles, the domain of the "Mama Benz." These vigorous business women usually ride in shining Mercedes cars, hence their name. Impressive by their girth and the sumptuous cloth they wear, their spectacular success has been built on the sale of colorful textiles, most of which they import from the Netherlands. (514)

In indigenous Africa, the occupational system and the family structure were functionally related. Women have always dominated market activity on the continent. A benighted attempt to destroy or reduce the scale of operations of an indigenous African market and the consequent decline in female participation in market activity would send shock waves through the entire family system. The market was so important in indigenous Africa that Skinner (1962) asserted emphatically that: "No African chief can refuse to hear a case brought to his attention at market (though he may postpone it until a regular court hearing). These courts may be the same as—but are often different from—the arbitrating facilities for settling disputes which arise among sellers and customers within the marketplace itself" (63).

MARKET PRICES

To effect trade, direct barter was the medium of exchange in the early stages of African market development. Goods were exchanged directly.

In many communities, however, various commodities were used as currency, including cloth, cattle, salt, iron bars, cowrie shells, beads, firearms, mats, and gold dust.

Every African today will declare that prices in the village markets are generally not determined or fixed by the village chief or king. This is a fact that has been true for centuries and must be stated emphatically, since many modern African governments are ignorant of it.

Prices in indigenous markets traditionally have been influenced by several factors: the forces of supply and demand, scarcity, time of day, status of the consumer, relation with the seller, quality of the product, its degree of necessity, bargaining skills, and competition. In general, prices are determined by the normal forces of supply and demand; the other factors merely shave off or add a few pennies so that two different consumers do not pay exactly the same price. Thus price discrimination exists in indigenous African markets.[3] It is the traditional practice.

Skinner (1964) observed that "Mossi merchants were very aware of the principles of supply and demand and held goods out of the market when prices fell, in order to obtain later higher prices" (222). Ian Vansina (1962) also found that prices on Kuba markets in Zaire, "behave in exactly the same way as prices do in European markets. The price is set by the relation of supply and demand. When shrimps first appear on the market, they fetch a high price. Later on, the price falls" (235). On the Konso markets of southern Ethiopia, Richard Kluckhorn (1962) discovered that, "supply and demand was the basic adjustment mechanism for prices" (86).

Marguerite Dupire (1962) observed that on Fulani markets, "The price of millet and of salt, essential elements in the life of the nomad, vary in proportion to their scarcity. That of millet is at a minimum after the harvest and at a maximum just before the next harvest—variations on the order of one to four—while salt is less expensive at the return of the caravans which bring it back from the salt mines of the Sahara" (36).

The status of the buyer also affected how much one paid for a commodity. Europeans would affirm that in indigenous markets they paid higher prices than the natives. That was one reason why many sent servants to make purchases for them. The price of an item was often influenced by the time of day. Toward the end of the market day, most

---

3. Price discrimination, technically, means charging different prices to different customers for the same product.

traders were in a hurry to get home or reluctant to carry home unsold goods. Africans knew that was the best time to obtain good bargains.

In most indigenous African markets, haggling was the process by which prices were determined. Prices were not fixed by any village government authority—people bargained over them. Tardits and Tardits (1962) provided a description of such a bargaining process on South Dahomean markets:

> Bargaining is the rule. Prices asked by sellers as well as buyers are always higher or lower than those which are finally agreed upon. Long debates ensue in which praise and insults have their place.
>
> A customer looks at a fish tray; the merchant asks 425 francs for 40 fish; the customer offers 350 francs. After a short discussion, the merchant is ready to sell. The customer then withdraws the offer and proposes 300 francs; the discussion goes on till the seller has accepted; the buyer thinks it over a second time and says: "275 francs." The merchant finally agrees but the customer drops the proposed price down to 200 francs. At this point, the merchant refuses to sell. Discussion starts again until at last the bargain is concluded for 225 francs. (106-107)

In sum, prices on indigenous markets generally fluctuated in accordance with the forces of supply and demand. When tomatoes were in season, the price fell, and vice versa. Peasants and chiefs understood these price gyrations. If the price of an item was too high, the traditional response was to bargain down the price. If it did not come down enough, a substitute was purchased, especially in the area of farm produce. For example, cocoyam, cassava or plantain could be substituted for yam. One was not "forced" to buy yams if they could not afford it. When the price of a commodity remained persistently high, the natives either produced it themselves, as often happened in the case of yams, or traveled to the source to obtain it more cheaply. Tales of traders trekking long distances to buy goods more cheaply at the source are legion. Similarly, various meat substitutes could be purchased if the price of, say, chicken was too high.[4]

---

4. It may sound strange to the reader that I am belaboring such an obvious point here. But many postcolonial African governments did not understand this facet of indigenous economic culture. They imposed price controls on peasant farmers and traders and arrested violators, charging them with "economic sabotage."

African chiefs did little to interfere with the day-to-day operations of the village market. Nor did they impose price controls on the market. It was never the traditional role of chiefs to police how prices were set. Even wages were not fixed by any village authority (Hill, 1987, 110). To all intents and purposes, the African village market was an open and free market, however "primitive." Only rarely did a chief intervene in market transactions.

Role of Women in Distribution

Upon close study of Africa's rural economy, one cannot fail to be impressed by the participatory role of women. Today the majority of Africa's peasant farmers—about 80 percent—are women. Women also dominate rural markets and trade. In Yoruba, "local farm produce—either cash crops or food crops—are marketed at the local market, almost invariably by women" (Hodder, 1962, 43). These are not recent phenomena. Female participation in market activities has always been a tradition. It was the result of the traditional division of labor on the basis of sex.

The object in trading, as everywhere, is to make a profit. The Yoruba women "trade for profit, bargaining with both the producer and the consumer in order to obtain as large a margin of profit as possible" (Bascom, 1984, 26). And in almost all West African countries, women kept the profits made from trading. "A Ga woman also makes money by her trading. . . . A man has no control over his wife's money, but any extra money she can extract from him for herself can never be reclaimed" (Field, 1940, 54). "In South Dahomey, commercial gains are a woman's own property and she spends her money free of all control. . . . Trade gives to women a partial economic independence and if their business is profitable they might even be able to lend some money—a few thousand francs—to their husbands against their future crops" (Tardits and Tardits, 1962, 110).

Traders frequently reinvest part of their gains to expand their trading activities and spend part to cover domestic and personal expenses, since spouses have to keep the house in good condition, replace old cooking utensils, buy their own clothes and educate their children. Historically, another important use of trade profits was the financing of political activity. According to historians M. J. Herskovits and M. Harwitz (1964), "support for the nationalist movements that were the instruments of political independence came in considerable measure from the donations of the market women" (377).

In fact, it can be validly asserted that there is no black African leader, past or present, whose mother or grandmother did not engage in trade, the traditional role of women in Africa. Clearly, any event, whether government policy, a civil war, or a calamitous occurrence, that disrupts agriculture or diminishes the scale of market activity would have a disproportionately adverse effect on African women. That in turn would have ramifications throughout the family structure and the entire society.

The Role of Government in the Indigenous Economy

Indigenous African economies were based on agriculture, pastoralism, markets, and trade. Both the rulers and the natives appreciated the importance of these activities. Indigenous governments created the necessary conditions for their subjects to conduct their activities. Even with agriculture, the tribal government did not interfere or dictate what crops the peasants should raise; the peasants decided what to cultivate. The role of the chief or kings in agriculture was to ensure that access to land was not denied to anyone, even strangers. Supervision or regulation of access did not constitute control over production.

In most cases in Africa, "there was no direct interference with production" (Wickins, 1981, 230). The tenet of African law that maintained that any harmful action against another individual was a threat to the whole society applied to the realm of economics. A restriction on an individual's economic activity placed severe constraints on the economic welfare of the whole society. If the individual prospered, so did his extended family and the community—so long as his success did not conflict with the interests of the community. The society's interests were paramount. Unless an individual's pursuit of wealth or prosperity conflicted with society's well-being, the chief or king had no authority to interfere with it. This was a well-nigh universal African belief.

With trade, the historical evidence does not suggest government intervention. It would hardly make sense for the chiefs prevent their own subjects from engaging in trade. Traders were free enterprisers, taking the risks themselves. As Kwame Y. Daaku (1971) observed: "Those who so desired and ventured into distant places in pursuit of trade could rise to higher positions in the traditional setup. Along the coastal towns, successful traders began to display their affluence by surrounding themselves with a host of servants. Some were raised to the status of headmen or elders. They built themselves magnificent houses on which some of them even mounted a few cannon. The rise of these people was not only a coastal phenomenon. In practically all the forest states there came into prominence men like Kwame Anteban of Nyameso in Denkyira, whose wealth became proverbial" (179).

Occasionally, the kings and chiefs had farms and other economic enterprises operated for them. For example, the Asante kings had royal gold mines, and the chiefs in East and southern Africa had some goats and cattle. But they were mainly for the consumption of royalty and guests—not purposefully for the people as a whole. This point is crucial. Nowhere in the history of Africa is there evidence of chiefs and kings operating tribal government farms to feed the people. The natives fed themselves, built their own huts, and provided for themselves.

Nor did the kings and chiefs operate tribal government enterprises. The craft industries were owned by individuals or families, not by the chief or the state. The ruler might choose to have an enterprise but, again, it was mostly for his own benefit, not that of the natives. It was the same with trade. As Daaku (1971) noted in the case of the Akan of the Gold Coast, "Apart from the occasional trading organized for and on behalf of the chiefs, trading, like all other vocations, was primarily an affair of individuals. Much of it was conducted by a man and his family, that is, his wives and children and/or with his sister's sons. It was never an affair of the state" (174).

Only in very, very few instances was trade monopolized and controlled by the state. The exceptions include the kingdoms of Dahomey, Asante, and Mossi. The Dahomey kingdom was centrally planned, and Dahomeans were the most heavily taxed West Africans in the nineteenth century. Inevitably, the kingdom collapsed under the weight of its bureaucracy and maze of regulations. In fact, throughout Africa's history, fewer than 20 out of thousands of commodities were reserved strictly for chiefs. According to Robert Bates (1987), the most frequently mentioned objects of chief's monopoly were ivory, kola, slaves, cattle, skins, and parts of game killed (55). Everything else was a free commodity.

In conclusion, state intervention in the economy was the exception rather than the rule in precolonial Africa. As Bates (1987) observed, "In precolonial Africa, the states underpinned specialization and trade; they terminated feuds; they provided peace and stability and the conditions for private investment; they formed public works; and they generated wealth, if only in the form of plunder. In these ways, the states secured prosperity for their citizens" (40).

The Indigenous System: A Summary and Assessment

Foreign observers who came upon African natives' profit-sharing schemes hastily denigrated them as "primitive communism." Many African leaders also considered the same schemes as proof that the indigenous system was "socialism." Both groups were wrong. Many tribal societies had no state planning or direction of economic activity. Nor were there state enterprises and widespread state ownership. The means of production were privately owned. Huts, spears, and agricultural implements were all private property. The profit motive was present in most market transactions. Free enterprise and free trade were the rule in indigenous Africa. The natives went about their economic activities on their own initiative and free will. They did not line up at the entrance of the chief's hut to apply for permits before engaging in trade or production. The African woman who produced *kenkey, garri,* or *semolina* herself decided to produce those items. No one forced her to do so. Nor did anyone order the fishermen, artisans, craftsmen, or even hunters what to produce.

In modern parlance, those who go about their economic activities on their own free will are called free enterprisers. By this definition, the *kente* weavers of Ghana, the Yoruba sculptors, the gold, silver, and blacksmiths as well as the various indigenous craftsmen, traders, farmers, and all were free enterprisers. And the natives had been so for centuries. The Masai, Somali, Fulani, and other pastoralists who herded cattle over long distances in search of water and pasture to fatten them also were free enterprisers. So were the African traders who traveled great distances to buy and sell commodities—an economic, risk-taking venture.

The extended family system offered them security they needed to take the risks associated with enterpreneurial activity. Many development experts overlooked these positive economic aspects of the much-maligned extended family system. Although this system entailed some "sharing" (not forced or proportionate), it also provided the springboard for Africans to launch themselves into highly risky ventures. If they failed, the extended family system was available to support them. By the same token, if they were successful, they had some obligation to the system that supported them. The Fanti have this proverb: *"Obra nyi woara abo"* (Life is as you make it within the community).

State intervention in the economy was not the general policy, except in the kingdoms of Dahomey and Asante. Even in commerce, African states lacked state controls and ownership. In Gold Coast, for example, gold-mining was open to all subjects of the states of Adanse, Assin, Denkyira, and Mampong. Some chiefs taxed mining operations at the rate of one-fifth of the annual output. In some states, all gold mined on certain days was ceded to the throne. But the mines were in general not owned and operated by the chiefs. Rather, they granted mining concessions.

Much of the indigenous economic system still exists today, where African governments have not destroyed it through misguided policies and civil wars. Female traders still can be found at the markets. They still trade their wares for profit. And in virtually all African markets today, one still bargains over prices—an ancient tradition.

Rather strangely, postcolonial African leaders and elites came to believe that they had to abandon their traditional heritage in order to develop. It is worth noting, however, that the economically vibrant Japanese did not do so. "Its postwar success is not due to Westerniza-tion. Although Japan has modernized spectacularly, it remains utterly different from the West. Economic success in Japan has occurred through pure discipline—the people's ability to work in groups and to conform; it has nothing to do with individualism" (editorial in *Bangkok Post* cited by *The Washington Times*, 9 November 1996, A8). In fact, the traditional Japanese heritage of working in groups bears remarkable similarity to Africa's.

STATISM

After independence, the economic systems established by African leaders and elites, just as the political systems, bore no resemblance to the indigenous systems. In the aftermath of independence, the nation-alist leaders were in a hurry to develop Africa. They needed an alternative ideology, as they uniformly rejected those that had under-pinned the colonial structures. Four distinct official ideologies emerged. The first was African socialism, espoused by such leaders as Kwame Nkrumah of Ghana, Ahmed Sekou Toure of Guinea, Modibo Keita of Mali, Gamal Abdel Nasser of Egypt, Julius Nyerere of Tanzania, and Kenneth Kaunda of Zambia. These leaders advocated the creation of an egalitarian, just, and self-sufficient polity. The mechanism for the attainment of these goals was the state, which would furnish the pivot of critical identities, organize the economy, and supervise the second, societal phase of decolonization (Chazan et. al., 1992, 155). They extolled political centralization and mobilization as the vehicles for real transformation.

The second ideology was political pragmatism, espoused by such leaders as Felix Houphouet-Boigny of Côte d'Ivoire, Abubakar Tafawa Balewa of Nigeria, Hastings Banda of Malawi, and Daniel arap Moi of Kenya. Declaring themselves to be nonideological, they stressed economic growth and prosperity. In their countries, the state was charged with the task of fostering entrepreneurship, attracting foreign investment, and creating a climate conducive to material advancement. The pragmatists were as statist as the socialists, although they wanted to use the state more for the preservation of elite privilege than for social or political transformation. "Centralization, therefore, was delineated not in a social or political but in an administrative sense; it nevertheless was as deeply ensconced in the political attitudes of pragmatists as in those of self-proclaimed socialists" (Chazan et al., 1992, 156).

The third ideology, military nationalism, was supplied by the first batch of military leaders who burst onto the political scene in the late 1960s and early 1970s: Idi Amin of Uganda, Jean-Bedel Bokassa of Central African Republic, Mobutu Sese Seko of Zaire, and Gnassingbe Eyadema of Togo. Mobutu, for example, wrote that "We in Zaire spent a lot of time building a strong central state which could resist Soviet aggression quickly and effectively. This enabled us to decisively make the uniform decisions that were necessary to fulfill our national defense obligations and our commitments to the United States" (*The Washington Times*, 14 June 1995, A23).

These military strongmen exhibited a dictatorial bent. They had not been central to the independence struggles and felt the need to develop alternative ideologies to supplant those of the leaders they overthrew. They glorified the African warrior tradition, shunned foreign ideals, and revived certain traditional practices. In the economic arena, they exercised full control over national resources, not only to deflect pressures from external creditors but also to account for statist monopolies. But their ideologies were scarcely impressive. "They are by and large bereft of intellectual content, they are replete with contradictions, they address key issues haphazardly. These orientations, at best, may be viewed as feeble attempts to legitimate their purveyors; in most instances, they have provided the cover for the exercise of brute force. Manifestations of this sort of military nationalism resurface periodically, as insecure leaders with dwindling support bases find refuge in cultural symbols in a desperate effort to gain some loyalty and legitimacy" (Chazan, et. al., 1992, 158).

The fourth ideology was Afro-Marxism, which was the official policy of Angola, Mozambique, Congo, and Ethiopia. It attributed the malaise of African economies to the lingering effects of imperialism and the continuing machinations of neocolonialism, both within and without Africa. It envisaged the creation of a totally new social order, in which private ownership of the means of production would be abolished and the state would become the supreme patron of economic destiny.

However, the application of such labels as "pro-capitalist," "military-nationalist," "Afro-Marxist" and "socialist" to postcolonial African governments is not particularly useful and probably more apt to create confusion. The relevant ideology always has been statism.[5] State hegemony in the economy was the common feature, although its precise

---

5. It should be emphasized, however, that the roots of statism can be traced to colonial administration policies. The Portuguese in Guinea-Bissau, for example, discouraged internal trade to persuade peasants to concentrate more on the production of cash crops for the export trade. In Mozambique, during the Estado Novo era, both large company plantations and the African population became heavily dependent on the state for their prosperity and economic security (Libby, 1987, 219).

In the 1930s, government in the French and Belgian colonies was a formidable power and essentially autocratic. Over the years, it took on greater powers. The most widely known aspect of this growth of government was the postwar development plans of the French and Belgians. These involved huge expenditures on public works: ports, airports, roads, public buildings, dams. The French program was known as FIDES, an acronym chosen to mean "faith." The Belgian campaign for public investment in its colonies was formally adopted in the 1952 Ten-Year Plan.

Along with the growth of public works projects, the central state apparatus grew as well. And in response to growing nationalist criticisms, the colonial administrations began more active interventions in African economies to meet their demands. Marketing boards, for example, were set up during the colonial era with the declared purpose of protecting small African peasant producers from the vagaries of the world market. Marketing boards fixed prices well below world market levels; the difference was to be used for rural development. Nevertheless, regardless of the colonial precedents, African leaders were, in general, disposed toward statism, or, according to official language, socialism.

characteristics and rationale varied according to the social, economic, and political conditions within particular countries and also over time in response to changing internal and external pressures. Virtually all African countries operated a system in which power was concentrated in the hands of the state and ultimately one individual. This had never been the case in indigenous Africa.

The only differences between the African nationalist leaders lay in two areas: how they proceeded with development and the nature of their state intervention. While Houphouet-Boigny and Kenyatta were willing to proceed slowly, Sekou Toure of Guinea and Kwame Nkrumah of Ghana were impatient. Nkrumah, for example, declared: "We shall achieve in a decade what it took others a century" (Nkrumah 1957, 398).

The other difference was in the degree of statism. Only a few African leaders, such as Banda of Malawi, Houphouet-Boigny, and Kenyatta opted for the "capitalist" road. The overwhelming majority of African leaders adopted "socialism" or some convoluted variation of that ideology. Even so, there was hardly any real practical difference other than the extent to which the operations of private foreign companies were encouraged or tolerated. In "capitalist" Ivory Coast, Kenya, Liberia, Malawi, Senegal, and Zaire, they were welcome. In the socialist countries they were generally not, and most foreign companies were nationalized.

More generally, the colonial experience propelled most nationalist leaders and the intelligentsia toward statism or socialism. During the struggle for freedom from colonial rule in the 1950s, many African nationalists harbored a deep distrust of and distaste for capitalism, which was falsely identified as an extension of colonialism and imperialism, much as Lenin said it was. Freedom from colonial rule was consequently interpreted as freedom from capitalism as well, and socialism—the antithesis of capitalism—was adopted as an alternative ideology.

A proliferation of socialist ideologies emerged in postcolonial Africa. Doctrinaire socialism, however, was eschewed. Many African leaders spurned becoming a satellite of the Soviet Union or China in the early 1960s. Socialism in Africa was to be a distinctive ideology based on the continent's unique social and cultural traditions—"African socialism." Nkrumah of Ghana, widely regarded as the "father of African socialism," was convinced that "only a socialist form of society can assure Ghana of a rapid rate of economic progress without destroying that social justice, that freedom and equality, which are a central feature of our traditional life" (Seven-Year Development Plan, 1963/64–1969/70, 1).

Nkrumah declared that socialism was his ideology and that his "Convention People's Party is the state and the state is the party. . . . The Party has always proclaimed socialism as the objective of our social, industrial and economic programmes. Socialism however will continue to remain a slogan until industrialization is achieved." He went on to say, "Let me make it clear that our socialist objectives demand that the public and co-operative sector of the productive economy should expand at the maximum possible rate, especially in those strategic areas of production upon which the economy of the country depends." Furthermore, he surmised that "socialist transformation would eradicate completely the colonial structure of our economy" (Nkrumah, 1973, 189).

Nyerere of Tanzania, on the other hand, claimed his socialist ideology was based on African cultural traditions. He was first exposed to socialism, as were many African socialists, in the West, during his schooling in Scotland. He castigated capitalism, or the "money economy," because, he believed, it "encourages individual acquisitiveness and economic competition." The money economy was, in his view, foreign to Africa, and thus could "be catastrophic as regards the African family social unit." As an alternative to "the relentless pursuit of individual advancement," Nyerere insisted that Tanzania be transformed into a nation of small-scale communalists ("Ujamaa") (Nyerere, 1966, 10-11). Nyerere conceived of "ujamaa" as a sort of extension, into the national and even international realm, of the traditional African extended family:

> The foundation and the objective of African socialism is the extended family. The true African Socialist does not look on one class of men as his brethren and another as his natural enemies. . . . He regards all men as his brethren—as members of his ever extending family. That is why the first article of TANU's creed is: *"Binadamu wore ni ndugu zangu, na Afrika ni moja."* If this had been originally put in English, it could have been: "I believe in Human Brotherhood and the Unity of Africa." "Ujamaa," then, or "Familyhood" describes our Socialism. It is opposed to Capitalism, which seeks to build a happy society on the basis of the exploitation of man by man; and it is equally opposed to doctrinaire socialism which seeks to build its happy society on a philosophy of inevitable conflict between man and man. (Bell, 1986, 117)

According to Morag Bell (1986), Nyerere "claimed that the traditional African economy and social organization were based on socialist principles of communal ownership of the means of production in which kinship and family groups participated in economic activity and were jointly responsible for welfare and security. The socialist system of co-operative production appeared to be more compatible with African culture than the individualism of capitalism, and on the basis of these cultural roots Nyerere sought to emphasis the distinctive characteristics of African socialism" (117).

Nyerere, however, misunderstood his own African heritage. His claim of "communal ownership of the means of production" was incorrect. As I made abundantly clear earlier, all the means of production in indigenous Africa were privately owned.[6] Three economic factors of production—labor, capital, and the entrepreneur—were owned by the peasants, not their chiefs or the state. Land, the other factor, belonged to the ancestors. The chiefs and kings held land only in trust, it did not belong to them or the state. Furthermore, the African emphatically does not "regard all men as his brethren." Otherwise, there would be no tribal wars or tribalism. Like many other African leaders, Nyerere displayed a woeful lack of understanding of his own black African heritage and culture. Such leaders attempted to graft an ideology onto an African culture they did not understand.

Regardless of the justification for its adoption, socialism in Africa was understood to mean increasing the state's participation in virtually every sector of the economy. Nkrumah was quite emphatic: State participation as a domestic policy was to be pursued toward "the complete ownership of the economy by the State" (Seven-Year Development Plan, 1963/64–1969/70, 3). There was to be a rapid expansion of the state sector, and "various state corporations and enterprises were to be established as a means of securing our economic independence and assisting in the national control of the economy," because "capitalism is too complicated a system for a newly independent state; hence the need for a socialist society" (Nkrumah, 1957, 398-399).

---

6. The source of this confusion is individual ownership versus family ownership. Whereas in the West, the individual is the basic economic and social unit, in Africa it is the extended family. Farms, for example, are family owned, but the family is a private sector unit, not a governmental one. Additionally, family ownership is not the same as communal ownership. A park or a river may be communally owned.

Many African governments followed in Nkrumah's footsteps: They not only nationalized European companies ostensibly to prevent "foreign exploitation" but also debarred the natives from many economic fields. For example, after Ghana gained its independence, the state took over European companies. It monopolized mining operations and declared indigenous gold-mining *(galamsey)* illegal. In fact, "Anyone caught indulging in illegal gold prospecting, popularly known as *'galamsey'* (gather them and sell), will be shot, a PNDC representative announced to a workers' rally in the Western Region" (*West Africa*, 1 March 1982, 618).

In many other African countries, the natives were squeezed out of industry, trade, and commerce, as the state emerged as the dominant, if not the only, player. Indigenous operators were not tolerated. Indeed, there was a time when the director of the Club du Sahel, Anne de Lattre, would begin her meetings with the frightening remark, "Well, there is one thing we all agree on: that private traders should be shot" (*West Africa*, 26 January 1987, 154).

Recall that in precolonial Africa, the natives had been trading freely before the colonialists arrived. But under Sekou Toure of Guinea's nonsensical program of "Marxism in African Clothes," "Unauthorized trading became a crime. Police roadblocks were set up around the country to control internal trade. The state set up a monopoly on foreign trade and smuggling became punishable by death. Currency trafficking was punishable by 15 to 20 years in prison. Many farms were collectivized. Food prices were fixed at low levels. Private farmers were forced to deliver annual harvest quotas to 'Local Revolutionary Powers.' State Companies monopolized industrial production" (*The New York Times*, 20 December 1987, 28).

Two perplexing questions continue to engage the minds of analysts: Why did African nationalist leaders and elites spurn their own indigenous systems? And why did they turn against the very people they were sworn to lift out of poverty? We turn to chapter 4 for some answers.

The Functionally Illiterate Elites

It is a sad commentary to call Nigerians "the most unintelligent intellectuals on the face of this planet." Although Nigerians are an academically brilliant group of people, according to the U.S. State Department, applying the "books" to real life issues and dilemmas has been a big problem for Africans in general and Nigerians in particular.
—Bayo Awokoya, Nigerian scholar in Oakland, California, in *African News Weekly,* 26 August–1 September 1996, 23).

Despite profuse declarations of pride in African dignity and culture, the nationalists and elites never really went back to their indigenous systems after independence from colonial rule. Chiefs were stripped of much of their traditional authority. All unoccupied land—customary land—became government property, including agricultural land in Nigeria. The elites shunned the existing economic system and imposed alien systems on the people, who were almost everywhere in Africa held in contemptible disdain.

The elites are an amorphous group of "educated" Africans, within which three subclasses may be distinguished: the super elites, the professional elites, and the subelites. The super or ruling elites are the heads of state, ministers, chief justices, governors of central banks, and other personalities, such as chairmen of state-owned corporations and vice—chancellors of the universities, who wield considerable political power and influence. The professional elites are those for whom administrative and political power are just within reach. This group, at the periphery of the administrative decision-making process, is composed largely of professionals: lawyers, medical doctors, university lecturers, military officers, university graduates, and secondary school principals and teachers. This group generally supplies the political leaders and candidates, both elected and defeated. The final group, the subelites, is composed of secondary school dropouts, ordinary soldiers (staff sergeants), and office clerks and typists. The subelites generally outnumber the other two groups combined by far.

However, the most vociferous of the three are the professional elites, who at the fringes of political power, are most strident in their demands and criticisms of the ruling elites. These professional elites, perhaps because of their educational achievements, have an overrated sense of self-importance, believing that only they are qualified to rule the country. Feeling shut off from power or denied its rewards, they constantly challenge the legitimacy of the regime in power and undermine its authority. Their primary objective is to remove the super elites and replace them with themselves. To accomplish this goal, they may establish "unholy alliances" with political leaders, other professionals, workers, or students. Indeed, much of the political instability that characterizes Africa emanates from internal power struggles within the elite class itself, in particular between the super and the professional elites. If they fail in their bid to unseat the ruling elites, the professional elites may sell off themselves to the ruling elites or engage in acts of sycophancy or collaboration, calculated to win the favor of the government in power. Such acts ensure that the professional elites also can partake of the fruits of power.[1]

In most African countries, the elites as a group make up less than 20 percent of the population. Yet they regard political power as their prerogative and government as their property. Political power is not to be shared with the "backward masses," who are too uneducated to understand such esoterica as "constitutional rights." The elites deem it the responsibility of the government to provide and care for themselves. The government must provide them not only jobs but also everything from houses, cars, refrigerators, television sets, to even their own funerals at subsidized rates. Naturally, to win their political support, African governments have been obliged to grant many of these demands. Moreover, governments themselves are run by the elites. Therefore,

---

1. This is often defended by references to such expressions as "If you can't beat them, join them" and "Man must eat."

providing perks and subsidies to one section of the elite class enables the super elites to grab an even larger piece of the pie for themselves. In all of this, the interests of the masses seldom count. What distinguishes the elites from the masses is the possession of pieces of academic paper: university degrees, diplomas, and army titles.

THE SHIBBOLETH OF EDUCATION

Colonization initiated a process of acculturation. Through contact with European colonialists, African natives came to learn of the former's way of life, such as mannerisms, habits of dressing and eating. The process was accelerated by education, the military might of the colonialists, and the general disparagement of African traditional beliefs and customs.

Denigration of Africans and their traditions was a common feature of colonialism, and references to Africans as "primitive" and "backward" punctuated scholarly work. The European colonialists constituted a super-elite group (reference group). They seldom socialized with the natives; they ran their own social clubs and organizations (Rotary and Polo clubs) and generally held the natives in contempt. E. E. Hagen (1962) referred to this treatment as "withdrawal of status respect."[2] Accordingly,

> When such disparagement impinges upon a man, his traditional occupation no longer yields the satisfaction it used to. . . . Disparagement demonstrates that that role is not sufficiently valued by the reference group to validate other aspects of his traditional behavior. He may be as diligent a cultivator or petty manufacturer or shopkeeper as anyone could possibly expect, yet he is still disparaged. . . . Groups whose opinions he has learned to respect no longer look on his role as entirely worthy.
>
> For peace of mind he must feel that the position which defines his position in the social structure is worthy and he must also defer to the attitudes of the reference group. These two inner attitudes are now contradictory; he cannot do both. (206)

These inner conflicts produced anxiety and frustration, which in turn caused irritation and rage. The victim could not vent this rage on

---

2. In what follows we borrow extensively from Hagen (1962). His analysis greatly facilitates the understanding of the socioeconomic dynamics of Africa.

his oppressors because they were too powerful.[3] The anxiety, frustration and hostility produced by acculturation tended to create three general types of personalities: retreatists, malcontents, and ritualists (conformists). The retreatist was the individual who, apparently baffled by the complexity of the new culture, retreated into the sanctity of his traditional world. By fleeing to the rural areas, such an individual escaped the unrelenting onslaught of denigration by the colonial administrators residing in the urban areas.

The malcontents were generally highly educated and professional. They found the very fact of colonialism unacceptable and were never satisfied with the colonial status. Infused with the ethos of liberty and humanism, this group rejected the subjugation of one human group by another. Although they possessed the qualifications required to work in the colonial administration, most chose, out of high moral and intellectual principles, not to. Instead, they waged a relentless crusade against colonial rule. Out of this group came African nationalist leaders of the anticolonial struggle: Kwame Nkrumah of Ghana, Kenneth Kaunda of Zambia, and Julius Nyerere of Tanzania, among others.

The ritualists were by far the most predominant type of personality. In experiencing extreme derogation, the victims sought to protect themselves by a psychological reaction mechanism known as identification with the aggressor. They persuaded themselves that if they had characteristics identical to the aggressors', they would not be harmed or destroyed by them. So ritualists modeled themselves after the aggressors (the colonialists), slavishly imitating their external traits. If the colonial masters wore white shirts and ties, so did they, notwithstanding Africa's hot and humid climate. If the colonialists consumed sardines and drank tea at 4:00 P.M. and Ovaltine at night, so did they. Not only did the ritualists copy the colonialists' habits and ideals, they did it in such a manner that they became more "British" than the British actually were themselves. Given the opportunity, the ritualists will study at the same schools of the master; pursue the same jobs, especially by obtaining entry-level positions in their companies (Hagen, 1962, 419).

In their frenzied attempts to imitate the colonialists or imbibe their alien incomprehensible traits, the ritualists never questioned or sought to understand *why* the colonialists drank tea at 4:00 P.M. or behaved the

---

3. Hagen suggests that such pent-up rage was often unleashed on the victim's wife and children.

way they did. Ritualists just aped them—a mimic syndrome that Africans call "monkey dey see, monkey dey do." Thus, their behavior was by rote or mechanical rather than alert and rational, a fact that often resulted in a confused emotional state.

Although the ritualists were naturally predisposed toward conformism, the colonial government also demanded conformist behavior for the preservation of the status quo and took steps to ensure that the educational system served this purpose. While missionaries were concerned primarily with teaching people to read so that they could absorb the lessons of the Bible, the colonial governments needed only obedient clerks. No large demand for technical skills was envisaged, as the colonies were conceived to be purveyors of raw materials and foodstuffs. "Adapted to the purposes of forming clerks, ministers of religion and later lawyers and officials, the educational institutions in Colonial Africa laid stress on literary and legal studies and neglected industrial and commercial training, not to speak of the agricultural, shunned by everybody and stigmatized by the notion that anything to do with the cultivation of the soil is fit only for a poor and uneducated rustic" (Andreski, 1969, 204).

Students were taught the French constitution, the British parliamentary system, the geography of the British Isles and France, British history, and French literature. The subjects' relevance was seldom questioned. To ritualist students, education was a passport to white-collar employment, prestige, and the status that had been denied them. What mattered to them most was the acquisition of the magic piece of paper. Indeed, for a placement in the post office, instruction in the British constitution was a requirement.

Gradually an educated class, an elite *(evolues),* began to emerge distinct from the populace. These African graduates enjoyed salaries that, although well below those of the colonial administrators, were extremely high by African standards. They acted like the European colonialists because to be called *"obroni"* (white man) was a term of praise. To have obtained part of one's education in Europe or America or even to have merely visited there carried the prestigious label "been to." To live in a bungalow (however small) in the European residential area carried prestige. Eating European dishes, inviting Europeans to your home, or generally associating with Europeans was prestigious.[4]

---

4. Social luminaries bragged about their foreign exploits as in "Oh, I have been to London. I have been to Paris." Hence the derisive term "been to."

To the elites, Westernization offered a way to gain acceptance or equality. Accordingly, African elites wore Western clothes, spoke Western languages, drove Western cars, and talked about Western art and culture. In Westernizing themselves, they believed that discrimination at the hands of the colonialists would ease. And in proving that they were more "French" than the French, the ritualists hoped that they would be accepted.[5]

INDEPENDENCE AND ITS AFTERMATH

The malcontents led the struggle against colonial rule, and the immediate effect of independence was to catapult them into power in Anglophone, and, later, Lusophone Africa. In Francophone Africa, with the possible exception of Guinea and Algeria, ritualists, such as Leopold Senghor of Senegal and Felix Houphouet-Boigny of Côte d'Ivoire, came to power. The malcontents tended to be anti-Western, while the ritualists were more pro-Western. Nonetheless, both groups quickly moved into positions vacated by the departing colonial administrators. The ritualists had little difficulty continuing where the colonialists left off. The malcontents, however, had it rough, for the inner psychological contradictions they had long suppressed burst into the open. During the liberation struggle, the malcontents had characterized colonial rule as "alien" and the colonialists as "infidels." Imbued with a deep sense of African pride and dignity, they felt, on the one hand, the need to eradicate all the vestiges of the hated system of colonial rule. But, on the other, they could not reject everything Western. After all, they had obtained their education in the West. In addition, they were in awe of the trappings of Western culture and craved the finest the West had to offer. Nor could they reject all the emoluments and perquisites endowed with the colonial posts.[6]

---

5. When President Leopold Senghor of Senegal—the author of *Negritude*—retired in 1980, he settled with his French wife in southern France to help "improve the French language."

6. It is important to note that this constant psychological conflict spilled over to the development arena. Inconsistencies and schizophrenic posturing were most notable in agriculture. Despite the "pride in African culture," this group of elites provided little assistance to traditional, peasant agriculture. The psychological torment also forced many to seek refuge in the East (socialist ideology).

Denigration, Oppression and Exploitation of the Peasantry

For the masses, independence altered little in their lives. All that changed was the skin color of the new masters. Black masters, or more appropriately, black neo-colonialists continued the invidious treatment the masses suffered at the hands of the colonialists. The masses belonged to a "lower class" to be handled at arm's length by the elites. The neocolonialists kept and reserved exclusively for themselves the various European clubs. A guard usually was stationed at the entrance of these clubs to shoo away the curious illiterate folks. "If a distant member from the village called on an elite unannounced, a separate table was set in the kitchen. The elite family supped with knives and forks at its regular table in the dining room. When the elite visited his village he took along some eggs, sugar, tea and coffee" (Lloyd, 1964, 135).

Nkrumah once referred to cocoa farming as a "poor nigger's business" (Killick, 1978, 63 n. 97). Why should the masses be treated any better? After all, colonialists treated them contemptuously. What made *that* treatment morally repugnant was the fact that the perpetrators were whites or foreigners.[7]

What evolved was blatant de facto segregation between the elites and the masses. The elites did not shop at Africa's traditional markets but at modern, air-conditioned supermarkets. Should they need an item unavailable at the supermarket, they sent their servants to the traditional markets. They would not be seen taking public transportation. They used either their own cars or transportation provided by the government. Nor was public housing fit for them. Even dance bands that played for the illiterate masses were not good enough for the elites. Consequently, the army, the police, and other state corporations all had their own resident bands.

The elites developed a peculiar taste for the best the West could offer and showed them off as status symbols. Accra, Lagos, Kinshasa are full of Mercedes Benzes and BMWs—even Maseratis. Name any luxury car and it can be found somewhere in Africa—out of commission. Never mind that the roads on which these luxury cars would be driven hardly

---

7. This kind of twisted logic provided the intellectual cover for the brutal tyrannies that came to be established in much of postcolonial Africa. Black African leaders could do no wrong—only the colonialists or the whites of apartheid South Africa.

exist. In Ghana even the police cruise around in BMWs. They claimed they needed cars fast enough to catch fleeing criminals.

Two Systems of Justice

After independence, a peculiar system of justice came to be established in Africa: a lenient one for the elites and a harsh and brutal one for the peasant masses. Ghana's adopted national motto was "Freedom and Justice." However, what its courts handed down to the illiterates was anything but. Consider the following cases from there:

> A 31-year-old shoemaker of Agona Swedru was been sentenced to life imprisonment by a Cape Coast High court for robbery involving 45 *cedis* (about $15). (*Daily Graphic*, 8 August 1981)

> A 36-year-old Niger national, Hamidu Zabrama, was jailed for 30 years with hard labor by a Ho Circuit Court that found him guilty of robbery with violence involving 189,720 *cedis* (about $33,000). (*Daily Graphic*, 11 August 1981, 1)

> A 27-year-old housewife Philippine Addo, who told a Ho Circuit Court that she attempted to smuggle 12 *cedis* (about $4) worth of cocoa into the Republic of Togo to enable her to buy soap was jailed five years with hard labor. The same court sentenced a 22-year-old farmer, Geze Rose Adzo, to six years imprisonment with hard labor for illegally attempting to export a basketful of cocoa valued at 100 *cedis* to Togo. (*Daily Graphic*, 3 July 1980, 8)

> On 27 September 1981, a 43-year-old woman, Kporkporvie Dada, was beaten to death by border guards for taking a gallon of kerosene to a relative residing in the Republic of Togo. (*Daily Graphic*, 23 September 1981, 3)

When peasants violated the law, punishment was swift and brutal but when the elites ran afoul of the law, recourse was made to all sorts of Latin writs, such as *habeas corpus* and legal technicalities. On 5 December 1980, Mr. Samuel Sagoe Nkansah, an agricultural officer of the Ghana Commercial Bank—an elite—drove his car through a candle procession of students of St. Augustine's college in Cape Coast, and knocked ten of them down, killing one Emmanuel Sam on the spot. He was jailed for four years (*Daily Graphic*, 23 July 1981, 8).

One may argue that the cases above covered different crimes. If so, how about cases where an elite and a peasant infringed exactly the same laws? In such cases, one would expect stiffer penalties on the elites because they were supposed to "know the law." But consider:

Peasant: A magistrate at Sunkwa-on-Offin, Mr. Kwadwo Asumadu-Amoah, jailed a 43-year-old petty trader, Madam Abena Amponsah, for three years with hard labor for making an illegal profit of 13.50 *cedis* on six cakes of Guardian soap. The same magistrate also handed down a three-year jail term with hard labor to an 18-year old student who made an illegal six *cedi* profit on a packet of matches. (*The Ghanaian Times*, 18 June 1980, 1)

Elite: For diverting 80 percent of the 1,000 bags of maize meant for distribution in the Eastern Region and selling the diverted maize for between 200 and 300 *cedis* per bag instead of 90 *cedis* (making an illegal profit of at least 88,770 *cedis*), Mr. A. K. Baah, the Regional Manager of the Food Distribution corporation, was only ordered transferred by the Eastern Regional Minister, Mr. Felix Amoah. (*Daily Graphic*, 18 June 1980, 7 [note the page number].)

Peasant: Issifu Moshie, a 50-year-old farmer, was jailed for ten years with hard labor by a Mampong-Ashanti Circuit Court when he was found guilty of possessing Indian hemp (marijuana) seeds and cultivating them. When the seeds and plants were sent to the Police Forensic Laboratory for examination, they were found to be Indian hemp that weighed 227 and 11,350 grams respectively. (*Daily Graphic*, 22 July 1981, 5)

Elite: A police corporal attached to the Police Striking Force in Accra was sentenced to a seven-year prison term with hard labor by a Kumasi Circuit Court for possessing 22,700 grams of Indian hemp. (*Daily Graphic*, 3 October 1981, 4)

Peasant: The magistrate at Dunkwa-on-Offin, Mr. Kwadwo Asumadu-Amoah imposed a 1,000 *cedi* fine (or three years if in default) on a 28-year-old petty trader, Miss Akua Afriyie, for making an illegal 1.40 *cedi* profit on four sticks of 555 cigarettes. In addition, she was banned from trading for 12 months and would, in default of the order, be fined an additional 1,000 *cedis*. The magistrate said he would have sent her directly to prison for three years had she not been a nursing mother. (*Pioneer*, 13 June 1980, 8)

Elite: Emmanuel Yaw Mensah, a marketing officer of the State Fishing Corporation at Dunkwa was brought before the same magistrate for making on illegal profit of 45 *cedis* on a carton of fish. The magistrate sentenced him to jail for six months and banned him from trading for 12 months, in default of which an additional three months would be imposed. (*Pioneer*, 11 July 1980, 8)

Within the elite class itself, justice is selectively or partially administered to the various subgroups. A witness, Anthony Ofori Boateng, told the Azu Crabe Commission that although both senior and junior officers were involved in a fraudulent deal at the Agricultural Development Bank in 1980, only the junior officers were punished, with two of them dismissed outright and a third suspended indefinitely (*The Ghanaian Times*, 20 July 1980, 1).

Of course, there have been super-elite crooks, bandits, and smugglers. But when caught, they are shown even more favoritism or leniency. Consider the following cases:

> G. O. Ampau, ex-minister of health in the Busia regime is to forfeit to the state a little over 100,000 *cedis* illegally acquired during his tenure of office. The money may be connected with the part he played in a transaction that enabled International Generics Ltd. to win a 3 million *cedis* order for drugs from the Ministry of Health. (*Daily Graphic*, 14 November 1978, 1)

> The Taylor Assets Committee has ordered that six houses unlawfully acquired by Mr R. A. Quarshie, Minister of Trade in the Busia government, should be forfeited to the state. The Commission also ordered Mr Quarshie to refund to the government a total of 62,762.45 *cedis* he unlawfully acquired. (*Daily Graphic*, 16 November 1978, 1)

Legal experts, of course, would argue that there is a difference between an unlawful or illegal acquisition and theft or robbery. Nonetheless, these cases dramatize the fact that an illegal acquisition of government property was not a criminal offense.

More bizarre were cases involving African heads of state. The late I. K. Acheampong was alleged to have mismanaged Ghana's economy and robbed the country of several million pounds sterling that he stashed away in Swiss bank accounts. Yet when he was arrested, lawyers spent days arguing whether economic mismanagement was a criminal offense. Back in 1971, the late Dr. Kofi Abrefa Busia, the president of Ghana, passed legislation requiring all members of parliament to declare their assets, but when subsequently asked to do so he refused to testify before the Taylor Assets Committee. The clear message was that the head of state in Ghana was above the law.

In Nigeria, the Okigbo Commission disclosed in 1994 that Nigeria's military rulers had squandered $12.4 billion of the country's oil revenue between 1988 and 1994. Yet not one single bandit was brought to justice. Meanwhile Nigeria's military regime executed illiterate armed robbers by firing squad. This glaring anomaly prompted Stephen Okoye, a Nigerian journalist, to write in *African News Weekly* (15–21 July 1996), "It is becoming increasingly difficult to distinguish between the Nigerian armed forces and the Nigerian armed robber. They both use the same operational tactics, resorting to fear, intimidation, and violence to achieve their objectives" (22).

Furthermore, when dealing with super-elite crooks, justice wavered from one regime to the next. What was unlawful under one government suddenly became legal when the government changed. One excellent example was provided by the legality of the property of Krobo Edusei, a minister in the regime of Kwame Nkrumah. His assets and physical property were seized when Nkrumah was overthrown in 1966. They were partially returned when Colonel Acheampong came to power in 1972, only to be seized again in 1978 when Acheampong was ousted. They were released in 1979, and then seized and he himself jailed in 1982.

It soon became clear to the African people that the ruling elites had transformed themselves into an arrogant bunch of oppressive kleptocrats, who were in many countries worse than the European colonialists. The blatant miscarriages of justice provoked military "revolutionaries" such as Flight-Lieutenant Jerry Rawlings of Ghana, Captain Thomas Sankara of Burkina Faso, and others to seize power and attempt to correct what they perceived to be grave injustices against the people. In the beginning of his 1981 "revolution," Rawlings claimed he represented the "poor masses," but actually he represented the subelites: workers, students, and junior army officers. Suddenly finding power thrust upon them, the subelites also abused their power and directed much of their pent-up vengeance at the super elites. Ghana's law courts were shunned because they favored the superelites and professional elites. The subelites established peoples' courts and public tribunals to try the other subgroups of the elite class. Stiff sentences were handed down in those tribunals amid widespread human rights violations.

Rawlings executed by firing squad former heads of state, including I. K. Acheampong and Lieutenant-General F. W. Akuffo, on charges of corruption and mismanagement. Stephen Heenke, a rich businessman (a super-elite), was sentenced to 60 years imprisonment by an Accra Public Tribunal for "outwitting the Bank of Ghana and collecting foreign exchange worth thousands of dollars and pounds sterling" (*Daily Graphic,* 24 September 1982, 1).[8] As it turned out, the Rawlings regime itself, despite its "revolutionary" rhetoric, became the most corrupt and brutally repressive in Ghana's history. Strangely, the oppression of ordinary Ghanaians continued under the Rawlings regime.

The period 1981 to 1983 may be termed the "Red Terror" era, during which Ghanaians were mercilessly brutalized and terrorized. For example, peasant farmers who had formed a queue to cash their "Akuafo" cocoa checks were beaten by police for being "disorderly" (*Daily Graphic,* 4 December 1982, 1). For three years a curfew was imposed on the country, providing the police with an opportunity to fleece the public. In fact, some policemen "deliberately set their watches ahead of time in order to get innocent people to harass" for breaking the curfew (*Graphic Review,* 9-16 July 1982, 15). There were complaints of "disgraceful acts" of some policemen who entered people's houses during curfew hours, threatened those relaxing in the yard with arrest, and extorted money from such "curfew breakers" (*West Africa,* 20 December 1982, 3316).

The Rawlings military regime unleashed barbarous atrocities against the ordinary Ghanaian people. At Kumasi, a student was shot dead by a soldier at a barrier near the University of Science and Technology; a porter at Ejura was shot and killed by a soldier; a civilian was beaten to death at Bantama; and some policemen attacked the people of Adunku, Ejisu District, on their farms, injuring many of them (*West Africa,* 31 January 1983, 295). Then soldiers "swooped down on a number of people, including girls and women, some with babies on their backs, who had queued at some department stores at Adum, and put them on a CMB truck operated by personnel of the People's Army to help in the cocoa evacuation exercise" (*West Africa,* 15 February 1982, 482). Also, "military personnel bundled innocent civilians into articulated trucks and seized 'tro-tro' vehicles at gunpoint to load fertilizer at Tema in the night" (*Graphic,* 11 December 1982, 4). Forced labor?

The Rawlings regime's campaign to impose and enforce price controls was even more insane. For selling one bottle of Sprite soft drink at 7 *cedis* instead of 1.50 *cedis,* an Accra petty trader, Umaro Shaibu, was jailed for four years by the Price Control Tribunal (*West Africa,* 28

---

8. Actually, anyone who outwits the Bank of Ghana should be commended and decorated and those incompetent officials who allowed the bank to be duped should be jailed.

February 1983, 576). And for charging 2 *cedis* for a trip from Accra to Labadi instead of 1 *cedi,* a driver and his assistant were placed in custody at Cantoments Police Station and their vehicle was impounded (*Daily Graphic,* 4 January 1983, 4).

Such widespread violations of human rights prompted *West Africa* (25 October 1982) to complain:

> These violations are now assuming disturbing dimensions before the People's Courts, where proceedings, under the direction of laymen, are anything but decent and lawful: sentences range from 10 years to 60 years, with half of each sentence slated to be served carrying human excreta and the other half as a forced labourer on farms; some of the trials last as long as five minutes. . . . A case in point was Emmanuel Ohene Obeng, charged with "dishonestly" receiving and "stealing" 40 bundles of galvanized gauze and 40 bundles of cottonwood, "property of the people." He bore marks of torture: a cracked lower lip, black eyes and a plastered wound on the left temple. . . .
>
> Ohene Obeng was given 10 years—half of the sentence to be spent collecting human excreta and the other half on the Kadamoso Oil Palm Plantation. (2773)

Of course, when the subelites—then wielding power—broke the law, they treated themselves leniently. For example, Osei Yaw, a member of the Offinso Interim District Coordinating Committee, was sentenced to two years imprisonment "for diverting goods and selling above the controlled price; he pleaded guilty of selling a packet of Ever-Ready batteries at 360 *cedis* instead of 38 *cedis* (*Daily Graphic,* 5 January 1983, 8). Compare that sentence to the four-year imprisonment handed down to Umaro Shaibu for selling a bottle of Sprite at 7 *cedis* instead of 1.50 *cedis.* Or the following:

> Two top officials of the National Youth Council, Major Anthony Avomyotse and Mr. J. S. Nketsiah, have been sacked for condoning and conniving with businessmen of doubtful integrity to purchase stationery, Renault and Peugeot cars over and above controlled prices. (*Daily Graphic,* 2 October 1982, 8)

> The entire executive of the PDC [People's Defense Committee] at Kyebi has been dismissed for abuse of power, indiscipline and extortion, according to a resolution passed by the people at Kyebi. The resolution

cited the case of a woman who was fined 50 *cedis* for not wearing sandals or shoes and another who was fined 4,000 *cedis* for disagreeing with a member of the PDC. (*Daily Graphic,* 4 January 1983, 8)

How different were these crackpot "revolutionaries" from the "belly-comfort" politicians they overthrew in 1981? It is the same African story of betrayal.

SOCIO-ECONOMIC EFFECTS OF ELITE MEGALOMANIA

The African masses never protested against the invidious treatment meted out by the elite aristocracy because, as in the colonial period, they did not have effective political power. To gain social acceptability and cessation of denigration, the masses too perceived it expedient to emulate the conspicuous consumption life-style of their oppressors, the ruling elites. After all, this was how the elites won "acceptance" from the colonialists. Although the effects of elite megalomania on the masses have been pervasive, we single out the following for special attention.

Imported Consumer Goods

Because of unfamiliarity with African food, the European colonialists imported their food into Africa in tins—tinned milk, sardines, corned beef and even bottled water. Unfortunately, the elites believed that consumption of these imported consumer items earned one a special distinction, and they soon became status symbols. Therefore, when the elites took over after independence, it was only natural and logical for them to consume these imported items. Even more incredibly, the government of Ghana went further, labeling these imported food items "essential" and setting up administrative structures to control their prices.[9]

In this way, the masses came to perceive corned beef, tinned milk, milo, Ovaltine, and other imported food items as the elites did. Consumption of these goods was symbolic of status. During the 1960s

---

9. Designating them "essential" carried an implicit acknowledgment that Ghana's own native diet was "inferior." If so, why were so many of the Africans who subsisted on it in the seventeenth century strong enough to be enslaved and transported across thousands of miles of ocean under the most deplorable conditions?

and 1970s, these items were often in chronic shortage in Ghana. A rumor that a government shop had some of these items in stock set off a stampede. Fights and scuffles often broke out in queues.[10] Shortages of these "essential commodities" were a factor in the overthrow of the Nkrumah regime in 1966. In fact, at the Ollennu Commission of Enquiry, Kwesi Armah, former minister of trade under Nkrumah, testified that "Further allocations of import licences were necessary to some areas hit seriously by shortages of essential goods and threatened with collapse into chaos. To meet the problems I foresaw, I made representation to the cabinet for a small supplementary vote in October 1963" (Ollennu Report, 1967, 75).

Elite obsession with imported consumer goods affected the masses. Cameroon, for example, acquired the rather dubious distinction of being the world's highest consumer of champagne per capita in the late 1980s. A public mentality had evolved that held imported items to be of better quality than the locally produced ones.[11] This strange preference system set African government officials up for swindle—even by the so-called socialist countries.

In the 1960s, Ghana signed several bilateral trade agreements with such socialist countries as Czechoslovakia and Hungary. But according to the Abraham's Report (1965), "A whole consignment of corned beef, obtained under bilateral trade agreement, had to be condemned as unsafe for human consumption by Port Health Authorities at Tema in 1964. . . . Another brand supposed to be corned beef surely suffers from a misnomer. It appears to have been fobbed off on the people of this country as "corned beef" when, in fact, it is pork luncheon meat with a minute dash of corned beef in the middle of most tins" (18).

---

10. In 1974 one Ghanaian, who had been up at 4:00 A.M. to queue for sugar, fainted, collapsed, and never regained consciousness. Another was stabbed for trying to take someone else's place in the queue; he died later. Another was shot by a soldier for attempting to jump the queue.

11. Ghana produces java prints (a type of cloth) locally, but the Ghanaian masses have constantly spurned them as inferior to the imported brand. An enterprising white merchant operating in Ghana decided to take advantage of the situation. He bought bundles of the local prints, shipped them out of the country, erased the "MADE-IN-GHANA" labels, resmuggled them into the country, and Ghanaians scrambled to pay five times the market value for these "imported" prints.

ʾect result of the acquisition of foreign tastes and the
ِ the elites was a phenomenal growth in the demand for
ᵤᵣts. During the 1970s, imports in most African countries careened
out of control. A battery of administrative and legislative controls failed
to check the stratopheric rise in imports. With limited foreign exchange
earnings, imports could be financed only with foreign loans. Thus, trade
imbalances precipitated chronic balance-of-payments problems and
foreign debt crises. Nigeria provides an excellent example of an African
country that found itself in this foreign debt trap, despite its immense
oil wealth.

In the late 1970s, Nigeria reaped an oil bonanza, with oil revenues
pouring in at the rate of $13 billion a year. The windfall, however, was
squandered on imports. By 1981 Nigerians were spending a third of their
household budgets on foreign food items. Local agriculture fell into
neglect as Nigerians, flush with oil money, splurged on food imports.
Agricultural production, which grew at 10 percent annually in the 1960s,
grew at less than 3 percent in the 1980s. As *New African Yearbook* (1993-
94) put it, "The volume of food imports increased dramatically. The
main increases were in wheat, rice, fish, meat, milk, sugar, oils and fats;
Nigeria was once one of the world's most important exporters of the last
two. The volume of Nigeria's agricultural exports fell simultaneously:
cocoa output declined, and exports of groundnuts and palm oil collapsed
to nothing" (282).

Other consumer items, from Maseratis and to Rolls-Royces, flowed
into the country to satisfy elite vanity. The government of Nigeria itself
went on a spending spree, spending lavishly on grandiose and ambitious
development projects: multiple-lane highways, fly-overs, steel mills, and
a brand-new capital at Abuja, prompted more by delusions of grandeur
than by economy and rationality.

In this way, much of Africa's resources that could have gone into
real development was wasted by the elites on useless prestige projects and
a benighted bid to prove racial equality or gain international acceptance.

Housing

When in Africa, the European colonialists were concerned primarily with
shelters that would provide maximum protection against not only the
elements and the African physical environment (floods, termites, etc.)
but also foreign interlopers and native insurgents. With this primary
objective in mind, the British built fortified castles strong enough to

withstand cannon-ball attack and lived in stilted, whitewashed, cement houses with cement walls, called "bungalows" in Africa. The houses were whitewashed because it was then easier to spot intruders lurking around them in the pitch-black tropical night. Security considerations dictated against the use of tropical wood in home building.

However, to the elites, castles and whitewashed bungalows were part of the perquisites of power. Therefore, after independence, living in them was a logical extension of the process of gaining political independence. In Ghana the elites went even further. They renovated and extended the Osu Castle—where African slaves were kept in the eighteenth century—painted it in splendid white, and made it the official residence of the head of state.[12]

In postcolonial Africa, house came to mean a cement-built structure. Ghana's State Housing Corporation's vision of "low-cost housing for the masses" was a fully-detached house built of cement. As with other "essential commodities," cement was in constant shortage in many African countries. In 1978 the Ghanaian Government banned cement walls in an apparent effort to save foreign exchange (*Daily Graphic*, 16 May 1978, 1). The elites never realized that the cement content of houses could be drastically reduced, with even greater foreign exchange savings achieved, through liberal substitutions of wood, bricks, and other equally durable local materials. But then of course the elites would not condescend to consider such substitutions. After all, the colonial "masters" never lived in such inferior or "mulatto" houses, so why should they?

In this way, the dietary requirements and housing needs of poor African countries became dependent on the very inputs and materials the country could not produce itself. They had to be imported, fueling demand for imports and aggravating the foreign exchange and debt crisis.

---

12. Hordes of black American tourists visit Ghana to pay homage to their "ancestral homes" and to "come to terms" with the dark part of their history: the slave trade. Visits to the castle dungeons that dot the West African coast are often an emotionally wrenching experience for them. Accordingly, the Elmina Castle in Ghana has been restored as a fitting memorial of the thousands of black slaves who were kept there before transshipment across the Atlantic. Imagine that about 150 miles from the Elmina Castle sits the Osu Castle, which is the seat of the government of Ghana.

POSTCOLONIAL DEVELOPMENT

The Religion of Development

The African nationalists and elites who took over power from the departing colonialists suffered from impatience, feelings of inferiority, the religion of development, and economic illiteracy. The first malaise, which affects almost all Africans, is the predisposition to "catch up" quickly with the rich countries, to narrow the gap between the rich and the poor.

As we noted earlier, after independence the object of Westernization shifted toward gaining international acceptance and equality for the new nation (Lloyd, 1964, 45). If Accra, Lagos, or Nairobi looked like London or New York, perhaps the new nations' status would be readily accepted. The elites brought this same unimaginative aping to the field of development. Foreign metropolitan symbols were mimicked. London had double-decker buses; so too must Africa. American farmers used tractors and pesticides; so too must Africa. Rome has a basilica; so too must Ivory Coast.

In 1963 Nkrumah demanded a bylaw from the Accra-Tema city council requiring all advertisements in Accra to be illuminated by neon lighting so that the main streets of the city would resemble Picadilly Circus. The city council approved the bylaw despite the insistence of the Ghana Chamber of Commerce that the lights were impractical in a country where most businesses had few employees and limited capital (Wherlin, 1973, 261). When Sir Arthur Lewis pointed out to an African prime minister that he was proposing to spend 50 percent of his entire development budget on his capital city, which had only 5 percent of the population, the prime minister was surprised. "But why not?" he asked. "Surely when you think of England you think of London, when you think of Russia you think of Moscow and when you think of France you think of Paris" (Lewis, 1962, 75). The most bizarre instance of this so-too-must-we syndrome occurred in 1976, when President Bokassa spent $20 million, or 20 percent of the GNP of the Central African Republic to crown himself "emperor" to prove that, like France, black Africa too can produce emperors.

Hardly any attempt was made to understand *why* London has double-decker buses or *why* American farmers use tractors. The concept of development became perverted. The developed countries were industrialized and used modern scientific techniques. Therefore, development was equated to industrialization and the use of modern scientific methods. This sort of reasoning is an example of the fallacy *post hoc ergo propter hoc* or what social psychologists call the "refrigerator fallacy."[13] The prevailing tendency to equate industrialization and modernism with development is a manifestation of a pathological condition known as the religion of development. This religion, which shapes or directs much of the elite's development effort, is characterized by the following:

- An excessive preoccupation with sophisticated gadgetry, signs of modernism, an inclination to exalt anything foreign or Western as sanctified, and a tendency to castigate the traditional as "backward"
- A tendency to emphasize industry over agriculture
- A misinterpretation of the so-called characteristics of underdevelopment as causes of economic "backwardness," and the belief that development means their absence
- A tendency to seek solutions to problems from outside rather than from inside Africa
- Attempts to model African cities after London, Paris, New York, or Moscow.

Negative imputations are made to the characteristics of underdevelopment as if there were something intrinsically wrong with having 60 percent of the population engaged in agriculture. Underlying this religion and facade of Westernization are innate feelings of inferiority. As Andreski (1969) put it:

> Anxiety about imputations of inferiority internationally fosters an obsessive concern for collective and individual status symbols. On the individual plane this manifests itself in the preoccupation with cars and other mechanical gadgets, punctilious attention to dress and great concern for decorum. On the collective plane this tendency leads the rulers of Africa

---

13. The Latin expression translates as: Because an event B follows another event A, then B was caused by A. The "refrigerator fallacy" states that, because university professors, for example, have refrigerators, you must be a professor if you own one. Or, in a bizarre twist, to become a university professor all one has to do is to acquire a refrigerator. We will explore this issue in connection with functional illiteracy shortly.

to give priority to obtrusive symbols of modernity—such as show-hospitals, airports, big industrial projects, television stations, assembly halls—and to disregard more important but less conspicuous matters like fostering small workshops. The economic planners would advocate for the importation of ruinously expensive tractors but not for introducing wheelbarrows and scythes, which would bring more palatable benefits. (87)

This religion of development contributed to the neglect and consequent decline of African agriculture. Agriculture was too "backward" and simply did not feature in the grandiose plans drawn up by the elites to industrialize Africa. Of African leaders, the late Kwame Nkrumah of Ghana epitomized this "religion." He was quite clear on the thrust of his development drive: "Industry rather than agriculture is the means by which rapid improvement in Africa's living standard is possible" (Nkrumah, 1957, 7). In exile after he was overthrown in a 1966 coup, Nkrumah asked, in response to charges of mismanagement: "How can the obvious evidence of modernization and industrialization of Ghana, such as new roads, factories, schools and hospitals, the harbor and town of Tema, the Volta and Tefle bridges and the Volta Dam, be reconciled with the charge of wasted expenditure. You only have to look around you to see what we achieved. We built more roads, bridges and other forms of national communications than any other independent African state. We built more schools, clinics and hospitals. We provided more clean piped water. We trained more teachers, doctors and nurses. We established more industries" (Nkrumah, 1973).

Tragically, only the quantity mattered, not the quality. Furthermore, in industry African elites showed a consistent tendency to opt for "modern" capital-intensive techniques and projects that emphasized grandeur rather than economy. For example, conveyors were installed in the State Footwear Corporation factory to move shoes during manufacture, although conveyors were little used elsewhere, even in the United States (Killick, 1978, 229-33).

Abiding Faith in the Potency of the State

During the struggle for independence, the nationalist leaders made extravagant promises to the populace, including free education, and free housing. After independence, they not only had to deliver but also had to meet the demands of their own lieutenants, who demanded the same high salaries, perquisites, and benefits as the colonialists. Never mind that the colonial governments had to offer attractive salaries and considerable fringe benefits, such as free transportation, medical care, and housing, as inducements to get their citizens to serve in the colonies, and that such inducements were clearly unnecessary in the case of Africans living in their own countries. But to the elites, if the colonial administrators were entitled to them, so too must they be. The new African governments capitulated to these demands. When those down the ladder—the subelites—agitated, they too were provided with such amenities as corporation buses and subsidized housing. In this way, the state came to be seen as "the provider."

The elites also perceived the state as "the protector," "the problem solver," and "the entrepreneur." It could protect the new African nation against the avaricious propensities of the multinational corporation. It could solve all economic problems, including underdevelopment. It could do so with a myriad of legislative controls, regulations, and edicts. Through such devices, massive resources would be transferred to the state for national development. But as we shall see in the next chapter, this never happened.

Price controls and various legislative instruments soon became tools for the systematic exploitation of the peasants. The prices peasants received for their produce were dictated by elite-run governments, not determined by market forces, as in traditional Africa. As we saw in the previous chapter, African chiefs did not fix prices. Bargaining was the rule in all village markets, as it is today. But under an oppressive system of price controls administered by the elites, Africa's peasants came to pay the world's most confiscatory taxes. In 1981 the government of Tanzania, for example, was paying peasant maize farmers only 20 percent of the free-market price for their produce. In 1984 cocoa farmers in Ghana received less than 10 percent of the world market price for their crop. In Ethiopia, Guinea, Tanzania, and many other African countries, peasant farmers were forced to sell their produce to the state at ridiculously low prices.

Soon the state became a cash cow—a vehicle for elite enrichment. Resources extracted from the peasants by the state were used by the ruling elites to develop the urban areas for themselves and to spend in conspicuous consumption. As Victor Owusu said in 1961, when "half-starved people are being daily admonished to tighten their belts, members of the Ghanaian aristocracy and their hangers-on who tell them to do this are fast developing pot bellies and paunches and their wives and sweet-hearts double their chins in direct proportion to the rate at which people tighten their belts" (LeVine, 1975, 1).

Africa's ruling elites secure their wealth by misusing their political authority, the color of their office, and manipulating the labyrinth of state controls and regulations. Consider this typical case in Ghana. Ghanaians returning from overseas owe hefty duties on personal vehicles brought into the country. Many who cannot pay the duties have their cars seized. In 1996 thousands of such cars were confiscated by the Commissioner of Customs, Excise and Preventive Services (CEPS). But, as *The Ghanaian Chronicle* (22-24 July 1996) reported:

> Beneficiaries of the CEPS largesse are mainly people who do not need the bonanza—Ministers, Parliamentarians, Castle Security personnel and NDC supporters and their friends. Ministers who obtained such confiscated cars at ridiculously low prices include Dr. Ayirebi-Acquah, Deputy Minister of Defence, and Mr. Victor Selormey, Deputy Minister of Finance, who has been silent since he was exposed as an accessory to fraudulent acquisitions.
>
> In May 1996, The *Chronicle* fingered Selormey for acquiring a luxurious Mercedes Benz 280 S at 2 million *cedis* from CEPS which had confiscated it for a tax default of 17 million *cedis*. The barracuda, estimated at 50 million *cedis,* later found its way to the car market going for 35 million *cedis*. (1)

In one fraudulent transaction, the deputy minister reaped a 32 million *cedi* (or $28,000) profit, more than four times his yearly salary of less than $6,000. Quite apart from the illegality of the transaction, the implications for development were awesome. The minister got rich not by producing anything, he merely used his position in government to secure a vehicle cheaply and resell it to make a profit—a practice known in Ghana as *kalabule.* Such an activity did not result in one extra tuber of yam being added to the country's gross national product.

There is nothing unethical about wanting to be rich. Only the process of *how* one becomes rich is important. In fact, a crude and unscientific way of distinguishing between "rich" and "poor" countries is by examining how the rich got their wealth. Whereas the richest persons in the advanced countries earn their wealth in the private sector, in Africa the richest persons are heads of state and ministers who earn their wealth in the state sector. The government does not produce real wealth; it only distributes wealth.

After only a few years or even months in office, top African politicians and ministers amass personal fortunes several hundred times their salaries. Many politicians extort illegal commissions on government contracts. Senior civil servants divert funds and materials to their own personal use. Public property is misused, official cars used for private pleasure, and public office is used for personal aggrandizement. The susceptibility of the elites to venality percolates to the subelites. Clerks who deal with innumerable small formalities expect gratuities before they carry out their service to the public. Otherwise they attend to the matter with deliberate lethargy or invent an excuse for shelving it forever. Even the police are notorious for imposing on-the-spot fines for fictitious traffic violations, fines that end up in their pockets. It is probably more accurate to describe them as disciplined extortionists than law enforcers.

Collection of taxes, excise, and custom duties offers ample opportunities for ignoble personal enrichment. A company that owes a substantial amount in back taxes can get off the hook by paying about one-tenth of that to the "right" civil servant, who will ensure that the tax assessment records mysteriously disappear. Similarly, private citizens can escape the payment of income taxes or excise duties with the payment of an appropriate bribe.

Venality and peculation have become so pervasive in Africa as to be legal iniquities. All too often, politicians and their intellectual cohorts find themselves co-opted by an administrative system in which probity is a constant casualty. Under such circumstances, the government or the state ceases to perform its functions for the people.

Education

Although acculturation during the colonial era was a Westernization process, its purpose was to gain respect from the colonialists and fend off denigration. Ritualists' ability to westernize themselves was limited by their income. After independence, Westernization and education assumed a new purpose. Ashamed of the high rate of illiteracy, which had become an international symbol of low status, or perhaps convinced that economic development would be expedited with a literate population, or merely succumbing to mass pressure, the new leaders and the elites embarked on massive programs of rapid educational expansion. In 1960 universal primary education was introduced in Ghana. By 1964, 1.4 million students, or 18 percent of the population, were in school compared with 6 or 7 percent in 1960. By the end of Nkrumah's regime in 1966, enrollment in primary schools had increased by 200 percent over the level in 1957; that of middle school had increased by 140 percent; secondary schools increased their enrollment by 480 percent (Lofchie, 1971, 82).

The educational curricula, however, followed the colonial pattern. The thought of restructuring them toward instruction in farming or vocational skills was anathema to the new leaders; "only the best in Britain—the Oxbridge model—was good enough for Africa; no longer should one be fobbed off with colleges giving inferior qualifications with the argument that these were more suited to Africa's needs" (Lloyd, 1964, 23).

Universities were built to adopt the characteristic features of the Oxford-Cambridge model; indeed, in many parts of Africa, universities built after independence were exact replicas of Oxford or Cambridge. Besides this, the universities also became proud symbols of nationhood, political independence, and emancipation from colonial subjugation. To fulfil these symbolic functions, university campuses were ornamented with resplendent architecture and well-manicured gardens. The head of state often was the university chancellor.

A university degree quickly became a status symbol, and even attending a university became prestigious. Even more prestigious were the academic gowns, which distinguished the "future leaders" of the country from the "backward masses." Out came these gowns at the slightest opportunity, even during student demonstrations against government policies or apartheid policies of South Africa.

Undue emphasis was placed on titles and degrees, especially those acquired abroad. The longer the string of degrees, the better. The Nigerians took this to the extreme, purchasing even traditional titles. For example, Chief Moshood Abiola had 98 titles. Military rulers conferred upon themselves titles upon titles, from general to field marshal. Flight-Lieutenant Rawlings of Ghana was not content with one Ph.D., so he acquired a second. This preoccupation with degrees and titles, like the belief that imported items were "better," exposed African elites to ridicule and fraud.

Furthermore, the obsession with degrees and titles gave a clear message to the masses that, without those degrees, they had little social status and nothing to contribute to economic development. Education, therefore, came to be perceived by the masses as the gateway to prestige, affluence, and white-collar jobs. So intense was the pursuit of academic papers that one Ghanaian took his own life after failing his General Certificate of

Education Ordinary Level (the equivalent of a U.S. high school diploma) twice. Another who lost his "Standard 7" school certificate took the exam over again instead of writing for a replacement copy.

Consequently, Ghanaian governments have been under massive pressure to expand educational services. In the 1970s there was such a phenomenal expansion in the educational system at all levels that education took the largest chunk—about 23 percent—of Ghana government expenditures (*Economic Survey*, 1972-74, 24).

Generally, an African country that spent such a large proportion of its budget on education might be expected to reap substantial returns. Unfortunately, this has not been the case in Ghana and many African countries, for three reasons. First, the wrong type of education was pursued: the literary type. The educational system was geared to produce more graduates in the arts (law, history, sociology, political science, among others) than in the sciences and the vocations. For example, in the 1973-74 academic year, enrollment in the various levels of Ghana's educational system totaled 1,599,789, of which 1,014,964 were in primary, 440,065 in middle, 72,036 in secondary, 12,800 in technical, 14,299 in teacher training institutions, and 5,625 in the universities (Five-year Plan, 1975/76–1979/80; Part 2, 292). From these statistics, it can be seen that of the students in middle schools only 0.029 percent continued with technical education. Certainly lawyers, historians, sociologists, and artists are needed, but too many of them were being produced.

As James Morton (1994) noted in the case of the Darfur society in the Sudan, "Even with regard to education, it is far from self-evident that a lack of formally educated human capital has much to do with Darfur's problems. Sudan still has illiterate millionaires. More important, perhaps, is the fact that as much as two-thirds of the country's educated force has already emigrated. Education in Sudan runs a great risk of merely providing the key to the door marked Exit" (8).

Africa urgently needs vocational education, which teaches students skills or some trade so that they can go out into the real world with practical skills and support themselves—instead of relying on the government that provided their education to also be responsible for their employment, as the literary graduates do. The vocations taught can be many and varied; they may range from carpentry, woodworking, fish smoking, cultivating plantations, and small fishing boat manufacturing to auto mechanics and gari-making (a local dish made out of manioc or cassava). More important, vocational students can be taught in the vernacular. In fact, the early missionaries in Africa learned the local languages in order to teach native carpenters, goldsmiths, and farmers various trades and skills. Unfortunately, the elites do not see things this way. To them, education means the ability to read and write English and the acquisition of a degree.

Second, the general type of education pursued in postcolonial Africa is of the "consumption variety." It equipped students with foreign tastes and knowledge about foreign phenomena. It teaches African students how to consume foreign goods without teaching them how to *produce* these items. In economic jargon, education is a consumption as opposed to an investment good.

Third, the ritualists perceived education as an end, not as a means to an end. The academic degree is the passport to a prestigious government post. Once a person acquires that degree, affluence, prestige, and power are expected to flow automatically. What is important is the degree; how it is obtained or what courses are taken is irrelevant. Education is not perceived as a means by which the student would acquire knowledge, venture out into the world by himself, and use or apply his knowledge to solve problems or be successful on his own. Upon graduation, he entered government service. Such a graduate is said to be functionally illiterate. He cannot apply his "book knowledge" to everyday practical problems.

Functional Illiteracy

Of all the obstacles that thwart Africa's development efforts, "functional illiteracy" is perhaps the most daunting. The functionally illiterate is "educated," possessing a degree, diploma, or some military title, but does not understand its import or the meaning of things. He is imbued with symbolism and characterized by rote behavior. He mimics his teacher and regurgitates what was taught in class because he is incapable of independent thought or rational reasoning and lacks initiative. If the teacher had a blue refrigerator, he would also buy one of the same color.

In the classroom, the functionally illiterate was taught that LAND + TRACTORS = BOUNTIFUL AGRICULTURAL HARVEST. Upon graduation, he finds that the "food equation" in traditional Africa is: PEASANT FARMER + LAND + SHIFTING CULTIVATION + MANURE + INCENTIVES = LIMITED AGRICULTURAL OUTPUT. Where are the tractors or fertilizer? "Tractors there must be! Even if they must be imported from Jupiter!" Else, there could be no agricultural revolution. Accordingly, tons of sophisticated agricultural machinery were imported into Africa, costing huge amounts of scarce foreign exchange or credit. In the 1970s Tanzania was using combine harvesters to grow wheat. Much of this agricultural machinery operated for a few months, then broke down and was abandoned in the fields.

Fishing is another example. To the functionally illiterate elites, the only way to catch fish is by a trawler, and the catch is preserved through refrigeration. Never mind that Africa's native fishermen have been fishing in dug-out canoes and preserving fish by smoking and salting it—techniques which require no foreign exchange expenditure. But to the elites, the traditional methods are not good enough. Only cold storage would do. And what happened when the cold stores broke down and there was no foreign exchange to import ammonia freon 22 (used as refrigerant for cold storage facilities)? The *Daily Graphic* supplied the answer: "The result is that the cold stores of the State Fishing Corporation which have been incapacitated by lack of refrigerant cannot take in any more of the bountiful catch being made by local fisherman. Fishing vessels of the corporation which would also be on the seas at this time of the year (bumper season) to haul in fish cannot move for the same reason" (*Daily Graphic*, 10 August 1981, 1).

Consequently, when the fishing season rolled around, Ghana could not increase its fish catch and distribution. Said the *Daily Graphic* in another editorial:

> Since time immemorial, July/August have always been bumper peaks for herring, and one would expect that our policy makers should make the surplus catch not only for a dry day but for distribution to other parts of the country since the whole country has been in a terribly lean period the past one year. The authorities are aware of fish that are fast rotting along the country's coasts. It started in the Western and Central Regions and we should have planned for and expected it along the eastern coast too.
>
> We are reliably informed that the State Fishing Corporation (SFC) is unable to store the abundant fish for technical reasons. The SFC could redeploy its workers to smoke, by traditional methods, all the fish brought ashore. (*Daily Graphic*, 4 August 1981, 2)

Health care is yet another example. "About 70 percent of the Ghanaian population relies on the traditional healers for treatment of their ills. Only 30 percent benefit from modern medical service provided in the hospitals. Professor C. O. Easmon, who gave these figures, predicted that for the foreseeable future, the bulk of the population would still be dependent on traditional healers" (*Ghanaian Times,* 20 July 1981, 1). "About 1,628 patients have been cured of various diseases at the Kwame Nkrumah Memorial Herbal Clinic at Takoradi since its inception 7 years ago. The ailments include hypertension, stroke, hernia, tuberculosis, lits, male impotency and barrenness in women. Dr. Joseph Nyamikeh, who is in charge of the clinic, said it was now generally accepted that herbal treatment was the answer to some diseases which medical science had been unable to cure" (*Daily Graphic,* 13 October 1982, 5).

Yet for years, traditional medicine was never taught in Ghana's medical schools. Nor did the government of Ghana assist or recognize traditional healers. The elites, afflicted with the religion of development, frowned on the traditional. Kwame Nyanteh, a Somanya-based industrialist, described Ghana's educational system as "bogus." "He pointed out that over the last two and half decades, the country's educational policies and performance had been one of confusion and purposelessness, adding that 'the time has come for a re-appraisal'. Mr. Kwame Nyanteh said the present educational system was completely out of tune and was even responsible for the creation of social problems. He therefore called on the government to bring the system in line with the developmental needs of the country." (*Ghanaian Times,* 20 July 1981, 1).

Similarly across Africa, the educational system produces graduates who spend more time arguing over the causes of Africa's problems than about how to fix them. The enormous expenditures on education hardly made any difference in increasing agricultural production or solving Africa's problems. Pini Jason, a Nigerian journalist, described a typical "elite": "There is a Nigerian called Alhaji Maitama Sule. He is from Kano state. Among other important government posts he has held, he was also once Nigeria's permanent representative in the United Nation. Outside government posts, which could come his way without any effort, he is hardly remembered for any other personal achievement, except that at public fora, he speaks about little things with such profundity and says little about profound things" (*New African,* April 1994, 8).

Nigeria, by its sheer size, has more graduates than any other African country. Bragged Chieke Evans Ihejirika of Temple University in Philadelphia: "One thing nobody can say that Nigeria lacks is a class of some of the best scholars the world has ever known" (*African News Weekly,* 3 March 1995, 17). And how have they tackled their country's problems with all that intellectual prowess?

In April 1994 Nigerian intellectuals held a conference to honor Dr. Nnamdi Azikiwe at Lincoln University in Pennsylvania. After presentations by featured speakers such as Professor Ali Mazrui, Chinua Achebe, Edward Blyden III, and Martin Kilson, the floor was opened up for general discussion on the future of "Zikist World View." According to *African News Weekly*, 27 May 1994:

> As usual, many people started talking about the problems of Nigeria. Then a man who claimed to be a medical doctor took the podium and stunned the audience with what he learnt from his recent trip to Nigeria after a 20-year absence. He said that Nigeria's problems are polygamy (allowing men to marry more than one wife) and the fact that women are denied their rights. Many people, who before then had been talking about the annulment of the 1993 presidential election and Nigeria's lack of democratic rule, stared in amazement, wondering how polygamy could be Nigeria's biggest problem at the moment. Of course, others quickly jumped on the man [verbally] shouting him down. (2)

In May 1994 Nigerian intellectuals held another conference at Howard University Inn, Washington. The purpose was to "form a national union to purge Nigeria of and save it from military tyranny." How did the conference go? According to *U.S.-Nigerian Voice*, June 1994:

> It was almost foiled by six big fools, who acted like thugs. They wanted to deny free speech to those they despised. They asked asinine questions but would not even wait for an answer. When they waited for an answer, it had better be the answer they are looking for, or, they would go rabid again. They wanted to supplant the *raison d'être* of the conference with their own selfish, political agenda. They shouted like maniacs what everybody in the room already knew: that [military dictator] Abacha was a brutish opportunist; that our leaders are corrupt; that Chief Abiola, who won the [1993] presidential election was robbed; that our folks back home were suffering, and so on. (8)

The next conference held by Nigerian intellectuals at the same Howard University on 10 December 1994 resulted in an exchange of fisticuffs. The occasion was an International Roundtable Conference to introduce Nigeria's National Democratic Coalition (NADECO), which was in the forefront of the struggle against the military dictatorship of

General Sani Abacha. After presentation by the panelists, the floor was open for questions. A Washington D.C. delegate asked a question about the leadership of the organization and was immediately shouted down by the delegation from California. Heated words were exchanged and soon blows were flying all over the place. The British wife of the late Tai Solarin, an invited guest, was thoroughly embarrassed.

A Nigerian journalist in Oakland, California, Bayo Awokoya, wrote a scathing indictment entitled, "Nigerians: The Unintelligent Intellectuals." He wrote:

> Nigerian intellectuals lack the critical thinking ability to incorporate their book knowledge to real life, such as in the case of Nigeria's political, economic and social woes. One of the major problems confronting many Nigerian intellectuals today lies with our inability to translate knowledge into problem-solving. One would expect that during our years in college, we would have learned the meaning and application of the following words: leadership, organization, coordination, implementation and opportunity. For example, let us examine opportunity. Our inability to recognize an opportunity demonstrates the ineffectiveness of our intellectual capability and ranks next in order to our social problems. While we are preoccupied by the frustration and hopeless circumstances that we find ourselves in, we have overlooked the opportunity to unite and combine our "intellectual," political and financial resources to change the present political model in Nigeria. (*African News Weekly*, 26 August–1 September 1996, 23).

To be fair, not all Nigerian intellectuals lack the ability to seize opportunity. One Nigerian intellectual, Dr. Chukwuemeka Ezeife, the former governor of Anambra State, saw an "opportunity" and rose to the occasion, calling on "all Nigerians to stand in their yard every 6:00 A.M. and 6:00 P.M. and shout, 'Go Abacha [military] government, go!' three times for 12 continuous days. Should this approach fail to dislodge Abacha from power, Dr. Ezeife called on all Nigerian women to organize their 'very traditional march' [marching stark naked] to the government house. He observed that no human being has survived this" (*African News Weekly*, 10 November 1994, 23).

His "doctorate" should be repossessed. If Nigerian intellectuals claim they have "some of the best scholars" in the world and proclaim their country to be "the giant of Africa," then they ought to provide Africa with better intellectual leadership than this.

CHAPTER 5

The Vampire African State

How safe is the state of Ghana in the hands of Rawlings and
his gangsters at this critical moment when they are seeking
the mandate of the people to continue their corruption,
misrule, contempt for public opinion, and disregard to
public property. Indeed, the record books are overflowing
with evidence of Rawlings' wanton misuse of state property
and abuse of power.
—Editorial, *Free Press* (4-10 October 1996, 6).

The [Nigerian] military has perfected the use of intimidation
and disinformation to keep a passive population calm. In the
process, a timid population became quiet and in some cases
conspiratorial and accommodating of dictators for too long.
The result is what you see today: a bunch of idiots terrorizing
the nation, intimidating opponents and harassing dissidents.
It is the equivalent of gangs taking over a whole town.
Imagine John Gotti or Al Capone as President of the United
States. Well, welcome to the reign of thieves and vagabonds,
welcome to our Nigeria today, a gangster's paradise.
—Ikenna Anokwute in *African News Weekly*
(16-22 September 1996, 6).

Those who came toting guns and brandishing cutlasses
[machetes] and shouting, "The 31st December Revolution
in Ghana is the culmination of the struggle of our people
against injustice, indignity and exploitation," are themselves
today meting out the worst injustice and indignities to us,
and sucking the blood of the nation to the last drop.
—Kwame Ashaai in *Free Press*
(30 October–5 November 1996, 5).

On the African contemporary scene, two striking phenomena are inescapable. The first is the towering importance and intrusion of politics into all spheres of human activity to the extent that politics and economics are inseparable. Of particular significance is the fusion of the political and economic systems. Those who wield political power are invariably the same people who make decisions regarding the allocation of resources: which factories or development projects are built, where they are located, who gets employed in those factories. Therefore, the success or failure of a business venture very much depends on one's political connections or "whom you know in power."

The second is the peculiarity of the institution of government. "Government," as it is known in the West, does not exist in much of Africa. Leaving aside the democratic requirement that a government must be by the people and for the people, one expects at a minimum a "government" to be responsive to the needs of the people. Or at least, to perform some services for its people. But even this most basic require-ment for "government" is lacking in Africa. "Government" as an entity is totally divorced from the people, perceived by those running it as a vehicle not to serve but to fleece the people.

Dishonesty, thievery, and peculation pervade the public sector. Public servants embezzle state funds; high-ranking ministers are on the take. The chief bandit is the head of state himself. President Mobutu Sese Seko of Zaire was not satisfied with his personal fortune of $10 billion; he stole an entire gold-mining region, Kilo-moto, which covers 32,000 square miles and reportedly has reserves of 100 tons of gold (*The Washington Times,* 3 January 1997, A14).[1] Ghana's Interior Minister, Colonel (retired) Emmanuel Osei-Owusu, "has been unable to account for 33 million *cedis* ($27,000) in excess income," according to a 1996 Report by the Commission on Human Rights and Administrative Justice. Another minister (of Trade and Industry), Ibrahim Adam, gave

---

1. The true extent of Mobutu's wealth is unknown. Estimates range from $4 billion to $15 billion. "The low figure was offered in the late 1970s by Mr. Mobutu's former minister Nguza Karl I Bond. The higher figure comes from exiled Zairean opposition figures based in Switzerland, who say Mr. Mobutu keeps part of his wealth in France and Belgium" (The Washington Times, 4 January 1997, A8).

undeserved waivers of customs duties and other taxes to fishing companies. "This has occasioned the loss of billions of *cedis* to the state" (*African
News Weekly,* 28 October–3 November 1996, 26). Kwame Ashaai, a
newspaper columnist in Ghana, complained bitterly: "Almost all P/NDC
top people are alleged to have put up mansions, each costing hundreds
of millions of cedis. And almost all of them, it is alleged, do their serious
shopping in North America and Europe. Public properties or assets—
vehicles, buildings, businesses, machinery—even ships—are sold out to
party members, friends, and relatives for peanuts. More than 400 billion
cedis (about $230 million) have been dumped in a bank in Angola. The
P/NDC government is conveniently keeping quiet over it" (*Free Press,*
30 October–5 November 1996, 7).

    Even diplomats cannot resist the occasional plunge into frenzied
banditry. In 1993 a Nigerian envoy to the United Nations was suddenly
recalled by his government. A snap audit revealed unbridled embezzlement of large sums of money at the diplomatic mission. In 1994 the
Ugandan ambassador to Nigeria, James Juko, vanished with $3.5 million
intended for the renovation of his embassy premises. Then on 10
October 1994, the Rwandan foreign minister, Jean-Marie Ndagijimana,
disappeared with about $187,000 he was carrying in a suitcase to fund
his country's United Nations mission in New York. Claude Dusaidi, the
director-general of Rwanda's Foreign Ministry, complained that, as a
result of the theft, the U.N. mission was left with "zero" cash, unable to
pay its bills and with no means to pay salaries or hire a lawyer (*The
Washington Post,* 19 October 1994, A37). Earlier in July 1994, Rwanda's
ambassador to the United States absconded with about $2 million.

    It is disheartening and shameful when Africa's own ambassadors,
who incessantly appeal to the international community for humanitarian
aid, themselves exercise no scruples whatsoever in grabbing what they
can from the little aid meant for poor, starving peasants. One would have
thought that of all people, Rwanda's ambassadors—the very people who
appealed for humanitarian aid—would comport themselves in a way that
would encourage others to help their country.

    But in Africa, government officials do not serve the people. The
African state has been reduced to a mafia-like bazaar, where anyone with
an official designation can pillage at will. In effect, it is a "state" that has
been hijacked by gangsters, crooks, and scoundrels. They have seized and
monopolized both political and economic power to advance their own
selfish and criminal interests, not to develop their economies. Their
overarching obsession is to amass personal wealth, gaudily displayed in

flashy automobiles, fabulous mansions and a bevy of fawning women. Helping the poor, promoting economic growth or improving the standard of living of their people is anathema to the ruling elites. "Food for the people!" "People's power!" "Houses for the masses!" are simply empty slogans that are designed to fool the people and the international community.

In Sierra Leone, "Although houses in the Kissy Low Cost Housing Estate were meant for low income earners, many of their occupants do not fall within that category" (*West Africa*, 7-13 June 1993, 952). In 1991, the government of Zimbabwe passed the Land Acquisition Act, the object of which was to achieve a more equitable distribution of land, since the white minority held over 70 percent of Zimbabwe's arable land. At independence, the government of Robert Mugabe had made such a promise to the landless peasantry. Accordingly in 1994, 20 farms were secured from white farmers for distribution to the peasants, but they were immediately grabbed by high-ranking government officials: "The local press revealed that the Secretary to the President and Cabinet, Dr. Charles Utete, the Deputy Secretary for Commerce and Industry, James Chininga and Harare's first black mayor, Dr. Tizirai Gwata, are among those involved. Moreover, money provided by the British government to facilitate the resettlement of landless peasants has been used to purchase land for wealthy individuals" (*New African*, September 1994, 32).

Similarly, in Sierra Leone, the former Inspector-General of Police, James Bambay Kamara, was said to own 37 pieces of land, with the most expensive valued at Le 7.5 million. His salary, according to the ministry of finance, was Le 182,250 a year. Kamara told the Beccles-Davies Commission that he had three bank accounts—two in Freetown and one with Barclays Bank in London (*New African*, September 1992, 17).

A more dramatic disclosure at the Beccles-Davies Commission, however, concerned the former Minister of Transport and Communications, Michael Abdulai:

> It transpired that he was being paid $100,000 a year by the German-based Hamburg Port Consulting (HPC) for having made sure that the company got the 5-year contract to run the Sierra Leone Ports Authority in Freetown in 1987. What this meant was that this money was added to the annual bill HPC presented to the government. The German general manager of HPC, Captain Helmut Friedrich, told the Commission that Abdulai received 10 percent of the total value of all overseas contracts. The Commission produced a letter from a bank in Geneva (Switzerland)

acknowledging receipt of $50,000 deposited by Abdulai to open an account. (*New African,* September 1992, 17)

In case after case, African government officials get rich by misusing their positions. Faithful only to their foreign bank accounts, these official buccaneers have no sense of morality, justice, or even patriotism. They would kill, maim, and even destroy their own countries to acquire and protect their booty because, as functional illiterates, they are incapable of using the skills and knowledge they acquired from education to get rich on their own, in the private sector. Needless to say, they are "derided by some African experts as 'the extractors,' people who squandered wealth without building for the future" (*The Wall Street Journal,* 10 December 1996, A1).

The inviolate ethic of the vampire elites is self-aggrandizement and self-perpetuation in power. To achieve those objectives, they subvert every key institution of government: the civil service, judiciary, military, media, and banking. As a result, these institutions become paralyzed. Laxity, ineptitude, indiscipline, and lack of professionalism thus flourish in the public sector. Of course, Africa has a police force and judiciary system to catch and prosecute the thieves. But the police are themselves highway robbers, under orders to protect the looters, and many of the judges are themselves crooks. As a result, there are no checks against brigandage. The worst is the military—the most trenchantly perverted institution in Africa. In any normal, civilized society, the function of the military is to defend the territorial integrity of the nation and the people against external aggression. In Africa, the military is instead locked in combat with the very people it is supposed to defend. Ibrahim Ibn Ibrahim, a Sierra Leonian journalist, was furious: "Apart from the corruption, the army under Captain Valentine Strasser's government has become totally incompetent, and is conducting a war against the people. The countryside is nothing but destruction upon destruction. Whole towns and villages have been destroyed" (*Akasanoma,* 31 July–6 August 1995, 38).

The September 1996 issues of Nigeria's news magazines, *Tell* and *This Week,* screamed about "How [Military] Administrators Plundered the States." Ike Nwosu, the ex-administrator of Abia State, "spent some 16.875 million *naira* ($214,000) on himself between March 1995 and March 1996" (*African News Weekly,* 28 October–3 November 1996, 17). A retired army officer, Major Kojo Boakye Djan, even admitted that: "In more than one sense, armies in Africa are a major cause for worry. Literally, in every African country, defense establishment takes the largest

share of national resource allocation" (*Akasanoma,* 31 July–6 August
1995, 45). Even the soldiers of traditional (precolonial) Africa were far
better, according to Major Boakye Djan: "In their alleged rudimentary
forms, precolonial African armies are now acknowledged to have been
functionally relevant, both in concept and organization, to the need of
the communities that created and sustained them."

Wole Soyinka (1996) handed the postcolonial soldiers a blistering
rebuke: "The military dictatorships of the African continent, parasitic,
unproductive, totally devoid of social commitment or vision, are an
expression of this exclusionist mentality of a handful; so are those
immediately postcolonial monopolies that parade themselves as single-
party states. To exclude the sentient plurality of any society from the right
of decision in the structuring of their own lives is an attempt to anesthetize,
turn comatose, indeed idiotize society, which of course is a supreme irony,
since the proven idiots of our postcolonial experience have been, indeed
still are, largely to be found among the military dictators." (139).

Prince Oduro of Ghana was equally scathing:

> A critical look at contemporary African military would bring one's eye closer
> to tears and one's mind nearer to insanity. The caliber of people found in
> the military is an obloquy to the belated institution. Today, soldiers of most
> African countries are known as brutes, bullies and buffoons. Soldiers are
> always supposed to be in the barracks, either training or doing something
> profitable. But in Africa, the case is totally different and appalling. Come to
> Accra and you will see soldiers moving about, wielding guns, pistols,
> harassing citizens and causing needless trouble. Go to Lome and you will
> see them. Go to Burkina Faso. To Lagos. To Kinshasa. O! what a
> degradation of the military! Ghana has seen varied types of uncouth and
> undisciplined soldiers. (*Free Press,* 4-10 August 1995, 4).

A simple rule of thumb on African development has emerged: The
index of economic well-being of an African country is inversely related to
the length of time the military has held political power. The longer it stays
in power, the greater the economic devastation. Said *African News Weekly*
in its 1 September 1995 editorial: "No military coup in Africa has produced
a vibrant economy to replace the bankrupt one it set out to redeem. In
almost every case, the army boys have imbibed the ways of the corrupt
politicians they pushed out of office and even taken their crookedness to
a higher level" (7). The following African countries are in the worst shape

economically and socially: Angola, Benin, Burkina Faso, Ethiopia, Ghana, Guinea, Guinea-Bissau, Liberia, Nigeria, Somalia, Togoland, Uganda, and Zaire. Most of them have been ruined by "military coconutheads," as West Africans aptly describe them; West Africa has the largest collection of them. Said W. D. Ansong of Abetifi-Kwahu of Ghana:

> Poverty is rife in Africa because African military despots have raped our economies. Soldiers have no knowledge about the art of government. Soldiers who have ruled countries in Africa have not been able to bring about any meaningful development.
>
> Soldiers only enrich themselves when they seize power. It is now the onerous duty of African civilians to organize themselves and force all soldiers ruling in Africa to hand over power to competent civilians. If they refuse, we must organize boycotts and civil disobedience to free ourselves. We have had enough military rule. (*Free Press*, 30 August–5 September 1996, 2)

Fed up with their antics, *West Africa* magazine, in its 20-26 June 1994 issue, offered them this advice: "Military people belong in the barracks not in the corridors of political power. Since independence, Nigeria has had an obscenely high number of military governments; they cited corruption and waste if taking over from a civilian government and something else if overthrowing another military junta. Needless to say, the Nigerian populace is fed up. The armed forces cannot claim not to realize this. If a soldier should become bored, he can always go and play ping pong; it is good for keeping fit" (1078).

Time and again in Africa's postcolonial history, all sorts of characters wielding bazookas and AK-47s have seized power or embarked on a crusade to clean up government or bring real freedom to their people. And time and again, these so-called saviors and liberators have turned out to be perfidious scoundrels and bandits, robbing innocent peasants and unleashing mayhem on the people. Remember the warlords of Somalia and Liberia, Mohamed Farah Aidid and Charles Taylor, who set out to liberate their respective countries of tyranny? How genuine was their cause?

Research shows that the late Aidid might have had a more personal ulterior motive for waging a civil war to oust the former and late dictator, Siad Barre, whom Aidid once served. Barre's regime developed a cozy relationship with the Italian Socialist Party, whose leader, Bettino Craxi, became the Italian prime minister in September 1985. The relationship was nurtured by the Italy-Somali Chamber of Commerce, which brokered many of the Italian-sponsored construction projects in Somalia in the 1980s According to Wolfgang Achtner, an Italian journalist, kickbacks became a routine part of doing business through the Chamber. "In a lawsuit filed against Craxi and Pillitteri in the spring of 1989, General Mohamed Farah Aidid, a former aide to Siad Barre, alleged that the Socialists had promised him and another Somali official a '50-50 split' of the 10 percent commission on all deals settled through the Chamber. The two Somali claimed they were owed billions of *lira*" (*The Washington Post*, 24 January 1993, C3).

Miffed, Aidid set out to get even. It soon became apparent that the liberation of Somalia and the restoration of true freedom was the least among his priorities. After Barre was ousted in January 1991, Aidid turned his attention to relief aid, extorting payments for taxes and protection from food relief agencies. In 1995, the World Food Program pulled its staff out of bandit-ridden Mogadishu. The aid agencies that were helping feed starving Somalis became the target of warlords and roving bandits, intent on wringing more money out of them. The United Nations exited also in 1995, ceasing its United Nations Mission in Somalia (UNISOM) operations and pulling its peacekeepers out in disgust.

When relief aid as a source of revenue evaporated, Aidid turned his attention to the lucrative banana export trade to Europe. A "banana war" erupted between Aidid and another Somali warlord, Ali Hassan Osman, known as Atto. Merca, the scene of the fierce fighting in 1996, is a small and ancient port about 52 miles south of Mogadishu. The port was renovated by two foreign firms, an Italian company by name of Somali Fruit and an American company called Sombana. "The two companies pay Aidid 20 cents for every carton they export. That comes roughly to about $800,000 a month during the peak season from April to August. Additional levies bring in an additional $200,000 to Aidid's coffers each month. Fighting flared again in March, 1996, when Atto demanded that the warlord either share the revenues from Merca or see that port closed" (*The African Observer*, 9-22 May 1996, 12).[2]

Did Charles Taylor really set out to "liberate" his native country, Liberia, or was he just another political entrepreneur? According to U.S. Deputy Assistant Secretary of State for African Affairs William Twadell, Taylor possibly made $75 million per year since he began the

---

2. In the ensuing battle, Aidid was killed in July 1996.

war in Liberia in 1990 from the sale of Liberian diamonds, gold, iron ore, and timber to European and Asian companies. The "booty" was in addition to Taylor's share of the "$16 million to $20 million" in ship registry revenues which Taylor and the five other members of his Council of State shared among themselves in 1995, said Twaddell (*The African Observer*, 18-31 July 1996, 2).

The goals and modes of operation of the late Mohamed Farah Aidid and Charles Taylor were no different from those of other African despots, such as General Sani Abacha of Nigeria, the late General Mobutu Sese Seko of Zaire, and Daniel arap Moi of Kenya: using the coercive apparatus of the state to extract for themselves the wealth and vitality of their people.

The Origins of the Vampire State

The evolution of the predatory state began innocently after independence; "innocently" because it is doubtful if the nationalist leaders knew what they were creating in the 1960s. These leaders did face enormous social problems and political dilemmas on the eve of independence. They had inherited fragile colonial structures that lacked the institutional basis of legitimate authority. Improvisation was necessary. They all had to consolidate and entrench the political center. But they also lacked experience in government and, therefore, policy mistakes were bound to be made. All this is granted, but that should not excuse their dogged obstinacy, intolerance of criticism, and adamant refusal to change course when things were going glaringly wrong. Hundreds of editors, journalists, writers, and ordinary citizens were jailed or killed for voicing even a whiff of criticism. Many fled into exile.

As was discussed in Chapter 3, there were four prevalent ideologies in postcolonial Africa: African socialism, political pragmatism, military nationalism, and Afro-Marxism. These African ideologies were decidedly nationalistic and sought to assert an independent African posture in the global arena. They were all infused with the ethos of anticolonialism and dependency theories.[3] But they all have a primary concern with overcoming poverty and underdevelopment. Politically, the vindication of

---

3. According to dependency theories, the status of the Third World countries is largely determined by their interrelationships with the rich countries. Dependency theorists sketch a bipolar global world: the center occupied by the rich

state power, with rare exceptions, was a major preoccupation until recently (Chazan et. al., 1992, 161).

Most African political systems have exhibited various shades of the "Big Man" patrimonial rule. Three distinct types of leadership surfaced in the postcolonial era. The first type was the charismatic, associated with such leaders as Nkrumah, Nyerere, Toure, Kaunda, and Mugabe. Their support was based largely on popular appeal of their message and their role in the decolonization struggle. As Chazan et. al. (1992) put it: "Charismatic personalities tended to emerge in situations of political uncertainty and social fluidity. The political style fostered is consequently autocratic: Leaders of this sort chose to dominate rather than compromise, to dictate rather than to reconcile. Charismatic leaders in Africa therefore bore the external trappings of omnipotence. In the case of Nkrumah of Ghana, it was exaggerated to the point of endowing the leader with godlike attributes." (162)

The second type of political leadership was the patriarchal, exemplified in such leaders as Jomo Kenyatta, Leopold Senghor, Felix Houphouet-Boigny, Julius Nyerere, and Kenneth Kaunda. They acted as the "father of the nation," and their style was that of adjudicator, conciliator, instigator and peacemaker. As fatherly figures, they expected to be revered. Although they seldom became embroiled in the conspiracies of daily political maneuvering, they could play one group against another to their advantage and even co-opt opposition members. In the initial stages of their rule, they were trusted and accorded a god-like devotion because it was assumed by the general populace that whatever they did was in their countries' best interest.

The third type, revolutionary or populist prophetic, emerged in the 1980s as near-perfect clones of the earlier-day charismatic leaders: Flight-Lieutenant John Jerry Rawlings of Ghana, Yoweri Museveni of Uganda, and the late Captain Thomas Sankara of Burkina Faso. They were impatient and angry at the appalling social misery, economic mismanagement and flagrant injustices in their countries. Each considered himself "revolutionary," a term which was improperly understood. Thus their style of rule differed remarkably, ranging from the erratic to the

---

countries with the poor countries on the periphery. The poor countries "depend" on powerful and rich countries that dominate the center and write the rules of the game to their advantage.

genuinely populist. In contrast to earlier stodgy nationalist leaders, these "revolutionary leaders" initially related to, and identified with, the concerns of their people. They could roll up their sleeves and pick up a spade to dig a trench. They spoke the language of the common man and were even willing to eat the common man's food. But for the most part, their authority and style of governing were despotic.

Generally, the autocratic and patriarchal types of leadership often resulted in tyrannical rule. As Chazan *et. al.,* (1992) noted, African dictators chose a method of rule that was domineering and, at times, sultanic. The state was their private domain—the people and resources were at their disposal. There was no distinction between private ambitions and public goods. Any opposition to their political stronghold was eliminated; repression and violence replaced entreaties, cajolery, or emotional fervor. These leaders maintained and enjoyed a strongman image—warriorlike, defiant, and ultimately invincible (167).

This type of "warriorlike," sultanic image became noted for its viciousness, impulsiveness, unpredictability, and buffoonery as with Idi Amin, Marcias Nguema, Jerry Rawlings, and Samuel Doe. In fact, most of Africa's cruelest tyrants, such as Mengistu and Samuel Doe, were from the military, having shot their way to power. They were generally illiterate, or possessed little formal education, rose through the ranks in the army and seized political power when the opportunity presented itself. The late Samuel Doe, for example, sought to improve his English by reading the old speeches of President Ronald Reagan.

The dictatorial mode of operation in postcolonial Africa was characterized by its coercive, idiosyncratic, and whimsical nature because of chronic feelings of insecurity. Leaders such as Amin and Eyadema were always suspicious and sought to tower above all others. If the army could not be trusted, private mercenaries were hired to protect the leader and partake in the spoils. State coffers were looted, human rights were violated, and fear was instilled to maintain loyalty and domination. But despite outward appearances, the strongman is often weak internally or psychologically. An economic illiterate, he cannot distinguish between a budget deficit and a trade deficit. To cover up his inadequacies, he craves—and demands—veneration, adulation, and obedience. He surrounds himself with followers who constantly reaffirm their faith in his exceptional wisdom and generosity. But he does not and cannot know whom to trust or whether his advisers tell him the truth. As such, he renders himself vulnerable to sycophantic and opportunistic adventurers who sing his praises even when his tail is on fire.

The Drift toward Statism

After independence, the nationalists and the elites all shared two basic common objectives. The first was to seek recognition and respect for the newly fledged African nations and win their deserved seats in the hall of nations. This objective was readily achieved with the acquisition of seats in the United Nations General Assembly, diplomatic recognition, and the procurement of foreign aid. The second was to develop Africa in the light and experience of Africa, not of Europe—an objective that proved far more difficult to achieve. One reason was that the nationalist leaders lacked an operational understanding of how an economy operates. Somehow, they believed an economy is run on emotions. That is, economic growth or investment could be spurred by incessant exhortations, appeals, threats, and orders. Addressing a large crowd at a rally at Cape Coast on 9 November 1996, President Rawlings said that "the opposition politicians were deliberately discouraging foreign investors to come into the country to invest" (*Ghana Drum*, December 1996, 35).

Another reason was that they misconstrued the notion of development, as we saw in the previous chapter. Afflicted with a religion of development, they castigated the traditional and exalted the foreign, and placed undue emphasis on industry to the neglect of agriculture, resulting in the unimaginative imitation of foreign paraphernalia. To compound the problem, they all had an abiding faith in the potency of the state and envisaged a large role for it.

A battery of arguments—ideological, pragmatic, and situational—was adduced to justify state interventionism. Most African nationalists misidentified capitalism with colonialism and opted for socialism. The African state was "to spearhead development" and "to protect the people against foreign exploitation." Tanzania's Julius Nyerere stated as one of his principles of socialism that: "It is the responsibility of the state to intervene actively in the economic life of the nation so as to ensure the well-being of the all citizens" (Fieldhouse, 1986, 174). After 1967, the Tanzanian state became predominant in all spheres. The state took over all commercial banks, insurance companies, grain mills, and the main import-export firms, and acquired a controlling interest in the major multinational corporation subsidiaries and the sisal industry.

In Kenya, Jomo Kenyatta's Kenya African National Union (KANU) adopted socialism as its policy objective (Sessional Paper No. 10—"African Socialism and its Application to Planning in Kenya," Republic of Kenya, 1965). The role of the state was expanded accordingly: "As a proportion of GDP, the state's share increased from 11 to 20 percent from 1960 to 1979, while private consumption decreased from 72 to 65 percent. Between 1964 and 1977 public employment rose from 32 to 42 percent of total wage employment. The state also took controlling position in agriculture. In form, at least, Kenya therefore adopted much the same state-centered approach to development as most other African countries." Kenya established such state monopolies as the Maize and Produce Board, the Kenya Tea Development Authority, the Kenya Meat Commission, and other state bodies with near-monopoly control over the distribution of food crops. Its government also drew up national plans and adopted an import-licensing system, the hallmarks of a state-controlled economy (Fieldhouse, 1986, 165).

In comparing KANU's Sessional Paper No. 10 with Tanzania's Arusha Declaration, Bell (1986) found that "Both documents display a commitment to equality and social justice, and to reducing international and internal inequalities" (118). For example, the Kenyan document stressed at the outset that "In African socialism every member of society is important and equal. . . . The State has an obligation to ensure equal opportunities to all its citizens, eliminate exploitation and discrimination, and provide needed social services such as education, medical care and social security" (Republic of Kenya, 1965, 4).

Similarly in Tanzania the Tanzania African National Union Constitution acknowledged as the first socialist principle "that all human beings are equal" and pledged that the government would give "equal opportunity to all men and women," and would eradicate "all types of exploitation" so as to "prevent the accumulation of wealth which is inconsistent with the existence of a classless society" (Republic of Tanzania, 1967, 1).

Although Nigeria is often touted as "capitalistic" and "open," its basic economic strategy and policies were decidedly statist and typical of postcolonial Africa. As Fieldhouse (1986) described: "Lagos, exactly like Accra, aimed to concentrate the largest possible share of the national product in its own hands, to expand the public sector and to develop import-substituting industry by means of tariffs, import licensing and other stimuli. At the same time, agricultural prices were to be kept down by marketing boards to benefit both industry and the urban consumer and to provide government income" (151).

In 1954 the Talakawa Party declared that: "Only a free and independent Nigeria can establish a socialist system of production; and that only such an establishment of socialism can enable our people to plan the use of our material and productive resources in such a way as to guarantee to every Nigerian citizen real security, the right to work and leisure, a rising standard of living, liberty, and equal opportunity for a full and happy life" (Olaniyan 1985, 177).

The state apparatus was also to be used to protect Nigerians from foreign exploitation. The First Development Plan (1962-68) called for economic independence and stated that indigenous businessmen should control an increasing portion of the Nigerian economy. The 1963 Immigration Act and the government's 1964 statement on industrial policy, when taken together, were designed to encourage personnel and local-content indigenization (Biersteker, 1987, 71). Three years later an Expatriate Allocation Board was created in part because of a large influx of Lebanese and Indian merchants engaged in both wholesale and retail sales of textiles goods in the Lagos trading area.

In April 1971 the state acquired 40 percent of the largest commercial banks, and the Nigerian National Oil Company (NNOC) was established with the government keeping a majority participation. Four years later the government acquired 55 percent of the petroleum industry and 40 percent of National Insurance Company of Nigeria (NICON). The following year the acquisition was extended to other insurance companies when the government took 49 percent of their shares.

Nigeria's Second Development Plan (1970-74) was unequivocal, declaring that:

> The interests of foreign private investors in the Nigerian economy cannot be expected to coincide at all times and in every respect with national aspirations. . . . A truly independent nation cannot allow its objectives and priorities to be distorted or frustrated by the manipulation of powerful foreign investors. . . .
>
> It is vital therefore for Government to acquire and control on behalf of the Nigerian society the greater proportion of the productive assets of the country. To this end, the Government will seek to acquire, by law if necessary, equity participation in a number of strategic industries that will be specified from time to time" (The Second National Development Plan, 1970-74: Program of Post-War Reconstruction and Development, 1970, 289).

According to *The Washington Post* (12 September 1995), Zambia under Kaunda fit the classic mold of the command economy: "Through companies it controlled, the state ran virtually everything, from the cultivation of maize to the baking of bread to the mining of copper. Payrolls were heavily padded, with employees receiving housing, cars and free airfare on the national airline. Even food was subsidized." (A12). State interventionism was also the order of the day in Francophone Africa, drawing much impetus from French socialists. According to Patrick Manning (1988), "In Guinea, a state-dominated socialist economy was set up beginning with independence in 1958, in Congo-Brazzaville, a similar decision was taken in 1967, and Benin, a socialist state was proclaimed in 1975. At the same time, the economy of Ivory Coast, which may be labeled one of state capitalism (since it draws private investment funds, but invests them under state control) is in some ways very similar" (129).

Thus, regardless of their professed ideology, the development stance of virtually all the post colonial African governments has been basically statist. The destiny and fate of millions of Africans have been in the hands of a fragile state, whose assumed role was to initiate development, protect the people against foreign exploitation. To assure state participation in and control of the economy, a myriad of state controls were enacted and executed by a small cadre of inexperienced and incompetent bureaucrats. But as it turned out, the development that took place occurred only in the pockets of the vampire elites; the state controls imposed on the economy served only to protect the interests of the gangsters. We now discuss in detail the mode of operation of the African mafia state.

MODE OF OPERATION

The Decision-Making Process

Despite their economic illiteracy, Africa's strongmen insist on taking all important decisions. In most African governments, the decision-making process is "closed" and centralized—it has been so in the Afro-Marxist systems, which touted "consultation with the people," as well as in those countries, such as Kenya and Malawi, that had parliaments. In the highly personalized systems, such as those of Moi in Kenya and Abacha in Nigeria, the head of state makes all final decisions. The late Houphouet-Boigny said it best when he remarked, "There is no number two, three or four In Côte d'Ivoire there is only a number one: that's me and I don't share my decisions" (*West Africa*, 8 August 1988, 1428). In the highest echelons of Zaire's ruling class was an inner core of former President Mobutu's family and close associates. The small clique of political allies included members of the powerful Central Committee of the People's Revolutionary Movement of Zaire (MPR) and advisers to the president, many of whom originated in the president's own Nord Ubangi subregion in northern Equateur (Libby, 1987, 273).

Elsewhere, although the degree of participation in the decision-making process varies, it is generally limited. Decisions are taken by the head of state and a tiny cabal of advisers, cronies, and trusted lieutenants. Advisers may be renowned in their own fields of work and brought in to assist the leader. However, they are frequently dismissed or replaced when the need or the whim arises. The leader often creates a cadre of followers with personal loyalty to himself and to the ideology he espouses. For these "followers," it is not their conviction to his ideology but the expectation of sharing in the spoils of office that keeps them faithful to the chief. "Eyadema's Kabye people, who make up no more than 15 percent of the population, scooped up the best government jobs; the army was nearly two-thirds Kabye as well. But three times as many Togolese belong to the southern Ewe and Mina peoples, who loathe the president" (*The Economist*, 5 September 1992, 47).

The spoils must be jealously protected. Rivals are systematically crushed, imprisoned, or exiled. Meanwhile, most of the population does not benefit from the spoils and is subject to repression. Popular participation, as in village meetings in traditional Africa, is rare. Where parliaments exist, they simply rubber stamp decisions that have already been taken.

In this mode of operation, decision making is politicized: The test of inclusion is fealty to the leader, ethnicity and strength of "conviction" to his precepts. But since these are difficult to assess, the politics of court intrigue flourishes in such settings: Conspiracies, rumors, plots, purges, and reshuffling become the political order of the day.

Insecurity breeds a craving for support and drives all the strongmen to place a premium on trust. Thus, the bulk of strategic positions in the political, bureaucratic, police and military hierarchies are filled with personally loyal individuals: brothers and cousins, friends and classmates, kinsmen and tribesmen. Spoils, used to buy political support, come in basically two forms. First, "Big Men" can provide their followers with access to state resources, handing out "jobs for the boys" in the civil service, government boards and public corporations. But the "boys" become unproductive charges to the state: "In 1984, 20 percent of Ghana's public sector workforce was declared redundant by the Secretary of Finance" (*West Africa*, 27 January 1986, 178).

Strongmen can channel low-interest loans and contracts from public agencies to their friends and allies. According to Kwame Ashaai, a columnist, "In Rawlings' Ghana, procurement or public works contracts are awarded to contractors, not on basis of ability to do the jobs well, and at the lowest costs, but on basis of affiliation and connections with the ruling NDC party or its top brass, or on basis of agreement to pay for the contracts" (*Free Press*, 30 October–5 November 1996, 5).

Soldiers can be bought with pay increases, subsidized housing, commodities, and faster promotions. In 1993 for example, General Ibrahim Babangida gave nearly 3,000 of his most loyal military chiefs new Peugeot sedans, which cost the equivalent of $21,000 each in Lagos, five times the yearly salary of a senior university professor, who earns about $4,000 a year. A nurse or mechanic is lucky to bring home more than $1,000 (*The New York Times*, 2 December 1993, A3). State workers may be provided with subsidized housing, and subsidized transportation or given "essential commodities" (sardines, corned beef, tinned milk) at government-controlled prices. Some patrons may supply their clients with opportunities for illegal gain from public office. Corruption is another such opportunity—accepting or extorting bribes for decisions or actions taken in a public capacity. Others include theft of public property, the illegal appropriation of public revenues (fraud), and nepotism.

Second, "Strongmen reward their clients by granting preferential access to resources which are subject to government regulation, permits. For example, favorable allocation of import or other licenses. All these allocations of non-governmental benefits can become counters in the game of factional manoeuver. Corruption and misuse of public office has reached exceptional levels also in Nigeria" (Sandbrook, 1993, 94). "One of General Abacha's main sources of patronage is the system that enables a lucky few to buy foreign exchange at 22 *naira* to the dollar, while others pay 80" (*The Economist*, 9 November 1996, 46). And "In Rawlings' Ghana, import permits, bank loans, etc. are awarded on orders of ministers, and only to friends, relatives, NDC members, or those who pay huge bribes. Businessmen and women who have NDC connections often enjoy tax exemption, penalty waivers, or get their tax obligations reduced. They may even be left to go free when caught evading taxation, or to have made false declarations regarding tax liabilities" (*Free Press*, 30 October–5 November 1996, 5).

Essentially, the model of governance is based on patronage: the monopolization of political power by one individual or a group and the dispensation of patronage (spoils) to cronies, loyal supporters and tribesmen. All others are excluded—the politics of exclusion, as we saw in chapter 2.

To facilitate the dispensation of patronage and reduce any threat to his power, the strongman usurps control over all key state institutions: the army, police, civil service, state media, parliament, judiciary, central bank, and educational system. Each of these must serve his dictates. To ensure this, he packs these institutions with his own supporters or tribesmen. Those who remain must sing his praises in order to keep their jobs. Professionalism in these institutions is destroyed and replaced with sycophancy.

After securing the support base, the next item of priority is legitimacy. It is important to demonstrate to the rest of the world that his regime is "popular" and supported by a large section of the people, including the educated class. A smattering of fawning lawyers, doctors, engineers, and professors accord the despotic regime a veneer of respectability and legitimacy. This intellectual support may be purchased outright with a Mercedes Benz or a government post. Indeed, many of Africa's intellectuals succumbed to these enticements and eagerly sold off their principles and integrity to serve the dictates of Africa's tyrants.

Foreign recognition and support is a crown jewel and actively sought. This support comes in the form of diplomatic recognition, and military and development assistance or aid. The leader may use weapons supplied under military assistance to suppress the opposition and to strengthen his grip on power. He may use development aid to fund projects for his supporters or his tribal region and thereby buy loyalty or political support. In competing for influence in Africa, especially during the Cold War, external patrons, wittingly or unwittingly, helped prop up African dictators and buttressed their repressive capacity. In the process, foreign governments promoted governmental irresponsibility, oppressiveness and venality in Africa.

Social Control

The interactions between the rulers and the people form the crux of the political process in most societies. Laws and rules must be enforced and complied with. Social control must be exercised to maintain order. To achieve these objectives, African autocrats devised various techniques in view of the immense diversity of ethnicity, religion, language, income, and occupation. The purposes of these techniques have been to consolidate the power of the rulers, to promote their legitimacy, and to execute their vision for the country. One technique involves building coalitions and granting representation or participation to key interest groups whose support is necessary to keep them in power.[4]

In the postcolonial period, African autocrats achieved both objectives by destroying structures or groups that potentially could pose a threat and by creating alternative organizations that effectively limited competition. Traditional institutions were eviscerated, ethnically based organizations were prohibited, and independent economic organizations and trade unions were curbed. Alternative structures and organizations were created in their places; for example, the single party system. Here "popular participation" was allowed but subject to the control of the ruler. Thus, although elections were held, they were of the nonsensical type where the President always won 99.999 percent of the vote.

Another technique entailed deflating demands for full participation in the political process from opposition groups by allowing and even encouraging their participation in innocuous and politically inert organizations and meticulously monitoring their activities. This strategy was first introduced by Houphouet-Boigny, Kenyatta, and Banda, and subsequently adopted by military leaders in Ghana and Nigeria. Thus, each group is accorded some freedom to pursue its own interest but within the parameters laid down by the rulers. Groups accorded such limited autonomy included chiefs, elite professionals and occupational associations, and religious communities.

Still another technique is the age-old carrot and stick—a combination of coercion and enticement. In Côte d'Ivoire, for example, the late President Felix Houphouet-Boigny tried to stamp out growing opposition to his rule among the Betes in the northwest. That October 1970 operation took an estimated 4,000 lives. He then tried to win over the Betes with promises of development; failing that, he denied the area development funding (*The African Observer*, 15-28 November 1994, 15). In Ghana,

> The people of Pramkese in the Kwebibirim District of the Eastern Region have accused the NDC government of bypassing them in the supply of electricity because the NDC lost in the town during the 1992 presidential elections. . . .

---

4. A much more detailed discussion of these techniques can be found in Chazan et. al., 1992, 174.

> Speaking at a meeting, two NDC operatives, Messrs Abrokwa and Yenning, were alleged to have told the people in the presence of the chief that the name of Pramkese was deleted from the towns slated to be supplied with electricity because the youth of the town do not support Rawlings, based on the 1992 election results, which showed the NDC lost in the town. (*Free Press*, 11-17 October 1996, 7)

Also struck off the list for connection to the national electricity grid was the town of Bomaa in the Tano District of the Brong Ahafo Region, which did not vote for Rawlings. Its roads were in such terrible shape that they were impassable for three days after it rained.

The ruling party may co-opt groups by showering rewards on their established leaders. Military regimes in Ghana, Nigeria, and Niger targeted traditional leaders, traders, civil servants, army officers, and sometimes even key foreign entrepreneurs. For example, even though General Babangida of Nigeria had signed a Structural Adjustment Program agreement with the International Monetary Fund in 1986 to rein in extrabudgetary spending and escalating defense expenditures, he showered army officers with gifts of cars worth half a billion *naira*.

The success of this technique, however, depends on the ability of the center to generate the resources required to appease or purchase the support of the major social groups. Such resources may be capriciously seized through exorbitant taxes, steep hikes in excise duties on imports, gasoline, and through various legislative edits and structures, such as price controls, value-added tax (VAT) and marketing boards. Or the strongman may attempt to generate such resources artificially—on paper, by printing money. The net result is declining production, tax evasion, escalating government expenditures, recourse to the central bank for financing, and ultimately, inflation.

Very narrow social support base and weak administrative structures have thwarted efforts to maintain social control. Consequently, African tyrants resort to personal and coercive techniques. The personal mode of control, as employed by Idi Amin, Bokassa, Mobutu, Doe, Rawlings, and Sani Abacha, has been particularly cruel and brutal. Dissent is not tolerated and all forms of expression are severely restricted. No critical monitoring of government policy is permitted. Stringent controls are placed on political activities, on the judiciary, on middle-level interest groups and on the military.

The populist-revolutionary (Afro-Marxist) approach to governance has not fared better than the personal-coercive ones. Although popular participation was touted, the expression of individual choice was not tolerated. The "Big Man" was omniscient. Existing associations were impugned, and new institutions—farmers' cooperatives, collective villages, worker controlled enterprises—were erected. But governments that adopted this technique, such as Angola, Mozambique, and Ethiopia, participated not only in direct military operations but also, increasingly, population relocation, resettlement schemes, and conscription. Only a select few had the ability to influence government power; informal and insurrectionist modes of political activity were more commonplace (Chazan et. al., 1992, 176).

The Support Base

Regardless of the specific strategies used to construct alliances and maintain social control, African leaders must find ways to carry out their decisions, to extract resources, and to maintain their support base. In general, they rely on patron-client and patron-patron relationships. Sycophants and hatchetmen may be employed as clients to execute the dictates of the strongmen. Hatchetmen may be ruthless thugs who may be hired to carry out dastardly deeds; for example, "eliminating" a political rival or dissident. For a more worthy goal, however, a direct appeal to the populace may be made. For example, to garner support for the struggle for independence, the nationalists promised to distribute the benefits of independence—free education, health care, affordable housing, and jobs—to the people. In 1957, Nkrumah, for example, spoke of a "veritable paradise."

Nevertheless, the dispensation of patronage to buy political support has resulted in soaring government expenditures and bloated, inefficient African bureaucracies that waste scarce resources. "This country had 50,000 civil servants who were consuming 51 percent of the nation's wealth," complained Guinea's reformist prime minister, Sidya Toure (*The Washington Times,* 17 October 1996, A19). But trimming these bureaucracies, as demanded by the imperatives of economic reform (or structural adjustment), has been anathema to the ruling elites since it cripples their ability to maintain their political support base. In Ghana, the total number of cabinet and deputy portfolios reached an astonishing 88 in 1995. Similarly, President Robert Mugabe of Zimbabwe increased his cabinet by two to 28, which took the number of officials with ministerial status to 54. This is due to an entrenched system of patronage. By comparison, Zimbabwe has a cabinet larger than those in the United

Kingdom, France, or South Africa but its population is only a fraction of those countries. (South Africa has a 25-member cabinet and 17 deputy portfolios) (*The African Observer*, 23 May–5 June 1996, 23).

Another type of clientelistic exchange is organized on the basis of solidarity ties, such as ethnicity, religion, or racial group. Patrons at the center funnel resources and funds to members of a particular group in exchange for the group's support. Thus, one finds African strongmen surrounding themselves with such kinsmen, who are placed in key positions in ministries and government posts, not on the basis of qualifications or merit but rather on the basis of political loyalty and tribal solidarity. Efficiency suffers and government institutions fail to do what they were supposed to do. According to Kwame Ashaai, a columnist, those Ghanaians who don't fall in any of these categories—relatives, tribesmen, party members, or friends—pay huge bribes to get employed or promoted, or are left to suffer and rot (*Free Press*, 30 October–5 November 1996, 5).

Similarly, in Kenya, President Daniel arap Moi has relied heavily on the Kalenjin, an ensemble of 12 of Kenya's smallest ethnic groups, giving members of the community top posts in the military, the civil service, state banks, and parastatals. For example, the Chairmen of the Kenya Posts and Telecommunications Corporation, the Cooperative Bank, the Post Bank, and the Kenya Creameries Corporation are all Kalenjin, as are the head of the Criminal Investigating Department and the governor of the Central Bank of Kenya (*The African Observer*, 25 April–8 May 1996, 13).

In Côte d'Ivoire President Henri Konan Bedie launched a xenophobic campaign of *"Ivoirite"*—Ivorian-ness—ostensibly to check the influx of foreigners. But opposition leaders said the campaign is a way for the president to promote his Baoule ethnic group and win support of hardliners in his party, which has ruled since independence in 1960. "After 1994, after Ouattara left, all [Muslim] northerners lost important jobs," said sociologist Abdou Toure. "I was fired from UNESCO, Ali Coulibaly was fired as main television broadcaster, General Abdoulaye Coulibaly was fired as air force commander. We were replaced by Baoules," (*The Washington Times*, October 10, 1996, A17).

In Nigeria, this insidious tribalism has retrogressively evolved into what Nigerian columnist Igonikon Jack called a "full-blown tribal-apartheid," in which people of a particular tribal, regional, or religious origin enjoy more privileges than their fellow indigenous compatriots, the Christian Ibos of the Southeast. The Ibos, who lost the Biafran War, are the most disadvantaged and discriminated against. The Northerners, who are of the Hausa-Fulani ethnic group and predominantly Muslim, have ruled Nigeria for 31 out of 35 years of independence and the military, has also been dominated by the Northerners for 25 years.

Nigerian journalist, Pini Jason, concurred: "Since the North controlled political power, it also controlled, decided and manipulated the allocation of posts, resources and values. And with this power it kept the competition for the crumbs alive in the South and the cleavages and political disunity very wide. The fact that the North, like the Tutsis of Burundi, controls the military and uses its military might to monopolize political power, and is not willing to part with the privileges power has brought the North over the years, make many Nigerians fear a possible blood-bath *a la* Burundi" (*New African,* April 1994, 8).

Wole Soyinka (1996) attacked this "infinitesimal but well-positioned minority," exposing the multifarious ruses and tricks they employ to enrich themselves, repress other Nigerians and perpetuate their rule. "In denouncing the activities of this minority, described variously as the Sokoto Caliphate, the Northern Elite, the Kaduna Mafia, the Hausa-Fulani oligarchy, the Sardauna Legacy, the Dan Fodio Jihadists, et cetera, what is largely lost in the passion and outrage is that they do constitute a minority—a dangerous, conspiratorial, and reactionary clique, but a minority just the same. Their tentacles reach deep, however, and their fanaticism is the secular face of religious fundamentalism" (8).

In Ghana, Ewes head most of the financial institutions, major corporations, and institutions, including the Bank of Ghana, the Social Security and National Insurance Trust, the Ghana Reinsurance Organization, the Home Finance Corporation, the Ghana National Petroleum Corporation, the Ghana Ports and Harbors Authority, the Ghana Supply Commission, and the Ghana Water and Sewerage Corporation. "In the military, the General Officer Commanding the Ghana Armed Forces and the Army Commander are all Ewes. In July, over 90 percent of the more than 100 new recruits who joined the Commando Unit of the Forces Reserve Regiment were all Ewes. The C.O. of Unit 64, the FRB, is an Ewe, and the President's Presidential Guard are all Ewes (*The Ghanaian Chronicle,* 7-9 August 1995, 1). Chris Atakpo of Ghana wondered why "almost all the key positions in the airports, harbor, the military, police force and corporations are filled by Ewes, although they make up only 9 percent of the population (*Ghana Drum,* June 1994, 4).

What then is the difference between white colonialism and black neo-colonialism? Nigerian human rights activist Ropo Sekoni saw no difference between the British indirect rule and the postcolonial system in which 35 years later, a small band of black people [Northerners] now takes on the colonial master's position of ruler and chooses to recognize the others as workers only. Domestic colonialism, whether practiced by Black soldiers or civilians from a certain part of the country, is no better than the now-defunct apartheid system in South Africa. "Nigerians must realize that colonialism has nothing to do with the color of the colonizer and the colonized. Any group of people that uses the advantage of power—military or material—to oppress, exploit, and interiorize another group of people can be justifiably described as a colonizing group" (*The Isokan News,* Spring 1995, 19).

A third type of clientelism is of the associational sort. Although leaders at the center denounce the patronage system, as Rawlings did in 1981, they do not dismantle the system. Instead, they expand its scope by creating new organizations, such as defense committees or the December 31 Women's Movement in the case of Ghana, which became vehicles for the disbursement of benefits.

Regardless of their forms, the effects of clientelism are the same. Politics is viewed as essentially extractive. The state sector becomes fused with the political arena and is seen as a source of wealth, and therefore, personal aggrandizement. "This kind of thinking, in many places, encourages a vicious cycle of competition for access to and control over national resources. It also frequently nurtured a zero-sum approach to politics. Winners take all to appease their backers and to make use of their position before other patrons take control and divert resources to their own ends. Patron-client modes of exchange do not draw sharp distinction between the public and private domains" (Chazan, et. al., 1992, 180).

The other major instrument (apart from patronage) for establishing and maintaining the strongman's grip on power is a personally loyal armed force. Because of weak legitimacy and the constriction of the charmed circle with access to the spoils, the strongman must increasingly rely on the threat or use of coercion for his survival. But he cannot trust the military; it could overthrow him. So he creates a Special Battalion and equips it with weapons far superior to the military's. But even then, the loyalty of this Special Battalion is not a certainty. Accordingly, he creates an Elite Presidential Guard, with troops drawn from his own tribe or from a foreign country to ensure reliability. "As in other undemocratic African countries, Abacha's presidential guard is drawn from his own ethnic group in his home town. The guards often get the best equipment and the best training" (*The Washington Post,* 23 July 1994, A16). In this way, the strongman creates a multitude of security organs—not only to watch the populace but also each other.

As they grow increasingly insecure and paranoid, African autocrats spend enormous sums on the military and security forces. Africa spends close to $8 billion a year on the importation of weapons and maintenance of the military. But all these expenditures do not buy them an iota of security or any peace of mind. In fact, the more they spend on security, the more insecure they become. In the end, however, despite the awesome arsenal of weapons they accumulate, they are booted out of power—often by their own security operatives: Moussa Traore of Mali and General Ibrahim Babangida of Nigeria, for example. Comrade Mengistu Haile Mariam once had the largest army in Africa at 300,000 men. He was routed by a ragtag army of rebels and fled to Zimbabwe. How safe was he in Zimbabwe? "Former Ethiopian dictator Mengistu Haile Mariam panicked and ran yelling for help when a would-be assassin fired a single shot at one of his guards last fall, a Zimbabwe court was told. The Eritrean suspect, Solomon Haile Ghebre Michael, 36, pleaded not guilty Monday in the attack on the exiled Colonel Mengistu, given asylum by President Robert Mugabe in 1991 after he fled Ethiopia" (*The Washington Times,* 11 July 1996, A10).

Dealing with the Opposition

Although the ruler himself may not be personally wicked, opposition to his regime builds rather quickly due to the activities and pronouncements of his hirelings. They tend to exude arrogance and flaunt their wealth, which invariably incites the envy and resentment of those excluded from the spoils of power. Dissidents or opponents may plot various ways of overthrowing the regime and replacing the ruling elites.

Autocrats employ a variety of techniques, ranging from the subtle to the ruthless, to deal with the opposition. Co-optation may be tried first. A harsh government critic may be offered a high-level appointment to silence him. Cases abound, as hundreds of intellectuals and opposition leaders have fallen prey to this tactic. In Zimbabwe, Joshua Nkomo, Mugabe's rival, was effectively silenced with the offer of an inconsequential post as deputy leader of their merged parties, the Zimbabwe African National Union and the Patriotic Front (ZANU-PF). Between 1993 and 1996 Kenya's ruling party, KANU, "bought the backing of opposition deputies, 15 of whom have joined the party" (*The African Observer,* 5-18 September 1995, 8).

In Cameroon, the Movement for Democracy and the Republic (MDR) campaigned vigorously in the early 1990s against the dictatorial rule of President Paul Biya. In the 1992 legislative elections, MDR won six seats in the north. Suddenly MDR joined Paul Biya's party in a coalition government and was rewarded with five cabinet posts. Among the new MDR appointees was Dakole Daissala as minister of state in charge of postal services and telecommunications. Dakole Daissala had been released from jail only a year earlier, after seven years in detention during which he was neither formally charged or tried.

The professional elites have been relatively easy to buy off. Their purchase price can be any one of the following: a ministerial post, a diplomatic posting, a directorship of a state corporation, a Mercedes Benz, or a government bungalow. Of all the various groups that aided and abetted the destruction of the continent, Africa's intellectuals stand out as the vilest traitors and accomplices.

Since independence, the majority of the African population—mostly rural communities—has looked to the educated minority for leadership. The educated people who have not disappointed their people are only a select few. The rest continue to take advantage of their trust by overindulging in a get-rich-quick bonanza, rather than trying to contribute to the meaningful socio-economic development of their countries. They have simply become tools of economic paralysis and political doom. To most of them, education means no more than power and wealth at the expense of their poor uneducated compatriots. This has resulted in untold hardship and misery for the innocent African masses who continue to bear the brunt of the social tension and economic mess left behind (M.I.S. Gassama, *West Africa,* 17-21 March 1994, 495).

If the elites cannot be bought, a silent and effective method is to pauperize them. Poverty, hunger, and destitution will force them over to the tyrant's camp. In Ghana, such quislings are derided as the "MMEs" ("man must eat"). In Zimbabwe, Robert Mugabe increasingly resorted to this tactic.

When such subtle tactics fail to work, African dictators resort to terror and intimidation. The secret police or paramilitary organizations are another way to suppress any signs of dissent or revolt and to ruthlessly pursue critics. The latter may be arbitrarily detained or even killed. On 24 December 1995 Nigeria's popular news magazine *Tell* featured a cover story titled "Abacha Is Adamant." "Palpable insult!" Nigeria's security agents— known locally as "kill-and-go" vagabonds— roared and sprang into action. "Security agents raided the homes of the two leading editors of the popular news magazine and confiscated the entire print run of its latest edition before it went to newsstand. *Tell's* editor in chief, Nosa Igiebor, was picked up at his home and taken to State Security Service headquarters. Later in the day, more than a dozen security agents forced open doors at the magazine's offices and searched the premises, according to a statement by *Tell's* managing editor, Onome Osifo-Whiskey, who went into hiding after his home was raided" (*The Washington Post,* 25 December 1995, A26).

A civilian or military agency, or often both, conducts intelligence and surveillance to sniff out conspiracies. Such an agency also may infiltrate opposition organizations to report on their activities, plant malicious disinformation, or even destroy the organization from within. Moles are generously rewarded. In Ghana, Nkrumah created the Young Pioneers to spy on people—a tactic adopted by Hastings Banda in Malawi as well. In Rwanda, *interahamwe* was the secret police that incited Hutus to slaughter Tutsis in 1994. An enormous amount of resources is spent on security forces, eating up a large chunk of the budget. Economists have a concept called "opportunity cost" that is relevant here. An opportunity cost is the cost of a foregone alternative. All those resources spent on security could have gone into development. Therefore, the opportunity cost of military expenditures is the development that African countries have sacrificed. The opportunity cost is even greater in times of national crisis. In 1993, for example, Ghana spent 26,599 million *cedis* on defense while 21,150 million *cedis* was spent on agriculture at a time when the country was importing food to feed its population. In Nigeria, the Petroleum Trust Fund was set up to administer more then 30 billion *naira* ($370 million) realized from the fourfold increase in domestic fuel prices in 1994. The fund was to be used to repair Nigeria's dilapidated public infrastructure. But military ruler General Sani Abacha had other ideas; he wanted to use part of the funds to reward the armed forces and the police: "We are convinced that a demoralized military cannot be motivated to peak performance. Herein lies the importance of the issue of welfare" (*African News Weekly,* 22-28 July 1995, 3).

"Divide and conquer" is an ancient stratagem employed by the colonialists. But in the postcolonial period, African tyrants have employed it with brutal relish to keep the opposition divided and ineffective. Since most African countries are polyethnic—only Somalia is ethnically homogenous—African dictators have played one ethnic group against another to maintain their grip on power: Kikuyu versus Kalenjin in Kenya, Hutus versus Tutsis in Rwanda and Burundi, and

Ewes versus Akans in Ghana. Nigeria's military rulers employ a slightly different tactic: creating new states.

On October 1, 1996 General Sani Abacha created six new states, bringing the total to 36. According to *African News Weekly* (7-13 October 1996), "The states created were chosen from 72 requests made by communities all over the country. Some 183 new local governments were created, bringing that total to 776" (2). Eventually Nigeria may end up with over 250 states—the same number as its ethnic groups.

The tactic may even be employed along occupational (workers versus employers) or professional (students versus lecturers) lines. President Moi not only uses tribalism as an instrument of tyranny but also divides his countrymen using the institutions of the state: the police, the courts, and the powers of arrest and detention. Writes Bill Berkeley (1996), an American journalist, on Kenya: "President Daniel arap Moi, who is 71 years old and widely loathed, presided for years over a predatory single-party regime that was made possible by the patronage of the West. No longer a Cold War asset, and pressured to democratize, Moi has clung to power by playing dirty. Skillfully manipulating the levers of coercion and bribery, he has sabotaged Kenya's monetary system, emasculated the rule of law, and stoked the destructive fires of ethnicity" (33).

In former Zaire, Mobutu's regime deliberately fragmented the army to play one faction off another and thus reduce the threat of a coup. "Zairian President Mobutu Sese Seko, who has been in power for over three decades, has run down the regular army to 20,000 men while forming a succession of strike forces to use against internal threats. He presides over 6 specialized security forces, hand picked for loyalty, including the 10,000 strong Civil Guard" (*The African Observer,* 17-30 October 1996, 31).

ECONOMIC MANAGEMENT: STATE CONTROLS

To perpetrate their nefarious activities of pillage and oppression, Africa's strongmen found a convenient ally in the ideology of socialism. Recall that virtually all the nationalist leaders, for a variety of reasons, saw the state as the primary initiator of development. State intervention in the economy was pursued with a whole battery of controls on prices, exchange rates, interest rates, and other economic variables. These were exactly the controls the strongmen needed to punish their rivals and enrich themselves. Officials administering state controls, however, quickly discovered that the controls could also be used for selfish and sinister purposes and to advance their own selfish economic interest as well as those of their kinsmen and supporters, and to silence their critics and to punish political opponents.

The byzantine maze of state controls and regulations provided the elites with rich opportunities for self-aggrandizement. Revenue collection, passport control, and even government stationery all presented an environment for illicit gain. Civil servants exploited their positions in government and manipulated the state's regulatory powers to supplement their meager salaries. Almost every government regulation and nuance of policy could be "exploited." "Because every permit has its price, Nigerian officials invent endless new rules. A guard outside a ministry demands a special permit for you to enter; a customs inspector invents an environmental regulation to let in your imports; an airline official charges passengers for their boarding cards" (*The Economist*, 21 August 1993, Survey p.5).

Officially, price controls were supposed to make commodities "affordable to the masses." But only the ruling elites and their cronies could purchase commodities at government-controlled prices. They later resold them on the black market to reap a huge profit, a practice known as *kalabule* in Ghana. In Rwanda, the late President Juvenal Habryimana ran lucrative rackets in everything from development aid to marijuana smuggling. "Habryimana and his in-laws operated the country's sole illegal foreign exchange bureau in tandem with the central bank. One dollar was worth 100 Rwandan francs in the bank or 150 on the black market. The president and his brother-in-law took dollars from the central bank and exchanged them in the exchange bureau. Habryimana was also implicated in the poaching of mountain gorillas, selling skulls and feet of baby gorillas" (*The Washington Post*, 18 April 1995, A17).

The richest opportunity, however, was offered by import controls, which were intended to curtail the volume of imports and thereby conserve the scarce foreign exchange needed to import machinery and other equipment essential for development. To import an item, a permit or a license was required from the Ministry of Trade. The licenses quickly became scarce. Ministers and government officials at the trade ministry demanded bribes—10 percent of the value of the import license—before issuing them. The withholding of licenses was used to punish political rivals and businesses associated with the opposition. In the late 1980s, import licenses were denied to *Free Press* and *Ashanti Pioneer* in Ghana and *Footprints* in Liberia for their criticism of government policies. In 1967 Ayeh-Kumi, Nkrumah's Special Consultant on Economic Affairs, gave dramatic testimony before the Ollennu Commission of Enquiry. He stated that it is common practice to gradually stifle the big businessmen and the small Ghanaian businessmen in this country and to replace them with State Corporations. The steps taken against them were various types of taxation and import licensing restrictions; African businessmen were not given licenses and if they persisted they were given licenses that would make them incapable of doing business (Ollennu Report 1967, 10).

This kind of policy was implemented elsewhere as well. In Kenya, for example, the Kikuyus were forced out of manufacturing and other industrial business for their opposition to the Moi regime. Development projects were started in those tribal areas that supported President Moi; opposition areas were neglected. Resources had been extracted from the rural areas through various legislative devices and controls, such as marketing boards, development levies, and taxes. The resources, it was claimed, were to be used for the development of the whole country, and would benefit the farmers too. But it never happened that way.

In Malawi, former Life-President Hastings Banda extracted economic surplus from peasant producers and transferred it to the state sector through two commercial banks, his holding company—Press Holdings—and the parastatal Agricultural Development and Marketing Corporation (ADMARC) (Libby, 1987, 191). He then used the resources to reward his political supporters by transforming the latter into commercial agricultural estate owners whose prosperity and economic security depended on their personal loyalty to the president.

Over time, the African state evolved into a predatory monster that used a convoluted system of regulations and controls to pillage and rob the productive class—the peasantry. The perpetrators and beneficiaries of this heinous larceny were the elites. The seriousness of the crime would have been somewhat mitigated if the elites had invested the booty in their own countries, to build factories and railroads for example, as did America's "robber barons" in the nineteenth century. But Africa's vampire elites spent the booty lavishly on mistresses, luxurious automobiles, fabulous mansions—on consumption, not productive ventures.

The rest of the loot was spirited out of the country into foreign bank accounts to develop the already advanced countries—a double whammy. "One Nigerian banker guesses that Nigerian [kleptocrats] have at least $25 billion in foreign bank accounts. A recent World Bank survey reckoned that capital flight during the 1980s may have reached $50 billion" (*The Economist,* 21 August 1993, Survey, 10). "A Nigerian man and a banker accompanying him were arrested at the Lagos airport after trying to board a London-bound jet with $800 million in cash. Customs officials said the seizure was the biggest recorded in Nigeria. The banker accompanied the other man apparently so that customs officials would not ask questions. The money has since been deposited in the Central Bank of Nigeria" (*The Washington Times,* 29 July 1995, A7).

In Kenya, "Many people in government have the biggest accounts in foreign banks. Critics of the Moi government say there is more money from Kenyans in foreign banks than the entire Kenyan foreign debt, which is about $8 billion. Kenya's situation is not unique to the country. It is a reality found . . . throughout Africa" (*The Washington Times,* 3 August 1995, A18).

Said Emma Etuk, a Nigerian scholar in Maryland, "Something is terribly wrong with the modern African psyche and spiritual moorings. Are we so stupid that we are incapable of learning any lessons from the histories of slavery and colonialism? How many whites are saving money in African banks, money they have stolen from their Western treasuries?" (*African News Weekly,* 28 October–3 November 1996, 28).

The post colonial state sector became the arena for the accumulation of private wealth. To become rich in Africa, one does not have to produce anything. All one has to do is to enter politics, become a government official, and use the office to amass a huge personal fortune. According to American journalist Howard French,

> In each [African] country, the formula for enrichment differs. In Senegal, World Bank officials have said that Government imports of rice, the staple food, have constituted a major source of unaccounted for revenue for ruling party leaders for years. In Congo, top officials and their relatives sign deals that mortgage the heavily-indebted country's oil earnings years in advance [to 2012], in exchange for quick cash. In Nigeria, the Government awards so-called "lifting contracts" to its political friends that amount to little more than gifts of handsome commissions on oil contracts. Based on realities like these, a confidential report prepared in 1995 by the French Foreign Ministry warned of the "criminalisation of sub-Saharan Africa" by the elites. (*The New York Times,* 4 February 1996, 4)

After a mere three-year tenure as minister of transport in the Shagari government in Nigeria, Alhaji Umaru Dikko managed to amass a personal fortune reputed to exceed $1 billion.[5] "Nigeria's problems are the few rich people in positions of power who divert huge amounts of money—that should have been used to develop the country—to foreign accounts for their selfish interests," said Gordon Adele, a civil servant in Lagos (*African News Weekly*, 16 June 1995, 7).

Writing in *African News Weekly* (27 May 1994), Anthony Ebeh explained the conception of public office in Nigeria, saying that the main problem is that Nigeria's leaders do not have a progressive view of the meaning of holding public office. In civilized nations—including non-Western ones—public office is seen as a way to provide selfless service to one's nation. It is held in very high regard, with the knowledge that those in public office are accountable to those they serve. To Nigerian officials, it is merely an opportunity to enrich self and kindred, which explains why Nigeria is now one of the poorest nations in the world (7).

The same follows for Kenya, where cabinet members continue to do disservice to the entire nation by playing favorites with certain ethnic groups and ignoring others. In September 1996 two Kenyan banks, the Kenya Finance Bank and the Heritage Bank, owned by members of the respected elite, including President Moi's son, Raymond Kipruto Moi, collapsed because of gross mismanagement and outright fraud: "Bad loans were at the center of Kenya Finance Bank's woes. . . . But what is, perhaps, most ironic is the inclusion of [the ruling] KANU on its list of bad debtors. The ruling political party is yet to repay debts amounting to a total of Kshs 42 million (about $750,000)" (*African Business*, November 1996, 31).

In 1994 in Zambia, three top ministers; Deputy Speaker Sikota Wina, Foreign Affairs Minister Vernon Mwaaga, and Community Development Minister Princess Nakatindi Wina, resigned to allow an inquiry into their alleged drug-trafficking activities. The three then

---

5. He fled to Britain after the 31 December 1983 coup by Major-General Muhammadu Buhari. On 5 July 1984 the Buhari regime unsuccessfully attempted to kidnap Dikko and bring him back to Nigeria to face justice. He was seized at gunpoint in London, drugged, and bundled into a crate for shipment back to Nigeria. His wife alerted London police, who intercepted the crate at Heathrow Airport, creating a major diplomatic row between the two countries.

demanded that some of their cabinet colleagues should also resign on the grounds that they were equally guilty of drug trafficking and other forms of corruption. The Winas named four other ministers and deputies and linked them with specific acts of corruption. . . .

One minister was accused of using grants from foreign countries and agencies to benefit his personal business. Another deputy minister who appeared penniless and living in poor quarters suddenly began to indulge in a lavish lifestyle and buy expensive machines.

Mwaanga said, "There are people in the cabinet who have enriched themselves through the abuse of donor aid and the dismantling of the pipeline at the Bank of Zambia and they should be investigated too."

Another minister is accused of pocketing some money that came from a housing project which was awarded to a South African company. Another is alleged to have given nationality papers to Lebanese traders in return for hefty payments. Another is said to be involved in shady deals concerning the issue of game licenses. (*New African*, April 1994, 32)

"Everyone in Zaire wants to be a minister before Mobutu falls so they can make money," said Duilleaume Ngefa, head of an association for human rights (*The Washington Times*, April 15, 1997, A13). Some of Sierra Leone's most senior state officials, including ministers, began a thriving business selling the country's passports to wealthy Hong Kong businessmen. "One such deal fetched about $350,000 for two highly placed functionaries" (*Akasanoma*, 31 July–6 August 1995, 38). In Ghana, the 1993 Auditor General's Report detailed a catalogue of embezzlement and corruption totaling 400 billion cedis. The rot at the Ghana National Procurement Corporation cost over 200 billion *cedis*. Yet not a single soul was indicted.

A year after taking office, Niger's president Maharanee Ousmane had tripled his personal fortune. As required by law, President Ousmane had declared a fortune of 51 million CFA ($89,000) and three houses when he took office in April 1993. A year later, "The poor West African country's Supreme Court said on April 28, 1994, that Maharanee had declared 160 million CFA ($280,000), with 57 million CFA held in cash and the rest in a local bank. Maharanee's list of property was 10 houses in Niger, livestock and poultry, three cars, two television sets, two video recorders and two gold watches" (*African News Weekly*, 20 May 1994, 8).

When Kwame Nkrumah exhorted Africans to "Seek ye first the political kingdom" (independence from colonial rule), he probably had no idea how this dictum would be perverted. The burning obsession of the "educated" African is to seek the political kingdom (government office) to enrich himself. Unfortunately, only one person can be the president or minister of finance at a time, so a fierce competition erupts for these posts. And once they are secured, by means fair or foul, they must never be given up because expulsion from the state sector can mean an economic death sentence. Thus, the occupants of these government positions must do all that they can to remain in these posts forever: "presidents-for-life," "ministers-for-life," or "ambassadors-for-life." And they will defend these positions and perks even to death.

On 6 June 1995 university students in Ghana peacefully marched to the Ashanti Regional Administration in Kumasi seeking to find out why payment of their academic expenses had been delayed and subsidies had been withdrawn from the regional commissioner. Nana Tuffuor, a student who participated in a peaceful demonstration, gave this report: "We started peacefully but had a shock when we went to the Ashanti Regional Administration to present our petition to the Minister. We were waiting patiently when we saw his Land cruiser coming. Amidst cheers we moved in the direction of the car—bought by the people—which we were not going to destroy. To our surprise, the Regional Minister, Ohene Agyekum, pulled a gun and threatened to shoot if we dared *touch the car* and shouted 'nkwaseafo' (fools) at us, on climbing upstairs" (*Statesman*, 30 June–7 July 1995, 9).[6]

The elites act this way because, in their strange scheme of things, there is no life outside the state sector—literally. "One of the five top officials of Mozambique's ruling FRELIMO party who were sacked four days earlier committed suicide, a party spokesman said on July 27, 1995. The

---

6. Another government official in the same city who tried the same tactic was taught a bitter lesson. On 27 August 1996, Nana Akwasi Agyeman, the chief executive of the Ashanti Metropolitan Assembly, ordered that a 30 million cedi ($24,000) building belonging to Amama Akyea, a strong supporter of the opposition party, be demolished. Protestors marched off to his office, demanding that he rescind his decision. But Nana Akwasi Agyeman pulled out a gun and fired a warning shot to scare the protesters. "Incensed and determined to take their pound of flesh, the protesters disarmed him and deflated the tires of his vehicle. They then set the vehicle ablaze. Sensing danger, Nana Akwasi Agyeman took to his heels with all the speed he could summon while his helmet flew off" (*The Ghanaian Chronicle*, 29 August–1September 1996, 12).

spokesman for FRELIMO's policy-making Central Committee said Eduardo Arao, who had been party secretary for administration and finance, shot himself in his home" (*African News Weekly*, 11 August 1995, 5). Another pathetic case was that of Mohamed Hassan Said, Somalia's ambassador to China. After his government collapsed in January 1991, he stayed on and on and on, surviving on occasional handouts from friendly Islamic embassies. "I came here to serve my nation, but I'm not doing much of that because there is no government as far as I can see," said the 56-year-old lawyer and veteran diplomat. "I've been marooned here for 8 years" (*The Washington Post*, 17 December 1996, A15). "I am here waiting for the situation to stabilize," he said. "We cannot but hope." He stayed on because the title "ambassador" was prestigious and more important than getting out of hopeless situation.

Even among Africa's expatriate community, politics still remains very attractive. Thousands of African exiles in Europe and North America do nothing—not even write a book—patiently waiting for the chance to become the next president of their countries. The older they grow, the more desperate they become, despite the hazards of the presidency. Recall this quote from *Africa Insider* (August 1995): "Becoming a Tanzanian presidential wannabe could be bad for your heart. Kghoma Ali Malima, leader of Tanzania's main opposition group, recently died of a heart attack at his son's home in London just months before landmark multiparty elections. Tanzanian journalists compared his death to that of Stephen Kambona, a would-be candidate who collapsed and died in Washington in 1994. Both men lacked a history of illness or heart problems." (6).

As we saw in Chapter 4, a crude rule of thumb that may be used to distinguish rich and poor countries is determining how the rich got their wealth. In Africa and other parts of the Third World, the rich got wealthy by exploiting their positions in government. By contrast, the rich in the rich countries got rich by producing and selling a commodity or a service. Bill Gates of the United States earned his wealth in the computer industry. Similarly, many of the U.S. politicians, who were elected in November 1994, arrived in Congress with considerable wealth made through business ventures, lucrative professional practices or profitable investments, according to their financial disclosure statements for 1994. "Nearly one-fourth of the GOP newcomers to the House and Senate reported holdings worth at least $1 million, documents released show. A similar proportion of the freshmen House Democrats who managed to prevail amid the Republican onslaught—3 of 13—were similarly wealthy (*The Washington Post*, 15 June 1995, A1).

Even in Africa's own supposedly backward indigenous system of government, people do not serve on the council of elders or become chief to enrich themselves. True, the chief is wealthy and lives in opulent style: gold rings, sandals, and other royal paraphernalia. Custom requires that he lives in such style to inspire respect for the tribe. But the wealth does not belong to him. It is considered "stool property," which the chief cannot take away with him if he is destooled. Furthermore, the "illiterate" peasants of Africa use their raw, native intelligence, imagination, talents and resources to produce cocoa, gold, corn, kenkey, and many other commodities. They do not use tribal government posts or connections to make their wealth.

Shamefully, the modern elites of Africa have turned the process of wealth creation and accumulation on its head. Using a government post to embezzle or steal money is not only criminal but also has deleterious developmental and personal consequences. First, such an activity does not create wealth for the nation. It merely transfers wealth from the productive sector into private pockets and there is no net gain for the country. In fact, the net result may well be negative when those whose wealth are sequestrated curtail their economic activities. Second, no African government lasts forever. Probes and commissions of inquiries usually follow changes of government and former government officials, found guilty of embezzlement and corruption charges, are given long prison terms and, in some cases, shot by firing squad. Obviously, it would be safer for the elites to make their wealth on their own, in the private sector; that way, when the government changed they would not be hauled before a commission of inquiry to explain how they accumulated their wealth. Above all, African elites should pay heed to American philosopher Ayn Rand, who once noted:

> Money is the barometer of a society's virtue. When you see that trading is done, not by consent, but by compulsion—when you see that in order to produce, you need to obtain permission from men who produce nothing—when you see that money is flowing to those who deal, not in goods, but in favors—when you see that men get richer by graft and pull than by work, and your laws don't protect you against them, but protect them against you—when you see corruption being rewarded and honesty becoming a self-sacrifice—you may know that your society is doomed (quoted by F. Brian Hiestand, *The Wall Street Journal*, 5 July 1995, A9).

Several countries in Africa are already doomed.

CHAPTER 6

The Inevitable Implosion

Crisis, chaos, famine, diseases, civil wars, coups, dictatorships, social disorder, corruption and legitimizing military
regimes seem to be the most outstanding elements of post-
independence Africa. The mood of optimism, hope and high
expectation has today been overtaken by frustration and
pessimism.

—Kofi Adusei-Poku
(*West Africa*, 1-7 March 1993, 320).

THE DESTRUCTIVE CONSEQUENCES OF THE MAFIA STATE

The system of governance described in the previous chapter is inherently
unstable and explosive. Sultanism (one-man rule) is potentially highly
destructive. It unleashes forces of instability, chaos, and violence that may
eventually consume the country, as in Burundi, Liberia, Rwanda, Sierra
Leone, Somalia, Sudan, and Zaire. While it is agreed that the state has a role
to play in development, what obtains in many African countries cannot be
called a state or government. It is a "state" that has been hijacked by a cabal
of crooks and gangsters. Africa cannot use such a "state vehicle" for the
development journey, as we saw in chapter 2. This state vehicle is defective
and broken down. Little progress can be made on the development journey
unless the "vehicle" is overhauled or discarded. Similarly, the system of
governance currently prevailing in Africa is a crisis-producing machine:
agricultural crises, debt crises, budget crises, environmental crises, population
crises, and so on, inevitably emanate from it.

The Development Environment

Development is a creative activity that results in the production of goods
and services. In Africa, the people who produce the bulk of these goods

and services are the peasant majority. They are the producers of Africa's real wealth: cocoa, coffee, gold, diamonds, and other commodities. The elite minority constitute the parasitic, extractive class who use the government machinery to milk the peasants.

The true challenge of development is to spur and release the creative energies of Africa's peasants. Creative activity, however, does not occur in a vacuum but in an environment. Various government legislation, policies (taxes, duties, and subsidies), institutions, and attitudes shape this environment. Thus, politics, ecology, and culture all form part of what may be called the development environment.

This environment must be such that it encourages or induces people to greater effort. Such an environment is described as "enabling" or "conducive" to productive effort. Although an "enabling environment" is an intangible, amorphous concept, certain pertinent features can be isolated for purposes of study with respect to their impact on development. The World Bank (1989) identified "incentives and the physical infrastructure" as crucial. But a more expansive set of requirements for an "enabling environment" would include the following:

- Security of persons and property
- System of incentives
- Rule of law
- Basic functioning infrastructure
- Stability: economic, political, and social
- Basic freedoms: intellectual, political, and economic

Since the importance of these may not be obvious to many African government officials, it is necessary to spell them out briefly.

Security

Security derives from the commonsensical fact that a person's first interest is survival. Let us imagine a peasant farmer named Amna. If she were in fear for her life, she would not go to her farm and double agricultural output. Nor would she if her maize harvest were repeatedly stolen. The harvest is her own personal property. How she disposes of it is her own business. Similarly, if an entrepreneur or investor establishes a company, it is his own personal or commercial property, which cannot be arbitrarily seized.

A System of Incentives

There are two ways of inducing greater productive effort from individuals. One is to provide them with *incentives*. For example, people may be praised, honored, or rewarded for certain patriotic acts. The other is to remove *disincentives*. Consider, for example, a worker who has been subjected to a constant barrage of insults, taunts, and abuses. He might become more productive if the pattern of abuse ceases, just as Africa's peasant farmers might do if the pattern of exploitation, repression, denigration and castigation subsides. Similarly, an exorbitant tax, such as a 90 percent profit tax, can act as a disincentive. Reducing the tax rate can in itself provide an incentive to produce and curtail tax evasion. Nothing rewards people better than enjoying the fruits of their own labor.

People do not engage in economic activity for altruistic reasons. Amna does not break her back in the hot sun to produce maize because of patriotism. She does so because she wants to earn a living, to feed her family and survive. She cannot supply all her family wants from the farm, so she produces a surplus, which she sells at the market. She uses the proceeds to purchase the things she cannot produce for herself. If she wants a sewing machine or television set, then she must produce more on her farm. Thus the market performs a vital role in enabling her to feed her family's wants other than food.

Further, the market's price mechanism operates as a system of incentives. If the price of maize were to rise, she would have a greater incentive to produce more. And if the price were to drop drastically, she might consider switching to the cultivation of, say, cocoyam, the price of which may have been rising. Price changes also send "signals" to consumers, giving them incentives to alter consumption patterns. For example, if the price of chicken rises, a consumer may purchase fish instead.

By rising and falling, prices perform an important economic function. The "signals" prices transmit influence the allocation of resources. The price mechanism also provides people—both producers and consumers—with a system of incentives. Anything that interferes with the operation of the price mechanism, therefore, not only reduces the effectiveness of incentives but also leads to distortions in the allocation of resources. Price controls, security checkpoints (or roadblocks), and poor road conditions that impede the free movement of goods are examples of such interferences. The removal of these impediments may induce greater production.

A host of other noneconomic disincentives may be identified: civil strife, insecurity, instability, and an absence of due process that allow people to be deprived of the fruits of their labor. Consider the situation in Burundi, where "coffee production has declined . . . because of civil strife that has engulfed that small country of 8 million people for the past two years. In 1994, Burundi produced about 41,000 tons of coffee. Production dropped to 30,000 tons in 1995, with the 1996 harvest expected to be even smaller. Coffee farmers in Burundi's rich western provinces of Cibitoke and Bubanza are most affected. Once the agricultural heartland of Burundi, these two provinces and a third in northern Burundi, Kayanza, have been deserted because of the fighting" (*The Washington Times,* 18 April 1996, A12). Thus, when world coffee prices rose in 1996, Burundi could not cash in. By contrast, after the civil war ended in Mozambique in 1992, its GDP grew by an annual average of 6.6 percent for next four years.

Rule of Law

A well-functioning legal system offers security of persons and property. It also ensures that the laws of the land are obeyed by all, with no exceptions. Individuals cannot do what they please outside their homes. In their interactions with others, they must follow the law. In other words, the law "rules," taking precedence over the whims or caprices of individuals. For example, the law may say that it is larceny to acquire property by stealing it from someone else. Anyone guilty of such a felony, whether that person is a doctor, a chief, or even the president of the country, shall be prosecuted and punished for all to see. Embezzlement or theft of public funds falls into this category, since the victim is the taxpayer. And when one's security is threatened or one's property is stolen, one does not "take the law into one's own hands" but follows laid-down procedure to seek a redress, usually by hauling the culprit, even if it is the government, into a court of law. When these conditions are met, the rule of law, which means respecting and following established ways of doing things, is said to prevail. Why is the rule of law important for economic development?

The constitution and the system of laws define the parameters or the legal framework within which economic activity or competition takes place. If the parameters are constantly being shifted or violated, confusion, uncertainty, or even chaos may result. Economically, it is difficult to make investment plans when laws are suddenly abrogated and new decrees issued without notice and to take immediate effect. People cannot be expected to follow the rules when the authorities themselves flout the law or apply it capriciously to favor one person over another. It would not be fair to a competitor to see a rival company blatantly violating the law while the authorities look the other way. And yanking a company's license to operate simply because the president of the country dislikes the owner's political views or ethnicity can have a chilling effect on business investment.

To ensure that the rule of law prevails, the most fundamental prerequisite is the existence of an independent and impartial judiciary. That is, the bench must be free from government control or manipulation. The judges must not all be appointed by the president or hail from his ethnic group. And judges must be free to deliberate on issues without fear of incurring government displeasure and even to reach verdicts against the government without fear of being abducted and murdered— as happened to three Ghanaian judges in 1982.

Basic Functioning Infrastructure

In production, inputs have to be procured and labor trained and employed. The finished product must be marketed. Telephone calls have to be made to contact prospective customers. Goods have to be shipped and deliveries made on time. Some basic infrastructure, such as roads, schools, electricity, water, and telephone services, are essential to facilitate this process. More important, they must function reliably. A factory will have difficulty with production if there are frequent interruptions in the power supply. And if factory owners must install their own power generators, water supply or mobile telephone systems, the cost of production will increase and be passed on to the consumer in the form of higher prices. Even then, such prices would place the business at competitive disadvantage, making it difficult to compete with imports.

Stability

People and businesses need a stable world in which to conduct and plan their daily activities. People cannot make production decisions or increase agricultural production when bombs go off in the middle of the night and everything is in chaos. Production activity—and therefore development—is sustainable only in a stable environment. Stability has several aspects: political, economic (monetary, price), and social. "To attract investment, a stable economic and political environment is essential" (World Bank, 1989, 9).

A system is stable if, after an initial disturbance or sudden change, it returns to its original position. A pendulum at rest is stable. If knocked, it eventually returns to its former position. Thus, a political system is stable if, following an election, the system returns, not necessarily with the same head of state but instead to the same bedrock of principles on which it was founded: democracy, rule of law, accountability, freedom of expression, and so on. That is, the system must have the capability to sustain itself year after year without violent and chaotic change. Political stability is not assured by having one buffoon declare himself president-for-life and keep all power to himself. That kind of "stability" is artificial because groups excluded from power-sharing and decision making will plot to overthrow or battle the government for inclusion. These activities result in violence and civil strife—hardly the environment that encourages development.

Economic stability is also required for development. Both producers and consumers need assurances that the economic system will not suddenly be overthrown and replaced with a convoluted one, that banks will continue to exist and function, and that the currency they have stashed under their mattresses will continue to have value. Peasant farmers need to be assured that markets will still be there and that they will not be uprooted and forcibly resettled on government farms or ordered to sell their produce to government agencies.

Price stability means that the currency, say the *zonga*, will have a stable value, so that when Amna goes to the market she will not find that a chicken, which cost 5 *zongas* yesterday, today costs 10,000 *zongas*. Planning one's productive activity is exceedingly difficult, if not impossible, when prices are increasing rapidly. Hyperinflation undermines confidence in the currency, discourages savings, and stimulates capital flight. A zero rate of inflation is impossible since the cost of producing things always rises due to declining resources, population increases, and various other factors. Consequently, price increases on the order of 5 percent are considered "normal." But a rate of inflation in excess of even 15 percent creates serious economic problems.

Monetary stability means that the currency, banks, and the monetary system as a whole continue to function smoothly without major upheavals. It means, for example, that Barclay's Bank will still be there tomorrow and its depositors will be able to withdraw money. It also means that Amna will not find that the *zonga* is no longer legal tender because overnight the government had replaced it with a new currency without giving people time to exchange the old for the new currency.

A sound monetary system is vital for the smooth functioning of an economy. An economy without money will grind away at a snail's pace, as people will be forced to exchange goods by barter, which is cumbersome, inefficient, and time consuming. Yet a monetary system operates largely by confidence. People will use and hold money if they have confidence in it. If they do not, they will rid themselves of their money by purchasing commodities. Of course, if everybody does this, the result will be inflation—rising prices. The resultant inflation, if excessive, would reduce the value of the currency, eventually rendering it worthless. Few people would keep their savings in such a currency. They would rather hold dollars or foreign exchange. Nor would people keep their savings in banks, as their value would be eroded by inflation.

Economic (price and monetary) stability and confidence in the banking system as well as the economy are all intricately tied up with how the government manages the economy. Of particular importance are the government's policies, statements, budget deficits, and development priorities. What the government says or does can have a major impact on investment and therefore development. For example, a government that is hostile to private business and rails against private companies as "corrupt" and "exploiters" will not have much luck attracting foreign or domestic investors.

How the government manages its own fiscal affairs is also extremely important. Chronic and ever-expanding budget deficits are manifestations of fiscal indiscipline. Such deficits may be financed by raising taxes, borrowing, or simply by printing money. In raising taxes, the government appropriates more and more resources to satisfy its voracious appetite. But if the tax base is narrow, such tax hikes increasingly fall on a small group who might eventually rebel or evade them. And if the government slaps an 80 percent profit tax on businesses, they would hardly have the incentive to continue operations.

Thus, government management of its own budgetary affairs has an important impact on the development environment. A government that recklessly manages its fiscal policies and makes persistent forays into the banking system to scoop up liquidity will inject more money into the economy and fuel inflation. And rapidly rising prices will play havoc with savings, investment, and production decisions. Mexico did this in the

1980s; according to *The Economist* (26 August 1995), "The financial crisis of the 1980s cost Mexico more than five years of lost development" (19).

Freedom

Economic actors (producers and consumers) must have some measure of freedom to make decisions. At the individual level, a farmer, for example, must be free to determine what type of crops to cultivate, how much of his produce to consume with his family, where the surplus must be sold, and at what price. The government cannot make these decisions for millions of farmers. Similarly, consumers must determine for themselves what products to purchase and at what prices. If an item is too expensive, a consumer may decline to purchase it, buy a substitute, or produce the item himself. Nobody knows what is best for the consumer better than the consumer himself. Consequently, economic actors must have the freedom to make these decisions for themselves.

The purpose of development is to raise the living standards of the people. Common sense mandates that those whose lives are being improved ought to have a say or participate in the development decision-making process. How does one know what peasant farmers want and if their needs are being satisfied? A February 1990 conference in Arusha, Tanzania, hammered home precisely this theme. The Conference stated in its *African Charter for Popular Participation in Development Transformation:*

> We affirm that nations cannot be built without the popular support and full participation of the people, nor can the economic crisis be resolved and the human and economic conditions improved without the full and effective contribution, creativity and popular enthusiasm of the vast majority of the people. After all, it is to the people that the very benefits of development should and must accrue. We are convinced that neither can Africa's perpetual economic crisis be overcome, nor can a bright future for Africa and its people see the light of day, unless the structure, pattern and political context of the process of socio-economic development are appropriately altered. (*Africa Forum,* 1991, 14)

Accordingly, structures must be established to permit the people's "full participation" in the development process—from the bottom up. People are not robots but human beings with emotions, thoughts, beliefs, customs, and aspirations. And as such, they must have the freedom to express themselves, their beliefs, thoughts, and ideas; freedom to live where and when they choose; freedom to worship a religion of their own choice; freedom to produce and market goods of their choice; freedom to belong to or form any association—trade, religious, economic or political; freedom from arbitrary arrest; and freedom from tyrannical rule or despotism. These may be grouped into intellectual, economic, and political freedoms as well as human rights.

THE PREVAILING DEVELOPMENT ENVIRONMENT

It is obvious to even the most casual observer that the requirements for an "enabling environment" that allows people to participate fully in the development process and attracts foreign investment have not been met in most African countries. The mafia African governments have recklessly banished the rule of law and wreaked mayhem across the continent, scattering human debris and wanton devastation in its wake.

Security of Persons and Property

In most places in Africa, people live in fear of their lives and property. In 1996, civil war and strife raged in at least 17 African countries: Algeria, Angola, Burundi, Central African Republic, Chad, Congo, Djibouti, Egypt, Liberia, Mozambique, Rwanda, Senegal, Sierra Leone, Somalia, Sudan, Uganda, and Zaire. These senseless wars uprooted millions of peasants and caused severe dislocations in agricultural production. By that year, Africa's refugee count had reached 22 million—about the third of the world's total. The cost of these wars are impossible to calculate, but most experts believe that Africa's agricultural production would increase by as much as 30 percent if the civil wars would end.

African governments do provide security—not for the people but for the ruling gangsters. According to General Ibrahim Babangida, the former military despot of Nigeria, "State security, in government parlance, is any measure, offensive or defensive, taken to protect the state from acts or whatever that even annoy the head of government. You can take any measure to stop the country from being subjected to acts of sabotage or terrorism. You can take any measure to make sure that the head of government or state or the president does not get annoyed. It's all part of security" (From an interview in *Tell* magazine, 24 July 1995). Note that it is the state which is being protected against the people.

For the people, "security" has been a pattern of heinous brutalities. The worst offenders have been military rulers. According to the World

Bank (1989), "Sometimes the military have deposed unpopular regimes. But often this had led to more, not less, state violence and lawlessness. Occasionally it has led even to civil war. These disruptions have driven many to become refugees, both directly by threatening lives and indirectly by making drought and other natural calamities harder to cope with" (22).

Consider the following:

The Osolu family complained to the Nigeria Air Force headquarters that their house in Afube village, Amichi in Nnewi-South Local Government Area of Anambra State, was recently invaded by Air Force personnel. The airmen allegedly shot a gun in the air and chased everybody out after beating them up and vandalizing their property.

NAF director of public relations, Wing Commander Alex Usifoh disclosed to the *Daily Champion* that the NAF has identified the officer who led four other armed airmen to the Osulus' house. All of them came from the 81 Air Center, Benin, Edo State. Usifoh said if found guilty, the airmen might be dismissed and handed over to the police for persecution. [They never were.] (*African News Weekly,* 3 March 1995, 13)

Sudan. Villages were burned; food stocks destroyed and animals stolen to make life impossible; civilians were robbed, kidnapped and tortured; women raped. (*The Washington Times,* 27 July 1995, A19)

When students of Khartoum University marched in 1992 against the rising cost of education, soldiers moved onto the campus, shot several demonstrators, arrested others, and closed the university for the rest of the year. (*The Atlantic Monthly,* August 1994, 32)

In order to rid Mauritania of the independent-minded black population and to consolidate control over the River Valley, the regime of President Maouya Ould Sid'Ahmed Taya carried out systematic human rights violations against the black ethnic groups, including arbitrary arrests, extrajudicial executions, expropriation of land, and denial of cultural identity. Two campaigns were particularly shocking: the massive deportations of some 70,000 blacks from Mauritania in 1989-1990, which targeted professionals in the cities, land-holders along the Senegal River, and nomadic herders; and the massacre of over 500 blacks in the late 1990/ early 1991. This latter group was among the 2,000-3,000 black Africans in the military and civil service who were arrested without charge, held

incommunicado in detention, and subjected to vicious physical abuse
(*Africa Report*, January/February 1994, 45)

People suffer brutalities not only from the "forces of law and order"
but also from the so-called liberators. Consider Liberia in September
1996 for example:

> Tubmanburg, Liberia—In a small shack in the countryside, a young
> woman with both arms sliced nearly to the bone flapped her paralyzed
> hands about and wailed in bewilderment, "I can't do anything with them."
> Blood oozed from the festering wounds, inflicted by ropes used to bind
> her arms behind her back during a rebel attack.
>
> An emaciated old woman was sprawled on the filthy floor nearby,
> pleading for the grown sons she said were somewhere in America.
>
> This is what passes for peace in Liberia. (*The Washington Post*, 24
> September 1996, A12)

Next door in Sierra Leone, the people have been trying to pull
themselves up by their bootstraps. Alpha Jallon, the national registrar of
cooperatives, recorded that people had established more than 1,200
cooperative societies, whose activities ranged from savings to farming, from
fishing to handicrafts. In 1991 the total membership was about 100,000,
mostly women with aggregate savings of about $353,000. But the coop-
eratives were laid to waste by the insurgents and renegade soldiers.

In April 1995, rebel soldiers raided the town of Port Loko and hit
the Kamuyu Rural Income Generating and Vocational Center, a cooperative. They kidnapped 60 girls and destroyed the center. According to
Alpha Jallon the Center had been founded in 1982 to provide women
and girls with vocational skills so that they could set up small businesses.
"'The April attack forced the Kamuyu Center to close down,' says
Patricia Forkoi Sonkoi, who fled to Freetown along with other instruc-
tors and some of the remaining trainees. 'We could not continue in the
face of serious insecurity to our lives,' she said. The Young Rising
Women's Cooperative at Magburaka, 272 kilometers from Freetown,
collapsed after a rebel attack on the town early in 1995. 'They destroyed
everything at our factory,' says Aminata Kamara. 'We were lucky to have
escaped'" (*The African Observer*, 22 August–4 September 1995, 5).

In the Central African Republic in February 1996, soldiers at the Alpha
Yaya military camp went on the rampage to demand a salary increase. "To
show they meant business, they fired shots in the air and seized vehicles from

innocent civilians. . . . Foreign investors have been thoroughly frightened by the violence and insecurity. Many Lebanese who were victims of the looting have packed their bags and left" (*New African,* May 1996, 26). Over 50 civilians were killed with more than 100 wounded. But what have innocent civilians got to do with salary increase for soldiers?

System of Incentives

Largely absent in postcolonial Africa has been a system of incentives to induce greater production. Most people aspire to be rich and live comfortably. Africans are no exception. After all, the object of development is to lift them out of poverty. In traditional Africa, peasants wanting to be rich seek to produce more on their farms. But in modern Africa, politics has emerged as the passport to opulence; almost every educated African who aspires to be rich wants to be the president or a minister. "Politics is seen as a way of gaining access to fantastic wealth, and this government [of Babangida] has taken it to extreme," said Beko Ransome-Kuti, frequently jailed a civil-rights leader in Nigeria (*The Economist,* 21 August 1993, 6). Whoever wields state or political power ultimately controls the allocation of resources.

In Kenya, "politics has always been a means of securing 'access to the meat.' Rampant corruption has sapped the economy and widened the gap between a rapacious few and the sullen *wanachi* (the common folks). Companies with links to Moi have skimmed monumental sums off government contracts in wheat, oil, and land, and particularly off foreign aid. Budget allocations are sold to the highest bidder. One series of scams in the early 1990s cost Kenya the equivalent of 10 percent of its annual Gross Domestic Product" (*The Atlantic Monthly,* February 1996, 33).

An intense struggle for political power erupts that is so absorbing that it overshadows the development imperative. "All the problems Nigeria contends with today have to do with the struggle for power," said Andrew Uchendu, a constitutional delegate from oil-rich Rivers State in the southeast of the country (*The African Observer,* 2-15 May 1995, 11). Often this competition for power degenerates into political violence, civil strife, or war.

Rule of Law

African governments arbitrarily seize people's private property with impunity. People cannot obtain relief from the court system, because the judiciary is just another organ of the kleptocratic government, which appoints judges and justices of the peace. The police, the military, and security forces that are supposed to protect the citizens are themselves the abductors, the killers, and the thieves. In July 1995 the Lagos government closed the Ojota toll gate to ease traffic and redirected traffic to two mini-toll plazas on the Sagamu and Abeokuta roads. The police, however, saw it differently. "With pullovers covering their name-tags, they immediately moved into the abandoned toll area and began harassing motorists, collecting bribes—particularly targeting commercial drivers carrying cargoes of electronics." (*African News Weekly*, 28 July 1995, 14)

Looting and arbitrary seizures of property by undisciplined soldiers have become rampant in much of Africa, discouraging not only foreign but domestic investment as well. Finally an African official spoke out. At the African Business Round Table in Cairo (1 March 1990), Babacar Ndiaye, president of the African Development Bank, warned that "in order to improve the flow of foreign investment into Africa . . . African governments [must] focus more on areas such as ownership law, settling of disputes, exchange controls, incentives and political stability" (*West Africa*, 12-18 March 1990, 423).

Even in Africa's so-called backward and illiterate society, chiefs could not arbitrarily dispossess people of their property. According to Louw and Kendall (1987), "In precolonial Africa, there were no powers of arbitrary expropriation, and land and huts could be expropriated only under extreme conditions after a full public hearing" (18). Shamefully, no such safeguards exist in most "modern" African countries.

In many African countries today, there is no rule of law. Public property is brazenly stolen. This culture of bribery and corruption costs Africa dearly. "Corruption is a normal business cost in Zimbabwe," says *The Economist* (2 March 1996, 44). "Virtually all government contracts now require some form of kickback or 'commission' to those with political influence or to the bureaucrats who stand guard over regulations."[1]

---

1. This same issue of *The Economist* reported the case of Strive Masiyiwa, whose application to operate a cellular network was withheld because of his refusal to pay a bribe. It reported similar stories about "a planned new international airport, the purchase and lease of unsuitable planes for the state-owned Air Zimbabwe and the troubled Zimbabwe Iron and Steel Corporation" (33).

More maddening, the loot is not invested in Africa to build factories and create jobs, but shipped out of Africa (capital flight) to develop the already rich countries. Said an irate Bedford N. Umez, a Nigerian professor of government at Lee College in Texas: "Even wild animals protect their own territories. These wild beasts, as we call them, use their own common sense to hunt together, share the price of their bounties together and, most importantly, protect their territories together. Not so the embezzlers of our public funds. A man who denies himself, his parents and his children good roads, hospitals, education, clean air and water by providing such amenities to his enemies [the rich countries] needs help—he is sick in the head" (*African News Weekly,* 7-13 October 1996, 24).

"Nigeria is the most corrupt nation in the world," according to Transparency International (*The Houston Chronicle,* 28 July 1996). Between 1970 and the early 1980s, when oil prices collapsed, $100 billion in oil money flowed into Nigerian government coffers. Nigerians are now asking what happened to the "oil money." According to *The Washington Post* (21 July 1992), "corruption robs Nigeria's economy of an estimated $2 billion to $3 billion each year" (A16). It also lurks behind the government's reluctance to abandon grandiose, wasteful projects because government officials loathe an inspection of their finances. According to *The Economist* (August 21, 1993):

> The junta will reveal neither how much it spends on projects like the Ajaokuta Steel Works, peacekeeping in Liberia or the new capital in Abuja, nor how much it earns from oil. The NNPC [the Nigerian National Petroleum Corporation] has no published accounts. International economists calculate that, given known Nigerian oil production and world oil prices, the gap between what the NNPC should have earned and what the government says it earned was about $2.7 billion in 1992. This suggests a huge amount of money—nearly 10 percent of GDP—is disappearing each year out of government coffers. (Survey, 8)

Bribery, embezzlement and theft—sometimes on a grand scale— divert enormous resources from public coffers to private hands. In the mature African mafia state, corruption becomes systemic: "Unrestrained corruption pervades the civil service, statutory boards and public corporations; what began as occasional acts of public misconduct spread like a cancer. The result is a pathological condition of 'systemic corruption'— an administration in which 'wrong-doing has become the norm,' whereas the 'notion of public responsibility has become the exception, not the rule.' Corruption is then 'so regularized and institutionalized that organizational supports back wrong-doing and actually penalize those who live up to the old norms' (Chazan, et. al., 1992, 180).

This pattern of looting has become so deeply ingrained that it would be difficult to eradicate. In Ghana, for instance, commissions of inquiry into official wrongdoing have accompanied each new regime and each set of commission unearthed, not unexpectedly, massive corruption and graft. Every commission recommended stiffer penalties and/or special police agencies to ferret out these practices. In 1983 Jerry Rawlings, the new ruler, had people found guilty of major acts of corruption shot. Yet the corruption actually increased.

In the most pernicious types of kleptocracy, such as Angola, Kenya, Nigeria and Zaire, the head of state and his entourage systematically loots the wealth of the country. As mentioned, this sort of governance was never acceptable in the supposedly "primitive and backward" Africa; therefore, foreign analysts should never excuse it. Traditional African rulers were held accountable at all times. For example, *Mantse* Obli Taki was destooled in 1918 by his Labadi people for a number of offenses, chief of which was the selling of Ga land in the name of the Ga people without consulting the owners of that land and pledging the stool itself as security on a loan. More recently, Chief Barima Adu-Baah Kyere of Ghana and his supporters fled following assassination attempts on them. The dispute concerned accountability regarding the village's revenue (*Ghana Drum,* June 1994, 12).

Corruption in modern Africa has several deleterious effects on economic development. First, it breeds inefficiency and waste. Who you are and how big a kickback you offer matters more than how well or efficiently you perform a job. As a result, work done is shoddy: Roads are poorly constructed and wash away at the first drop of rain. Telephones refuse to work, postal service is nonexistent, and the entire communication system is in shambles, costing the country billions in lost output.

Second, corruption aggravates the budget deficit problem. Expenditure figures are padded. Ghost workers proliferate on government payrolls: "An audit task force appointed by the Nigerian Government said on 1 November 1996 that it had discovered 28,000 'ghost workers' on the state payroll . . . The 'ghost workers' are either fake, retired or dead persons whose names remain on the payroll for fraudulent officials to claim their wages" (*African News Weekly,* 11-17 November 1996, 17). Revenue collectors are notoriously corrupt, pocketing part of tax proceeds, waiving taxes if they receive large enough bribes.

Third, corruption drives away foreign investors: "Government contracts in Nigeria, say international businessmen, are among the most expensive in the world 'mainly because of excessive margins built into such contracts for personal interests.' Those personal interests can be seen as attending expensive schools in Britain, or parked outside plush government villas: a Maserati or Lamborghini is quite normal for an army chief" (*The Economist*, 21 August 1993, Survey, 5).

Fourth, corruption, nepotism, and political disorder feed on themselves to create institutional break-down as we shall see in the next section.

Basic Functioning Infrastructure

African governments have little appreciation for the importance of infrastructure, and the word "maintenance" does not exist in the official lexicon. Infrastructure has crumbled in many African countries. The educational system is a shambles. Roads are potholed. Hospitals lack basic supplies, and patients are often asked to bring their own bandages and blankets.

Of Zimbabwe, *The Economist* said that the "phone system is notoriously bad . . . many businesses use messengers and personal visits instead" (2 March 1996, 44).

But the situation in Nigeria is not hopeless. Says Helen Okpokowu-ruk, editor of *African News Weekly* (16 September 1994):

> There is at least one service that is efficient and on time. It is the phone bill, if you happen to be among the lucky ones in Nigeria who own a phone. NITEL's phone bills are completely computerized and are delivered on time every month. Even though your phone may have been out of order for over half of the month due to technical problems at NITEL, you are expected to pay your phone bill promptly or your line will be "tossed" [disconnected]. If your line is disconnected, it could be given to someone else and you will have to get on the waiting list again to get a new phone line. How long would you have to stay on the waiting list? It depends on how much bribe you are willing to pay to the people at NITEL.
>
> The electricity bill too is computerized and delivered on time. People are not so afraid of having their electricity disconnected. Some would not notice the difference. (2)

Even Abuja, the vaunted new capital, must often go without electricity: "Toll gate operators have had to signal motorists with flashlights at night to collect tolls. No illuminated warning signs exist to indicate the presence of the toll booths to oncoming motorists" (*African News Weekly*, 1 September 1995, 12).

And does the mail get delivered in Nigeria? "Joshua Bamigbele, acting Postmaster-General for the federation, said that pilfering and mail theft are most common at ports due to heavy traffic of mail from abroad" (*African News Weekly*, 4 November 1994, 3). Nigerian cities have fire departments, but often there is no equipment. When a three-story apartment building and a bakery were destroyed by fire in Umuahia "one volunteer, Mr. Timothy Nwachukwu, said that the fire service did not help because they had no working vehicles" (*African News Weekly*, 24 February 1994, 12).

The Nigerian military government solves these pesky little problems by launching glitzy media campaigns and glossy advertisements! According to *Africa Insider* (15 July 1995), "The Nigerian government began a media campaign to persuade Nigerians not to use the port of Cotonou in Benin, which is about 16 miles from Lagos. Nigerian importers can import their goods there, then move shipments over land routes into Nigeria. This allows them to avoid delays and higher costs at Nigerian ports. For example, it costs $1,875 in port customs fees to move a fairly used car through Lagos. And $437.50 to move the same car through Cotonou" (4).

Stability

Stability, especially political stability, has been elusive. Groups excluded from power agitate for inclusion and may resort to civil disobedience. Chaos and strife ensue. The chaos may even be deliberately planned: "'Don't be deceived by the chaos,' said one experienced Western businessman. 'Mobutu likes it this way. With hyperinflation it's easy for foreigners to make money, and it's the cut from foreigners that fills his pockets. With no roads, the army can never topple him. With no communications, the opposition can never organize. With total corruption, it's every man for himself and people can be picked off one by one'" (*Vanity Fair*, November 1994, 95).

A peculiar form of stability prevails in many African countries—stability wrought by impoverishment and repression. In Zimbabwe, according to Paul Taylor, an American journalist, "There's big enough patronage base in the civil service and parastatal companies, which together account for about 35 percent of the economy, for the Mugabe government to keep a firm grip on power. Ministers get rich, political opponents get weary, the masses get poorer. The country is stable" (*The Washington Post*, April 9, 1995, A23).

To rebuff any threats to its authority, insecure African regimes invest heavily in the military and security forces. Their wages and salaries consume a huge portion of the budget. But the tax base is small. To generate revenue, the government slaps a tax on anything that moves. The regime may seek foreign aid or loans, but much of it is used to pay the salaries of civil servants, to import consumer goods and weapons for the military. If access to foreign credit is tight, the regime may simply print the necessary money to finance government expenditures and political campaigns. For example: "In the 1992 election campaign, Moi's cronies established a network of 'political banks' that siphoned money out of the Central Bank and pumped it into the ruling party's campaign. This brazen abuse of the monetary system to finance the campaign almost doubled the money supply in six months, creating 100 percent inflation" (*The Atlantic Monthly*, February 1996, 33).

And how much confidence do Africans have in the banking system? "No sense putting money in the bank," says Hilal El-Jamal, a refrigerator merchant in Ghana. "Dig a hole and bury it, or better, build something with it" (*West Africa*, 8-14 May 1995, 718). Economists estimate that 50 percent of Ghana's money supply lies outside the banks.

The situation was exacerbated during Ghana's 7 December 1996 elections, when the ruling NDC regime was alleged to have printed fake *cedi* notes to buy votes in the north. Imagine a regime debauching its own currency in order to win an election. Lenin once said that the best way to wreck the capitalist system is by debauching its currency. Rawlings, a neo-Marxist, appeared to be creating a "capitalistic system" on one hand and wrecking it on the other.

In Nigeria, the banking system is on the verge of collapse. Most banks are unable to meet their obligations to customers. Depositors often are not allowed to withdraw amounts in excess of 1,000 *naira* ($110), irrespective of their credit balances. In June 1995 hundreds of irate depositors took action. At the Onitsha Branch of the Mercantile Bank, they held the staff hostage and demanded to withdraw their money from the bank. They wanted to close their accounts and accused the bank of being on the distressed list. "The bank manager maintained that there was not enough cash on hand to satisfy this great number of customers. In response, the depositors blocked all entrances to the bank and would not permit staff members to leave" (*African News Weekly*, June 2, 1995, 12). Depositors were infuriated by a notice on the door to the Ikolaje/Idi-Iroko Community Bank stating that "we have been forced to close shop as a result of external auditors' certification. . . . A team of auditors had examined the bank's records and found them wanting" (*African News Weekly*, 9 June 1995, 15).

Monetary stability, however, was achieved in Francophone Africa, where the currency, the CFA *franc* (Communaute Financiere Africain) was pegged, in 1948, to the French *franc* (FF) at 50 CFA to 1 FF and devalued on 11 January 1994 to 100 CFA to 1FF. The common currency (CFA) and its link to the FF stabilized prices in Francophone Africa but at a tremendous geopolitical cost. By linking the CFA to the French *franc* and by insisting that Francophone African countries keep 30 to 35 percent of their deposits with the Bank of France, French banking connections were able to exercise "a far more effective system of control than any form of colonization" (Biddlecombe, 1994, 30).

Furthermore, the linkage of the monetary system accelerated flight of capital out of Francophone Africa: "over $500 million worth of local CFA currency was being illegally shipped out every year, about one-third of all the notes in circulation" (Biddlecombe, 1994, 34).

Elsewhere in Africa, where there was no such monetary linkage to assure "economic independence," African governments simply overissued their currencies, by printing money to finance ever-soaring budget deficits. But too much money in circulation results in inflation, leading civil servants and workers to demand pay increases. If granted, the salary increases will further increase government expenditures, which will necessitate additional injection of new money into circulation—a never-ending cycle, continuously feeding inflation. What is maddening is that these problems, as well as the solutions, are known. Said Ismail Yamson, chairman of Unilever of Ghana,

> There is no reason why Ghana should not achieve the consistently high growth rates of certain parts of Asia. All the favorable conditions that we see in such fast-growing economies are to be found here and even more. Yet we are not growing. The reasons are not far-fetched. They can be found in the deteriorating macro-economic environment and the poor performance of the manufacturing sector as well as weaknesses in the management and control of government expenditure.

Budget deficits in 1992 and 1993 pushed the inflation rate to around 25 percent, halved the value of the *cedi,* and forced the Bank of Ghana to raise interest rates to over 40 percent to check the expansion of money supply. Just what any country needs to scare away investors and destroy industry. (*Africa Report,* March/April 1995, 36).

Basic Freedoms

The three types of freedoms relevant for our study are intellectual (freedom of expression, of thought, and of the media), political, and economic. On each type, Africa scores worse than other regions in the Third World. Most African nations are members of the United Nations, which, in 1948, promulgated the Universal Declaration of Human Rights. Article 19, in particular, asserts: "Freedom of expression is not the product of any political system or ideology. It is a universal human right, defined and guaranteed in international law. . . . Everyone has the right to freedom of opinion and expression; this right includes freedom to hold opinions without interference and to seek, receive and impart information and ideas through any media regardless of boundaries."

African governments are supposed to observe October 21 each year as Africa Human Rights Day. But do they? According to *West Africa* (1-7 March 1993): "Since the African Charter of Human and Peoples' Rights came into force on October 21, 1986, after being ratified by a majority of member states of the OAU including Ghana, it became mandatory for OAU member states to observe the day as a way of sensitizing the people on human rights issues. In Ghana, as in many other African countries, the day is not observed" (327).

Actually, the day's purpose should sensitize the government, not the people. But trust the Organization of African Unity to get even this mixed up. According to New York–based Freedom House, of Africa's 54 countries, only seven have a free press. Of the 20 countries throughout the world where the press is most shackled, nine are in Africa: Algeria, Burundi, Egypt, Equatorial Guinea, Libya, Nigeria, Somalia, Sudan, and Zaire. Countries in the "not-free" category include Angola, Cameroon, Central African Republic, Chad, Eritrea, Ghana, Guinea, Ivory Coast, Kenya, Liberia, Mauritania, Rwanda, Sierra Leone, Swaziland, Togo, and Tunisia (*The African Observer,* 6-19 June 1996, 25).

A similar situation exists on political freedoms. Of the 54 African countries, only 14 are democratic: Benin, Botswana, Cape Verde Islands, Central African Republic, Madagascar, Malawi, Mali, Mauritius, Namibia, São Tomé & Principe, Senegal, Seychelles, South Africa, and Zambia.

Political tyranny is still the order of the day. Steve Mallory, publisher of *The African Observer* (May 2-15, 1995), put it succinctly:

> Three decades after independence, uncertainty and fear still rule the African continent. The freedom and justice that many people sacrificed their lives for have been replaced by tyranny and oppression. And the promise of a decent living has been betrayed by misgovernment and corruption.
>
> Most Africans fought so hard to liberate themselves from colonial rule only to be used and abused and their nations ruined by their own leaders. . . . The future of a half-billion people still looks gloomy as some despots have cleverly ducked the democratic wave blowing over the continent and others have taken undue advantage of it, legitimizing their brutal regimes via the ballot box. (3)

Africa is the most economically unfree continent in the world. The Heritage Foundation of Washington, D.C., compiled an Index of Economic Freedom for the world and concluded that: "Of the 38 sub-Saharan African countries graded, none received a score of free. Only 10 received a score of mostly free, 22 scored mostly unfree, and six were rated repressed. Of the 19 countries [worldwide] categorized as repressed, the majority are in sub-Saharan Africa" (Holmes et. al., 1997, xv).

In sum, the greatest obstacle to Africa's development is the absence of an enabling environment. Note that this obstacle is man-made— created by mafia African governments themselves. As such it can be removed only by *human action from within Africa*. Colonialism, Western imperialism, the slave trade, and other external factors have nothing to do with the creation of such an environment. The colonialists did not expunge the rule of law from postcolonial Africa. Even during the hated period of colonialism, there was law and order, not the lawlessness that is the norm in several African countries today. American "imperialists" did not order Mobutu to plunder the Zairean treasury. The Soviet Communists did not initiate the savage war against the people of Ethiopia. Nor did the World Bank tell Jerry Rawlings to unleash his security forces on peaceful demonstrators on 12 May 1995.

Political Instability: Coup Attempts

Most of Africa's tyrants are military men, with Idi Amin, Samuel Doe, Sani Abacha, and Mobutu Sese Seko being the most notorious and brutal. Because they seized power by staging a coup d'etat, other military officers may entertain similar designs on the presidency. Some do try, although many attempts have been unsuccessful. But the very attempt itself adds to the paranoia and insecurity of the regime, leading to even more repression and surveillance. Sandbrook (1993) captured this dilemma well: "The armed forces are generally the strongman's Achilles' heel. To capture and neutralize the army, the ruler has two options. He can transform it into a force led and, perhaps, manned by his followers, or he can build up a personally loyal counterforce. But there is a catch. Either route may provoke the officer corps if they perceive a threat to their prestige or professional autonomy" (99).

Paranoia and Overreaction

Because the tyrant knows he has done evil, he is afraid of his own shadow. One of his most nettlesome problems is how to guard his claim to the presidency. No potential challenger must be permitted to gain a power base. Even successful businesspeople must be kept under his leash. Everyone else must vie for his patronage. At Victoria Park during a political rally on 9 November 1996, President Rawlings of Ghana asked: "Where is the moral justification to support private enterprise when most of the opposition members were part of the problem?" (*Ghana Drum*, December 1996, 35). Therefore, he would starve or strangulate the private sector, sacrificing economic development for the political expediency of impoverishing the opposition.

He may resort to legislation to debar potential rivals based on their parentage. In Zambia, President Chiluba's government passed a law to disqualify former autocrat, Kenneth Kaunda, from running for the presidency because his parents were Malawians. In Côte d'Ivoire, President Henri Bedie passed a similar law—not only did it debar Alessane Ouattara, a former prime minister, but it also divided "the country for the foreseeable future into an entrenched inner circle and a group of outsiders" (*The Washington Times*, 17 October 1996, A19).

Even in that inner circle, suspicion, intrigue, and jostling flourish. Sycophants may outdo each other in proving how indispensable they are to the head of state. In their zeal, they may discredit associates, overstate their claims, fabricate and feed him false information. "At the opening of an annual agricultural show in President Daniel arap Moi of Kenya's home district of Baring, Agriculture Livestock and Marketing Minister Simeon Nyachae, accused unnamed Kenya African National Union bigwigs of *misinforming and misleading the president*" (*The African Observer*, 12-25 October 1995, 7).

Sycophants may tell the president such things such as: "The people love you," "In every village they call you the Messiah!" "As for the opposition, they have no support at all. You will beat them all!" Even if there is no good news to tell the president, the sycophant will manufacture one. "Don't mind the opposition, the foreign investors are coming. I saw them," he would say. Only sycophants would claim to have seen foreign investors.

Sometimes the information the sycophant passes on the president may be malicious and dangerous. "I saw this opposition leader and some men at a secret location, loading some boxes in the trunk of a car," he might tell the president. The sycophant may also snitch on business rivals and even neighbors he may dislike. The information he provides may be totally false but the paranoid president may conclude that the said person is plotting something against his regime and could have him "picked up" or, worse, disposed of. But what goes around comes around. Sooner or later, the president would realize that he is being fed false information and may decide to dispense with the sycophant.

Paranoia and overaction characterize personal rule. The overaction often emanates from sycophants and security personnel who suddenly find themselves overtaken by events they did not foresee. Such miscalculation may cost them their jobs—or even their lives. In Ghana, for example, sycophants had been telling President Rawlings how popular he was with the people.[2] On 12 May 1995 about 80,000 *Kume Preko* ("You might as well kill me") demonstrators marched through the streets of Accra to protest the imposition of a value-added tax that was popularly derided as "vampire tax." Sycophants and security personnel panicked and concluded that the president must not be allowed to see the protest, which must be dispersed immediately. So they unleashed ACDR (government-hired thugs) who opened fire on the peaceful demonstrators, killing four.

Nigeria held a presidential election on 12 June 1993 that was adjudged to be the freest and fairest in its history. The election was apparently won by Chief Moshood Abiola but was annulled by former military despot, General Ibrahim Babangida, who was himself ousted by General Sani Abacha. On the first anniversary of the annulment, Chief

---

2. President Rawlings himself found to his chagrin that "people who hitherto cheered me up in villages now insult me because the opposition politicians have been peddling lies against me in the newspapers" (*Ghana Drum*, December 1996, 35).

Abiola belatedly declared himself "president" and was immediately arrested on charges of treason. Unhappy, oil workers in the south staged a series of strikes that crippled oil production. The military regime's hysterical response was brutal repression. Pro-democracy protesters were gunned down; oil unions were proscribed and their leaders arrested—political leaders of a different persuasion—more than 100 senators, ex-governors, and human rights activists were detained. Nobel laureate Wole Soyinka fled the country. *The Guardian, The Concord, Newswatch,* and other newspapers were shut down and their editors arrested. On 27 September 1994 all civilians were expelled from the Provisional Ruling Council (PRC). About 40 people, including former head of state General Olusegun Obasanjo were arrested in March 1994 on trumped-up charges of plotting to overthrow the government. It is hard to imagine that all this brutality and repressive crackdown was occasioned by a simple dispute over an election result.

In Libya, Colonel Moammar Gadhafi, who seized power in a military coup in 1969 at the age of 27, has been grooming his son, Saidi, as his heir apparent. On 9 July 1996,

> At least 20 persons were killed at the Tripoli soccer stadium after spectators chanted slogans hostile to Colonel Gadhafi's son, Saidi, patron of one of the soccer teams. Saidi's retinue shot some of the spectators to death, others were killed in the crossfire or in a stampede to get out of the stadium.
>
> Exiles say the incident shows how sensitive Libya's rulers are to criticism and how public discontent has picked Saidi as a substitute for Colonel Gadhafi himself.
>
> "The people are just no longer interested in continuing on the course that Gadhafi has set for the last 27 years. They can't go on, and they reject the suggestion that Saidi might one day be put in charge," said one of the exiles. (*The Washington Times,* 17 July 1996, A13)

Decay of State Institutions

The African despot maintains his power base by dispensing patronage or by appealing to "tribal solidarity" from his kinsmen, who in return receive key government jobs There is no meritocracy—corruption runs rampant throughout the state. Very quickly, institutions such as the civil service, the judiciary, parliament, and the police break down and fail to function because they have all been perverted. Says Kenyan scholar Tom Ochieng, based in Charlotte, North Carolina: "Today in Kenya there is no rule of law. If you commit a crime, traffic offense or anything else, you only have to bribe the police. Your lawyer will even tell you to take something to the judge presiding over your case and the case will be delayed and eventually thrown out" (*African News Weekly*, 4 August 1995, 6).

The rot is not confined to one area but seeps into all areas of government. Parliament becomes a joke—rubber-stamp. The police, the military, and the civil service—all are hopeless. Even though the state soaks up scarce resources (through heavy taxation), it fails to fulfill its role in facilitating economic growth or delivering essential services. "Nigeria has many fine lawyers, but the judiciary is tainted by trials settled with bribes. It has fine academics, but universities are tarnished by the trade in diplomas. It has respected chiefs, but the nobility has been mocked by the sale of chieftaincy titles. In many ways, the institution which has suffered the most under this military regime is the military itself. 'Military men are not soldiers anymore' is a common Nigerian observation" (*The Economist*, 21 August 1993, Survey, 6).

People react by withdrawing from the state sector because it cannot provide even the most basic services, such as education and health care. As they withdraw from the state sector, they take their taxes with them or evade them altogether by bribing tax officials. The minister of finance then finds that, despite tax hikes on the order of 30 percent and the introduction of vampire taxes, government revenues still cannot cover expenditures. Kofi Apraku, a Ghanaian opposition member of parliament, reminded his colleagues that "The efficiency rate in tax collection is about 16 percent; and the Ministry of Finance itself projects that we can attain 22 per cent with a little bit of effort. But there is a long way to go yet" (*Ghana Parliamentary Debates*, 29 January 1997, 238). Because out of every tax dollar owed, only 16 cents tax are collected, projected budget surpluses turn out to be huge deficits. The central bank then covers the deficits by printing new currency and fueling inflation.

People begin to scoff at the pious utterances of the vampire elites regarding probity, accountability, unity, hard work, and sacrifice. As Sandbrook (1993) noted, "Political institutions such as the presidency, the parliament, the party, even the judiciary, lose whatever public esteem they commanded. Bureaucratic institutions also become ineffective and lose their technical rationality. Nepotism and patronage swell the bureaucratic ranks with incompetents and time-servers. Those civil servants who are competent and honest are demoralized by the graft, fraud, and theft of public property. Indiscipline and lassitude paralyze the bureaucratic apparatus" (113).

Administrative capability deteriorates. Institutionalized bureaucratic norms and practices are flouted. Simple routine tasks that normally
would require a day's work by a civil servant take weeks, if ever.
Accounting controls are often non-existent and two departments within
the same government ministry may not even know what the other is
doing. The capacity to execute plans, to implement reform (restructuring
plans), or even to manage the budget collapses. While in office, Ghana's
finance minister, Kwesi Botchwey, berated members of his own government of mismanagement, lack of satisfactory accountability, lack of
transparency, and corrupt procurement practices:

> He blamed the Accountant General for laxity and lapses which he said was
> making his ministry unable to monitor government spending. He said
> ministries were even breaching basic financial and administrative regula-
> tions that require monthly expenditure returns to his ministry. He said
> even when they did submit the returns, they were erratic. Although the
> Ministry of Finance had appointed consultants to straighten things up,
> officials were still being reckless and irresponsible.
> "They see their role as spenders and not keepers of accounting data.
> ... Many in the civil service do not consider budget management as part
> of their work," he lamented. (*Ghana Drum*, January 1995, 14)

Declining Investment

Africa has remained a wilderness to foreign investors for a variety of
reasons: weak currencies (except notably in extractive industries, where
output is priced in dollars), exchange controls, a feeble local private
sector, poor infrastructure, small domestic markets, stifling bureaucracy,
political instability, uncertain legal system, and corruption. Despite
fanciful ads, elaborate investment codes, and guarantees of profit
repatriation, Africa "attracts less than 5 percent of the direct investment
going to the developing countries, an estimated $2.5 billion or so in
1994" (*The Economist*, 12 August 1995, 11). In 1995 when a record
$231 billion in foreign investment flowed into the Third World, Africa's
share fell to a miserly 2.4 percent.

Crumbling infrastructure, chronic instability, and the mafia govern-
ments' penchant for terror and violence have deterred foreign investors.
According to Stephen Buckley, a black American from the *Washington
Post* (31 December 1996): "The continent's lack of preparedness for a

new model of global economic growth is linked to a history pocked with wars, coups and counter-coups. Since the late 1950s, 25 African countries have undergone at least one violent government change, with some entrenching coups as political rituals. Meanwhile, many longtime dictators and strongmen have held their economies hostage, maintaining unprofitable state-owned enterprises, keeping high tariffs and price controls and explicitly supporting corruption" (A12).

Even French investors are shying away from Africa for precisely the same reasons. According to the *African Observer* (4-17 April 1995), "Africa's share of French overseas investment dwindled from $500 million in 1983 to $170 million in 1992, [Jean-Pierre] Ranchon [vice president of the Council of French Investors in Africa] said. Asia's grew from $4 million to $600 million over the same period" (22).

With the help of the World Bank and Western donor agencies, which touted the country as "Africa's economic star," Ghana launched an ambitious effort to draw foreign investors in the mid-1980s, revamping its once-onerous investment code and offering generous incentives to outside entrepreneurs. It established export processing zones. Having embraced the free market/private enterprise formula that brought prosperity to countries from the Philippines to Chile, Ghanaians waited, waited, and waited for their own economic takeoff.

With the exception of the mining sector, where investment is not politically sensitive, Ghana's campaign for foreign capital foundered. Critical areas such as agriculture and manufacturing, both with the potential to produce large numbers of jobs, have attracted relatively little investment. Overall, foreign investment comprises only 4 percent of Ghana's gross domestic product. A government campaign to woo foreign investors with ads in major Western newspapers failed miserably, as did the campaign to export nontraditional exports, such as pineapples. Stephen Buckley analyzed the reasons why foreign investors stayed away from Ghana and much of Africa: "Potential agricultural investors, like foreign investors generally, are often scared off by the country's unreliable infrastructure, especially in rural areas, which often do not have telephones, electricity or water and where many roads are impassable. . . . Electricity is sporadic, even in parts of the capital. Some sections of Accra are without water most of each week. . . . Education is critical to foreign investors. In Ghana, as in many other African countries, there is no critical mass of workers with secondary school education."

There are 3.5 phones for every 1,000 Ghanaians and to get one may take months of entreaties and bribery.[3] Ghana offered foreign investors a patina of incentives. They included 8 percent income taxes for companies that invest in nontraditional exports; tax writeoffs for those that invest in agriculture and manufacturing; and some exemptions on customs duties. One hundred per cent foreign ownership was even included in the package. Yet in 1996, foreign investment outside the mining, petroleum, and timber sectors dropped sharply, from $94 million for the first half of 1995 to $41.2 million for the same period in 1996 (*The Washington Post,* 31 December 1996, A12).

Government officials themselves have admitted that elegant foreign investment codes and numerous conferences on investment opportunities failed to bring foreign investors. Emma Mitchell, former Minister of Trade and Industry, told a forum during President Rawlings' visit to Britain in July 1995 that since they established the Ghana Investment Promotion Center, they had signed close to $1.5 billion of investment contracts but none of the investors seemed to be coming back—because there was no decent infrastructure for doing business in Ghana (*Free Press,* 20 July–3 August 1995, 12). She could have added the following: bureaucratic red tape, soaring inflation, declining value of the local currency, and schizophrenic posturing on private enterprise. One day, the regime "welcomes" foreign investors and then the next day launch vituperative insults against them for "exploiting Africa."

Nigeria's military government also took a naive, mechanical approach to foreign investment, issuing in March 1995 "The Nigerian Investment Promotion Decree" to guarantee foreign investment against nationalization or expropriation by government. The decree supposedly would establish a framework for encouraging foreign investment by providing a deregulated and debureaucratized atmosphere for foreign investment. Nothing was said about ensuring the reliability of basic essential services, which affect domestic production too: "The high cost of foodstuff and other essential commodities in Jalingo, the Taraba State capital, has put food out of the reach of many. . . . The reasons for the high cost of essential goods in the state are many. They include lack of a good road network, linking the state with commercial cities and towns, inadequate electricity and portable water for industrial services and the

---

3. Sub-Saharan Africa averages 4 phones per 1,000 people, compared to 4 per 100 in Asia and 6 per 100 in Latin America.

ineffectiveness of the Taraba State Consumers Protection Council. In the past, Taraba has been the food basket of the nation" (*African News Weekly*, 1 September 1995, 15).

Finally the military regime came to its senses. On 30 May 1995 Finance Minister Anthony Ani said that the military government was determined to redress constraints such as inadequate infrastructural and market facilities by providing and improving infrastructural facilities such as electricity and roads (*African News Weekly*, 16 June 1995, 8).

Indeed, according to a 1995 report by the Nigerian Institute of Social and Economic Research, the country was losing foreign invest ment because the *naira* had little value abroad and because there was little foreign exchange available to meet the investor's demands. In an 18-month period, from January 1994 to mid-1995, at least 12 foreign partners pulled out of Nigeria. In 1994, there was almost no new investment in the country. Other reasons besides poor infrastructure included high inflation, low purchasing power of consumers, safety and security of life and property, high tariffs, and political instability.

During a symposium on 18-19 September 1996 in Brussels, Zaire's prime minister, Kengo wa Dondo, tried to persuade representatives of some 130 companies to invest in his country. But legal security of investments weighed heavily on investors' minds. "Many still shudder from the memory of the wholesale 'Zairanization' of foreign assets in the early 1970s . . . While investment prospects in Zaire are tempting, many investors would prefer to see political stability take shape first before they risk investing" (*African Business*, November 1996, 30).

These considerations were important even to China, which in the early 1990s was providing the bulk of foreign investment in Africa while other nations stayed away. "'China State Construction Engineering Corporation had a two-year delay on a Zaire stadium project because of political instability,' says Luo Chao, a deputy general manager. 'Only if the countries remain stable can we make even a small profit,' he says" (*The Wall Street Journal*, 19 July 1996, A9). The International Finance Corporation, the private-sector arm of the World Bank, designed to act as a banker to businesses investing in poor countries, has written off all its loans to Zaire and has made none since 1992 (*The Economist*, 9 November 1996, 95).

However, the emphasis on foreign investment is totally misplaced. The focus ought to be placed on domestic investors. Said Brehane Mewa, vice president of Addis Ababa Chamber of Commerce and president of the Ethiopian Industries Association: "In order to bring change to this country, the economy should be built by local investors. . . . The bottom line is that the private sector is the engine of growth. If it is indigenous, the result will be more fruitful. You only need to look at South Korea to realize the importance of the local entrepreneur" (*African Business,* November 1996, 32).

If Africans themselves won't invest in their own countries, why should foreigners? Even Nigerians are unwilling to risk locking their capital into long-term investments. "The Manufacturing Association of Nigeria says that 700 of its 1,500 members have closed their doors since 1987" (*The Economist,* 21 August 1993, Survey, 7). Do foreign investors know more than Nigerians or the locals? And have African governments drawn up investment codes to spur domestic investors?

The case of Ghana is also typical. Few local investors are ready to put money into job-creating industries like fishing, farming and manu-facturing because "Jerry Rawlings annoys businessmen by denouncing commerce as corrupt. After he and his small band of soldiers took power in 1981, they accused private companies of 'economic sabotage' and confiscated their assets. Although they embraced the IMF two years later, the government still sends soldiers to deal with people suspected of 'economic crimes,' mostly meaning bribery of officials, which is com-mon. Arbitrary attacks do little for business confidence: businessmen still fear that Mr. Rawlings himself, or another band of plotters, will change the rules again" (*The Economist,* 22 August 1992, 34).

In 1989, there were two prominent cases of such confiscation in Ghana. In the first case involving Dr. Kwame Safo-Adu, an African Development Bank and World Bank credit was secured to establish a pharmaceutical factory at Kumasi that employed about 30 Ghanaians. Strangely perceived as a political threat, his home was attacked by two brigades of military personnel in February 1988. Both groups were disguised as "armed robbers" and, apparently mistaking the other as real robbers, shooting erupted between them. Before it was over, two of them lay dead. On 3 November 1989, the pharmaceutical factory was cordoned off and closed by a battalion of 400 armed soldiers.

The second case involved International Tobacco (ITG) Ghana Limited, which was established in 1976 by a Ghanaian, B. A. Mensah, of Ghana International Tobacco. In 1988 the company fell into custom and excise arrears. The Ghanaian government claimed the company collected 993 million *cedis* ($3.2 million) in excise duties and sales tax but failed to pay it to the government. The company cited structural adjustment and its deleterious impact on the working capital of many indigenous entrepreneurs. The PNDC appointed a committee on 29 September 1988, to examine the peculiar nature of the financial and operational problems facing ITG with a view of finding ways of assisting them to overcome their problems. The committee consisted of officials from National Revenue Secretariat, the Ministry of Finance and Economic Planning, the Ministry of Industry, Science and Technology, and the Ghana Investment Center.

The committee accepted Mensah's proposal to reconstitute the company into a tripartite equity participation arrangement. The other two partners were to be Rothmans International, which is London-based, and Ghana's State Security and National Investment Trust (SSNIT), with participation ratios of 33 1/3 percent. The arrangement was to enable an infusion of external cash of £ 975,000 pounds sterling from Rothmans International for the settlement of the customs excise tax arrears.

But suddenly on 26 July 1989 Mensah was ordered to have nothing to do with ITG. The Customs Service seized the plant, equipment, buildings, and other property and closed the factory. A new company, Meridian Tobacco Company, was incorporated in its place to produce ITG's products but without assuming any of ITG's liabilities and staff. The government's SSNIT share was raised to 56 percent with Rothmans International holding the remaining 44 percent. In this way, a wholly private company became a joint-venture with the state holding majority shares.

African governments provide few incentives to local investors. They often harbor deep suspicions toward successful local businessmen because they might pose a political challenge. "Accordingly, fairly successful entrepreneurs are watched and harassed for fear that they may become centers of opposition; and this happens even when they do not show signs of political ambition" (Ake, 1991b, 322).

After ten years of economic reform in Ghana, *The Washington Post* (7 September 1992) noted: "So far, private business remains wary of Ghana. There has been scant new investment, Ghanaian or foreign, except in mining. . . . Part of the problem seems to be Rawlings himself. Upon taking power, he emulated previous military regimes and labeled private business people as agents of corruption" (A24).

President Rawlings even went further:

> In a flush of emotion, President Rawlings made what should pass as the most disastrous dampener on private enterprise when he harangued against some of Ghana's distinguished businessmen at a mini-rally held in Accra

on June 4, 1993. He told his glum-faced audience to be wary of rich
businessmen who had amassed wealth over the years, some of them
through stealing, and lamented that the businesses that would have
belonged to those in the audience in Nkrumah's time "are now in private
hands, which use the money for all sorts of things including financing
political parties."

But the eye-popping climax of what was seen as his campaign against
private initiative was when he got personal with Kwabena Darko, Appiah-
Menka and Dr. J. A. Addison and exposed them to ridicule and contempt.
In the most savage dig at Appiah-Menka, the soap king, the President
lamented that he was using his money from the proceeds of his soap to
finance a political party and reasoned that when people buy his soap they
are giving him money to finance his party. (*Ghana Drum*, July 1993, 6)

President Rawlings subsequently urged Ghanaians not to buy Apino
soap or any of the products of the Ghanaian entrepreneurs who worked
for the opposition. Imagine a president telling his people not to patronize
the products of his own country. Whose business is it what a private
businessman chooses to do with his own money? Some Ghanaian
entrepreneurs accuse Rawlings himself of still harboring disdain for the
private sector.

Economic Contraction and Collapse

The mafia African government cannot attract foreign investment or spur
domestic investment. The prevailing environment, characterized by
oppression, brutality, cruelty, absence of rule of law, corruption, political
instability, and a deteriorating infrastructure, deter investors, both
foreign and domestic. The government is forced to rely more and more
on foreign aid, but foreign aid does not provide the key to self-sustaining
growth. "In many cases, foreign aid has sustained governments in their
pursuit of economically counterproductive political and economic policies" (Congressional Budget Office, 1997, 8).

To secure investable resources, recourse is made to the coercive
apparatus of the government. Like the colonial state, the vampire
African state is also extractive. But the fact most analysts may find
uncomfortable is this: The vampire African state is as bad, if not worse
than the hated authoritarian colonial state that Africans overwhelmingly rejected in the 1960s. Under colonialism, Africa's resources and
wealth were plundered for the development of metropolitan European

countries. Today the tiny, parasitic ruling elites use their governing authority to exploit and extract resources from the productive members of the society, which are then spent lavishly by the elites on themselves. The similarities, however, end there. As Robinson (1971) asked plaintively: "What incentive does the peasant have to produce more when through taxation the surplus is siphoned off to be spent in conspicuous consumption?" (43).

People become alienated, as the Nigerian scholar Claude Ake (1991b), noted eloquently. "Most African regimes have been so alienated and so violently repressive that their citizens see the state as enemies to be evaded, cheated and defeated if possible, but never as partners in development. The leaders have been so engrossed in coping with the hostilities which their misrule and repression has unleashed that they are unable to take much interest in anything else including the pursuit of development. These conditions were not conducive to development and none has occurred. What has occurred is regression, as we all know only too well" (14).

The economy limps along or contracts. The contraction is accelerated by large-scale flight out of the formal economy. People lose faith in the ability of the government to provide basic services (housing, health care, water, and electricity) and jobs and to combat corruption. A growing sense of alienation and disaffection among the larger population sets in. A huge credibility gap emerges between the people and the leadership

Desperate, people turn increasingly to clandestine economic transactions in the parallel or informal economy to keep their incomes and assets out of the reach of the state. These are survival mechanisms. The parallel economy is called *magendo* in East Africa and *kalabule* in Ghana, but everywhere its activities are similar. They involve hoarding, exchange of goods above the official price, smuggling, illegal currency deals, bribery, and corruption (Sandbrook, 1993, 139).

With time, larger and larger segments of the economy slip out of the control of the government. It soon finds that its control does not extend beyond a few miles of the capital—as was the case for the late Samuel Doe regime in Liberia, the late Siad Barre regime in Somalia, and Mobutu Sese Seko of Zaire.

Angry Peasants Battling the Predatory State

During the liberation struggle in the 1960s, the masses were promised a "veritable paradise" after independence. But for many "the veritable paradise" turned out to be a starvation diet, unemployment, and a gun to the head. "Everything we have has been taken from us by the military," says Ken Anamudu, a geologist in Lagos, Nigeria. Disaffection and alienation have soared. African masses are restless and angry. All sorts of groups are fighting against the naked rape of their resources by mafia governments. In Ghana, Yaw Amoafo expressed this very well in *The Daily Graphic* (17 February 1982):

> Despite noises being made about the exploitation of the people, it is the STATE, as the Chief Vanguard, and her so-called Public Servants, Civil Servants which actually exploit others in the country. The money used in buying the cars for Government officials, the cement for building estates and other Government bungalows which workers obtain loans to buy, the rice workers eat in their staff canteens, the soap, the toothpaste, textiles cloth which workers buy under the present distribution system all come from the farmers' cocoa and coffee money. . . .
>
> This STATE-MONOPOLY CAPITALISM has been going on since the days of the colonial masters and even our own Governments after independence have continued the system.
>
> The farmers realising this naked exploitation decided unconsciously that they would no longer increase cocoa and coffee production, they would not increase food production and any other items which the State depends on for foreign exchange. In effect, there will be no surplus for the State to exploit. (3)

Those who are exploited economically or excluded from the spoils of power may seek remedies in several ways. Farmers who are exploited by artificially low producer prices may withdraw (exit option) from the formal economy, reduce production, or smuggle their produce out of the country. Smuggling of cocoa, coffee, diamonds, gold, and other commodities is a daily phenomenon in Africa. For example, in 1982, Ghana's cocoa production hit its lowest until reforms were adopted in 1983 that increased the producer price to farmers. Prior to that, Côte d'Ivoire surpassed Ghana as the largest producer of cocoa, but much of the former's output was in fact cocoa smuggled from Ghana. Cash crop farmers also may switch production—from cocoa to, say, maize. Or they may even desist from producing altogether and move to the urban areas for "a piece of the action." While these responses are passive, active options are available.

In Côte d'Ivoire, once touted by the World Bank as an African "success story," angry citizens took to the streets to protest hopeless life in perpetual poverty. In October 1992 university students boycotted end-of-year examinations to protest the government's new education policy, which required them to pay higher bus fares. Unemployed youths also went on the rampage, blocking midday rush hour traffic. Meanwhile, anger was seething in the countryside, where 80 percent of the country's 12 million population lives. They produce over 80 percent of the country's wealth—cocoa, coffee, cotton, banana, and pineapple. But years of neglect by the government and lack of development finally prompted them to take action. As *West Africa* (7-13 December 1992) reported:

> They held a meeting at Anyama, on the outskirts of Abidjan, after which they issued an ultimatum to the government to address their demands, which included better prices for their produce. A deadline of 15 October was set.
>
> Realising that things were getting out of hand, President Felix Houphouet-Boigny himself hosted the leaders [of the farmers] at his private residence in Yamassoukrou. . . . The angry farmers demanded that they should be involved in selling direct to the consumers, to ensure that they know how much the country is earning from abroad. The government agreed. (2098)

Nigeria's oil wealth is produced in the Niger delta, which has been the scene of one such rebellion. The entire delta area with 6 million people, consisting of 20 tribes, has been devastated. For instance, in Nembe, home to several thousand people on the edge of Nigeria's largest oil field, there is no electricity, clean water, or roads or other basic amenities. Gas is burned there, causing environmental pollution. Nor does the area have a major oil refinery. In a policy that defies economic sense, oil is piped from the delta area hundreds of miles to the north, where it is refined to provide employment and industrial activity to Hausa-Fulani who have monopolized political power since Nigeria's independence in 1960.

Hardest hit in the Niger delta are the Ogoni, who number 500,000 and sit on top of billions of dollars of oil reserves. But "we get no benefit from it, absolutely none," complained Chief Edward Kobani, a senior elder of the Ogoni. Their homeland is an environment mess. Gas—a by-product of the oil industry for which there is no use—is burned 24 hours a day, producing acid rain and toxic pollution. Air and water quality has suffered, crops damaged. The health toll is enormous: high levels of skin rashes, allergies, abscesses, and infections. Ken Saro-Wiwa started the Movement for the Survival of the Ogoni People (MOSOP), demanded $10 billion for environmental damage and royalties from the federal government and Royal Dutch/Shell, and threatened to secede from Nigeria. The group wrote an Ogoni national anthem, designed a national flag, and printed a national currency. Frightened of another Biafra, the military government attacked Ogoni villages. In May 1995 Saro-Wiwa was arrested; he and eight others were hanged on 10 November despite a chorus of international pleas for clemency. But the Ogoni have not given up their fight.

The 120,000 inhabitants of Cabinda, a tiny enclave that forms part of Angola, also have huge oil reserves from which they derive no benefit. The Cabinda Enclave Liberation Front-Armed Forces of Cabinda, known as FLEC-FAC, has been fighting since 1975 for independence for the region. "The rebels complain that people in Cabinda live in poverty while the Angolan government strips the region of its riches—diamonds, manganese, timber and most importantly oil. Cabinda produces more oil than any other region in Sub-Saharan Africa except Nigeria, and Angola receives more than $3 billion each year for its share of pumping operations run by U.S.-based Gulf Oil. '[But] our territory is completely underdeveloped, with no roads, no cities,' said Izias Mayo, minister of education and youth in a shadow government set up by the rebels" (*The African Observer,* 12-19 June 1996, 32).

Child soldiery has become an increasing problem in Africa. But economic conditions have become so precarious that adults would approve of any means to remove a hated regime from power. Similar conditions simmered at Obuasi, a gold-mining town in Ghana:

> Fears are mounting over the growing tension between the illegal miners and gold-mining companies in Ghana as unemployed youths become more desperate to grab a piece of the wealth they see being extracted from around their villages. . . . At least 1,000 illegal miners, known as *galamsey,* a local word that means "gather them and sell," armed themselves with blow guns, clubs, knives and machetes in June and attacked Ashanti Goldfields security men who tried to run them off a particularly rich site. The miners also stole about 50,000 chickens from the company's poultry farm, ransacked the building and injured three policemen. (*The Washington Post,* 16 July 1996, A10)

These examples can be multiplied a hundred times elsewhere in Africa, where the masses are stirring and have vowed not to sit idly by while they are being raped by vampire elites. Some African villagers are openly defying tax officers: "The Loulouni district chief was thrown out of the village when he tried to collect taxes on Feb. 2 1995. The chief returned on Feb. 9 with a battalion of police and paramilitary gendarmes. Enraged villagers met them with clubs and hunting rifles. Two peasants and eight policemen were wounded in the ensuing clash" (*African News Weekly,* 3 March 1995, 5).

Fed up with a deteriorating economy marked by a rising inflation and the hopeless inability of the elites to resolve the matter, peasant groups set up their own "parallel government" on 18 March 1995 in Madagascar. Two of their leaders, Andranalijaona Nuniamanampy and Francois Andrianantoandro, who had been named "coprime ministers," were arrested by the government. An official communique said the arrests were ordered because the group was confusing the public (*African News Weekly,* 7 April 1995, 5).

The African people are turning their wrath on the crocodile liberators who often are no better than the despots they set out to overthrow. In Liberia, the people were tired of the warlords. On 19 December 1994 thousands of angry Liberians marched through the capital carrying machetes to send a message to the warlords departing for yet another peace conference in Ghana not to return without a peace treaty.

At that conference, a six-member Council of State was proposed to govern Liberia until elections were held in November 1995. The conference immediately broke down under fierce jostling for the chairmanship. Frustrated, an irate Obed Asamoah, Ghana's foreign minister, expelled the Liberian delegates. When the news reached Monrovia, Liberia's capital, about 1,000 angry protestors, brandishing machetes and homemade bazookas, raced to the airport to meet the warlords. Flight plans were quickly changed in midair and the warlords headed for Côte d'Ivoire. Enraged, the protestors rioted for three days, blocking the main bridge in Monrovia, burning tires, and stoning vehicles. Eight people died in the rampage.

A year earlier Charles Julue, the former chief of the Armed Forces of Liberia, led about 100 disgruntled AFL fighters who briefly seized the seat of power on 15 September 1994 and declared himself president. They were forced out by a massive assault by the ECOMOG forces. But when Julue tried to slip out of the country, disguised as an Arab, the people recognized him. He was quickly grabbed, stripped, and beaten severely before being handed over to the ECOMOG forces.

THE IMPLOSION

The African mafia state cannot and will not endure. Its extractive and exploitative ethic is morally and philosophically indefensible. Africans fought against the relatively less rapacious form of exploitation under colonialism. So too will they fight against mafia African regimes—or black neo-colonialists. Nor can that "state vehicle" be used to take Africans on the "development" journey. Only a few live the charmed, opulent life. The rest of the population is excluded. But those excluded will take the abuse and the rape for only so long.

Angry peasants may not only withdraw, taking with them potential tax revenues, but also may fight back, sabotaging the property of the predatory state and attacking its officials. Fed up with incessant power interruptions, they wreaked vengeance on "NEPA equipment in protest against power failures starting around the time of the World Cup televised from the United States. They also allegedly vandalized property worth about 212,000 *naira* [about $2,500] at the water treatment plant in the area to protest the perennial water shortage" (*African News Weekly,* 4 November 1994, 12).

In every society, there must be an avenue for people to vent their frustrations and release excess pressure. In civilized societies, when people are angry at their government, they may protest, hold demonstrations, lambaste the government in the newspapers or on the radio, or toss out the errant regime at the ballot box. But in most African countries, the mafia government has blocked each of these avenues.

In Ghana there has been a pattern of brutalities and blockage. On 22 March 1993 university students at Legon began a boycott of classes to press their demands for an increase in student loans. They were attacked and beaten up mercilessly by thugs hired by the ruling NDC regime. Libel suits were another weapon. When newspapers tried to expose corruption and wrongdoing by NDC government officials, they were slapped with criminal libel suits. "At least 30 libel suits have been filed against the independent press by leading members of the government in what is seen largely as an attempt to stifle freedom of expression," said Kwesi Pratt, Jr., President of the Private Newspaper Publishers Association of Ghana (PRINPAG) (Free Press, 20 December–2 January 1997, 8).

On 4 December 1994 police raided the premises of Charles Wereko-Brobbey, seized the transmission equipment of Radio Eye, and arrested five persons, including two Britons. When supporters of the radio station marched to parliament on 8 December they were attacked by thugs and beaten up. On 12 May 1995 over 80,000 Ghanaians marched through the streets of Accra to protest the unbearable cost of living and demand the withdrawal of the VAT. ACDR thugs opened fire, killing four of them. On 28 December 1995 when Vice President Arkaah went to a cabinet meeting, he was beaten up. On 1 June 1996 the National Union of Ghanaian Students held a demonstration to protest deplorable conditions at the country's universities. They were attacked and beaten by government-hired thugs.

In all these provocations, Ghanaians were counseled to be patient and that they would get their chance to throw the vampire elites out of power at the 7 December 1996 polls. They turned out in massive numbers—about 80 percent of the registered voters—to vote. But the elections were rigged. As a result, a significant number of Ghanaians have lost faith in the electoral process. "They have vowed not to vote in any future elections if the voting pattern of Ghanaians remain the same. . . . After all, they know that even if the right man is there, he will not be chosen. Madam Ama Mensah, a trader of Obuasi Central Market, and a host of other tomato sellers in the market emphatically said in their remarks that they would never vote again in their lives because they had come to realize that truth does not matter in Ghana politics" (*Free Press,* 13-19 December 1996, 6).

If people lose faith in the ballot box, they may decide not to vote again or may seek alternate ways of removing a hated government from power. Several such options are available. People may decide to cheat the government, since the government cheated them of their vote. They may cheat on their taxes, refuse to recognize the regime or attend its functions. They may embezzle or sabotage government operations and generally make life miserable for the government, or render the country "ungovernable." Any of these methods would raise government expenditures and subsequently the deficit. They may also withdraw their services and refuse to deal with a government they regard as "illegitimate." Or they may resort to violence. Predictably on 10 December 1996 supporters of the ruling NDC reveled in the streets of Bimbilla, celebrating their "victory" in the election. They taunted opposition members, who went home to fetch machetes and butchered several of the NDC revelers.

People will not tolerate injustice, brutality, and abuse indefinitely. K. A. Britwum, the Ashanti Regional Secretary of the New Patriotic Party [Ghana's main opposition party], said that the organization will not allow the NDC to terrorize its supporters and members. "Referring to the brutalities meted out by certain military and NDC machomen to

NPP supporters during the Afigya-Sekyere parliamentary by-election, Britwum warned that the NPP will in any future elections match the NDC boot for boot in all aspects of the game of brutalities and intimidation, if need be, adding that 'After all, violence is not the monopoly of any one group or group of persons'" (*Free Press,* 25 June–1 July 1997, 3).

Similarly in Nigeria, the military rulers have blocked every avenue for redress of political and social grievances. Brutalities have been heaped on activists, who have therefore resorted to violence. A group calling itself the United Front for Nigeria's Liberation (UFNL) claimed responsibility for an 18 January 1996 plane crash in which head of state General Sani Abacha's first son and 14 others were killed (*The African Observer,* 1-14 February 1996, 2). The next day, 19 January 1996, two bombs went off at two locations connected to Abacha: the Kaduna Hotel, which he allegedly owned, and Kano Airport, which was the major transit point for people attending his son's funeral. Since then bombs went off intermittently in 1996, causing the U.S. State Department to issue an alert to Americans traveling to Nigeria.

In several other African countries such as Cameroon, Gabon, Kenya, Libya, and Sudan, political strife and discontent are brewing. As noted earlier, on 7 July 1997 church leaders, opposition politicians, student groups, and civic organizations demonstrated in Nairobi, demanding constitutional reform to level the political playing field before elections scheduled for later that year. The opposition claimed that free and fair elections could not be held unless changes were made. President Moi, who had been in power for 19 years, controlled all the levers of power: the parliament, security forces, judiciary, and electoral commission. His police shot, clubbed, and tear-gassed the demonstrators, including Reverend Timothy Njoya of the Presbyterian Church of East Africa. Eleven people were killed.

The politics of exclusion has been the basic cause of turmoil in Africa. Eventually, those excluded from the political spoils eventually will rise up and set out to either overthrow the system or secede. The Biafran War of 1967 is an example. Regardless, secession or insurgency degenerates into violence, chaos, and destruction. The Liberian civil war started in 1989 when the excluded group (Americo-Liberians, Mandingos, and Moslems) set out to remove Samuel Doe and his Krahnmen from power. The 1994 Rwandan massacre began when Tutsi rebels set off from Uganda to remove the Hutus from power. The disintegration of Zaire began with rebellion led by Laurent Kabila in 1996 with easterners excluded from power by Mobutu. Civil war and strife, together with famine, have claimed the lives of at least 5 million Africans since independence in the 1960s and have driven millions more into exile.

But Africa's mafia governments have learned nothing from all these civil wars and this carnage. They repeat the same foolish mistakes again and again in country after country. In the next chapter, we shall spell out what can be done to prevent the collapse of more African states.

CHAPTER 7

The Acrobatics on Reform

In Africa, political transitions are occurring without political
transformations. It is necessary, therefore, to distinguish
between mere demilitarization of politics and the democratization of politics. Military leaders have simply changed into
civilian leaders; the personalities and political culture have
not really changed. Nor has the African military given up its
traditional role. It has been and remains anti-people and
repressive.
—J. Kayode Fayemi, Deputy Editor, *Africa World Review*
(London), at the National Endowment For Democracy
Conference, 13 March 1995 in Washington, D.C.

INTRODUCTION

The state as usually understood, does not exist in Africa, as we saw in
chapter 5. It has been taken over by gangsters. All the important
institutions that are crucial for running countries have been debauched:
the army, police, civil service, state media, parliament, judiciary, central
bank, and educational system. Parliament is either nonexistent or a
charade. Each institution has been packed with the tyrant's tribesmen
and sycophants. Professionalism and accountability in these institutions
have been destroyed. The result is the institutional breakdown evidenced
in many African countries. A program of reform or a complete overhaul
of the defective state vehicle is needed.

Few would quibble with these imperatives, but nettlesome questions
emerge. Can the state vehicle be fixed, or must it be discarded? Who
should initiate and execute reform? And how competent, credible, and
committed is the reformer? Since scrapping is impractical, the state
vehicle must be reclaimed, the reckless driver tossed out, and each system
checked and rewired.

In practical terms, de facto apartheid systems must be dismantled; erected in their places must be democratic systems that admit open participation by those who have heretofore been excluded. The system whereby one group monopolizes both economic and political power is untenable and ultimately explosive. Further, the state's stranglehold on the economy also must be broken and economic power returned to the people. This requires market liberalization and privatization measures. The other major reform needed is institutional. The various institutions of society or government must be reformed and professionalism established in each. Soldiers must do what they are trained to do and not impose themselves on the political arena. The judiciary must learn how to dispense justice, fairly and without fear or favor and so on.

Because reform is required in so many areas, sequencing is critical. Broadly categorized, the areas in which reform must take place may be delineated as institutional, political, intellectual, and economic. Since Africa's political and economic systems are inseparable, most analysts affirm that economic and political reform must go hand in hand. However, they do not address where the institutional and intellectual systems should be placed in the sequence or where to begin. Perhaps by deductive analysis, we can make some headway.

Nobel-prize winning economist Milton Friedman made an important point: Political freedom is essential to a nation's economic success. Free press is vital for a free market because it enables people to make informed decisions. If that is missing, then the push for economic autonomy will surely fail because "you cannot have a free press and have a centralized, authoritarian government" (*The Wall Street Journal,* 12 February 1997, A16).

First of all, economic reform cannot be implemented in an African country where a civil war or strife is raging. Most of Africa's civil wars are really conflicts over yet-unresolved political issues pertaining to the right of participation in the decision-making process, a secessionist endeavor, or an effort to remove a despotic regime from power. Recall from chapter 2, that a dispute over some aspect of the electoral process— blockage, manipulation, subversion, and annulment—always triggers civil war. Had this process been blocked or subverted in South Africa, Benin, Zambia, or Malawi, each country would have blown up too. Clearly, the economies of Algeria, Angola, Burundi, Liberia, Nigeria, Rwanda, Somalia, Sudan, and Zaire cannot be meaningfully reformed until the political question has been settled.

The institution of democracy may not necessarily rescue the economy of an African country but it makes all the difference whether the country—and therefore, the economy—exists or not. Said Adebayo Adedeji, former secretary-general of the United Nations' Economic Commission on Africa, "People will never comprehend Africa's crisis so long as they continue to assume that it is an economic one.... What we confront in Africa is primarily a political crisis, albeit with devastating economic consequences" (*The Economist*, 7 September 1996, Survey, 4). The authoritarian postcolonial state assumed the roles of economic regulator, planner, and entrepreneur. Africa's experience suggests that economic reform under dictatorships is generally not sustainable. The continent is characterized by dictatorships or weak authoritarian regimes that maintain their authority through personalistic patron-client relations. These relationships are prone to sudden and erratic changes, which produce political instability. This instability impedes the correction of structural economic imbalances.

Indeed, many of the African countries the World Bank restructured into "economic success stories" did finally hit the "political ceiling" and began to unravel: They included Cameroon, Côte d'Ivoire, Ghana, Kenya, Malawi, Nigeria, and Zaire. In 1989 Côte d'Ivoire was declared a success story but its fortunes began to sink after 1990, with the decline in world commodity prices and even further with political turmoil after the 1991 elections.

After the death of its *Le Vieux*, Felix Houphouet-Boigny, in 1993, Henri Konan Bedie, the speaker of the parliament, assumed control. For the presidential elections in 1995, he rammed through parliament an electoral code designed to ensure his victory. Protests led to violent clashes with security personnel on 16 October 1995, and five lives were lost. "Only a politician like Bedie could have made such a mess of things," said an irate World Bank official. "Only he could have turned an economic success story into a political nightmare that this is turning out to be" (*The Washington Times*, 19 October 1995, A14).

Recall the statement by Andrew Uchendu, a constitutional delegate from oil-rich Rivers State in the southeast Nigeria: "All the problems Nigeria contends with today have to do with the struggle for power" (*The African Observer*, 2-15 May 1995, 11). Meaningful economic reform cannot occur under the watchful eyes of Nigeria's military coconutheads unless the power equation is resolved. A leader who is not willing to relinquish control over the economy or whose basic beliefs are antithetical to free-market philosophy creates more problems for investors by sending out contradictory and erratic signals. A new pro-market leader would make things easier.

In the same vein, significant institutional reform can be achieved more readily under a new leader. This was exactly the stance taken by the United States in regard to reforming the bloated U.N. bureaucracy. Dissatisfied with his ineffectual management style and ineptitude at reforming the United Nations, in December 1996, the United States vetoed a second term for Secretary-General Boutros Boutros Ghali. This paved the way for the election of Kofi Annan, who, as the new United Nations chief, would have a clean slate to implement needed reforms. If only the United States and Western countries would take a similar stance in regards to African reform. However, resolving the leadership and political issues requires "intellectual freedom," as Malawi's recent experience eloquently attests.

On 5 February 1993 the regime of Life-President Hastings Banda promulgated a series of regulations that would govern the 14 June 1993 referendum to determine the country's political future. The referendum question was: "Do you wish that Malawi remains with the one-party system of government with the Malawi Congress Party (MCP) as the sole political party or do you wish that Malawi changes to the multiparty system of government?" Could Malawians freely debate this question in a country where "in every village, party and police informers and the paramilitary Malawi Young Pioneers report the smallest expression of dissent and the president can use his powers, under the Preservation of Public Security, to detain people indefinitely and without charge" (*West Africa*, 24-30 May 1993, 867).

The 5 February regulations failed to permit freedom of expression and offered members of MCP immunity from prosecution for violence and intimidation during the referendum campaign, without a concurrent offer of immunity for the ordinary voter. Written police permission was required for any type of public political campaigning, even the handing out of leaflets. "School teachers who volunteered to be poll monitors for the opposition were promptly dismissed from their jobs. Local opposition organizers told of being rounded up at night by Youth League redshirts and whipped bloody" (*The New York Times*, 1 June 1993, A6). In addition, the mass media was firmly in control of the government. Amnesty International noted that "a crucial issue in the referendum campaign is the government's monopoly over the principal mass media" (*West Africa*, 24-30 May 1993, 867).

A free flow of information is vital not only for economic actors in a free market but also for sound economic management. The establishment of a free marketplace of ideas is necessary if reform is to be internally generated. This is hardly possible in a viciously repressive environment in which freedom of expression is not tolerated and editors are routinely harassed by a state that refuses to obey its own laws. A free and private press is an effective antidote for corruption and economic mismanagement.

At their annual meeting in October 1996, the Bretton Woods institutions came very close to admitting that economic reforms alone are insufficient. "James Wolfenson, president of the World Bank, bluntly stated that 'we will not tolerate corruption in the programs we support' and IMF's Michael Camdessus made numerous references about law, order and justice being prerequisites for funding at a closing press conference. The reaction? "Third World plutocrats who drink at the development trough felt so threatened by all this that they issued a separate G-24 communique warning the World Bank and the IMF to butt out of their internal affairs and 'proceed with extreme caution'" (editorial, *The Wall Street Journal,* 22 October 1996, A22).

It must be clear that intellectual reform must precede political reform, which, in turn, must precede economic and institutional reform. The latter can be implemented more readily under new leadership. Further support for the basis of this order is derived from the five steps in problem resolution discussed in chapter 2.

The first step is the exposure of the problem, which is the business of journalists, editors, writers, intellectuals, and novelists. A problem cannot be solved if it is swept under a rug. Recall the Ethiopian proverb: "He who conceals his disease cannot expect to be cured." Freedom of expression and to publish is required for problems to be exposed. More important, it is Africans who ultimately must devise their own African solutions to their African problems. But they need the freedom of expression to air, debate, and determine what solutions which would be optimal.

Radio and print media are particularly important in the democratization process. They expose human rights abuses, corruption, repression, economic mismanagement, and a host of other evils associated with dictatorship. A conference entitled "Limiting Administrative Corruption in Democratizing States in Africa" and sponsored by United States Agency for International Development came to a similar conclusion: "In general, participants agreed that openness, the free flow of information, and meaningful political choices were widely seen as the keys to accountability and resulting control of corruption" (*African Voices,* 4). The print media also afford forums for publishing and exchanging ideas and solutions to problems.

PROGRESS REPORT ON INTELLECTUAL FREEDOM

It is often easy to overlook the critical importance of "intellectual freedom"—a catch-all phrase embracing freedom of expression, press freedom, and free flow of information. A pertinent characteristic of totalitarian or tyrannical political systems is the rigid control exercised over the content and flow of information: what can be said, printed or disseminated by the people, editors, and publishers. The free flow of information is vital for an economy if investors are to make sound decisions. It is thought that the manipulation and control of information triggered the Mexican peso crisis in 1994.

In Africa, the flow of information is severely restricted. As mentioned earlier, of Africa's 54 countries, only seven had a free press in 1995. Kakuna Kerina, program coordinator for sub-Saharan Africa for the Committee to Protect Journalists, a New York-based group, sent a letter in 1996 to the OAU reminding it that injudicious detention, censorship, and intimidation of journalists work against the public's right to information and the right to hold and express opinions and ideas. Both rights are guaranteed under Article 19 of the U.N. Charter and Article 9 of the African Charter on Human and People's Rights, to which most African countries are signatories. Kerina pointed to Nigeria, Côte d'Ivoire, The Gambia, Zambia, Angola, Kenya, Liberia, and Cameroon as nations where the press is severely restricted.

Most bewildering, said Kerina, is the fact that press and general freedoms are most restricted in those African countries that are multiparty democracies. The strangulation of the press in the post–Cold War period has been most evident in West Africa, where "at least 12 journalists have been detained in Ivory Coast, The Gambia, Ghana, Sierra Leone and Nigeria in the past month. Since 1994, West African governments have seized dozens of magazines and newspapers, deported journalists, and closed independent radio stations in Cameroon, Togo, The Gambia, Mali and Gabon" (*The Washington Times,* 6 April 1995, A15).

Due to the explosion in the number of satellite dishes, electronic communications (fax machines, the internet, e-mail, etc.), much more information is now available in Africa. The new technology has severely hindered the ability of African dictators to control the flow of information and keep their people in the dark. In their desperate attempts to retain control, defamation or libel suits, heavy fines, and murder have become the choice tactics of corrupt regimes. "As discussed in the previous chapter, the Ghanaian government filed at least 30 libel suits against the independent press.

In Angola, BBC reporter Gustavo Costa was slapped with a defamation suit in June 1994 by oil minister Albna Affis after filing stories about government corruption. On 18 January 1995 Ricardo de Melo, the editor of the Luanda-based *Impartial Fax*, was killed for writing stories about official corruption.

In Cameroon, Emmanuel Noubissie Ngankam, director of the independent *Dikalo*, was given a one-year suspended sentence, fined CFA 5 million ($8,800), and ordered to pay CFA 15 million in damages after publishing an article alleging that the former minister of public works and transportation had expropriated property in the capital Yaounde. Also in Cameroon, staff at two other newspapers, *La Nouvelle Expression* and *Galaxie*, were sued for defamation by Augustin Frederick Kodock, state planning and regional development minister, over newspaper articles alleging that the minister's private secretary had embezzled large sums of money. Then "the Cameroonian newspaper which reported President Biya's marriage to a 24-year-old has been suspended by the government. When *Perspectives-Hebdo* ran the story on March 17, 1994, police quickly seized all available copies. Joseph-Marie Besseri, the publisher, said the official reason for the ban was failure to show the edition to censors before distribution, as the law requires. He denies the charge" (*African News Weekly*, 8 April 1994, 5).

Similarly in Sudan, journalists must register with a state-appointed press council or risk jail terms and fines. According to *The African Observer* (8-21 August 1995), "So far, more than 596 journalists have done so. However, 37 were rejected on the grounds that they were inexperienced. . . . Some of the rejects are graduates of journalism schools, others hold masters degrees in social studies. Those rejected were given a second chance. They were made to sit an examination in mid-July, but only 19 of the 37 passed the exam, which tested their knowledge of the achievements of el Bashir's government" (21).

In Nigeria police confiscated all issues of the 7 December 1992 edition of *Quality* magazine, for carrying an interview with Femi Falana, in which he discussed the transition program and the delay in the handover of political power. The next day in a radio broadcast, the inspector general of police declared that all human rights groups were being put under surveillance. *Nigerian Tribune* editor-in-chief Folu Olamiti and journalist Wole Efunnuga were arrested on 31 December

1992, apparently in connection with a front-page article by Efunnuga published on 29 December critical of the police.

The brutal repression continued for much of the early 1990s. In 1995 the government, in a major crackdown on the opposition, banned three newspaper groups, which own a total of 16 papers, from circulation for six months in 1995. They include *The National Concord,* published by Chief Moshood Abiola, *The Guardian* and *Punch.* "This renewed onslaught on the press makes a nonsense of the assurances by the minister of information, Professor Jerry Gana, that the government would not harass journalist," Nigeria's Media Rights Agenda organization said (*African News Weekly,* 29 April 1994, 5).[1] In August 1995, Nigeria's military regime planned a new decree that, according to information minister Walter Ofonagoro, "will instill discipline among [media] practitioners" (*The African Observer,* 8-21 August 1995, 20). Who needs more discipline in Nigeria: the private media or the military junta?

In Kenya, "Fotoform, a company that prints three independent newspapers, was closed in May, 1993, and parts of its machinery were removed by the police" (*The Economist,* 12 June 1993, 47). "Police in Kenya have charged two local journalists with subversion and detained six employees from the same newspaper, *Standard,* for reporting that 9 people had been killed and hundreds displaced in fresh ethnic fighting in the volatile Molo area of the Rift Valley region. Officials have strongly denied there was ethnic fighting in the Molo region" (*African News Weekly,* 6 April 1994, 5).

On March 28, 1996, Kipruto arap Kirwa held a press conference at Kenya's Parliament Building to complain about the stifling of alternative views with the ruling KANU party: "I had hoped President Moi would, on the basis of his wealth of experience and shrewdness as a political operator and a democrat, albeit reluctant one, find some accommodation [with] those of us with dissenting views. But I have now come to the conclusion that the President is not a democrat of any shade" (*The African Observer,* 25 April–8 May 1996, 13). Since he delivered that broadside, Kirwa has not been seen, fueling speculation that he might have paid the penalty reserved for overly outspoken critics of Moi. As

---

1. Note that the minister of information is a professor. The most tragic aspect of Africa's descent into tyranny is the active collaboration provided by the continent's own brains—an issue that will be explored later.

mentioned earlier, in 1990 former Foreign Minister Robert Ouko was murdered after threatening to expose corruption in the government.

In Tanzania, two newspapers were banned for "violation of journalistic ethics." One means to suppress the private press is "To establish a national register of journalists and expel those who transgress. Others see the recent bannings—and the government's refusal to grant licenses to other independent papers—as the state's way of eliminating the competition. Because the independent press is vulnerable economically, simply pulling one issue off the stands can kill a publication. Few have deep pockets; most are dependent on sales rather than advertising—particularly in those states with limited private industry—for income" (*Africa Report*, May/June, 1993, 62).

Sixteen years after independence in 1980, Zimbabwe continues to use the old tactics: "The *Financial Gazette* claimed that the government was discussing ways of frustrating the operations of the independent press by instructing companies not to advertize, and by placing tight controls on the allocation of newsprint" (*Index on Censorship*, February 1993, 41). The media in Zimbabwe is still primarily the government's mouthpiece. Only two independent weekly papers and a few monthly magazines do not religiously toe the government's line. "This is a pathetic situation which has stifled those who have views independent of the government, because the official press cannot bite the hand that feeds it," said Herbert Munangarire, former owner of the *Sunday Times*, which folded in 1995 (*The African Observer*, 6-19 June 1996, 25).

Most disappointing has been the government of President Frederick Chiluba of Zambia, who ousted long-standing patriarchal autocrat, Kenneth Kaunda, in 1991. Following a series of articles questioning the integrity of Vice President Godfrey Miyanda, the speaker of parliament, Robinson Nabulyato, declared on 27 February 1996 that editor-in-chief of *The Post* Fred M'membe, managing editor Bright Mwape and columnist Lucy Sichone had been "in contempt of parliament." He imposed a fine of 1,000 *kwacha* on the journalists and ordered them imprisoned until they apologized. Opposition parties said the incident showed that the ruling Movement for Multi-Party Democracy was no better than the one-party regime it replaced. "The government has finally shown what it really is," said a leader member of the Zambia Democratic Congress (*The African Observer*, 29 February–13 March 1996, 2). "President Chiluba is a worse dictator than his predecessor who, at his very worst, never did what this government has done. I did not know that the speaker had power to imprison anyone indefinitely," he added.

PROGRESS REPORT ON POLITICAL FREEDOM

The political situation in many African countries continues to remain distressing. The euphoria that gripped Africans as the "winds of change" swept across the continent following the collapse of communism in Eastern Europe has largely dissipated and been replaced with a sense of disillusionment. While a few African despots were toppled, in the large majority of African nations they successfully beat back the democratic challenge. In some countries opposition leaders were partly to blame. Their own divisiveness, fragmentation, and lack of imagination as well as their propensity to choose ineffective tactics played right into the hands of the dictators. As we saw earlier, out of the 54 African countries, only 14 are democratic.

In the postcolonial period, three scenarios have emerged in the ouster of Africa's dictators. In the Doe scenario, those leaders who foolishly refused to accede to popular demands for democracy risked their own safety and the destruction of their countries: Doe of Liberia, Barre of Somalia, Mengistu of Ethiopia, and Mobutu Sese Seko of Zaire (now Congo). (Doe was killed in September 1990; Barre fled Mogadishu in a tank in January 1991; Mengistu fled to Zimbabwe in February 1991; and Mobutu fled in May 1997.) African countries where this scenario is most likely to be repeated are Algeria, Cameroon, Chad, Djibouti, Equatorial Guinea, Libya, Niger, Sierra Leone, and Tunisia.

In the Kerekou scenario, those African leaders who yielded to popular pressure managed to save not only their own lives but their countries as well: Kerekou of Benin, Kaunda of Zambia, de Klerk of South Africa, Sassou-Nguesso of Central African Republic, and Pereira of Cape Verde Islands. Unfortunately, they are the exceptions.

The Eyadema scenario is by far the most common. In this scenario, the leaders yield initially, after considerable domestic and international pressure, but then attempt to manipulate the rules and the transition process to their advantage, in the belief that they can fool their people. In the end, however, they fool only themselves and are thrown out of office in disgrace. African countries likely to follow this route are: Angola, Burkina Faso, Burundi, Côte d'Ivoire, Gabon, Ghana, Gambia, Kenya, Mauritania, Niger, Nigeria, Rwanda, Tanzania, Uganda, and Zimbabwe. Recent events in Burundi and Kenya also show that the outcome of the Eyadema scenario is highly unpredictable and its impact on economic development deleterious. Political uncertainty and instability discourage business investment and trade.

Under both external and internal pressure to democratize, African despots resorted to various tricks and chicanery. Mobutu, for example, embraced multiparty democracy enthusiastically but created so many parties of his own that it became known as multi-Mobutuism. African dictators manipulated, controlled, or dictated the pace—as well as the terms—of the transition to democracy; excessively used their "incumbent advantage" to spring surprises on the opposition; and shut the opposition out of the state-owned media. Says Keith Richburg, an African American reporter: "Mobilizing the masses and pressing for political reform is one thing. Actually winning election is a far more difficult proposition in countries where ruling parties control the media and dominate virtually every phase of the election process, from registering voters to deciding the location of the polling places. . . . Africa's autocrats are proving far more durable than their counterparts elsewhere" (*The Washington Post,* 24 October 1992, A23).

The following quotations from two African newspapers add other perspectives:

> Governments developed new tactics to frustrate the opposition. Some like the Cote d'Ivoire and Gabon, dropping all their previous ideological objections, held elections so fast that the opposition found no time to organize. Houphouet-Boigny and Omar Bongo won huge majorities for the ruling parties as early as November and September 1990.
>
> Other astute operators adopted the opposite tactic to achieve the same end, the retention of power. They simply kept the whole apparatus of the modern state in their hands, controlling state expenditure, the party press, radio and TV, patronage, bribery, the police and security forces. . . . There is no attempt to have an interim government while all parties compete equally [as was the case in South Africa]. (*New African,* November 1992, 12)

> The programs have been designed by African despots in such a way that they lack full press freedom, judiciary and administrative autonomy and procedural guarantees for free and fair elections. . . . Biased electoral systems, cheating and intimidation by the incumbents, gray areas between state and party, as well as internal squabbles and disunity are among the multiple disadvantages that have dampened the opposition effectiveness.
>
> If some opposition movements were able to benefit from democratic openings and win polls in Zambia (1991), Congo (1992) and Malawi and South Africa (1994), this proves more difficult in countries like Zimbabwe, Ghana, Cameroon, Cote d'Ivoire, Burkina Faso, Nigeria, Kenya, and others. (*The African Observer,* 2-15 May 1995, 3)

We examine in detail two crass attempts at "hide-and-seek" bazooka democracy in Ghana and Nigeria. In the case of Ghana, up until 1990, the ruling PNDC consistently and openly stated its abhorrence of multiparty democracy. Intense pressure from Western donors and also internal opposition forced the regime to relent; even then, it refused to commit itself to a definitive timetable. It unilaterally defined the modalities of the transition process and set up a National Commission on Democracy (NCD). The Washington-based International Foundation for Electoral Systems (IFES), which went to Ghana under a grant from U.S. AID in May 1992, wrote in their report that "The transition to democratic rule in Ghana is a process characterized by control. Flight-Lieutenant Jerry Rawlings and the PNDC remain the obvious source of political initiatives, retaining their claim to the last word in decisions that affect the forward movement of Ghanaian policy" (*Ghana—Pre-Election Assessment Report, IFES,* 1992, 2).

At about the same time in South Africa, the whites and blacks had sat down together to hammer out a transition program under CODESA (Convention for Democratic South Africa). CODESA was not controlled by one side. Oddly, Ghana drew up a program and constitution for multiparty democracy without the participation of political parties, which were then banned. Imagine the whites of South Africa writing a constitution for a democratic South Africa without black participation. Not surprisingly, almost every important group in Ghana, including the Ghana Bar Association, the Kwame Nkrumah Welfare Society, the Catholic Bishops Conference, the Tema District Council of Labour, the Movement for Freedom and Justice, the National Union of Ghana Students, and the Africa Youth Command, and an alliance of eleven opposition groups called The Co-ordinating Committee of Democratic Forces of Ghana opposed the work of the NCD. In particular, *West Africa* magazine wrote: "The NCD is made of persons hand-picked by the PNDC and is chaired by the Vice-Chairman of the PNDC, Justice D.F. Annan. It is not democratically representative or accountable. Members of the NCD have regularly expressed partisan views on what should or should not be part of the country's political system. Many have expressed doubts that such a body can be expected to impartially collate and distil views of Ghanaians" (13-19 August 1990, 2270).

Despite these criticisms and misgivings about the NCD, the PNDC charged ahead and established a Consultative Assembly to draft Ghana's constitutional proposals for the Fourth Republic. That assembly was blatantly packed with government delegates: from the army, the navy, air force, committees for the defense of the revolution, December 31st Women's Movement, and district assembly representatives. The tiny Ghana army had four delegates while the huge numbers of teachers in the country had only two. Of the 260 delegates, more than 190 were "on the military government's side."

Then Sections 33, 34 and 36 were clandestinely inserted into the constitution without any debate to give the PNDC blanket and perpetual immunity from "any official act or omission [committed] during the administration of the PNDC." A regime that preached the gospel of "accountability," "transparency," and "probity," according to the World Bank, suddenly refused to be held to the same tests. Ghanaians abroad were disenfranchised at a time when other Africans could all go to their embassies and vote.

There were numerous other problems. The voter registry was riddled with inaccuracies. The IFES reported that "the total number of registered voters in Ghana listed (8,410,990) is improbable, given an estimated population of 16 million, of whom half are under 15 years of age. An estimate of a million erroneous entries is not inappropriate. Such inaccuracies open the list to such tampering as to affect the outcome of an election" (*Ghana—Pre-Election Assessment Report, IFES,* 1992, 45).

The list suffered from multiple entries, inconsistent name order, failure to record corrections, and ghost entries. No attempt was made to purge the list of voters deceased since 1987. IFES recommended that all eligible voters be reregistered as quickly as possible. This recommendation was ignored, and only two months were allowed for campaigning. The opposition participated in the presidential election, which they claimed was rigged, and boycotted the subsequent parliamentary elections, resulting in a de facto one-party parliament.

For the 1996 elections, IFES claimed that it registered 9.1 million voters, or 90 percent of those eligible. But IFES could not give the total population figure for Ghana. If half of Ghana's population was under the age of 15, and there were 9.1 million registered voters, its population would be between 18 million and 22 million. Yet its 1992 population was 16 million; its growth rate would have to be an astonishing 6 or 7 percent for the population to have grown so much in four years. (Ghana's population rate of growth was around 3.2 percent).

The source of the problem were the projections of voting age population provided by the Statistical Service, a government agency. Its 1 September 1995 projection of the voting age population was 2 million higher than that on 1 July 1995. In other words, within two months, the

Statistical Service suddenly realized that a whopping 2 million more people could vote in Ghana. According to IFES, the Statistical Service could not explain this 24 percent increase in estimated voting age population. Needless to say, the new voters' register also was inflated, and most of the flaws in the 1992 elections were repeated for 1996:

- Ghanaians living abroad continued to be disenfranchised.
- The registration period was shortened to two weeks (1-15 October), despite Ghana's Interim National Electoral Commission's own estimate of three months back in 1992.
- Aliens were registered to vote—exactly the same problem noted in the 1992 IFES Report.
- Large quantities of fake registration papers were discovered.
- The deputy electoral commissioner David Akanga reported over 2 million registration papers missing, although he later retracted this statement.
- The names of thousands of registered voters in opposition strongholds were deleted from the register; in other areas names had been inserted.

The 1996 election campaign was marred by violence at Tamale, Kyebi, Bibiani, Sabon Zongo in Accra, East Sraha in Tema, Offinso, Assisiwa, Peninpa, and Old Tafo. "In all these the NDC was the aggressor. Yet no arrests were effected," complained the Free Press (6-12 December 1996, 12). And 11 hours before Kufuor held a rally at Jackson Park in Kumasi, explosives were set off at regular intervals, leaving two large craters in the park (Ghanaian Chronicle, 4 December 1996).

NDC supporters purchased voter ID cards or the information on them and printed fake cards. Patrick Merloe, senior associate for the Washington, D.C.–based National Democratic Institute, an international observer team that was in Ghana, "noted that the purchasing of voter identity cards could be used to disenfranchise those who part with their cards, and called for effective investigations concerning such activities and voter education to prevent such activities. . . . In addition, news coverage of the incumbent political contestants is overwhelmingly positive while coverage of the other political contestants is often presented in a negative tone or not at all," Mr. Merloe added (Free Press, 22-28 November 1996, 12).

Indeed, "At Okaikoi South booth at the Kaneshie Police Station, Mr. Patrick Sosi, an electoral official, found to his shock and dismay that somebody had used his name to vote. . . . At Okaikoi South where Nana

Akomea won, the NDC losing aspiring parliamentary candidate, Mr. Ernest Agbemor Yeboah, refused to sign the declared results and instead pulled a gun to threaten those who pleaded with him to sign it" (*Free Press*, 11-17 December 1996, 3). Such is the obsession with political power, providing yet another reason why political reform must precede the economic.

Democratization of Nigeria

Nigeria, the comatose giant of Africa, appears to be in a perpetual state of transition to democratic rule. A five-year transition program was begun in 1985 under General Ibrahim Babangida but it turned out to be a sham. The program was stretched out with frequent interruptions, devious maneuvers, broken promises (at least four), and then complete nullification of the 12 June 1993 presidential election, which was considered the freest and fairest and apparently was won by the late Chief Moshood Abiola. (Previous missed handover dates were October 1990, October 1992, and January 1993.)

Most Nigerians, of course, were not surprised by the annulment and had long suspected General Babangida's desires to perpetuate himself in power. In fact, their suspicion and cynicism produced the moniker "Maradona."[2] In political parlance, a "Maradona" is a trickster, who deviously plots diabolical political shenanigans, resorting to subterfuge and chicanery to fool the people and advance his own secret agenda. Said Olusequn Obasanjo, Nigeria's former head of state: "It has now got to a stage that when the [Babangida] government says good morning, people will look out four times to ascertain the time of day before they reply" (*African News Weekly*, 2-9 April 1992, 3).

In the 1980s, Nigerians initially applauded the ouster of corrupt politicians by a succession of military leaders—Major-General Buhari (December 1983) and General Babangida (August 1985). The coup that brought Babangida to power aimed to get rid of those in the Supreme Military Council who had abused their power and failed to tackle the country's economic problems. But the "disciplined" military officers who were supposed to save the country seldom listened to the people.

---

2. The name was taken from the Argentine soccer star. The term is incisively double-edged. On one hand, it connotes charm and stardom but, on the other, a "dribbler." In soccer, a dribbler is a person who concocts false body maneuvers to fool and move a ball past an opponent.

Despite all the promises of probity, the military elite proved itself more corrupt than any regime that preceded it, taking huge kickbacks on contracts and diverting government funds. Allegations have been rife about corruption and illicit enrichment by members of Babangida government.

General Babangida was forced aside by the military top brass, led by General Sani Abacha in June 1993 and an interim civilian government under Ernest Shonekan was installed. But after barely three months in office, Shonekan was overthrown by Abacha in November 1993. Initially Abacha attempted to quell public dissatisfaction by co-opting the opposition (offering its leaders cabinet posts) and organizing a constitutional conference. It turned out to be another scam.

The public viewed Abacha's constitutional conference with a massive dose of skepticism and cynicism. That the general twice postponed its opening did not help matters. A day after the conference finally began on 27 June 1994, it was adjourned for two weeks. The official reason? The delegates' accommodations were not ready.

Moreover, the 396 delegates, who were to deliberate on the future of democracy, congregated at Abuja as "guests of the military." A fourth of their number (96) were nominated by General Abacha and the rest "elected" under suspiciously complex rules. Delegates were chosen by "people's representatives" who were themselves elected by popular vote on 23 May, postponed from 21 May. Candidates under 35 years of age were ineligible to run. In addition, they must not be "an ex-convict, must be sane, must be a fit and proper person and must not have been declared bankrupt by a court of law"—requirements that most of the ruling military elites themselves would fail to meet.

Logistical problems, inadequate publicity, and apathy bedeviled the electoral exercise. There was no campaigning; no voter register or cards. Confusion reigned. Voters did not even know whom they were voting for and for what purpose. And stunned by the annulment of 12 June elections, many chose to stay home. The general voter turnout across the country was scandalously low.

More suspiciously, the Constitutional Conference was not sovereign. That is, the Abacha regime reserved the right to reject or accept its recommendations. If the regime rejected them, the entire exercise would be a colossal waste and started anew. If the recommendations were accepted, the military regime would then draw up a timetable, perhaps another transition period for "civic education," voter registration, local, state and regional elections with still the possibility of interruption midstream.

Now compared with South Africa's 1991 Convention for a Democratic South Africa, the differences are glaring. Nigeria's conference was a meritricious charade that should have been dissolved. Political parties did not take part in the constitutional conference. Imagine de Klerk of South Africa banning the ANC and all political parties, arresting political leaders, clamping down on the news media, nominating 25 percent of the delegates to the conference, and declaring that its resolutions would not be binding on the white minority government.

On 12 June 1994, the first anniversary of the annulment, Chief Abiola belatedly declared himself "president," and was promptly arrested on charges of treason. This triggered a wave of strikes by oil workers, which disrupted oil production as was noted earlier. The paranoid military regime unleashed a wave of brutal reprisals. Pro-democracy protesters were gunned down; political leaders of different persuasions were detained. The Guardian, *The Concord, Newswatch,* and other newspapers were shut down and their editors arrested. And all civilians were expelled from the Provisional Ruling Council (PRC) on 27 September.

About 40 people, including former head of state, General Olusegun Obasanjo, were arrested on trumped-up charges of plotting to overthrow the government. The irony of charge is that it was the private press which reported rumors of an impending coup, whereupon military personnel sprang into action. These events culminated with the arrest and subsequent hanging of Ken Saro-Wiwa.

PROGRESS REPORT ON ECONOMIC FREEDOM

The record on economic reform (or structural adjustment) has been dismal. The problem has less to do with the "medicine" itself or its sponsorship by the World Bank but more to do with its implementation. African leaders themselves acceded to reform—on their own accord. In May 1986 they collectively admitted, in a rare moment of courage and forthrightness, before the United Nations Special Session on Africa that their own capricious and predatory management had contributed immensely to the continent's deepening economic crisis. In particular, they pointed to their own "past policy mistakes," especially the neglect of agriculture.

The OAU Report, which served as the core of the African sermon at the United Nations, urged African nations "to take measures to strengthen incentive schemes, review public investment policies, improve economic management, including greater discipline and efficiency in the use of resources." Most notably, the report pledged that "the positive role of the private sector is to be encouraged." Even a year before that, the African Development Bank and the Economic Commission for Africa had produced reports that had been adopted at the OAU meeting in July 1985. These reports stressed a change of direction of economic policy "toward more market freedom, more emphasis on producer incentives, as well as reform of the public sector to ensure greater profitability" (*West Africa,* 21 April 1986, 817).

African leaders subsequently agreed to the World Bank's structural adjustment programs (SAPs): to adopt a transparent management style; to dismantle the state interventionist behemoth; to liberalize markets; to devalue or float currencies; to sell off unprofitable state-owned enterprises; and to remove a plethora of controls on prices, interest, and rents. In return, the World Bank would provide loans to ease balance-of-payment, debt-servicing and budgetary difficulties. In June 1987 the leaders reaffirmed their determination to pursue the SAPs at a conference organized by the Economic Commission on Africa at Abuja, Nigeria. By 1989, 37 African nations had formally signed up with over $25 billion in Western donor support. As it turned out, however, while the leaders admitted the role of internal factors, they had no intention to address them. Rather it was a ruse to extract more foreign aid from the international community.

Under a structural adjustment program, an African country undertakes to devalue its currency to bring its overvalued exchange rate in line with its true value. Supposedly a more realistic exchange rate will reduce imports and encourage exports, thereby alleviating the balance-of-trade deficit. The second major thrust of SAP is to trim down the statist behemoth by reining in soaring expenditures, removing price controls, eliminating subsidies, selling off unprofitable state-owned enterprises, and generally "rationalizing" the public sector to make it more efficient.

In 1994 the World Bank evaluated the performance of 29 of these countries, concluding that although "no African country has achieved a sound macroeconomic policy stance," six had performed well: The Gambia, Burkina Faso, Ghana, Nigeria, Tanzania, and Zimbabwe. A year later this number had shrunk. In The Gambia, a military coup toppled Sir Dawda Jawara on 24 July 1994, quashing any hopes of economic recovery. Continuing political turmoil in Nigeria throttles economic reform. In the remaining four "success stories," reform is on the verge of collapse. The case of Ghana was even more traumatic; it had been hailed by the World Bank as a "success story" in 1992 but it dropped precipitously from "stardom" to opprobrium within a year.

World Bank loans of more than $2 billion, including more than $1 billion for adjustment operations, helped Ghana's economic progress over the past 13 years. But a new study by the World Bank's own Operations Evaluation Department warned that progress would not be sustained unless the country speeded up the implementation of a large unfinished agenda of policy reform.

In its December 1995 report, the department noted that although Ghana had been projected as a success story, prospects for satisfactory growth rates and poverty reduction were uncertain. Agricultural growth did not progress as necessary nor did it keep up with population growth. There were fiscal problems and high deficits and insufficient credit to the private sector. The combination of excessive credit to public enterprises and fiscal dilemmas have continued to depress private investments and savings and caused the resurgence of inflation in 1993 to 1995.

This dire prognosis for Ghana's economy was echoed by Joe Abbey, the former Ghanaian Ambassador to the United States and now the executive director of the Center For Policy Analysis (CEPA). He warned of "a full blown economic crisis unless there is an urgent review of the level and quality of government spending in 1996 and beyond. In a macroeconomic review and outlook for the Ghanaian economy, CEPA pressed the panic button and decried the off-tracking of the economy with the recent re-emergence of high inflation, budget deficits and low savings." Abbey believed that economic growth for 1996 would be no more than 3.5 percent (*The Ghanaian Chronicle*, 18-20 March 1996, 1).

Ghana's impressive 5 percent annual rate of growth of GDP over the period 1984 to 1990 is not sustainable as this was engineered with massive infusions of foreign aid. Subtract a population rate of growth of 3.2 percent and that leaves a miserly 1.8 percent rate of growth. Investment, both domestic and foreign, is the key to sustainable growth, but both categories are faltering in Ghana, which has had difficulty attracting foreign investment despite designation by the World Bank as "the economic star of Africa." In 1992 it received only $23 million—same as war-torn Mozambique. By 1997 the economy was a shambles. Inflation was raging at 60 percent, unemployment had reached 30 percent, and the currency was in a free fall. Worse, according to Michaels (1993), "Ghana's manufacturing sector, meanwhile, was left to decline, and as

Ghana increasingly becomes a 'buying and selling' economy, the only real growth is in the service sector. Its transportation, wholesale and retail sub-sectors now account for 42.5 percent of GDP, which generates little in the way of foreign exchange (or food). After nine years of structural adjustment, Ghana's total external debt had nearly quadrupled to almost $4.2 billion."

WHY STRUCTURAL ADJUSTMENT PROGRAMS FAILED IN AFRICA

A huge emotional debate has erupted over the success or failure of structural adjustment in Africa. Much of the controversy derives from the involvement of the World Bank and International Monetary Fund in Africa's adjustment programs. These two institutions, deservedly or not, have a rather poor image in Africa, and their involvement in any program on the continent draws automatic flak. This is unfortunate since the efficacy of a program should be assessed objectively, regardless of its sponsor.

A program may fail for a variety of reasons. It may be poorly implemented, and this may have nothing to do with the Bretton Woods institutions or the SAP itself, just as Africa's problems with democratization have less to do with sponsoring Western agencies or "the inherent flaws in principle of democracy" than with the manner in which the program was executed.

There were several reasons why SAP failed in Africa. They may be categorized into two broad areas: design flaws and sequencing. As designed by the World Bank, structural adjustment was beset with various internal flaws. (See Ayittey, 1992, chapter 13, for a full discussion.) First, in most cases in Africa, SAP amounted to reorganizing a bankrupt company and placing it, together with massive infusion of new capital, in the hands of the same incompetent managers who ruined it in the first place. Certainly that arrangement would not be tolerated in the West. Why, then, should the World Bank impose such a "solution" on Africa?

Second, SAP assumed that development takes place in a vacuum, that the senseless civil wars, environmental degradation, infrastructural deterioration, and general state of violence and terror in Africa have no effects on economic development. In 1993, for example, Mozambique's 12-year-old civil war had cost at least $8 billion and an estimated 900,000 civilian lives. Over a third of its population had been displaced. Yet Western donors and institutions sought to "restructure" Mozambican and Angolan economies without regard to the raging civil wars. The most ludicrous "restructuring programs" were in Sudan and Somalia, where the World Bank sought to restructure economies that did not exist. In both countries, ongoing civil wars had devastated the economies by the time the World Bank attempted to implement its adjustment programs.

Third, economic reform without a concomitant political reform is meaningless, especially in Africa where the political and economic systems are fused. However, the World Bank and the IMF did not pay much attention to political reform until after the collapse of communism in Eastern Europe.

Fourth, the reduction of the economic reform program to a few quantitative measures (devaluation, removal of price controls, sale of state-owned enterprises, etc.)—ostensibly for purposes of easy assessment of progress—rendered its implementation "mechanical." For example, the removal of price controls alone does not automatically establish a free market. Such a market requires the existence of supporting infrastructure and institutions that establish civil society, fairness, due process, and rule of law. These supports include a private press (for the free flow of information), freedom of expression, an independent judiciary/legal system (to uphold the rule of law, enforce market contracts, and protect private property rights), and an independent central bank. In Nigeria, the Central Bank, granted limited autonomy in 1989, was brought back into the finance ministry in January 1997.

Meaningful market reform cannot endure if the legal system is not functioning and has been replaced with tribunals or kangaroo courts. In the absence of the rule of law, commercial properties can arbitrarily be seized by the state without due process. Where the central bank is under the thumb of the government, the state can gun the money supply, wreaking disastrous inflationary havoc with fragile financial markets and business decision making. In short, the World Bank has not focused on the supporting institutions needed to make market reforms work.

Since SAP is often referred to as "the bitter IMF pill," perhaps a more fruitful way of assessing it is to use a patient-doctor analogy. A sick patient goes to see a doctor, who performs some tests. After determining the cause of the ailment and making a diagnosis, he prescribes a medicine. Whether the medicine cures the patient or not depends on a host of other variables that have nothing to do with the doctor. For example, to be effective, certain medications must be taken three times a day. It may not work if taken once a week. In addition, the medicine only will work under certain conditions. For example, it should be taken before meals and the patient, while on the medication, may not consume alcohol or coffee, which counteract the effectiveness of some drugs. Clearly, a patient who does not follow this regimen will not be cured.

By the late 1980s, it was clear that many African economies were "sick." Their governments saw the "doctor" (the World Bank/IMF), which prescribed SAP. Keep in mind that the World Bank was not the only "doctor" around. If an African government loathed the World Bank and its "fees," other "doctors" could have been consulted. After years of "adjusting," however, Africa's economies were not "cured." The reason was simple: Although the pill was the right medicine, it was prescribed by the wrong doctor (World Bank), administered by the wrong nurse (the mafia African state) and implemented using the will tactics. Note only one "right" but three "wrongs."

The "Right" Medicine

In the postcolonial period, African governments, as we saw in chapter 5, arrogated onto themselves the power to intervene in almost every conceivable aspect of their economies, ostensibly for "national development" and protect the new African nation against "foreign exploitation." Subsequently, state controls were used for the benefit of a tiny ruling elite. State hegemony in the economy became pervasive. The bureaucracy swelled with payrolls padded with government/party supporters. State controls created shortages and opportunities for illicit enrichment by the elites and bred a culture of bribery and corruption. In addition, they killed off the incentive to produce. The state sector became grotesquely inefficient and wasteful. The rot at the government house propelled the military to intervene in politics. Notwithstanding the fact that the soldiers often made matters worse, their primary objective was explicit: to clean house. The state sector had to be cleaned up and government operations rationalized. Most Africans would agree.

The basic thrust of SAP—to grant greater economic freedom to the people—is unassailable. The pervasive control African governments wield over their economies needs to be rolled back. Peasants who produce foodstuffs and cash crops should be allowed to keep a larger portion of their proceeds. Countries that move away from a state-controlled economy toward greater reliance on the private sector generally do better economically. Innumerable examples, from Asia to Latin America and the former Soviet bloc, can be adduced for testimony. As we noted in chapter 3, a more scientific effort was made to test this hypothesis empirically. The Heritage Foundation of Washington, D.C. and the Fraser Institute of Vancouver, Canada, attempted to find the correlation between economic freedom and wealth around the world over a 20-year period.

Essentially, economic freedom deals with property rights and choice. The two aforementioned organizations defined economic freedom thus: "Individuals are economically free if property that they have legally acquired is protected from invasions or intrusions by others, and if they are free to use, exchange or give away their property so long as their actions do not violate other people's similar rights." The concept may sound abstract and esoteric but is relevant in everyday activities. Perhaps, like democracy, it is easier recognize its absence than to define it. Economic freedom does not exist when a government arbitrarily can confiscate private property (residential or commercial); conscript individuals for military service or forced labor; can dictate prices at which commodities may be sold and purchased; can restrict access into certain occupations, economic sectors and markets; can prohibit the production and consumption of certain commodities and services; and even impose on its citizens the use of a currency rendered worthless by reckless monetary policies (*The Economist*, 13 January 1996, 21).

In terms of broad geographic regions, the study found that, "apart from a handful of Middle Eastern countries, sub-Saharan Africa was the only area of the world that enjoyed no appreciable improvement in its level of economic freedom between 1975 and 1995."[3]

As seen in table 7.1 , individual African countries may be placed in three freedom categories: borderline freedom, mostly unfree, and repressed.

It should be recalled that African natives enjoyed much economic freedom before the advent of the colonialists. They themselves determined what they produced and sold their surpluses on free village markets. Prices were determined by bargaining, not fixed by chiefs. Free trade and free enterprise were the rule, as they traveled long distances— along free trade routes—to trade freely. The tribal government played only a minimal role in the economy. But after independence, African governments stripped them of their economic freedoms.

---

3. This was also cited by Nicholas Eberstadt in *The Washington Times*, 7 October 1996, 19.

TABLE 7.1
Comparative Economic Freedom in African Nations

BORDERLINE	MOSTLY UNFREE	REPRESSED
(Score: 5.0)	(Score: 5.0–4.0)	(Score: Under 4.0)
Botswana	Cameroon	Algeria
	Central African Republic	Benin
	Gabon	Burundi
	Ghana	Congo Egypt
	Kenya	Côte d'Ivoire
	Malawi	Egypt
	Mali	Madagascar
	Senegal	Morocco
	Sierra Leone	Rwanda
	South Africa	Niger
	Tunisia	Nigeria
		Tanzania
		Togo
		Uganda
		Zaire
		Zambia
		Zimbabwe

Source: Compiled from *The Economist,* 13 January 1996, 22.

Where reform was implemented, the results were spectacular. A few African countries, such as Ghana, Tanzania, and Zimbabwe, performed remarkably well in the initial phases of reform. Once free of statist controls, Tanzania's agriculture expanded annually at 5 percent in the early 1990s. State-owned enterprises that Tanzania privatized also chalked up spectacular results. One was the state brewery that once produced the local Safari beer that one had to inspect carefully before drinking because of odd ingredients floating in the brew. A stray cockroach now and then could be spotted.

In 1993 the government sold part of its stake to a South African company in a privatization drive. The brewery was modernized and the bottles steam-cleaned. Production of Tanzania's Breweries Ltd. in 1995 recovered to 1985 levels, and the company paid its first dividend in two decades. "Privatization is very good," says Joseph Mbuya, a technician who has worked at the brewery for 17 years. "People get more money. There's more things to buy. That's what we want." His salary and benefits were boosted to about $310 a month from $53, as productivity gains let the company cut the payroll to 2,000 from 3,200. This enabled him to spruce up his small house and go out on an occasional night with his wife (*The Wall Street Journal,* 10 December 1996, A6).

The Ashanti Goldfields Corporation of Ghana is another example of privatization turning a moribund state-owned corporation around. The AGC, which accounts for 20 percent of Ghana's foreign exchange earnings, increased its output from 272,000 ounces in 1987 to 355,700 ounces by the end of 1989. "This represented an increase of 30.8 percent over the last 3 years" (*West Africa,* 5-11 February 1990, 190).

In agriculture, excessive rainfall and flooding hampered crop harvests and resulted in serious losses in the production of rice, maize, yam, and sorghum. Despite these losses, maize production rose by 19 percent between 1988 and 1989 while yam and sorghum, increased by 7 and 8 percent respectively. In fact, Ghana's national food balance showed surpluses of 52,000 tons of maize, 28,000 tons of sorghum, and 140,000 tons of yam. Part of the maize surplus, 17,100 tons, was exported to Angola, a major achievement since Ghana itself was a major recipient of food aid a few years ago.

In some areas, privatization of state-owned enterprises in Africa has worked remarkably well to improve productivity. Premier Breweries Ltd., an Anambra State-owned concern in Nigeria, is another excellent example.

In the first ten months of 1987-88 financial year, it recorded a loss of 3.1 million *naira* instead of a target profit of 9 million *naira* ($1 = 7.70 *naira*). Worse still, outstanding loans of 12 million *naira* were owed to First Bank, the United Bank of Africa, First City Merchant Bank, and many others. There were also outstanding overdrafts to the tune of 2.8 million *naira.* The monthly capital and operational payout was over 6 million *naira* while the monthly cash receipts were less than 5 million *naira*. This sounded like the typical loss-producing state enterprise that would swallow budgetary subventions at the rate of 12 million *naira* a year just to continue operations.

In 1988 the company was privatized by the Anambra State Government; it retained a 40 percent share holdings, down from 80 percent. Centerpoint Merchant Bank was contracted to raise 10 million *naira* through the issue of loan stock to the public. The shares were fully subscribed. In addition, the company's management structure was revamped. The board of directors were replaced and 31 management positions, deemed to be sinecures, were eliminated. "At the end of the 1989 financial year, directors of the Premier Breweries announced a turnover of N80.5 million, a pre-tax profit of N10 million and after-tax profit of N7.5 million with N3 million shared as gross dividends while N4.57 was retained as profit for the year" (*West Africa*, 15-21 January 1990, 64). Investors who bought Premier shares at 50 *kobo* (100 kobo = 1 naira) each received a dividend of 6 *kobo* on every share. Although the rate of return was 12 percent, Premier stock jumped in price to 87 *kobo*, producing substantial capital gains on sale.

These three examples—and many others exist—show that macroeconomic restructuring of an economy away from a state-controlled system (Ghana's case) and privatization (Premier's case) does work, if pursued with dedication, seriousness, and honesty.

Wrong Doctor

Although the medicine was "right," the World Bank and the IMF were the wrong institutions to prescribe it. Rightly or wrongly, they have been perceived as "imperialist institutions" or as "Trojan horses for the penetration of Western capitalism into Africa." In Kenya, "the bank's policies are viewed as a monster that no one wants to hear about" (*The African Observer*, 28 September–11 October 1995, 21). This kind of emotional rhetoric unnecessarily politicizes the debate and impedes the search for solutions. Additionally, it provides a convenient shield for incompetent African despots to conceal their own failures. African governments could have consulted other "doctors."

More serious, however, was the World Bank's own credibility. Back in the 1960s and 1970s, it funded disastrous statist policies in Africa. In the 1980s, imagine the World Bank telling African governments to dismantle the same statist structures it had helped them build. Even more bizarre, the World Bank itself was afflicted with the same ailment it set out to cure in Africa: corruption, nepotism, and bloated bureaucracy. While it was exhorting African governments to trim their bloated bureaucracies, its own bureaucracy was swelling. Recognizing the discrepancy, finally, as *The Washington Times* (24 August 1995) reported: "The World Bank is quietly eliminating 600 positions at its downtown headquarters. By the end of this year, the bank hopes to have identified all the positions that will be eliminated. By the end of fiscal 1997, which begins in July, the bank expects to have saved a net of $96 million over two years" (A1).

Wrong Nurse

To compound the problem, the "bitter pill" was administered by the wrong nurse. Too many African reformers lacked legitimacy, credibility, and trust. In fact, some "reformers" were the same incompetents who precipitated the economic crisis in the first place. In Burkina Faso, Ghana, Tanzania and Zimbabwe, the "reformers" were avowed Marxists and socialists, whose conversion to free market philosophy was at best dubious. Zimbabwe's president, Robert Mugabe, who in 1980 vowed to institute Marxist-Leninism, finally ditched socialism in 1990 and embraced the free market. Yet at ZANU-PF's preelection congress in Harare in September 1994, he declared ebulliently: "Socialism remains our sworn ideology" (*The African Observer,* 12 January 1995, 9).

In Ghana, the "nurse" was the Provisional National Defense Council (PNDC)—an unrepentant Marxist regime, heavily imbued with a "control mentality." The regime was closely associated itself with Angola, Cuba, the former Soviet bloc, Libya, and Nicaragua's Sandinistas. It did not believe in the "medicine," which entailed deregulation and loosening controls on the economy. Nor did it believe in private enterprise and free markets.

In the halcyon of the Rawlings revolution (1982-83), stringent price controls were imposed on most commodities and ruthlessly enforced by Price Control Tribunals. Private businessmen were attacked. Traders who violated price controls were hauled into jail and their wares confiscated. Some women traders had their heads shaved. Scores of markets, decried as "dens of profiteers and capitalists," were torched by revolutionary cadres. Makola No. 1—a free market in Accra—was dynamited. Traders were warned that if any were found with hoarded goods, they would be 'taken away to be shot by firing squad'" (Herbst, 1993, 26). Criticisms of these idiotic economic measures were mercilessly crushed with brutal abandon. Back in 1982, the World Bank and the IMF were denounced by the PNDC regime as "imperialist institutions dedicated to the oppression and exploitation of the Third World." In fact, Dr. Kwesi Botchwey, the former minister of finance, vowed that Ghana would never bow to the IMF. These economic inanities sent the economy reeling to its nadir in 1983. A 180-degree turn came in 1983 with the signing of the SAP agreement with the World Bank, which astonished even the PNDC's own Marxist supporters.

According to Herbst (1993): "As both the economy and civil society fell apart, it soon became apparent to the regime that it did not have the economic policies to cope with the crisis confronting Ghana. The Soviet Union and its Eastern European allies, which the PNDC had hoped would come to the aid of its revolution, told Ghana they had no money, suggesting that the Rawlings regime negotiate a program with the IMF" (29).

Thus, the PNDC agreed to implement SAP, which was known in Ghana as Economic Recovery Program (ERP), not out of conviction but out of economic necessity, with the hope that the program could be ditched when conditions improved.

To implement economic reform, the regime had to overcome its own self-doubts in order to take Ghana on an economic path fundamentally antithetical to its own borrowed Marxist beliefs. That it did not believe in economic reform was revealed by its often erratic actions and contradictory statements. As mentioned earlier, it assured foreign investors that they were welcome in Ghana and then lambasted them for "exploiting Africa." It preached "accountability" but refused to be held to same standard. It sought to wrap itself up in the mantle of Nkrumaism (socialism), while systematically dismantling Nkrumah's legacy. It also sought to "liberate" the economy but at the same time keep the control structures in place. All these served to confuse investors about the direction in which the PNDC was taking Ghana.

Nor did the regime have any clue as to the causes of Ghana's economic woes, which President Rawlings blamed on the opposition. During a November 1996 campaign tour of the Central Region, he scowled at opposition politicians, accusing them of "deliberately discouraging investors to come into the country to invest." He also charged that "Opposition politicians destroyed the banking system in the country by borrowing heavily and refusing to pay back" (*Ghana Drum,* December 1996, 35).

Said an irate Hawa Yakubu-Ogede, a former independent member of parliament and an opposition politician, "Ghana's economic malaise is not the result of lack of opportunities or of resources. Ghana suffers from the affliction of dishonest leadership" (*The Ghanaian Voice,* 12 February 1995, 8).

Lack of credibility did not arouse public confidence or support in the ERP, which jeopardized its success. The people did not enthusiastically embrace the program. More serious, perhaps, was the failure of the military regime to build a constituency for reform in urban or rural areas—that is, nurture a group or coalition of groups to support SAP, even among members of the regime itself. Said the Ghanaian newspaper *The Guide* in its 10-16 September 1996 editorial: "There was no attempt to convince anyone—not even members of the government—about the rationale for reform. . . . For many Ghanaians, the tendency was to view ERP as a short-term government program that was a basic requirement for receiving aid" (4).

Among the urban population, the important groups are industrialists, workers, professionals, students, and traders; each is at war with the regime. The PNDC frequently lashed out at workers and threatened to withdraw their right to strike. Nor was any attempt made to associate the Trade Union Congress (TUC) with the economic recovery program. One senior TUC official complained: "The impression given is that the TUC is part of the planning process but it is not. Since 1983 the TUC has not been consulted. We are not in a position to participate" (Herbst, 1993, 34). That the professional bodies (especially lawyers) and the student population have been thoroughly alienated from the program is already well known. Ghanaian industrialists did not openly embrace ERP because of stiff competition from imports and market traders did not easily forget the brutal harassment by city officials, and confiscation of their wares.

The rural population was the natural constituency for the PNDC to cultivate for support of ERP. Castigated as "backward," this sector traditionally has been marginalized or ignored by Ghana's political elite. Its fate worsened in the initial phases of the Rawlings' revolution, but after 1983 cocoa prices were increased, rural roads were repaired, and electricity extended. An attempt was made to give them a real voice with the institution of the District Assemblies. But the rural folks remained skeptical—justifiably so.

The PNDC made no effort to form peasant organizations. The People Defense Committees (PDCs) which were supposed to do that proved to be ineffective and a failure. Through their terrorist activities in 1983, the PDCs quickly earned the scorn of the rural population.

Many chiefs condemned the activities of the PDCs in their areas. Rather unwisely, the regime tried to use these same organizations to rally the peasants for a program that the PDCs themselves had rejected earlier.

Nor did the PNDC establish the environment conducive to investment. A well-functioning legal system is crucial for the success of any economic adjustment program. Both domestic and foreign investors need to be assured that there would not be arbitrary government actions against businesspeople. Such a legal system establishes an environment that promotes business confidence because it ensures that the economic rights of individuals would not capriciously violated and their commercial properties arbitrarily seized without due process of law. Strangely, the PNDC made no progress whatsoever in instituting real legal reform. Its frosty contempt for the legal profession is well known.

The absence of a well-functioning legal system and the PNDC's own policy blunders, reversals, and inconsistent rhetoric partly explain why the regime has had extreme difficulty in persuading foreigners to invest in Ghana.

In Tanzania, ex-president Julius Nyerere continued his frontal attacks on the structural adjustment program, sowing confusion and much uncertainty. Once, when asked to assess the economic situation in Africa and the options the continent had, Nyerere replied that African economies would not change unless the neocolonial relationship changed. Africa's foreign debt was a symptom and the result of the neocolonial relationship, not the problem (West Africa, 6 June 1988, 1034). This kind of twisted logic and harangue offered little in regard to fixing Africa's broken-down state vehicle.

After ruining the Tanzanian economy with "Ujamaa" socialism, he "retired" to be the chairman of Tanzania's ruling and sole legal party, Chama cha Mapindzi. In July 1988 the Tanzanian government under Mwinyi licensed six private companies to set up breweries. Here too, private-sector participation was to be allowed to break the decades-old state monopoly on breweries in a restructuring program. But after some companies conducted feasibility studies and arranged financing, the industry and trade minister suddenly abrogated the licenses, claiming that the private breweries would falsify output data and evade taxes.

There has also been the problem of credibility and commitment to reform. In 1996 George Mbowe became the head of Tanzania's commission to dismantle government-owned entities. But Mbowe was the same man who played a key role in the nationalization drive launched by President Nyerere in the 1960s, under the failed socialist program of

"Ujamaa." Most industries were nationalized and agriculture collectivized. But within a decade, more than half of the 330 state-run enterprises were broke and many people were hungry. Was Mbowe now convinced that *"Ujamaa"* was a failure and privatization was the right policy? "I would not say *Ujamaa* was a failure," he offered. "It's just that the government spread itself too thin, building schools and roads" (*The Wall Street Journal*, 10 December 1996, A6).

Wrong Tactics

Even worse was the manner in which the pill was administered. The method chosen by Ghana's PNDC regime was brutal and savage. No attempt was made to cajole or persuade the public to accept belt-tightening. In fact, there was no public debate. Five years after the program started, in 1983 the regime scheduled a public debate—which was canceled and then finally held in 1997.

Nigeria's privatization program was implemented half-heartedly, with little conviction. Hamza Zayyad, chairman of the Technical Committee on Privatization and Commerce, excoriated many state governments for not working hard enough to interest natives of their areas in the privatization program. He said that some state governments were even refusing to air advertisements about the project unless they were paid in advance by the TCPC, and that some state governments were unwilling to grant loans to their employees to allow them to participate in the program (*West Africa*, 19-25 February 1990, 284).

In January 1997 privatization was nixed altogether when Nigeria's military rulers sought to defy what they perceived to be Western free-market orthodoxy. In other African countries, the pill was administered intermittently or in cycles: aborted when the crisis abated and reinstated on reemergence (Sudan, Equatorial Guinea, Zaire, and Liberia). Even during restructuring, measures often were implemented perfunctorily without the conviction and the dedication needed to carry them through. Nigeria, which adopted SAP in 1986, suddenly abandoned its implementation in 1993. In Zambia, President Chiluba, who began "adjusting" the economy soon after his election in 1991, has begun to waver.

In many cases, trenchant dishonesty, shameless looting, and tomfoolery shattered public confidence in the program. For example, believing that economic development occurs in a vacuum, the government of Angola drew up a grandiose Investment Code (Law 13/1988) to attract foreign investors. Even *West Africa* magazine wondered why any foreign investor would choose to invest in war-torn Angola, when various apparently stable, structurally adjusting African countries as well as Asian and Eastern European countries offer better opportunities (13-19 March 1989, 407).

In Benin, reformist Nicephore Soglo railed against nepotism, lack of accountability, and transparency. Yet he was perpetrating the same malpractice: "His wife, a member of parliament, is accused of political tinkering. His brother-in-law is minister of state, the country's second-most powerful position. One of his sons is a special adviser. One of his brothers is an ambassador. Even his bodyguards are said to be relatives" (*The Washington Post,* 18 March 1996, A11).

In Ghana, the military government declared its willingness to allow private sector participation in the economy after decades of socialist management and ruin. But its actions proved incongruous with its pronouncements. Through its economic liberalization measures, it had sought to woo foreign investors by assuring them of the safety of their commercial properties and its commitment to private-sector development. But no such assurances were forthcoming to domestic investors. In 1989 there were three reported cases of arbitrary seizures of the commercial properties of burgeoning indigenous entrepreneurs without due process of law.

Hopeless inability to control their own budgetary expenditures did not help matters. For ten years, there was no audit of public accounts in both The Gambia and Ghana. An audit in 1994 revealed an embezzlement of 535,940 *dalasis* at the Ministry of Agriculture and misuse of 60 million *dalasis* by the Gambian Farmers' Cooperative Union. In Ghana, the 1993 Auditor-General's Report detailed a catalog of corrupt practices, administrative ineptitude, and the squandering of over $200 million in public funds. A 27 September 1994 audit in Nigeria revealed that a total of $12.4 billion—more than a third of the country's foreign debt—was squandered by its military coconutheads between 1988 and 1994.

The former minister of finance, Dr. Kwesi Botchwey, himself admitted of chaotic public expenditure management with the treasury and spending agencies operating at cross purposes (*Ghana Drum,* January 1995, 14). In Sierra Leone, President Momoh declared to parliament on 2 June 1989, that austerity and self-sacrifice must prevail—but not for his government. Large, uncontrollable expenditure items had rendered the budget meaningless. According to Momoh the government had continued to fund its activities by printing money, spending more than tax revenue would cover, and borrowing from the

Central Bank, while the nation's scanty resources were used for unnecessary imports (*West Africa,* 12-18 June 1989, 958).

Politically insecure reforming governments—even military ones—too easily capitulate to special elite interests. The Manufacturing Association of Nigeria opposed the closure of several inefficient industries and even demanded greater protection from the Babangida regime. Riots and demonstrations in 1988 prompted that regime to raise the minimum wage, unfreeze wages in the civil service, and remove the ban on civil service recruitment. The military was completely exempted from budgetary cuts; in fact, Babangida showered the officers of the armed forces with gifts of cars worth half a billion *naira.*

His military successor, General Sani Abacha, maintained the controversial dual exchange rate system, which allowed the government to buy foreign exchange at a quarter of its market price and suspended mass privatization of state-owned corporations. "Some say General Abacha bowed to the lobbying of those who gain from the phoney exchange rate and the patronage opportunities of state corporations" (*The Economist,* 25 January 1997, 41).

Elsewhere, top African government officials also exempted themselves from cuts. In 1995 in Zimbabwe, barely a month after Mugabe's government stipulated a 10 percent annual salary increases ceiling, top government officials awarded themselves increases exceeding 50 percent. In Tanzania, senior government officials and major politicians exempted themselves from taxes. In 1993 there were over 2,000 such exemptions, costing the treasury $113 million.

INSTITUTIONAL REFORM

Not much has been done in the area of institutional reform, even in Ghana, because of conflicts of interest and misplaced priorities. Top positions in key institutions—the civil service, military, judiciary, banking, and police—are all occupied by party supporters or kinsmen of the ruling despot and reform measures must be passed by a paranoid parliament. The military despot cannot reform the military; else the soldiers might overthrow him. The court system has been packed by government supporters and sycophants.

Nigeria's 35-odd universities have been starved of funds and destroyed by the country's military, who see no value in university education. Actually, military people see education as a threat, since it educates people about their rights. Ghana attempted an educational reform in 1988 with a $25 million World Bank grant; it was a monumental disaster.

In Kenya, the banking system cannot be reformed because the banks in distress "are owned by members of the respected elite, including President Moi's son, Mr. Raymond Kipruto Moi, who owns Heritage Bank" (*African Business,* November 1996, 30). Nor can the banking systems of Ghana and Nigeria be reformed by the ruling NDC and military junta respectively.

Ghana has meddled with its currency more than four times since independence in 1957. In February 1982 the military government, the PNDC, demonetized the 50 *cedi* note. The public was asked to deposit these notes in their banks in return for chits to be redeemed later; they never were. The official reasons for the demonetization were to mop up excess liquidity in the system, to crack down on tax evasion, to punish corrupt politicians, and to render useless large amounts of the currency circulating outside the country. This would crush currency smuggling and thereby shore up the external value of the currency. According to the authorities, "the withdrawal of the 50 *cedi* note was not against the poor or the genuine rich but rather it was meant to withdraw excess liquidity in the hands of a few greedy and corrupt businessmen" (*Daily Graphic,* 24 February 1982, 1).

On 13 February 1982 one day after the deadline for the deposit of the demonetized 50-*cedi* notes in Ghanaian banks, the PNDC announced that those whose bank balances exceeded 50,000 *cedis* would be subject to investigative probes to determine their compliance with tax obligations.

Similarly in Nigeria, "there was too much money in circulation. . . . Persons who had deposited up to 5,000 *naira* were informed they would have to produce their tax clearance certificates, showing that they paid their taxes over the last 3 years, before they could be allowed to withdraw any money" (*West Africa,* 28 May 1984, 1106, 1108). Nigeria's Central Bank Director of Domestic Operations, Chief Nwagu, argued that the change was necessary to demonetize the 2 billion *naira* illegally acquired by corrupt politicians and held outside the country.

When "the news of the exercise [50-*cedi* note demonetization] leaked out, many people in Accra and other parts of the country went on shopping spree before the February 12 deadline to get rid of their notes" (*West Africa,* 22 February 1982, 536). Exactly the same phenomenon was observed in Nigeria.

In Ghana, the demonetization of the 50-*cedi* note prompted speculation that the 20-*cedi* note would be next. Some traders even refused to accept the 20-*cedi* notes (*Graphic*, 12 February 1982, 4). A more enduring damage inflicted by the changeover, however, were the probes of individuals whose bank balances exceeded 50,000 *cedis* in 1982 or 5,000 *naira* in 1984.

The public reacted by withdrawing their cash balances from the banking system and conducting their businesses strictly on a cash basis. In Ghana, the state-owned *Mirror* reported "a sharp drop in the amount of money paid by the public into the various banks" (22 January 1982, 1). In response, the PNDC government ordered that "businesses are to be transacted in cheques, not cash" (*Graphic*, 27 May 1982, 1).

The banking system has never recovered from this economic inanity. Thirteen years after this misguided currency change, Ghanaians still shun the banking system and large amounts of cash are held outside the system. In Nigeria, the public responded similarly. To attract funds, banks offered fantastic rates for short-term deposits of six months or less. The banks have had considerable difficulty attracting long-term funds. In both countries, loss of confidence and flight from the currency also drove people to hold foreign currencies, which they could obtain only on the black market. "By Sept. 1, 1993, literally all the banks in Nigeria were unable to meet their obligations to customers. Depositors were in most cases not allowed to withdraw amounts in excess of N1,000 (in some cases, even less), irrespective of their credit balances" (*African Business*, October 1993, 17).

THE RESISTANCE TO REFORM

The commitment to reform has been weak in other African countries. Little progress was made in Tanzania—Africa's last haven for state-owned enterprises. In 1985 Tanzania was offering ideological asylum to 460 state enterprises—the largest collection of such "refugee" enterprises anywhere on the continent. Two years later, only three had been privatized in spite of the structural adjustment agreement signed with the IMF. In the public arena, there was much talk but little else. Finally in the early 1990s, Tanzania took some halting steps to reform its agricultural sector and privatize some state enterprises. The results were spectacular, as we noted earlier. So why the strong resistance to reform?

Structural adjustment required sacrifices and, naturally, the burden of adjustment was to be equally shared. But there has been fierce resistance to reform from three sources: the leadership, the tribes, and the elites. Austerity, transparency, and accountability all entail the curtailment of subsidies and the eradication of illicit income-earning opportunities. Civil servants opposed to reform may sabotage the program. Soldiers may simply take over the government while students and urban workers may riot or stage strikes.

For a variety of reasons, African despots, especially the patriarchal, charismatic, and military populist types, are loath to relinquish control or power. They would rather destroy their economies and countries than give up power.

Most African despots have built a cult of personality around themselves with an air of invincibility and infallibility. Their nation's fortunes and destiny are very much tied up with their personalities. Some of them get this absurd notion that the country belongs to them and them alone. Witness their pictures on currencies and in every nook and cranny in the country. Every monument or building of some significance is named after them. They love the self-idolization. Since accepting reform of any kind is an admission of failure or fallibility, they put up all sorts of arcane reasons to block reform. The most famous was President Daniel arap Moi's assertion that it took the United States 200 years after its independence in 1776 to establish genuine democracy, so Kenyans who just gained their independence in 1963 should not even dream of asking for it.

Even if they accept reform, these leaders do so reluctantly and do everything possible to undermine it to prove that the plan advocated by the reformers would not work. Again, President Moi predicted that if Kenya establishes multiparty democracy, it would degenerate into tribal rivalry and strife. Indeed, since 1991, when Moi bowed to external donors and instituted multiparty "democracy," more than 1,500 Kenyans have been killed—mostly Kikuyus but also Luos and Luhyas—and 300,000 have been displaced in ethnic clashes. Said Nairobi lawyer Gitobu Imanyara, "We have a President who is determined to fulfil his prophesy that the country is not cohesive enough for multiparty democracy. His desire is to prove that he is right, even if it means destroying Kenya as a country" (*The Atlantic Monthly,* February 1996, 32).

Second, as we noted in chapter 5, occupying the presidency is a lucrative business. Abacha, Eyadema, Mobutu, Moi, and the other kleptocrats have amassed legendary personal fortunes. Their business empires will collapse if economic reform strips them of state controls. Economic liberalization may also undermine their ability to maintain their political support base and thus prove suicidal.

The third reason is fear. Many of Africa's heads of state have their hands so steeped in blood and their pockets so full of booty that they are afraid all their past gory misdeeds will be exposed. So they cling to power at all cost, regardless of the consequences. Another source of resistance comes from the sycophants and supporters, often drawn from the leaders' own tribes. Ethnicity adds an even more dangerous element to the democratic reform issue. It casts the issue into tribal rivalry: one tribe, fearing that it may lose its dominant position in government, may oppose multiparty democracy, while the other excluded tribes may resort to violence to dislodge the ruling tribe from power.

As noted in chapter 5, other supporters are simply bought: soldiers, with fat paychecks and perks; urban workers with cheap rice and sardines (essential commodities); students, with free tuition and hefty allowances; and intellectuals, opposition leaders, and lawyers, with big government posts and Mercedes Benzes. In Nigeria, "Defense and police budgets enjoy the largest slice of the national cake (and even so the figures are understated, since the military imports are paid for with dollars bought cheaply at the government exchange rates)" (*The Economist*, 25 January 1997, 41). Thus, even when the head of state does contemplate stepping down, his supporters and lackeys fiercely resist any cutbacks in government largesse or any attempt to open up the political system.

The final potent source of resistance may come from the elites: high government officials, intellectuals, lecturers, teachers, editors, and civil servants. This class benefits immensely from government subsidies and controls. They may have access to free government housing and medical care and be entitled to government loans for the purchase of cars, refrigerators, and even their own funerals. They too would resist any cutbacks of such government largesse. Other members of this class may oppose economic liberalization on purely ideological grounds. In Guinea, "Progress [on reform] was slow because civil servants and others with a stake in the past sought to preserve it. Dissatisfaction produced a series of coups, the latest in February 1996, when a group of soldiers dissatisfied about going without pay joined forces with others in the military who sought Gen. Conte's ouster" (*The Washington Times*, 17 October 1996, A19).

In Zambia, resistance to reform is coming from within President Chiluba's own circle. Some clamor for the continued influence of state spending and patronage. For example, said Mundia Sikatana, a Chiluba adviser and a founder of the Movement for Multiparty Democracy, the government continues to provide vehicles and fuel to hundreds of civil servants. The government, he said, "cannot abandon the old habits. The structural adjustment program is not doing enough" (*The Washington Post,* 12 September 1995, A12).

Africa's intellectual community has a deep-seated aversion to capitalism or free markets. This attitude is a throwback from colonial days, when capitalism and colonialism were confused. The involvement of the World Bank, generally castigated by African intellectuals as an "neocolonial institution" does not help matters.

More important, perhaps, is the fact that a shrinking state sector shatters the elites' dreams. Recall that the ambition of most educated Africans is to become the president or a minister. The state sector is where one makes his fortune. As far as the elites are concerned, there is no life outside the state sector.

To skirt elite opposition, African governments opted for politically safe budget cuts: education, health care, and road maintenance. Sub-Saharan African governments cut spending on education by more than 50 percent in the 1980s. Guinea, Malawi, Tanzania, Zambia, and Senegal slashed education budgets by 18 to 25 percent during the late 1980s. Real per capita spending on health dropped below the 1980 level in over half of sub-Saharan African countries. Critics say those countries opted for politically safe budget cuts rather than slicing into their militaries or other bureaucracies. "They cut places like education because they knew the people wouldn't howl about that," said G. K. Ikiara, an economics professor at the University of Nairobi (*The Washington Post,* 23 July 1995, A23).

There is some chicanery involved here. African governments constantly lament that SAP "hurts the poor." Of course, SAP will do so when these governments exempt the elites and shift the burden of adjustment disproportionately onto the rural poor, especially women and children.

Worse, the cuts on social services and infrastructure undermined the success of SAP. Roads, schools, and telecommunications systems fell apart. The number of teachers declined as salaries failed to keep pace with inflation. Zimbabwe experienced a mass exodus of doctors (estimated at about 1,400) to neighboring Botswana and South Africa. Communicable diseases such as yellow fever, malaria, and cholera reappeared with a vengeance.

To compound the problem, the "politically safe" budget cuts were not enough to reduce budget deficits. With revenue collection systems in shambles, cash-strapped African governments resorted to printing money, which fueled inflation and provoked demands for wage increases. Between 1986 and 1991, Ghana's money supply increased at an astonishing average rate of 43 percent.

In sum, most African leaders lack the competence and credibility to institute real reform. Nor are they interested in it. They implement only the bare minimum cosmetic reforms that would ensure continued flow of Western aid. Africans deride the posturing, tricks and acrobatics as "Babangida Boogie": One step forward, three steps back, a sidekick, and a flip to land on a fat Swiss bank account. All much ado about nothing: "One day Nigeria's Finance Minister, Anthony Ani, talks of mass privatization. The next day privatization is merely an option to be considered by some government committee. . . . Lagos businessmen are appalled. 'Just as we were beginning to move forward, this will set us back years,' says a merchant banker" (*The Economist*, 25 January 1997, 41).

More scandalous perhaps has been the ready supply of Western dance partners. The Kenyan version of this ritual dance, the Moi massamba, was well described by *The Economist* (19 August 1995): "Over the past few years, Kenya has performed a curious mating ritual with its aid donors. The steps are: One, Kenya wins its yearly pledges of foreign aid. Two, the government begins to misbehave, backtracking on economic reform and behaving in an authoritarian manner. Three, a new meeting of donor countries looms with exasperated foreign governments preparing their sharp rebukes. Four, Kenya pulls a placatory rabbit out of the hat. Five, the donors are mollified and aid is pledged. The whole dance then starts again" (37).

Who is fooling whom? And who suffers at the end of the dance?

CHAPTER 8

How the West Compounded Africa's Crisis

> If we were to abandon all those states run by dictators in
> Africa, there would be no one left to cooperate with.
> —Socialist Italian Foreign Minister
> Gianni De Michells in 1990

INTRODUCTION

Africa is a tragedy in more ways than one. So many foreign governments, agencies, and institutions set out to help eradicate poverty in Africa. So much in foreign aid, loans, and credits were poured into Africa to spur development. More than $400 billion in aid and credits have been pumped into Africa since the 1960s, not to mention the massive expenditures for peace missions. The 1993 humanitarian mission in Somalia, for example, cost the international community a staggering $3.5 billion. Yet all these efforts have borne negligible results. The continent continues to sink deeper into an economic abyss.

In destroying their economies, Africa's tyrants had much help— direct and indirect—from the West. This help came in a variety of forms: foreign aid, diplomatic recognition, joint military exercises, intellectual support, and racial solidarity from black Americans. During the Cold War, the geopolitical and strategic importance of Africa attracted the attention of the superpowers. In the 1980s it was argued that, for its own interests, the West should not ignore Africa. Its geostrategic location, abutting Gulf oil sea lanes, will render it indispensable to the economic security of the West in the 1990s and beyond. It is further argued that, Africa will become an important source for such strategic and important minerals as cobalt, chromium, manganese, platinum, rhodium, titanium, and vanadium, especially when deposits elsewhere are depleted. "Without these critical minerals, all major industrial production could grind to a halt" (*World & I,* September 1988, 35).

With its rich supply of minerals and its large potential market for foreign goods, Africa became a terrain on which the Western and Soviet blocs and other foreign powers competed for access, power, and influence, often by playing one country against another. African leaders also benefited enormously from the Cold War game. They touted their ideological importance to both sides and played one superpower against the other to extract maximum concessions and aid. The continent thus became a theater of superpower rivalry, intrigues, and blunders.

Nigeria, for example, which was regarded as a substantial prize because of its size and mineral wealth, became the object of intense superpower competition. The East met West in 1988 in the hangars of Makurdi Air Base in central Nigeria. As the *Washington Post* (23 July 1994) reported: "Soviet military advisers hovered around two dozen MiG-21 fighter jets supplied by Moscow to Nigeria's long-serving military government. British advisers watched over 15 Jaguar fighter-bombers sold to balance the Soviet supplies. Americans ferried supplies for nine C-130 transport planes. Czechs tended approximately two dozen L-39 jet trainers they had sold. Italians carried spare parts for eight G-222 aircrafts" (A1).

Seduced by the charisma and the verbiage of Third World despots, the West provided them with substantial military and economic aid. "In the past, we have had, for national security reasons, to consort with dictators," admitted former U.S. Ambassador Smith Hempstone (*The Washington Post*, 6 May 1993, A7). But the heavy Western investment in these tyrants, who were blatantly corrupt and brutally repressive, often drew the ire of the people of the Third World. The subsequent overthrow of these dictators invariably unleashed a wave of intense anti-American or anti-Western sentiment. Tensions rose even further when these corrupt ex-leaders almost always managed to escape to the West with their booty.

Similarly, the West often obliged and supported pro-capitalist African dictators, despite their hideously repressive and neo-Communist regimes. For geopolitical, economic, and other reasons, the West propped up tyrants in Cameroon, Côte d'Ivoire, Kenya, Liberia, Malawi, and Zaire as Cold War allies to the detriment of democratic movements. To check the spread of Marxism in Africa, the United States in particular sought and nurtured alliances with "pro-West" regimes in Kenya, Malawi, South Africa, and Zaire and with guerrilla groups (UNITA in Angola). Substantial American investment poured into these countries and military support was covertly supplied to UNITA. At the same time, the U.S. government attempted to woo socialist/Marxist regimes in Ghana, Madagascar, Mozambique, Tanzania, and Zambia. U.S. Secretary of State Warren Christopher confirmed that "During the long Cold War period, America's policies toward Africa were often determined not by how they affected Africa, but by what advantage they brought to Washington or Moscow" (*The Economist,* 29 May 1993, 46).

WESTERN ACADEMICS AND DEVELOPMENT EXPERTS

In the 1950s and 1960s, the prevailing development orthodoxy held that poverty was a pathological condition in the Third World that needed to be eradicated. Although various causal factors were identified, the culprit was held to be inadequate rate of capital accumulation or investment. But more, however, could not be invested because savings were low. That, in turn, was due to low income, since savings are derived from income. But then income was low because investment was inadequate. Thus, the poor country was caught in a vicious circle or a "low-level equilibrium trap."

To break this circle, it was argued, private enterprise and markets could not be relied on. Markets in the developing countries were either nonexistent or underdeveloped; as such they could not provide reliable guidance for development. The only way out of the poverty trap was somehow to raise the national income to the point where savings and capital accumulation would flow in sufficient volume. A "big push" was needed to launch the economy into a takeoff of self-sustaining growth. These ideas were associated with such economists as Gunnar Myrdal, W. W. Rostow, S. Kuznets, Harvey Leibenstein, and H. W. Singer.

However, before the question of how to get the "big push" initiated was tackled, it was universally agreed that colonialism must end, since the colonial state lacked the legitimacy to undertake any fundamental social transformation. The onus, therefore, must be placed on the first successor states just beginning to emerge in Africa. As Fieldhouse (1986) aptly described it, "On these states and their character the economists—like the 18th century philosophies, with whom they had much in common, before them—placed great faith. Their rulers were assumed to be both enlightened and efficient, and so fit to be the main instruments of change and development" (88).

Because of the widespread belief that market prices in Africa were distorted and did not reflect true social values, development analysts placed great emphasis on economic management and planning as the alternative to the market. Under state planning, it was thought that development could overcome such deficiencies or market imperfections. Such theories as "The Big Push" and "Unbalanced Growth Models" of development proliferated at this time.

Scores of Western scholars and institutions provided the intellectual and moral grist for statism. As Bandow (1986) pointed out: "The London School of Economics, which promoted the socialist development model, was perhaps the most important educational institution for English-speaking colonial subjects . . . As a result, leaders throughout the underdeveloped world adopted this particular British economic philosophy as their own" (20).

Bandow continued that, as culpable as the menagerie of Western economic advisers who developed the statist philosophies adopted by developing nations were, the international aid agencies did worse. They paid Third World leaders to adopt the *dirigiste* model. Even the World Bank resorted to these influences—as much as it was reputed to be a pro–free enterprise and market-oriented organization, it encouraged state-run governments instead of attempting to promote capitalism and democracy (23).

The World Bank's support for statism was reflected in its lending policies. Most of its loans focused on government-devised infrastructure projects. For example, throughout the 1980s, the bank committed about 80 percent of its funds to government enterprises, or parastatals.

The IMF, on the other hand, provided less direct support for statism. Its focus was on balance-of-payment disequilibria, and its loans were subject to conditionalities such as devaluation, trimming budget deficits, and general macroeconomic management. However, IMF emphasis and insistence on conditionalities and macromanagement had the effect of reinforcing the notion of state management and control. An African government that followed IMF prescriptions would solve its country's economic problems. Nothing could have played more into the hands of Africa's statists. "For 30 years, Zambia's statist policies of import-substitution, subsidized food prices and state enterprises were backed by western economic advisers including the World Bank. True, the IMF always disliked them, but then, as one IMF official says privately: 'Why did we lend $1.2 billion to a government whose policies we disapproved of?'" (*The Economist*, 1 July 1995, 34).

Many Western governments and international aid agencies also supported or subscribed to this orthodoxy. Foreign direct investment was not considered capable of curing the vicious cycle of poverty. It was argued that this type of investment tended to be concentrated in "enclaves" that were insulated from the rest of the host economy. In economic jargon, foreign direct investment lacked forward and backward linkages. Thus foreign enterprises, it was concluded, did not contribute significantly to the process of capital accumulation or the creation of local skills and know-how. If anything, they caused a drain on resources. To deliver the needed "big push," foreign *aid* would be a better alternative. Coincidentally, at this time Europe was recovering splendidly from World War II with the Marshall Aid Plan. Why not a similar plan for postcolonial Africa to break out of the poverty trap?

As Whitaker (1988) noted: "From the early 1960s on, the World Bank and the International Development Association supplied at least 25 percent of the loans to Africa. U.S. aid fluctuated widely, doubling during the Kennedy and the Carter administrations, and receding in the mid-1980s when the United States itself became a major debtor nation. Yet throughout this period, the World Bank, the United States, and most Africans felt that development would occur by creating industries and services which would expand and diversify the economy. Governments themselves would move into areas that Europeans and Asians nearly monopolized. The United States and the World Bank actively supported national planning as the basis for government activity and their own projects" (66).

Said Stephen Thompson of Washington:

> Behind the World Bank's astounding incompetence is its basic economic philosophy, which is more in line with that of the old Soviet Union than of the West. Its preferred way of operating is to set up some Soviet-style development "project" that in one fell swoop is supposed to lift the economic status of the area to a higher plane. Of course, such projects are usually done more or less as government programs, resulting in theft, bribery, kickbacks and other corruption on the part of government officials. (*The Washington Times,* 20 June 1995, A18)

The World Bank committed numerous blunders in Africa. In 1987 it even sought to build a regional headquarters in Addis Ababa at a time when civil war was raging in the country. In June 1989 the bank advanced $33 million to Somalia for structural adjustment while a civil war in the north was expanding. Maren (1997) wrote: "These so-called development agencies [the IMF and the World Bank] kept right on financing the destruction of the country. Their actions were eroding Somalia's economy, making people poor, and, in a bizarre way, creating a need for more and more aid, more and more NGO [non-governmental organi-zation]. It was a cycle that eventually would consume itself" (175).

The same blunders were repeated in Rwanda, where a World Bank mission in September 1993 issued a glowing report in April 1994, the same time that Rwanda descended into savage anarchy. In Algeria, also wracked by civil war, the World Bank and the IMF were supporting economic reforms in 1994-95 (*The Washington Post,* 3 August 1995, 26).

Worse, the donor agencies seldom agreed among themselves. A case in point was Mozambique in 1995. The IMF demanded budget cuts to squeeze out inflation. On the other side, aid-giving governments argued that if the IMF went on squeezing, there would be nothing left to adjust. Western ambassadors in Mozambique, including U.S. Ambassador Dennis Jett, wrote a stiff letter to the IMF headquarters in Washington, complaining about "obsession with monetary targets and no interest in the lives of ordinary people" (*The Economist,* 28 October 1995, 46). The IMF did not back down.

The United Nations agencies also supported statism. For example, all United Nations Development Program (UNDP) funds go to governments, and the agency consciously avoids projects that do not involve close public sector involvement. Bandow (1986) would also include the United Nations General Assembly, the United Nations Conference of Trade and Development (UNCTAD), as well as United States AID and nongovernmental organizations in his indictment. "Throughout the postwar period, the Ford Foundation, the Harvard Institute for International Development, and the MIT Center for International Studies have all supported the local and central planning bureaucracies of India and Pakistan. Though the American economists generally advised the adoption of modest market incentives—such as higher prices for farmers—all three groups endorsed the transcendent goal of state planning" (25).

WESTERN MEDIA BIAS AND DOUBLE STANDARD

I am sick and tired of seeing Africa represented only in the white man's terms, as if Africans themselves are inarticulate about their own lives, lazy people waiting with a bowl in hand for help. Where are the African leaders, dissenters, economists and scientists?

—Tarzi Vittachi of UNICEF
(*TV GUIDE,* 24 May 1986, 3)

African despots probably found their greatest silent allies in the Western media. One would assume that if Africa's problems could not be exposed in Africa on account of censorship and intellectual repression, they could be exposed in the West for correct diagnosis and prescription of solutions. But excessive racial sensitivity, political correctness, ignorance, and even arrogance proved to be formidable obstacles to overcome. White editors and journalists who wrote about Africa's crises were attacked as "racist" and the Western media bludgeoned for their "negative coverage of Africa." The situation did not improve when black Americans were included on formerly white editorial boards. A practice evolved whereby white editors deferred African stories to black American editors for approval. Quite often these stories were spiked if they did not fit into the black American editors' racial and/or political agenda. In this way, both black and white editors seriously compromised the truth about Africa.

The racial sensitivity problem was compounded by ignorance. As Ungar (1985) complained: "American intentions in Africa have fre-quently been good, to the extent that there have been any at all. From colonial times to the present, the U.S. has almost ignored the African continent, maintaining a childlike innocence about the second largest land mass in the world, 11,635,000 square miles with a population now estimated to be approaching 500 million. . . . There are now more than fifty independent countries in Africa, but most Americans would be hard-pressed to name half a dozen" (20).

Then crookery set in. Over the past two decades, helping Africa became a growth industry. A swarm of fly-by-night "experts" emerged who falsely professed vast knowledge of the continent after a mere one day stay at an African airport and returned to dispense expensive vile counsel. In 1989, for example, technical assistance/cooperation amounted to $3.2 billion—or one-quarter of total official development assistance to sub-Saharan Africa, according to a 1993 UNDP study. This is not to suggest that all Western experts lack operational understanding of Africa's crises. But much of what many Western experts know about Africa is gleaned from outdated books and films. As a result, analyses of African issues often tend to be pitifully shallow and naive. Needless to say, Western assistance programs, though laudable and well intentioned, often ended up as enormous and costly failures because of faulty analysis.

The 1985 Ethiopian famine relief efforts brought this fact to the fore. Again, the efforts and intentions were noble but the approach and modalities, based mostly on obsolete paradigms and misconceptions, left much to be desired. Little effort was made to ask those in need what type of assistance was best suited for them. To help American farmers, one asks them what they need. Simple though this maxim may seem, it was not applied in the case of relief aid to Africa.

According to Joanmarie Kalter, TV's focus on Western relief mirrored the colonial conception of Africans as backward and helpless, a "white man's burden." "Of 117 quotes from analysts and professionals in network famine reports, only 18 came from of Africans; an over-whelming 94 were from white Americans or Europeans," she claimed. And what about the indigenous relief efforts? Djibril Diallo of the United Nations Office for Emergency Operations in Africa confirmed that Senegalese fishermen contributed 33 tons of fish to the hungry in Senegal and that Africans mounted musical fund-raisers in the Côte d'Ivoire and Sudan well before Live Aid concerts in the West for Ethiopian famine victims.

> [According to one Western correspondent,] "In many of my stories, I used interviews with African experts. They know more about these problems than anyone. But they would be cut, sometimes replaced with American or British experts. . . . It upset me. I interviewed the people who knew most about the region, but my bosses would want a young American who was there on his first trip."
>
> This "we-know-best" approach, say development experts, not only contributed to the crisis, but also bedevils our current efforts to help. Says Rep. Howard Wolpe, chairman of the House Foreign Relations Sub-Committee on Africa, "It's certainly one of the reasons why some of our development assistance programs over the years have been so monumen-tally unsuccessful. We don't listen to what Africans say about their own environment and experiences." And so what we offer can be wholly inappropriate. (*TV GUIDE,* 24 May 1986, 3)

Imbued with compassion, the Western media is naturally attracted to situations of "great human suffering." When an African crisis erupts, the media launches an appeal to the U.S. government and the interna-tional community for "humanitarian assistance to ease the suffering"— as in Somalia, Rwanda, Liberia, and Sudan. In so doing, the liberal Western media assumes it is "helping" Africa when in fact it is doing more harm and compounding the problem.

First, the liberal Western media seldom performs a coherent analysis of the internal causes of an African calamity, since doing so may lead it to blame African leadership. But that would not be "politically correct" or acceptable since it amounts to "blaming the victim"—a strange interpretation, since African leaders are in fact the perpetrators of vile deeds and the primary cause of the crises. Blaming African leaders also may draw the ire of black Americans and possibly evoke charges of racism. Thus, to play it safe, the liberal media chooses to focus on the "human suffering" rather than the internal causes and, in doing so, it absolves African despots of responsibility.

Second, by appealing to the international community for humanitarian assistance to ease human suffering in Africa, the liberal Western media perpetuates the offensive notion that solutions to Africa's problems cannot come from within Africa and always must come from external sources. This feeds into the mentality of incompetent African tyrants, who, when a crisis emerges, sit on their hands, appeal to the international community, and wait.

THE PERNICIOUS FAILURE OF WESTERN AID TO AFRICA

Foreign aid has done more harm to Africa than we care to admit. It has led to a situation where Africa has failed to set its own pace and direction of development free of external interference. Today, Africa's development plans are drawn thousands of miles away in the corridors of the IMF and World Bank. What is sad is that the IMF and World Bank "experts" who draw these development plans are people completely out of touch with the local African reality.

—David Karanja, a former Kenya
member of parliament,
in *New African,* June 1992, 20

That Western aid to Africa has been ineffective can no longer be disputed. U.S. AID itself admitted in 1993 that "much of the [Third World] investment financed by U.S. AID and other donors between 1960 and 1980 has disappeared without a trace" (*The Washington Times,* 10 October 1996, A19). "The African countries that received the most aid—Somalia, Liberia, and Zaire—have slid into virtual anarchy. Another large recipient, Kenya, inflicts unspeakable abuses of human rights on its own citizens while aid pays the bills" (Maren, 1997, 11).

In a letter to Secretary of State Warren Christopher, the U.S. House of Representative's International Relations Committee chairman, Representative Benjamin Gilman—a Republican—and Lee H. Hamilton, a ranking Democratic member, wrote:

Zaire under Mobutu represents perhaps the most egregious example of the misuse of U.S. assistance resources. The U.S. has given Mobutu nearly $1.5 billion in various forms of aid since Mobutu came to power in 1965. Mobutu claims that during the Cold War he and his fellow African autocrats were concerned with fighting Soviet influence and were unable to concentrate on creating viable economic and political systems. The reality is that during this time Mr. Mobutu was becoming one of the world's wealthiest individuals while the people of Zaire, a once-wealthy country, were pauperized." (*The Washington Times,* 6 July 1995, A18)

Similarly, the United States gave Liberia's late President Samuel Doe more than $375 million in aid between 1980 and 1985. But much of it was squandered and looted, forcing that country into a receivership on 2 May 1986.

Some analysts, such as Morton (1994), question the concept of aid itself. Others take aim at the administration of aid. A 1995 Foreign Aid study was conducted by the Freedom Support Coalition, chaired by former Congressman Dave Nagle and its 1,000-page report was released on 12 October 1995. "Mr. Nagle said in an interview that 80 percent of foreign aid is spent in the United States buying food, equipment, expertise and services. But he said many Americans wrongly believe most of the $13 billion a year the U.S. has been spending on foreign assistance goes directly to foreign leaders" (*The Washington Times,* 13 October 1995, A17). Even then, U.S. AID was plagued with cronyism: "Ninety-five percent of procurement went to a few firms that only did business with AID. They were inside-the-Beltway firms that employed former AID staffers," said Larry Bryne, the assistant administrator for management (*The Washington Times,* 19 August 1996, A8). Similarly, "an estimated 80 percent of French aid comes back in salaries, orders and profits," according to Biddlecombe (1994). So who is helping whom?

However, what contributed most to the grievous failure of Western aid to Africa was a donor culture of doublespeak, inconsistencies in policy actions to achieve a confusing, and an overlapping set of objectives. Foreign aid comes in three forms: economic development assistance, military aid, and humanitarian relief assistance for humanitarian crisis situations. Despite being cloaked in "development" garb, economic development assistance to Africa has over the decades been used as an instrument by the donors to achieve a variety of noneconomic (geopolitical and political) objectives, such as the containment of Communist expansionism in Africa, democratization, and promotion of human rights, among others. But some of these are also the stated policy objectives of U.S. foreign military aid, which seeks to promote stability, democracy, and human rights among U.S. allies. The two key elements of that program have been Foreign Military Financing, which provided allies with grants, military equipment, and related technical services; and International Military Education and Training, which provided extensive training of foreign military officers and police forces in a wide variety of operations. Such U.S. military aid went to brutal military regimes in Liberia (under the late Samuel Doe), Ghana (under Jerry Rawlings), Somalia (under the late Siad Barre) and Zaire (under Mobutu).

POST-COLD WAR WESTERN ECONOMIC AID TO AFRICA

After the Cold War, Western foreign policy objectives were overhauled. Greater emphasis was placed on promotion of democracy, respect for human rights, better governance, transparency, and accountability, among others. In May 1990, for example, the U.S. Congress and the White House reshaped the U.S. foreign aid program in light of global political changes and reordered priorities. President George Bush sought new flexibility to boost aid to emerging democracies in Eastern Europe, Panama, and Nicaragua. Assistant Secretary of State for Africa Herman J. Cohen announced in May 1990 that, along with economic adjustment and the observance of human rights, democratization would soon be included as the third prerequisite for U.S. development aid. Shortly after the establishment of the policy of tying bilateral aid to political conditions, the U.S. Congress called for institutions such as the World Bank to do the same for multilateral aid.

But beyond the rhetoric, nothing much changed underneath the surface. It was "business as usual." Old friends remained old friends. The reformist winds of change that blew across Africa in the early 1990s subsided rather quickly. As Michaels (1993) noted, "Economic reforms that promised to bring back foreign capital investment have thus far only deepened Africa's dependency on foreign aid. The pace of political transition that saw no less than nine leaders toppled by gun or ballot in the nine months following the fall of 1990 has slowed to a crawl, as many incumbent regimes have managed to maintain military control while outmaneuvering splintered oppositions" (34).

The West stood by and watched as wily autocrats honed their skills to beat back the democratic challenge. Africa's democratization experience in the 1990s has been marked by vapid Western pronouncements, truculent duplicity, and scurrilous abandonment. When the going got tough, the West cut and ran.

Although virtually all Western governments made lofty statements about the virtues of democracy, they did little to aid and establish it in Africa. There have been more than 170 changes of government in Africa since 1960, but one would be hard-pressed to name five countries that the West successfully democratized from 1970 to 1990. The record since 1990 has been dismal. Pro-democracy forces in Benin, Cape Verde Islands, Zambia, Malawi and other newly democratized African countries received little help from Western governments. Nor have democratic forces in Ghana, Nigeria, and Kenya for that matter. This was not the case in South Africa or Eastern Europe. In South Africa, the African National Council received funds and material from Western governments. Similarly in Poland, Solidarity received substantial assistance from Western governments. But the West seems incapable of abandoning its racialist way of thinking and apply one race-neutral standard to all of Africa.

Still wedded to old colonial paradigms, Western governments have yet to grasp the full import of current events in Africa. The struggle being waged now is for the second liberation of Africa. The "enemies" this time around are primarily "internal": black neocolonialists, crocodile liberators, military coconutheads, Swiss bank socialists, grasping kleptocrats, vampire elites, gaping sycophants, and intellectual prostitutes. In short, scoundrels, whose ruling ethic is self-aggrandizement and self-perpetuation in power. They care not an iota about their people or their country, only about themselves.

More maddening, the donor agencies *know* about these leaders' motivations and activities. In an interview, Edward Jaycox, the World Bank's Vice President for Africa, complained bitterly: "How many African governments put a top priority on alleviating poverty? I can't even think of three. When has the military given up it toys? When has a diplomatic mission been closed in the interests of poverty alleviation? When has the role of women been enhanced in any of these African countries, without outside interference?" (*Africa Recovery,* April-September 1994, 9).

Yet, the bank considers these same African governments as "partners in development." When the United Nations launched a $25 billion Special Initiative for Africa on 15 March 1996, to revive development on the continent, World Bank president James Wolfensohn gushed that "he was pleased that the Special Initiative is designed to be supportive of and a 'true partnership' with African leadership" (*African Recovery,* May 1996, 13). In a letter to the editor of *The Washington Times* (20 June

1995), Stephen Thompson was furious: "The infusion of cash strengthens corrupt ruling classes and encourages the continuation of disastrous socialist policies. Thus, the World Bank becomes, in effect, the partner of corrupt, oppressive, often brutal regimes" (A18).

World Bank loans and foreign aid to Africa have bailed out tyrannical regimes. After its economy was shattered by crass "revolutionary" policies in 1983, the Marxist PNDC regime in Ghana found its days numbered. The Soviets and Cubans could no longer provide assistance. It made overtures to the West, which responded with alacrity, eager to win one more "convert." The regime signed a structural adjustment agreement with the World Bank in 1983. Slight improvements in the economy were hailed hysterically and Ghana was declared a "success story," a "role model for Africa." Twelve years later and after the infusion of more than $2 billion in World Bank loans and credit, the World Bank itself admitted that "prospects for sustaining satisfactory rates of growth and poverty reduction are uncertain" (OED Report No. 99, December 1995). Subsequently, the Bank's own 1996 Country Assessment Report stated that declaring Ghana a "success story" was a mistake and not in the country's own best interest.

Similarly in Mozambique and Angola, whose economies had been devastated by years of senseless civil wars. The Marxist regimes in both countries, under siege from freedom fighters, were about to collapse. They did what any clever Marxist would do to survive: blamed apartheid South Africa for funding insurgency activity in their country, eschewed doctrinaire Marxism, expunged all references to this ideology from government documents, and signed a structural adjustment agreement with the World Bank. Eager to woo these countries from the Soviet orbit, Western financial and technical assistance poured into Mozambique in the late 1989, at the rate of $800 million a year. Britain even provided military assistance and personnel to help Zimbabwean forces crush the insurgents in Mozambique and to rebuild and reopen the Beira Corridor where goods flowed from the interior to the port city of Beira. Suddenly these resistance forces or freedom fighters, who for years put up a courageous struggle against brutal Marxism, were now characterized as "bandits" and forsaken by the West. The same fate befell the resistance forces in Angola. In July 1989, when Angola was faced with imminent economic collapse, President dos Santos took up membership of the IMF. A year later his government formally abandoned Marxist-Leninism and announced that it would introduce a market economy. The new Clinton administration cheered and the State Department made diplomatic exchanges with Angola. Dos Santos was invited to the United States, just as Jerry Rawlings was officially invited. The rehabilitation and bailout of Marxist "tin gods" was complete.

In this way, World Bank–sponsored SAP provided failing regimes with the door to redemption in the West and, more important, to their own survival. Had the World Bank insisted on signing SAP agreements with only democratic countries and those *at peace*, the course of history in Ghana, Mozambique, and Angola would have been different and their people would have breathed easier. The very act of signing such an agreement was an admission of failure. Johnson (1993) noted that:

> Western experts who had backed the rapid transfer of power argued that Africa, in particular, was going through a difficult transition, and that patience—plus assistance of all kinds—was imperative. That view is now discredited. During the 1980's it came to be recognized that government-to-government aid usually served only to keep in power unsuccessful, unpopular and often vicious regimes. By the early 1990's, some international agencies were beginning openly argue that, in crisis situations, like the famine in East Africa, a Western military presence was essential to supplement a largely nonexistent government. (7)

The relationship between Western donors and African governments is akin to that of a battered spouse. She (the World Bank) cannot make up her mind whether to leave or stay with the marriage. She might stay, hoping that she can change the abusive husband, which is often to no avail. Western governments naively assume that diplomatic talk or gestures can influence African despots. For example, when Nigeria's military despot, "the Butcher of Abuja," defied world opinion and proceeded to hang Ken Saro-Wiwa in November 1995, Western governments withdrew their diplomats in protest. But Abacha made no concessions and after a few months, the diplomats were quietly sent back.

Nor has the West been able to influence, let alone accelerate, the pace of democratic reform in Africa. For example on 29 December 1992, Kenya held its first multiparty elections in 26 years. Every indication pointed to a fraudulent outcome. Opposition parties were given barely two months to campaign. In his campaign speeches Moi, who has earned a reputation for political thuggery, vowed that he would crush his opponents "like rats." On 9 December candidates or their agents were required to hand in their papers in person. "Nearly 50 opposition activists were barred from doing do, by various means. They met illegal roadblocks, papers were snatched from their grasp, some were kidnapped. No KANU candidate [found] such obstructions" (*The Economist*, 26 December 1992, 52). Opposition candidates and their supporters were harassed, voter registration rolls were manipulated, opposition rallies were restricted, and the state media was biased in favor of the ruling party. Moi handily "won" the elections, although disunity among Kenya's opposition parties played a role. Yet U.S. response to this massive electoral outrage in Kenya was meek.

To be sure, Western governments cannot dictate the type of democracy that will be suitable for the African people themselves. But the West can indicate what it will not accept: democratic malfeasance (manipulation and control of the transition process by one side) or unlevel political playing fields (opposition parties denied access to the state media and stripped of state resources). Democracy is not dictated or imposed. It is a *participatory exercise*. In South Africa, all the various political parties and anti-apartheid organizations gathered together in a Convention for a Democratic South Africa to create a new society for their country. But in Cameroon, Ghana, Nigeria, Kenya, Togo, and many other African countries, incumbent governments drew up the transition programs by themselves without the participation of political parties, which were banned.

If Western governments will not help the pro-democracy groups, they should at the very least be fair, neutral, and consistent. In Poland, they helped Solidarity. In South Africa, they helped Mandela and the ANC. So why not help the Lech Walesas and Mandelas of the rest of Africa? Further, the standard applied to Kenya and Nigeria should be the same applied to Ghana and Togo. Unfortunately, official Western approach to democratization in Africa has been marked by blatant inconsistencies and doublespeak. Despite Britain's condemnation of military governments and denial of any possibility of military involvement with them, a December 1994 report from the British high commission in Sierra Leone recorded that a senior British diplomat, David MacLennan, told the Sierra Leoneans that the British government had decided to offer a military adviser, a short-term training team for senior officers, and a procurement expert to study defense purchase problems in their war against the country's rebels (*The Economist*, 8 July 1995, 40). Similarly in Nigeria, the British government claimed it had placed restrictions on arm sales. Yet in 1994, Britain issued 30 export licenses for "non-lethal" military equipment for the Nigerian junta.

The French, however, are the worst. In May 1991, 9 million rounds of ammunition arrived in Cameroon on a ship from France, destined for the authoritarian government of President Paul Biya (*The Economist,* 7 March 1992, 46). The ammunition helped Biya brutally suppress political opponents, enabling him to win the October 1992 presidential election in a vote that observers said was fraudulent. As *The Economist* (29 May 1993) observed, "Two months later France gave Cameroon FF600 million [$110 million] in new loans. In May 1993, Mr. Biya was welcomed in Paris by both Mr. Mitterrand and the new French prime minister, Edouard Balladur. In Rwanda soldiers loyal to President Juvenal Habyarimana have been responsible for atrocities against the Rwanda's Tutsi minority. Yet Mr. Mitterrand continues to help the regime" (46).

The late President Mitterrand was severely rebuked at a French-African summit at Biarritz on 8 November 1994: "Human rights groups said Mitterrand's decision to invite Mobutu, along with other notorious, long-standing leaders, such as Gabon's Omar Bongo and Togo's Gnassingbe Eyadema, was a betrayal of his promises at the 1990 summit in La Baule, in northwestern France, to terminate the autocratic rule of 'Africa's dinosaurs'" (*The Washington Post,* 9 November 1994, A41).

During a visit to Yaounde, Paris mayor Jacques Chirac, then campaigning for the presidency of France, declared that "the continent was not yet mature enough for Western-style democracy, which he called a luxury that Africa cannot afford now" (*The Washington Times,* 20 April 1995, A13). Guess who cheered hysterically at this insult to the people of Africa?

According to *The Washington Times* (16 July 1996), "Paris has tolerated a high level of corruption and economic mismanagement among the pro-French governments in Africa.... The French giant Elf-Aquitaine virtually operates Gabon's oil industry. France is by far Gabon's biggest trade partner, supplying 44 percent of its imports and 80 percent of its foreign aid. Three-quarters of all foreign investment in the country comes from France. Gabon and Elf's subsidiary there have long been a source of funding for French political parties, especially Mr. Chirac's Gaullists" (A11).

The French never equated decolonization with retreat. "Charles de Gaulle, assisted by a handful of competent and ruthless men, managed an incredible sleight of hand: not a termination of France's control over its former African colonies, but a transformation of its control into something quite original—a community of nations, sharing one currency, that was tied to France economically, politically, culturally and, of course, militarily," said Gerard Prunier of the Paris-based National Center for Scientific Research (*The Wall Street Journal*, 24 January 1997, A14). African children were taught that their ancestors were Gauls and that the deserving among them would gain French citizenship.

But as we saw earlier, France established a far more effective form of control over francophone Africa than any form of colonization by linking their currency to the French franc and by insisting that Francophone African countries keep 30 to 35 percent of their deposits with the Bank of France. These deposits are supposed to earn interest, but it is rarely paid and corrupt African government officials hardly notice. It is called the "interest rate dodge" (Biddlecombe, 1994, 37).

Disguised by bombastic gushing of "cooperation," France's real intention, however, was to protect its economic interests and gain access to Africa's minerals. And French economic interests were vast. Twenty percent of France's oil came from West Africa. Côte d'Ivoire buys 40 percent of its imports from France and the French own a third of the country's manufacturing industries (*The New York Times*, 23 February 1994, A6).

As *The Economist* (12 August 1995) put it:

> France has always regarded its francophone "commonwealth" in Africa as part of its ticket to world-power status. Since General de Gaulle's time, French presidents have maintained direct personal links with African heads of state, appointing a Mr. Africa as personal fixer and emissary (President Mitterrand sent his son). French officials, sometimes seconded from Paris ministries, sit behind the thrones of many African leaders. French political parties receive donations from African leaders; French companies, especially oil ones, are given extraordinary privileges in African states; French arms protect African allies. And aid has flowed freely. In 1993, France's budget for overseas aid was $7.9 billion. (35).

The United States also applies its own set of inconsistent criteria. In June 1993, for example, Amnesty International charged that the United States was spending billions of dollars on military and security assistance to countries that often used the money and equipment to oppress their own citizens. "Despite the fact that the stated goals for much of this assistance is the promotion of democracy and human rights, many of the recipients of U.S. security assistance continue to be responsible for gross violations of human rights," it said (*The Washington Times*, 9 June 1993,

A9). Among the African countries Amnesty International named were Egypt, Kenya, Malawi, Morocco, and Zaire. Also, "One [human rights] standard is applied to the special friends of the United States and another is applied to other countries," complained Jim O'Dea, director of Amnesty International's Washington office. "We would like to see the U.S. government get back on the road of credibility in its human rights policy" (*The Washington Post*, 9 June 1993, A23).

HOW WESTERN CHARITY HELPED DESTROY SOMALIA

Somalia is probably the most egregious example of Western patronage gone berserk. Huge amounts of economic and disaster relief aid was dumped into Somalia, transforming the country into the Graveyard of Aid. But the massive inflow of food aid in the early 1990s did much to shred the fabric of Somali society. Droughts and famines are not new to Africa, and most traditional societies developed indigenous methods of coping. These methods were destroyed in Somalia, and the country became more and more dependent on food imports. "The share of food import in the total volume of food consumption rose from less than 33 percent on average for the 1970-79 period to over 63 percent during the 1980-84 period, which coincides with Western involvement in the Somalia economy and food-aid programs" (Maren, 1997, 171).

Grain prices were depressed, giving local farmers less incentives to farm. It became easier for them to trek to the refugee centers for their food rations. The young, armed with AK-47s, saw an opportunity. Relief supplies could be looted. One Somali, Abdirahman Osman Raghe, complained bitterly:

> We would talk about how food aid destroyed our systems. For many years we weren't dependent on food aid. We had droughts before, but in the past there was a credit system; the nomads were coming to the urban areas and taking loans that they would pay back when times were good. There was a system among the nomads of sharing resources. People worked together.
>
> Look into drug donations and how they destroyed our developing health system. We once had so many pharmacies here. Pharmacists knew their jobs. Now there are people handing out drugs who are not trained, because of the donated drugs from the international community that are so cheap. (Maren, 1997, 166)

Between 1981 and 1990, Italy sponsored 114 projects in Somalia, costing more than $1 billion. According to Wolfgang Achtner, an Italian journalist, "with few exceptions (such as vaccination programs carried out by NGOs [nongovernmental organizations]), the Italian ventures were absurd and wasteful" (*The Washington Post*, 24 January 1993, C3). One example was the $250 million spent on the Garoe-Bosaso road that stretched 450 kilometers across barren desert that was crossed only by nomads on foot.

Piero Ugolini, a Florentine agronomist who worked for the technical unit of the Italian Embassy in Mogadishu from 1986 to 1990, revealed that most of Italian cooperation projects were carried out without considering their effects on the local population. "Italian aid program was used to exploit the pastoral populations and to support a regime that did nothing to promote internal development and was responsible for the death of many of its people," he said.

Italian construction and engineering companies that were given lucrative contracts for projects in Somalia provided kickbacks to politicians in Rome and Mogadishu. In fact, Italians colonies were divided up among the politicians. Ethiopia, another former Italian colony in the Horn of Africa, went to the Christian Democrats. The Socialist Party, which got Somalia, flooded it with millions of dollars of aid (*Washington Post*, 24 January 1993, C3).

Siad Barre used this aid to purchase arms and military advisers for his armed forces, which declared war against their own people. Northern Somalia, a hotbed of opposition to Barre's tyrannical rule, was bombed on several occasions, even with napalm. Burned-out buildings bore testimony to the depravity of Barre's rule. Barre's eldest son, Colonel Hassan Mohammed Barre, who handled the aid money, acquired property and bank accounts in Switzerland. Yet Rome maintained friendly relations with Siad Barre after the bishop of Mogadishu, Salvatore Colombo, was assassinated in July 1989, and even after an Italian biologist was beaten to death in the Somali Secret Services headquarters in June 1990.

When the Somalia crisis erupted in 1991, a swarm of foreign NGOs descended on the country. Why so many? According to Maren (1997), who was food assessment specialist for U.S. AID, "There was money available from donors, so they came. The Somali government loved it as well. More NGOs meant more headquarters in Mogadishu. Most of the major landlords in the city were relatives of the president or other high government officials. Even in towns such Beledweyne, homes were rented from government officials at preposterous rates. The government was pleased to have all the NGOs they could get." (95)

Very quickly, the aims of the humanitarian mission became perverted. Each group or organization involved in the relief efforts saw in the famine/war crisis an opportunity to advance their own sectarian agenda. Refugee aid became such an important source of foreign exchange that the Somali government grossly inflated the number of refugees. According to Maren (1997), "The million and half refugees who were allegedly in Somalia didn't exist. The Somali Government liked to say 1.5 million. Journalists liked to say 1.5 million. It looked good and added a weightiness to their stories. Several press reports even took the liberty of pushing the figure up to 2 million. My own rough estimates from the time spent in the camps made me suspect that even 400,000 was generous" (97).

Nor was the government interested in resettling or solving the refugee crisis, as that would eliminate its source of foreign currency. Political reasons were involved as well. Many refugees were from the Ogadeen clan, Siad Barre's mother's clan. They were grateful for being fed and also for being given land taken from the rival clans. If the relief food aid was halted, Barre could lose the political support of the Ogadeen clan. In addition, relief aid provided Somali soldiers with the means to supplement their income.

A large part of the donor funds goes to feed a hungry bureaucracy. Aggressive lobbying campaigns often are launched to provide justification for the continuation of food relief aid. Ken Hackett, director of Catholic Relief Services, pitching the idea of food aid, told the U.S. Congress: "Each food aid dollar has at least a double impact. First, the funds are spent primarily in the United States on U.S. commodities, processing, bagging, fortification, and transportation. This enhances economic activity and increases the tax receipts to the U.S. government. Second, the food is provided to people and countries which cannot afford to import adequate amounts of food on a commercial basis. Finally, when PVOs are involved, we leverage funds and services and gain broad public participation" (Maren, 1997, 201).

How much of the food actually reaches the needy? In the case of Save the Children, in 1994 less than 50 percent of the total of sponsors' dollars actually went in grants to field programs. Of that amount, about half was given in grants to other organizations, which also had their own salaries and expenses, to actually implement the programs. Thus, much smaller percentages of the money actually was devoted to field programs. Even then, not all the programs on the ground were defensible. Maren (1997) provided examples of such "idiotic projects":

> Oxfam was teaching refugees to grow onions and cabbages and peppers in the refugee camp. The two Oxfam agriculturists discussed their dilemma nightly: The idea behind their project was to make refugees more self-sufficient. But if the refugees were going to return to their nomadic way of life, these skills wouldn't be very useful. And if they were going to settle down and become farmers, they'd need to know a lot more about agriculture than how to grow just a few cash crops. The Oxfam team drank their whisky every night and wondered aloud why they were doing what they were doing that day. (98)

Because of Africa's social system of extended families, there is no such thing as an orphan. A child without parents can always find an aunt, cousin or some distant relative to serve as a guardian. Yet "a Canadian group arrived one day looking for orphans. They checked into the local office of the National Refugee Commission and were given permission to collect whatever orphans they found. Thirty or forty children were gathered together and loaded onto a truck and carted off to an orphanage in Mogadishu, while their clan elders protested" (Maren, 1997, 95).

THE ROLE OF BLACK AMERICANS

Black Americans constitute an important group that could help Africa get on the right and fast track. Historically, they were instrumental in the liberation of Africa from the yoke of colonialism. In the 1980s, their role in the struggle against and demise of apartheid in South Africa was widely acclaimed and appreciated by Africans. Yet in the rest of Africa, the involvement of black Americans in the postcolonial period has been more of a hindrance than help.

A large part of the problem derives from differences in perception, attitudes, and historical experiences. There are four such differences between black Americans and black Africans. First, black Americans—throughout their history and experience—have always seen their oppressors and exploiters to be white. Black Africans, on the other hand, have seen both black and white oppressors and exploiters. As such, they have no difficulty condemning the architects of apartheid in South Africa with as much venom as they would the tyrannical regimes elsewhere in Africa.

Black Americans have never lived under black tyrannical regimes and therefore cannot relate to black tyranny.

Second, black Americans analyze their problems—often justifiably—in a black/white or racialist paradigm, which they tend to use for Africa's problems as well. Unfortunately, the model is unsuitable because in black Africa, racism is not the issue, except in Kenya, Mauritania, South Africa, Sudan, and Zimbabwe. Rather, it is tribalism—for example, tribal apartheid in Burundi, Nigeria, and Rwanda—that is the problem, a fact that black Americans have difficulty grasping. In Sudan and Mauritania, black Africans are still enslaved by Arab masters. But black Americans pay no attention.

The Catholic bishop of southern Sudan, Macram Max Gassis, testified at an antislavery conference in May 1994 at Columbia University that southern Sudanese are bought and sold for as little as $15. Ushari Ahmad Mahmoud, author of "Human Rights Violations in Sudan," has confirmed such charges and others. Arab militias from Khartoum stage "ghazzus"—raids—in southern Sudanese villages and round up women and children after killing the men. To prevent them from escaping, they are branded, often on the ears. In his scathing 1994 report to the United Nations Commission on Human Rights, special investigator Gaspar Biro documented the "abduction of children and women. . . . They are kept in special camps where people from the north or from abroad come to purchase them for money or goods such as camels. Young girls and women are purchased as housekeepers . . . and wives. The boys are kept as servants" (*The Wall Street Journal,* 20 October 1995, A12).

During his assignment in Africa, American black Washington Post correspondent Keith Richburg happened upon a group of black Americans in Sudan in March 1994. This group was being feted by the brutal military regime of Omar el-Bashir at the Khartoum Hilton. Apparently some members of this group even berated the U.S. Ambassador at Khartoum over U.S. policy toward Sudan, claiming it was unfair to label Sudan a "sponsor of terrorism." "I was nearly shaking with rage," said Richburg. "Couldn't they see they were being used, manipulated by one of the world's most oppressive regimes?" he asked (*The Washington Post Magazine,* 26 March 1995, 30). Nation of Islam leader Louis Farrakhan has persistently dismissed the issue of slavery as a "Western conspiracy" against an Arab regime.

Third, most black Americans tend to look up to the U.S. Congress (or government) to provide solutions to their problems. Congress gave black Americans the Civil Rights Act, affirmative action, and other protections. But most black Africans see their governments not as the "solution" but as the problem.

Fourth, black Americans have been shut out of government—perhaps out of the racist belief that blacks are incapable of ruling and therefore cannot occupy high government positions. It is therefore gratifying when black Americans come upon black African presidents—living proof that blacks are capable of running a country. They lobby Congress and the U.S. administration to provide more aid to African governments and denounce any attempts to cut aid as "racially motivated," often serving as agents for African despots.

At conferences and summits in Africa, black American delegates exercise little restraint in their effusive praise of African tyrants. One example was the Second African–African American Summit (24-29 May 1993) in Libreville, Gabon. The black American delegation included Virginia's governor Doug Wilder, the Honorable William Gray III, the Reverend Jesse Jackson, Mrs. Coretta Scott-King, Joseph Lowery, Louis Farrakhan, and many others. At that summit, none of the black Americans ever mentioned—or even bothered to go meet—opposition leaders, such as Jules-Aristide Bourdes-Oguiliguende. And none of the black Americans ever mentioned the plight of Gabon's only private radio station, which was being blocked from transmitting. Or the peasants in the countryside who had thrown up barricades and staged protests against economic exploitation and political repression.

Instead, according to Keith Richburg, "what came out was a nauseating outpouring of praise from black Americans for a coterie of some of Africa's most ruthless strongmen and dictators" (*The Washington Post* Magazine, 26 March 1995, 30). When Sierra Leone's military despot, Captain Valentine Strasser, entered the meeting hall sporting camouflage battle fatigues and Ray-Ban sunglasses, "many of the black Americans went wild with applause, as if Strasser were a celebrity rap star. No one bothered to mention that Strasser seized power in a military coup in 1992, that he had yet to make good on his promise to return Sierra Leone to democratic government and free elections, and that in the last year of his rule this boyish-looking autocrat had presided over a violent purge of dissidents and ex-regime officials in his own country" (*The Washington Post*, 30 May 1993).

At that summit in Gabon, "Rev. Jesse Jackson praised Babangida as 'one of the great leader-servants of modern Africa in our time' and told him, in a speech, that 'you do not stand alone as you move with a steady beat toward restoring democracy.' Jackson was applauded when he said

Babangida should be rewarded with an official visit to meet President Clinton in Washington on what would be a 'triumphant tour as we herald the restoration of democracy' in Nigeria" (*The Washington Post*, 8 July 1993, A11).

When asked about African democracy movement, Benjamin F. Chavis, Jr., the former executive director of the National Association for the Advancement of Colored People (NAACP), replied: "The African-American community would like to see the process of democratization continue in Africa, but not try to dictate the character or pace of that democratization. It is for the people of Gabon to determine their destiny. It is not for outsiders to get involved in the internal political struggles of Gabon" (*The Washington Post*, 30 May 1993, C2).

Quite often, black American leaders do not realize they are being played for suckers by brutal African tyrants. For example, during his March 1996 visit to Ghana, a presidential jet was placed at the disposal of Minister Farrakhan and commandos assigned to accompany him without cabinet or parliamentary approval. This action provoked a blistering editorial from Ghana's crusading paper, *Free Press* (4-10 October 1996):

> Under normal circumstances, it is necessary in a transparent environment for the government to come out with a public statement that the cabinet (or Parliament) has approved a request from Minister Louis Farrakhan for the release of the jet and commandos, for stated reasons. That would give the people also the opportunity to state their stand through memoranda, letters or through the media. This is necessary because the state jet and the commandos are public property, and, therefore, one had expected Rawlings not to use them as he would use his smock, car or children. . . .
>
> One had least expected Afro-Americans, whose forebears suffered as much inhumanity in America as Ghanaians are suffering here today, to allow themselves to be used as dirty prostitutes against the interests of the people of Ghana. We only take consolation in the fact that it is only deadwoods of the Afro-American community in America who normally jump on the mischief bandwagon and come here to play the fool. (6)

The editorial was fierce because Farrakhan had infuriated many Ghanaians on a number of occasions. During a three-day visit to Ghana in April 1993 he spoke at a public forum organized by the du Bois Memorial Center for Pan-African Research. After listening to him, Kweku Sakyi-Addo, a columnist for *The Ghanaian Chronicle* wrote:

You know, I've heard the Leader of the Nation of Islam, Louis Farrakhan, speak on three occasions. I share his ideas that black people ought to get their act together. But some of the philosophies he put forward at one of his lectures at the du Bois Center in Accra did not quite sit well with me. The man was defending Dictatorship!

But listen to Farrakhan's analogy and defense: If a man engineers your freedom from slavery, then he has The Right to dictate to you; to tell you where to go and where to sit. Hey, wait a minute. That sounds like merely swapping slave masters, Louis. Try another one. And he did. He compared the relationship between newly Independent Ghana and Dr. Nkrumah to that of a Child and its Mother. Farrakhan argued, must not a Mother tell a child where to sit, and what to eat and when to go to bed and who its friends must be? Nope, you got it all mixed up, Louis.

Number one: That philosophy of parenthood is passe. And number two: A child does not elect its Mother. But citizens, even in a freshly-independent country, elect their President. "To Represent them." Repeat. To represent them, not to dictate to them, thank you very much.

Then there is this one about the Niceness of his Belongings. He said: "I drive a nice car, a very nice car; I live in a nice house, a very nice house; and I wear a nice suit, the best the Whiteman makes Until We (Black people) Can Make Our Own." Until we can make our own? Hang on a second. We were making and wearing our *kentes* and *batakaris* and *boubous* and *amoase* before suits and g-strings came this way, man!

The other thing was how he kept referring to us as "Followers" of some leader or the other. Now, let's get something straight here. The people of Ghana are not followers. We are Citizens. Our President is not a Cult Leader. He is an elected mortal President! What guides us is not Faith. It is a written Constitution. Ghana is not a Religion. It is a country.

Finally, there was the small, I mean small, matter of money. Farrakhan, after our taxes had hosted him and his 16-member entourage including his sons and daughters, made a donation to the du Bois Memorial Center for Pan-African Research. You know how much he gave? FIFTY DOLLARS! Five Zero! If you ask me, I think he can stuff it up in his wallet.

Of course, Black people will find it hard to make it if Men and Women with political and Religious influence insist on a life of combined opulence and stinginess. (*Ghana Drum,* July 1993, 7).

In 1994 the Christian Women in Leadership resolved to put pressure on President Rawlings to cancel a 5-9 Oct 1994 visit by Minister Farrakhan. In a protest note, the organization urged the government "for the sake of peace and tranquility in our land, to reconsider its decision and cancel Mr. Farrakhan's visit to Ghana. From what we have heard and read of Mr. Farrakhan's utterances and beliefs, we are apprehensive that his presence in Ghana at this time is likely to bring disunity, chaos and strife into the country" (*Ghana Drum,* April 1994, 12).

Black Americans' support of African despots appears to be based more on ignorance than anything else. Said E. R. Shipp, a black American columnist:

> Most black Americans have no firsthand knowledge of the going-ons in Africa, nor do they necessarily trust what limited news they may get from the media. Often they rely on public figures like Rev. Jesse Jackson and Randall Robinson of TransAfrica or on black-owned newspapers such as the 200 or so that constitute the National Newspapers Publishers Association (NNPA). Unfortunately, those who help shape those opinions often weasel out of exerting moral authority by saying it's a tribal thing and we cannot possibly understand. Or they compromise their moral authority by questionable financial dealings with those whose causes they advance. Many NNPA members have been bought off: Last fall, Nigeria paid for a 19-member delegation to visit for a "fact-finding" tour. When she returned, NNPA President Dorothy Leavell said: "We traveled throughout the country, but we found no evidence of a dictatorship or a so-called thug-ocracy that others who've never been there have charged" (*The Houston Chronicle,* 17 May 1996, A5)

A stultifying display of ignorance occurred in California, when the Board of Education of the Oakland Unified School District voted on 18 December 1996, to recognize "Ebonics" (the amalgamation of "Ebony" and "phonetics") as "black English" and seek federal bilingual funding for a programs to help children who use "black English" learn standard English.[1] The board's resolution read: "Now, therefore, be it resolved that the Board of Education officially recognizes the existence and the cultural and historic bases of West and Niger Congo African Language Systems, and each language as the predominantly primary language of African American students." But Ebonics is not related to any of the

---

1. "Black English" contains such expressions as "I axed him" (I asked him) and "I be gone" (I am going or I am gone).

1,000 languages of Africa, which can be classified into four stocks: Niger-Kordofanian, Nilo-Saharan, Khoisan, and Afro-Asiatic (Hamito-Semitic). Finally the whole idea was dropped quietly.

Confronting Nigeria's Military Despots

Black American leaders did make a concerted effort to bring about change in Nigeria—Africa's most populous nation. What triggered this was the arrest on 15 March 1995 of retired General Olusegun Obasanjo, a former Nigerian head of state, on suspicion of complicity in an alleged coup plot and black American realization that a disintegration of Nigeria could wreak cataclysmic repercussions, destabilizing the entire West and Central African regions.

Nigeria's military leader, General Sani Abacha, who seized power in a November 1993 coup, has been the most brutal of all of Nigeria's military despots. He is described by international company executives as the "most corrupt head of state in the world" (*The Economist*, 6 September 1996, Supplement 8). As the absolute ruler of Nigeria, he brooks no dissent. All seemingly democratic institutions have systematically been demolished and the economy ruined. Brutal repression has been rampant.

This blatant "in-your-face" political contumely in Nigeria finally provoked into action TransAfrica, the activist group that spearheaded the campaign against apartheid in South Africa and against Haiti's military thugs. Randall Robinson, TransAfrica's executive director, called a press conference in March 1995 to denounce Nigeria's military regime and urged an imposition of worldwide sanctions. "It is not easy to publicly criticize black leadership. It is uncomfortable and disquieting. But we are left with no choice," Robinson lamented (*The Washington Post*, 14 March 1995, A13).

This campaign for the institution of democracy included newspaper ads castigating the military regime in Nigeria and demonstrations at the Nigerian Embassy. The effort was backed by a cross section of famous African Americans, including poet Maya Angelou, NBC *Today* show host Bryant Gumbel, the Reverend Jesse Jackson, former welterweight boxing champion Sugar Ray Leonard, and Baltimore mayor Kurt L. Schmoke. This was the first time prominent black Americans had mounted a highly visible public campaign against a black African government.

"I think it would be inconsistent for us to express concern about repression and tyranny by the white dictators in South Africa and ignore the same thing in black Africa," said the Reverend Joseph Lowery, president of the Southern Christian Leadership Conference (*The Washington Post,* 14 March 1995, A13). "Either way, black Africans suffer."[2] Randall Robinson was blunter: "We shall oppose the Nigerian government with as much tenacity as we opposed the [former white] South African government, with as much tenacity as we opposed the military regime in Haiti" (*The Washington Post,* 14 March 1995, A13). "I think it's a high-water mark in maturity in the black community. The courage to call a thing like it is," he added.

However, the campaign was soon dogged by division and acrimony, and the facade of a united black American front against Nigeria's military collapsed. Following his successful Million Man March on 16 October 1995 in Washington, Minister Louis Farrakhan embarked on a World Friendship Tour, which took him to Nigeria, Sudan, Libya, Iraq, and Iran. On 7 February 1996 he issued an unabashed blanket endorsement of Nigeria's military regime. "I think the Abacha regime should be given a chance to move this country [Nigeria] toward democracy and if the words of General Abacha are true, he will step down in 3 years and turn it over to a civilian rule," Farrakhan said in Lagos (*African News Weekly,* 19-25 February 1996, 24). To add fuel to the fire, he "said military regimes are not necessarily bad."

Michael Eric Dyson, a black American professor of communications at the University of North Carolina, lambasted Farrakhan's forays on foreign soil and bizarre missions as a betrayal of the spirit of the Million Man March:

> When Farrakhan journeyed to Nigeria, instead of indicting the dictator, General Sani Abacha, for his cruel policies, he pleaded with human rights advocates to give Abacha 3 more years to live up to his promise to return Nigeria to civilian rule. Farrakhan ignored the detention of hundreds of pro-democracy activists without trial. He was silent about the executions

---

2. Ten years earlier when I made exactly the same comment in a *Wall Street Journal* editorial (22 July 1985, A12), I was vilified, denounced as an "Uncle Tom" and denied promotion at Bloomsburg University in Pennsylvania. "Let's free the blacks in South Africa first," said one black American to me. "Maybe too late for the rest of Africa," I retorted. As it turned out, we "won" South Africa but lost Burundi, Ethiopia, Liberia, Rwanda, Sierra Leone, Somalia, Zaire and more to come. Some victory.

of opposition leaders like Ken Saro-Wiwa. Farrakhan insulted Nigerians by telling them that severe discipline was sometimes necessary, and that Moses, like Abacha, had been a dictator as well. Thus, Farrakhan seemed to ignore the barbarous practices of Nigeria for no other reason than that the nation is black. (*The Washington Post,* 13 October 1996, C3)

Following on Farrakhan's heels was Senator Carol Moseley-Braun—the only black U.S. Senator—whose unannounced trip to Nigeria from 9-12 August 1996 outraged Africans and many human rights groups. She defended her trip as "just doing my job as I see it" (*The Washington Times,* 21 August 1996, A6). When in Nigeria, she visited Port Harcourt and chatted with military governor Colonel Dauda Musa Komo, who supervised the hangings of Saro-Wiwa and other activists. "Government-owned Radio Rivers State later reported that she praised Komo for bringing peace to the region" (*Newsweek,* 26 August 1996, 40). But she did not meet with pro-democracy leaders in Lagos. Adotei Akwei, government program officer for Africa at Amnesty International, slammed the trip: "This was just . . . the latest kind of blatant act of disregard of the Nigerian government's human rights violations, which she claims are not being backed up." Even Moseley-Braun's chief of staff, Edith Wilson, resigned in protest, claiming she was not informed about the Nigerian trip.[3]

ANGRY AFRICAN REACTION

It has become clear to the suffering African masses that Western governments, nongovernmental organizations and some black American leaders are not on their side but are in cahoots with the tyrants. This has provoked strong African reactions and a disturbing trend in the liberation struggle: warnings, threats, and reprisals against Western economic and diplomatic interests in Africa. Consider the following sample:

In January 1994 a group of over 300 U.S.-based francophone Africans sent a strongly worded open letter to France and its political

---

3. Apparently before Moseley-Braun was elected Senator, her former fiancé and campaign aide, Kgosie Matthews, had visited South Africa and Nigeria, where he met with military dictator General Ibrahim Babangida in 1992. Subsequently, Matthews went "to work as a lobbyist for the Nigerian government" (*The Washington Times,* 22 August 1996 A4).

leaders complaining about Paris's "deplorable policy and attitude in Africa." It accused France of supporting "some of the most ignominious dictatorships ever found in human history." The letter continued:

> It is difficult to understand why a respectable nation, a nation of culture, a nation as civilized as the French nation, would, at the end of this twentieth century, trade and ally itself with tyrants as inhuman as the ones that contemporary Africa has produced; tyrants who will, forever, haunt the memory of Africa. It is even more difficult to understand why successive leaders of a respectable people would collaborate with tyrants who, without scruple, unnecessarily maintain their people in almost beast-like living conditions. . . . Such failed foreign policy can be witnessed in all the countries where France is or was actively involved: Cameroon, Chad, Congo, Mauritania, Niger, Rwanda, and Zaire.
>
> One could be led to believe that France's foreign policy in Africa is based on purely racist considerations, and this policy will impede France's interests on the African continent, let alone in the world. (*West Africa*, 31 January–6 February 1994, 175)

Frustration is driving many Africans to take desperate action. In Nigeria, sabotage and damage to Shell Oil installations in Ogoniland in 1993 cost that Western company about $30 million. In March 1992 protesters in Niger burned the French flag in the streets of Niamey, denouncing France's "desertion" of the reformist government of Ama-dou Cheffou, the prime minister, in the face of an attempted coup. But at the same time, France was sending 150 paratroops to the assistance of Chad's Colonel Idriss Derby (*The Economist*, 7 March 1992, 46).

In Sierra Leone, Revolutionary United Front rebels seized 17 foreigners, many of them from Britain, the former colonial power. "Mr. Foday Sankoh, the elusive leader, says that his 'foreign guests' will be released as soon as Britain stops helping the current regime of army captains and majors. Britain insists that it has not given aid to Sierra Leone since Captain Strasser seized power in a coup in 1992" (*The Economist*, 11 February 1995, 39).

In Algeria, scores of French nationals were abducted, with some killed, for their support of the military regime since the civil war erupted in 1991. In Zambia, a shadowy group known as the Black Mambas wrote poisonous letters and made threatening phone calls to local politicians and foreign diplomats and their families in 1996. This was part of a campaign to get foreign aid donors to pressure the ruling

Movement for Multi-Party Democracy into sticking to the democratic course it embraced when elected in 1991. The ruthlessness of the campaign, which threatened the lives of cabinet ministers, the speaker of parliament, and foreign donors, forced the government of President Frederick Chiluba to put up a $3 million reward for the capture of Black Mambas: "Letters and calls at night issuing death threats to Swedish Ambassador Anders Johnson's wife, Anne-Marie, unless she convinces her husband to withhold aid, have left her so distraught, embassy staff say, that she has withdrawn from public life" (*African Observer*, 8 April–25 May 1996, 9).

In Rwanda, a Hutu rebel group called People in Arms for the Liberation of Rwanda offered "a $1,000 bounty for the head of every American killed in Rwanda, and $1,500 for that of U.S. Ambassador to Kigali, Robert Gribbin, senior Western diplomats said. U.S. Embassy officials in the Rwandan capital of Kigali, contacted by telephone from neighboring Burundi, confirmed the threat and said U.S. citizens in the country had been warned to take extreme care" (*The Washington Times*, 13 June 1996, A15).

Humanitarian relief workers in Somalia, Rwanda, and Goma, Zaire, also were attacked. Increasingly, Africans are beginning to vent their spleen at black American leaders. For example, in June 1994 President Clinton sent the Reverend Jesse Jackson as a special envoy to help defuse Nigeria's political crisis. But pro-democracy forces refused to meet with him due to of his support of the former military dictator, General Ibrahim Babangida. Perhaps no black American leader has drawn more fire from black Africans than Louis Farrakhan, leader of the Nation of Islam.

Minister Farrakhan's praise of Nigeria's military regime drew this angry reaction: "The Committee for the Defense of Human Rights (CDHR) condemns without reservation the unabashed pro-military stance of, and the provocative immoral endorsement of the General Sani Abacha-led military junta by, the visiting American Black Muslim leader" (*African News Weekly*, 19-25 February 1996, 24).

Upon his return from his African tour, Farrakhan gave a series of interviews, the contents of which baffled many Africans. An irate Evelyne Kinang Joe, a Cameroonian president of the International Africa Foundation, wrote:

> Minister Farrakhan launched a summary defense of African leadership, a brazen performance which puts all the lobbyists to shame, handing carte blanche to every brutal despot and trainees-in-the-wings. On Nigeria, the

Minister challenged the temerity of the U.S. to condemn human rights violations and lack of democracy. He promised to send his own black lawyers to study the judicial process that led to the hangings of Ken Saro-Wiwa and eight others. Meanwhile, he asked the U.S. to count how many people it has hanged. . . .

The tragic loss of lives of Mr. Saro-Wiwa and the eight others who were brutally murdered is certainly not material for public relations gimmicks. Minister Farrakhan's arrogant and insensitive statements were most irresponsible and exploitative. The sheer audacity of Mr. Farrakhan using it as another window of opportunity is diabolic. The average African will tell the Minister that his investigative proposal is "medicine after death," a crazy alien recipe for Africa. Africa, and Nigeria in this instance, has never lacked competent judicial minds or traditional arbitration to stamp out this level of insanity. An offer like the Minister Farrakhan's is a distracting waste and impediment to reason. The Minister would be within the confines of courage and wisdom if his judicial ensemble can, for starters, examine the processes that foster an environment for political repression in Nigeria. (*The Free Africa Review*, Summer 1996, 17)

Ropo Sekoni of the Action Group for Democracy in Nigeria (AGDN) based in Wheaton, Maryland, poured on more invective:

I am writing to express AGDN's utmost dismay and distress at the recent pronouncements by African American Islamic leader Louis Farrakhan, during his recent visit with Nigeria's tyrant, General Sani Abacha. Mr. Farrakhan's prescription: "Only in that military kind of way can a nation that has been down come up and get going," shows a lack of respect for the 100 million people of Nigeria. It is embarrassing that a few months after Mr. Farrakhan spoke in front of the U.S. Congress to 1 million fellow African Americans about the need for them to constantly demand justice from white Americans, he calmly recommended dictatorship for the most populous black nation on earth.

No respectable African-American leader has shown the level of contempt for fellow blacks in Africa that Mr. Farrakhan demonstrated in the statements attributed to him in Nigeria. . . . (*The Washington Times*, 3 March 1996, B2)

On Sudan, one of Farrakhan's minions, Abdul Akbar Muhammad, made matters worse by attacking the emerging abolitionist movement, including Sudanese groups in the United States. They charged that the stories of slavery in Sudan and Mauritania were nothing but a "Jewish conspiracy," part of a "Western plot" and a campaign against the spread of Islam in Africa. Such a reckless diatribe brought this response from Augustine Abulu Lado, a black Sudanese and president of Pax Sudani:

> We are flabbergasted and outraged at the charges and attacks directed against us and other American abolitionists. It is disingenuous and preposterous to down play the role of African Sudanese groups here and abroad who have always fought against slavery and gruesome atrocities perpetrated against Africans by Arabs. . . .
>
> While religion is a personal choice, we must emphasize that Islam and Christianity are not (and have never been) indigenous African religions. During colonial times in Sudan, Christianity and Islam conspired to brutally enforce and legitimize cultural superiority over Africans. British and Arab imperialists conspired to keep Arab slavery of Africans discreet. Arab slavers were camouflaged as masters and African slaves as servants. . . .
>
> Louis Farrakhan must act forthrightly to repair the damage that Abdul Akbar Muhammad has done to the Nation of Islam. He must fire Akbar from his ranks and apologize for this deputy's nefarious conduct. He cannot remain silent on the use of Islam to perpetrate slavery on black Africans in Sudan and Mauritania. He should also assume an active role in the abolitionist movement and use his mosque's pulpit to zealously speak out against the enslavement of black Africans. . . . Finally, anyone with a soul should stop building business ties with Sudan, Mauritania, Libya, and any country in Africa where Africans are being enslaved. (*Daily Challenge*, 19 June 1995, A4)

The pronouncements of Minister Farrakhan on Sudan after his February 1996 African tour added more fuel to the fire. Said Evelyne Joe:

> Minister Farrakhan stated that his trip to Africa was a private, fact-finding mission. But his public posturing and prescriptions were horrendous and insulting to the sensibilities of Africans who bear the brunt of organized mayhem, disorder and brutality orchestrated by unscrupulous African governments. . . . Minister Farrakhan relishes recounting how well he was received in Africa and beyond. This personal craving for adulation highlights the real lesson. If we learned nothing else, Mr. Farrakhan proved again that: Destiny and salvation of Africa lies primarily with Africans. (*The Free Africa Review*, Summer 1996)

CHAPTER 9

Alternative Solutions to Africa's Crisis

The world is washing its hands of sub-Saharan Africa, leaving its 700 million people to save themselves. They might yet succeed if, like the new South Africans, they can work together.
—Tony Thomas in *The Economist,* 7 September 1996, Supplement, 3.

INTRODUCTION

The crisis in Africa has become so serious and deep that all actors involved with African development have become disillusioned and exasperated. "Donor fatigue" has set in. Some in the international community are beginning to wash their hands of Africa. Various proposals and solutions have been bandied about which, unfortunately, do not go to the heart of the issue.

Recall from chapter 5 that the basic problem is the mafia state—government hijacked by kleptocrats and brutal despots. Their overarching ethic is self-aggrandizement and self-perpetuation in office. All power, both political and economic, has been concentrated in their hands, which they use to extract resources from the productive masses and spend them in conspicuous consumption. The current system of governance is untenable and eventually implodes, as we saw in Chapter 6.

Two policy objectives suggest themselves. The first is to prevent the implosion by instituting real intellectual, political, economic; and institutional reforms. But as we saw in chapter 7, African despots are not willing to reform, choosing rather to perform the "acrobatics." Under these circumstances, energies must be channeled into breaking or neutralizing the ruling elites' resistance to reform. If this resistance is unshakable, the second policy objective would dictate abandoning the state sector altogether but putting in place safeguards to ensure that the inevitable implosion does not consume the entire nation ("controlled implosion").

Unfortunately, most of the proposals that have so far been advanced do not address these fundamental issues.

AFRICAN GOVERNMENT AND OAU/ECA PROPOSALS

Proposals by African governments, the OAU, and the United Nations' agency, the Economic Commission for Africa, can easily be dismissed since they envisage external solutions, based on the premise that Africa's crisis is largely caused by external factors. These proposals, in the main, revolve around debt relief or cancellation and the provision of more foreign aid. In its 1996 *Report on the Economic and Social Situation in Africa,* the ECA noted that "Despite the fundamental and hopefully irreversible domestic reforms, Africa's medium-term prospects continue to be threatened by daunting external factors beyond its control, including the debt burden" (cited in *Africa Recovery,* May 1996, 13).

More distressing, African governments have found allies overseas to support their demands for these external solutions. Among them are France, the United Nations, black Americans, and some Western nongovernmental organizations and charitable organizations, such as OXFAM. Following the 7 October 1996 five-nation African tour by U.S. Secretary of State Warren Christopher, a skeptical France slammed the trip as politically motivated to pander to black American voters in the November 1996 presidential elections. Said Jacques Rummelhardt, a spokesman for France's Foreign Ministry: "All demonstrations of interest in Africa on the part of the industrialized countries, such as the recent visit by the American secretary of state, should be accompanied, especially if they can have the effect, with increasing aid to the continent" (*The Washington Times,* 15 October 1996, A11).

On 15 March 1996 the United Nations launched a $25 billion System-Wide Special Initiative on Africa to revive development, using the same defective state apparatus. The initiative, to cover the period 1996 to 2006, will develop programs in education, health, government, sanitation, and peace-building. The plan was hatched in consultation with African leaders at a meeting in Burkina Faso in January 1996. In announcing the initiative simultaneously around the world in Africa, Europe, and the United States, the U.N. Secretary General Boutros Boutros-Ghali warned that Africa was in danger of becoming the "lost continent" (*The Washington Times,* 16 March 1996, A9). But to most

Africans, the continent is already lost under its current leadership—just as an entire decade, the 1980s, has been dismissed as the "lost decade for Africa"—a lost continent under a lost leadership in a lost decade.

The New York–based *African Observer* (11-24 April 1996) dismissed the harangue as "a charade and . . . a pretext for U.N. Secretary-General Boutros Boutros-Ghali to run for re-election [in December 1996] as a supporter of African development" (2). A more scathing editorial came from Ghana's crusading newspaper, *Free Press* (20-26 March 1996), describing it as "U.N. Largess to African Dictators":

> We are dismayed that hitherto the U.N. and the nations that influence it most have refused to appreciate that Africa is a continent dominated by dictators, and that the tragedy which blights the continent today is the doing of these notorious dictators. It is the Abachas, the Mugabes, the Eyademas, the Mobutus, the Santos, the Biyas, the Gaddafis, the Jammehs, the Rawlings, like the Samuel Does, Bokassas, Nguessos, Amins, Mengistus, Babangidas, before them, that have been standing in the way of development and progress of Africa, and causing ruination that they, the U.N., and the donor countries are worrying about today. (6)

The Washington Times (16 March 1996) pointed out the U.N. plan "has no authority to stop African governments from using their money to build palaces or buy weapons" (A9). The director of the World Bank's own Poverty and Social Policy Department, Ishrait Husain, observed that: "Adjustment is failing in many African countries precisely because their governments misappropriated funds. They spend large sums of money promoting their own interests, building airports in their home towns, increasing military spending, and buying more fashionable cars instead of using the funds in the social sector which would benefit their people" (*The African Observer,* 28 September–11 October 1995, 21).

BLACK AMERICAN PROPOSALS

Lack of understanding of Africa's economic woes and blind "racial solidarity" support have often led black American leaders to support failed aid policies in Africa. On 3 February 1995, for example, prominent black American leaders, African diplomats, and development experts convened a summit on Africa to respond to Republican threats to end U.S. aid to Africa. The Reverend Jesse Jackson delivered a stinging response. Recalling "250 years of free labor" by African slaves in America,

Reverend Jackson called the Republican plan "a Tarzan policy—racist and immoral." "To ignore the pain of Africa comes from a vision blurred by racism," he added (*The Washington Times,* 4 February 1995, A7). The issue is not so much the morality of continuing U.S. aid to Africa but rather its effectiveness.

In May 1993 the Eminent Persons' Group of the Organization of African Unity organized its first Pan-African Conference on Reparations in Nigeria's new federal capital city of Abuja. Delivering a speech on behalf of then President Ibrahim Babangida, Nigeria's vice-president Admiral Augustus Aikhomu declared: "If history demonstrates that Africa has been injured through slavery and colonialism, and if morality demands that injury be compensated, then the logic of the reparations movement is established alongside its morality" (*West Africa,* 24-30 May 1993, 861).

Out of the conference came the paper "The Abuja Declaration," which called for a recognition that the damage sustained by the African people is not a thing of the past "but is painfully manifest in the damaged lives of contemporary Africans and the damaged economies of Africa." It urged the OAU to grant observer status to select organizations from the African diaspora to facilitate consultation with the continent and to call for monetary payment through capital transfers and debt cancellation. The Declaration entreated "Those countries that were enriched by slavery and the slave trade, colonialism and neo-colonialism to allow debtor countries total relief from foreign debt" (*West Africa,* 24-30 May 1993, 861). Interestingly, the conference did not call for reparations from Arabs, who ran the East African slave trade, in a traffic particularly noted for its savagery. Or even an end to the enslavement of blacks by Arabs in this day and age in Sudan and Mauritania.

Regarding reparations, said *West Africa* (18 April 1994) in an editorial: "Instead of calling for reparations from countries in the West, there should be a concerted effort to force Western banks to return the billions that have been stashed in their vaults by some African leaders who have, in the process, pauperized their countries. This is a more feasible proposition than that of reparations."(837) Author Anya O. Anya, observed that: "In Nigeria, it has been estimated that the assets of Nigerians transferred into Western Europe and North America is of the order of $120 billion–$160 billion. This is a colossal asset that needs to be put to use for Nigeria's development" (*West Africa,* 30 May–5 June 1994, 940).

WESTERN PROPOSALS

The international community is divided and at a loss over the appropriate policy measures to take in most African countries, where hope is fast fading. Two camps may be identified: those who are withdrawing from Africa and those who see some flicker of hope and wish to remain engaged. In the first camp are the "retreatists" and "Afro-pessimists." The retreatists are abandoning Africa because it has lost its strategic value after the Cold War. In 1993 the State Department's Bureau of African Affairs lost more than 60 posts. According to Michaels (1993), "Consulates in Kenya, Cameroon and Nigeria are to be closed, and perhaps also the U.S. Embassy in the Comoros Islands—bodies and budgets are needed in eastern Europe and the Commonwealth of Independent States. Over the last three years, the Africa desk for US AID has lost 30 to 40 staffers out of the 130 for the same reason" (94).

The United States has all but disengaged from Africa. It resolutely refused to send peace-keeping troops to Liberia, which was settled by former freed U.S. slaves. The U.S. Institute For National Strategic Studies spelled out the message quite clearly: "The United States has essentially no serious military/geostrategic interests in Africa any more, other than the inescapable fact that its vastness poses an obstacle to deployment in the Middle East and South Asia, whether by sea or air" (*The Economist,* 7 September 1996, Supplement, 4).

Afro-pessimists, on the other hand, have succumbed to donor fatigue after being overwhelmed by a torrent of Africa's intractable problems. Stung by costly (financial as well as human) miscues in Somalia and Rwanda, they have lost the appetite for future "African adventures." Put less diplomatically, most donor governments have become fed up with Africa's incessant crises, onerous misrule, and grotesque mismanagement and have been reducing their Africa aid budgets. Even such exemplary givers as the Canadians, the Dutch, and the Scandinavians have been hit with donor fatigue.

In the other camp are the "optimists," who wish to remain involved, not only for Africa's survival but also for their own. In this camp are the development agencies and humanitarian relief organizations that need crisis situations to remain in business. Although a few "thrive" on African humanitarian disasters, most are sincere, churning out various proposals under the mantra of "sustainable development." They advocate reform (economic and political) and, if everything else fails, recolonization.

Better Governance

In the past few years, a lively debate has erupted as to whether Africa needs "democracy" and whether democracy is even essential for successful economic development at all. During the Cold War, this issue was moot. Until the beginning of the 1990s, the donor community ignored democratic reform in Africa for a couple of reasons. The obvious one was geopolitical. The second reason was historical. Western conservatives pointed to the eighteenth-century industrial revolution in Europe and argued persuasively that economic reform would create a middle class that, as its numbers increased, would demand greater discretionary freedom in spending its wealth, greater protection of its property, and greater political rights and say in how their tax monies were spent. This argument was bolstered by the experiences of Chile and of South Korea, Taiwan, and the other "Asian Tigers," where successful development occurred under authoritarian regimes, provided the right type of economic policies (free market) were pursued.

American economist Robert J. Barro argued that the establishment of democracy in a poor country will tend to empower the "oppressed" poor and enhance the appeal of rich-to-poor redistributionist policies that will only stymie economic growth. Consequently, it would be counterproductive for the United States to seek to "export" democracy to such countries as Somalia and Haiti. Better for the United States to promote the establishment of free markets in poor countries. Barro remarked that "If economic freedom were to be established in a poor country, then growth would be encouraged, and the country would tend eventually to become more democratic on its own" (*The Wall Street Journal*, 1 December 1994, A18).

Furthermore, as we saw in chapter 5, Africa's economic and political systems are fused. One cannot be reformed without the other. Leaving aside the question of sequence, we saw in chapter 7 that the entire reform process has stalled. African despots simply are not interested in reforming their abominable systems, even though they have been bribed with billions in structural adjustment loans and foreign aid.

Civil Society

A society may be considered to rest on three tripods: government, the market, and civil society. According to U.S. Senator Bill Bradley, "Civil society is where Americans [the people] make their homes, sustain their marriages, raise their families, . . . where opinions are expressed and refined, where views are exchanged and agreements made, where a sense of common purpose and consensus are forged. It lies apart from the realms of the market and the government and possesses a different ethic. The market is governed by the logic of economic self-interest, while government is the domain of laws with all their coercive authority. Civil society, on the other hand, is the sphere of our most basic humanity" (*The Washington Post,* 18 May 1995, A30).

The ethic of civil society is defined by four "Cs": consensus, compromise, co-operation and co-existence. People come together and form various associations or clubs on voluntary basis. They exchange views, share experiences, and promote common interests. While the three legs of society interact with one another in complex ways, great ideas and innovation originate from the civil society. The government is supposed to pursue policies that are in the national interest. But more often than not, governments have their own bureaucratic self-preservation agenda. When government policy is "bad," the market reacts negatively and silently: Production is curtailed, shortages appear, and so on. But civil society reacts "noisily" by protesting, by denouncing the government measure in radio, television, and newspapers. Thus, while civil society serves as a barometer of government policy measures, it also acts as an important "watchdog" and brake on a reckless government. In fact, it is in the civil society that reformers and true revolutionaries are born.

For civil society to do its job, two key freedoms are critical: freedom of expression and freedom of association. People must not only have the right to form associations freely—whether political, economic, social, or religious—but also must have the right to express their views freely. However, the dynamics and propulsion of civil society are supplied by "a middle class." The "lower class"—or the poor—are too preoccupied with their struggle for survival to take any ardent interest in national politics or issues. And the "upper class" prefer seclusion to enjoy their riches. The middle class has enough to eat, a job, a house, and a car in the garage. Small business owners, insurance agents, engineers, lawyers, poets, professors, artisans, editors, for example, make up the middle class. But they are never satisfied. They want more—not only consumer goods such as high-resolution color televisions, mobile telephones, computers, and fancy cars, all of which the upper class has already—but also better and responsive government, safe neighborhoods to raise their children, better schools, better management of the earth's environment. Thus, the middle class organizes, clamors, pushes, creates, and innovates to achieve its desired goals. For example, American artist Linda Liotta worried privately that something was awry in America. She entered the electronic universe of fax networks and started a new grass-roots political movement. Its membership numbers in the millions, "linked by fax machines and united by a radical distrust of government borne of wide-ranging grievances about American society. Increasingly, they are making common cause out of what appears to be little common ground, building mushrooming fax and computer networks of angry taxpayers, property rights groups, states' rights groups, gun owners, home schoolers, right-to-lifers and Christian patriots" (*The Washington Post,* 20 August 1995, A22).

Thus, a society that lacks a middle class would be stale and moribund. Under such circumstances, the impetus for change would have to come from the outside, not from within. Historical analysis credits the industrial revolution to the emergence of the middle class in Britain; many development experts have bemoaned the lack of the middle class in Africa as a major agent of reform. The theory that the middle class will push for greater reform works, but perversely in Africa.

In Africa, a large part of the middle class is derived from the same "vampire" elite class that already controls the instruments of government. The ruling elites acquire their wealth not in the private but the state sector, by using the instruments of the state to enrich themselves. Thus, the ruling elites are satisfied with their positions and do not, in contrast to Linda Liotta, harbor any "radical distrust of government."

In the 1960s, the elites were small, generally constituting about 10 percent of the population. But as their numbers grew in the 1970s and 1980s, they became infected with a grab mentality that made them willing partners in the oppressive and kleptocratic system. As M. I. S. Gassama wrote:

> On account of greed and lack of conscience, the vast majority of the Africa elite, whether as politicians (Ministers, Ambassadors, party bosses, etc.) as academics (professors, lecturers), as professionals (lawyers, doctors, accountants, etc.), as civil servants (of all grades), or as military personnel (officers or men), only strove to transform themselves overnight into petty bourgeois or *nouveau riches* by massive embezzlement of public funds with impunity in a free-for-all rat race and, consequently and naively, lightened the burden of the white man by perpetuating the economic exploitation of their own continent, picking up from where the colonialists left off. (*West Africa,* 21-27 March 1994, 495)

Therefore, according to Ko'Oppong, "The African middle class has continued to miss the opportunity to become the catalyst for social change on the continent, for the precise reason that its habits and outlook remain pathetically alien. If this vital class transforms itself into a conscientious brigade for change by redomesticating itself, it will recognize its vital role in Africa and help—through ideas and commitment—make the lives of the ordinary people better than it is" (*Akasanoma*, 11-17 August 1995, 45).

The other truncated part of civil society that can serve as "a catalyst for change" are the excluded. And for a segment of civil society—regardless of its size—to perform its functions, freedom of expression and of association must be guaranteed.

Thus, pressure for political reform is more likely to come from the excluded groups but they have not served as catalysts for change for a variety of reasons. First, they have been susceptible to bribery and co-optation (intellectual prostitution). Second, they are often badly fragmented, as with opposition political parties. Third, the channels through which civil society can operate to effect change have been blocked systematically and insidiously by Africa's despots (the banishment of freedom of expression, of the press, and of association), with serious developmental consequences. Creativity is stifled, and, since reform initiatives cannot be generated internally, they must come from the outside: the World Bank, IMF, and other external organizations or governments. For example, on 7 October 1996 U.S. Secretary of State Warren Christopher embarked on a five-nation African tour to sponsor the creation of an African Crisis Response Force, which may be deployed in countries on the verge of a Rwanda-like meltdown. This initiative could not have come from African leaders or the OAU because civil society did not have the means to agitate for it.

Recolonization

Donor fatigue and frustration about lack of progress in arresting Africa's downward economic slide have led a few Western journalists to advocate "recolonization." If change cannot come from within Africa, then the continent's salvation lies in recolonization. We review four such arguments by American journalists.

This first is by Kaplan (1992), who argued that Africa is full of Haitis. Somalia and Liberia are only the first of many African nations doomed to go over the edge into anarchy and destruction for the same reasons Haiti has. He is skeptical that economic reform could save Africa. He said that one of two things could happen to some of the smaller West

African nations: they could end up as United Nations trusteeships, or as drug lord trusteeships. The economies of these countries are small enough and the young officers running them sufficiently corrupt that they can be bought for cash the way the Greek shipowners have bought Liberia mail drops—as sort of a fake, albeit legal, sovereignty (23).

The second argument is by Johnson (1993), who argues that many Third World countries, mostly in Africa, are just not fit to govern themselves and should be recolonized. This new form of "colonialism" will differ from the old-style in that it will be done under United Nations supervision by placing countries under trusteeships. African candidates for colonization by the "civilized world," according to Johnson, would be Somalia, Liberia, Zaire, Angola, and Mozambique. He argues that this trend should be encouraged on practical and moral grounds because there is no other course in nations where governments have collapsed and there is no evidence of even the most basic conditions for civilized life. This is the case in Africa, where normal government is breaking down in a number of states (6).

The third argument is by Michaels (1993), who was the Nairobi Bureau chief of *Time* magazine. Instead of helping to restructure African governments, economic reforms that were intended to encourage foreign capital investment have only served to make Africa more dependent on foreign aid. We no longer find one government takeover after another. Now there are military dictators who have developed political strongholds by violent means, instilling fear in the people and using divisive tactics on opposition parties to divert any governmental ousters. "The situation is so dire that one American diplomat said, 'In five years Africans will be begging to be recolonized.'"

The final article comes from Christopher Hitchens (1994), who wrote: "The word is recolonization. It's a decision that has been made for quite a few African countries. For obvious reasons, it's not called recolonization, out loud, in Africa itself. . . . But in country after country, with Mozambique as a salient case, you find that the local treasury is a branch of the World Bank, the armed forces are under the stewardship of the United Nations, the electoral register is in the care of international observers, and the distressed citizens apply for relief to outside charities and aid groups. . . . African states, and African peoples, being rescued for their own good. If the policy of outsiders is sound and consistent, they wait and live. If not, they wait and die" (92).

Recolonization, however cast, is politically unacceptable, economically impractical, and emotionally inadmissible. Even de facto recolonization is philosophically out of the question, assuming the West or the United Nations has the resources to undertake so mammoth an enterprise. First, taking over the administration of African economies, devastated by years of civil wars, corruption, and mismanagement, would be hugely expensive. The cost of the 1993 U.N. operations in Somalia alone was estimated at $3.5 billion. Second, recolonization would be tantamount to a humiliating admission of the failure of independence. Africans did not struggle for their freedom from colonial rule in the 1960s only to be recolonized in the 1990s. Third, recolonization perpetuates the offensive notion that nothing good can be found or done in Africa to save itself and that the solutions must come from external sources. The solutions to Africa's crisis lie in Africa itself, not in the West. More pointedly, it is not the World Bank, IMF, United Nations, or Western governments that have to save Africa. Africa must save itself since ultimately, it is the African people themselves who must solve their own problems. The United Nations and the donor community can help, but the initiative has to come from Africa itself, which, in turn, implies that African governments and leaders must allow their people to make their own decisions. The problem is *not* the people; it is the mafia African state or the leadership.

RADICAL ALTERNATIVES

Returning to Africa's Roots / Modernizing the Indigenous

The most maddening and unfathomable aspect of African reform is the fact that the very solutions required to save the continent are in Africa itself—in its own backyard. Africa does not have to copy the American, French, or Asian model.

As we have argued in chapter 3 and elsewhere, all Africa needs to do is to return to its roots and build on and modernize its own indigenous institutions.[1] There is now a greater awareness of the need to reexamine Africa's own heritage. A return to traditional institutions will ensure not only peace but stability as well:

> Malians are quick to remind visitors that they were a nation long before
> they embraced democracy. Their 12 ethnic groups governed themselves

---

1. For an extensive discussion of these institutions, see Ayittey (1991) and references contained therein.

for centuries before French colonization. Each ethnic group governed a region of the [Mali] empire. The governors of each region had to work together to preserve economic and political balance. The result: one of Africa's more stable and powerful empires.

Such history has helped Mali resist ethnic tensions: When the Tuaregs of northern Mali rebelled against this government, they found no allies among the other ethnic groups.

"Ethnicity cannot be manipulated in this society," said educator Lalla Ben Barkar. "The people may be from the north or the south, but in the end they realize they are one nation, and that is Mali." (*The Washington Post*, 24 March 1996, A28)

According to Carl M. Peterson and Daniel T. Barkely, a reason why Somalia imploded is that "The previous government [Siad Barre's] failed to incorporate the institutional aspects of Somalia's indigenous culture into a functioning national body. . . . [Therefore] a stable, viable and fair political system must comprise the essential characteristics of Somalia's complex society. This means revitalizing indigenous institutions, restoring traditional powers and giving clans a legitimate outlet for political expression" (*New African*, June 1993, 20).

The traditional institutions, often castigated as "outmoded," can be useful. Indeed, this was exactly what was found by the multinational force that was sent into Somalia in 1993 to maintain peace and ensure delivery of relief food supplies to famine victims. The centralized government structure and other institutions established by the elites, such as schools, the postal service, and the central bank had all collapsed. But Somalia's traditional form of local government survived, and the U.S.-led military force tried to use it to revive the others. In the traditional system, decision is taken by clan elders, gray-haired men who have won inherited status in their communities as scholars, clerics and business leaders. "'They represent legitimacy in this country,' said Colonel Serge Labbe, the commander of Canadian forces, who meets frequently with elders to discuss how to end lawlessness, reopen schools and generally restore some degree of normal life. 'They're considered to be wise, almost supernatural in what they say.'" (*The Washington Post*, 28 March 1993, A30).

Institutions that have helped Africans survive for centuries cannot be that deficient. At least, they are superior to the hastily imported systems that could not last for even 30 years. According to Hitchens (1994), "The Swahili word for this concept, now coming back into vogue after a long series of experiments with foreign models, is *majimbo*. It stands for the idea of local initiative and trust in traditional wisdom" (*Vanity Fair*, November 1994, 117). Adebayo Adedeji, former executive secretary of U.N. Economic Commission for Africa and director of the African Center for Development and Strategic Studies in Nigeria, would agree: "Unfortunately, the leadership that took over from the departing colonial authorities did not go back to our past to revive and revitalize our democratic roots. They took the line of least resistance and convenience and continued with despotism, autocracy, and authoritarianism. But the basic democratic culture is still there" (*Africa Report*, November/December 1993, 58).

E. F. Kolajo of Thoyandou, South Africa, concurred: "The Japanese, Chinese, and Indians still maintain their roots, and they are thriving as nations. Africa embraces foreign cultures at the expense of its own, and this is why nothing seems to work for us" (*New African*, February 1995, 4). In fact, according to *The Bangkok Post*, "Japan's postwar success has demonstrated that modernization does not mean Westernization. Japan has modernized spectacularly, yet remains utterly different from the West. Economic success in Japan has nothing to do with individualism. It is the fruit of sheer discipline—the ability to work in groups and to conform" (cited by *The Washington Times*, 9 November 1996, A8).

In view of their success, African leaders have been heading off in droves on tours of Asian countries, "Hoping to copy blueprints that allowed some Asian countries to leap from poverty to relative prosperity in little more than a generation, more and more African leaders are heading off these days on tours of countries like Singapore, Malaysia, Thailand and Korea. And along with their economic recipes, these leaders are returning home with authoritarian political notions" (*The New York Times*, 4 February 1996, 4).

It is hoped that the twenty-first century will find them heading off to Jupiter on a one-way ticket!

The Village Meeting / National Conference

In chapter 2, we noted the five steps that must be followed to solve a problem: (1) expose the problem; (2) diagnose its causes; (3) prescribe a solution; (4) implement a solution; and (5) monitor the solution. Recall that when a crisis erupted in an African village, the chief and the elders would summon a village meeting. There the issue was debated by the people until a consensus was reached. During the debate, the chief usually made no effort to manipulate the outcome or sway public opinion. Nor were there bazooka-wielding rogues intimidating or instructing people on what they should say. People expressed their ideas openly and *freely* without fear of arrest. Those who cared participated in the decision-making process. No one was locked out. Once a decision had been reached by consensus, it was binding on all, including the chief.

In recent years, this indigenous African tradition has been revived by pro-democracy forces in the form of "national conferences" to chart a new political future in Benin, Cape Verde Islands, Congo, Malawi, Mali, South Africa, and Zambia. Benin's nine-day "national conference" began on 19 February 1990, with 488 delegates, representing various political, religious, trade union, and other groups encompassing the broad spectrum of Beninois society. The conference, whose chairman was Father Isidore de Souza, held "sovereign power" and its decisions were binding on all, including the government. It stripped President Matthieu Kerekou of power, scheduled multiparty elections and ended 17 years of autocratic Marxist rule.

Congo's national conference had more delegates (1,500) and lasted longer than three months. But when it was over in June 1991, the 12-year old government of General Denis Sassou-Nguesso had been dismantled. The constitution was rewritten and the nation's first free elections were scheduled for June 1992. Before the conference, Congo was among Africa's most avowedly Marxist-Leninist states. A Western business executive said, "The remarkable thing is that the revolution occurred without a single shot being fired . . . [and] if it can happen here, it can happen anywhere" (*The New York Times,* 25 June 1991, A8).[2]

In South Africa, the vehicle used to make that difficult but peaceful transition to a multiracial democratic society was the Convention for a Democratic South Africa. It began deliberations in July 1991, with 228 delegates drawn from about 25 political parties and various anti-apartheid groups. The de Klerk government made no effort to "control" the composition of CODESA. Political parties were not excluded; not even ultra right-wing political groups, although they chose to boycott its deliberations. CODESA strove to reach a "working consensus" on an interim constitution and set a date for the March 1994 elections. It established the composition

---

2. Unfortunately, Gen. Sassou-Nguesso did not accept his defeat graciously and overthrew, with the help of France and Angola, the civilian government of Pascal Lissouba in October 1997.

of an interim or transitional government that would rule until the elections were held. More important, CODESA was "sovereign." Its decisions were binding on the de Klerk government. De Klerk could not abrogate any decision made by CODESA—just as the African chief could not disregard any decision arrived at the village meeting.

Clearly, the vehicle exists—in Africa itself—for peaceful transition to democratic rule or resolution of political crisis.[3] But the leaders in most African countries either are not interested or seek to control the outcome of such national/constitutional conferences.

The Leadership as the Primary Obstacle

As we saw in chapter 7, African dictators loathe reform; they will undertake only the minimum cosmetic reforms necessary to ensure the continuation of Western aid. Delusions of omnipotence, fear, and anxiety from sycophants impel African despots to resist reform whole-heartedly. This should not come as a surprise. According to Vladimir Bukovsky, a prominent dissident in the heyday of the Soviet Union, "The Communists cannot reform themselves. They cannot liquidate them-selves. They must be swept away, toppled by an alternative force, as they were in Eastern Europe. Even if Mr. Gorbachev were to become a radical democrat tomorrow, he could succeed only by dismantling his own rule. And even if he tried that, the people wouldn't trust him. What you need now in the Soviet Union is a clean, clear break from the past" (*The Wall Street Journal*, 24 March 1992, A14).

---

3. It should be noted, however, that a national conference is *not* foolproof. A conference can be hijacked by various groups to advance their own political agenda. In Togo and Zaire, for example, national conferences failed when some delegates misused the forum to launch their own personal vendetta. In Zaire, national conference delegates openly insulted President Mobutu and demanded his head while its deliberations were being broadcast live on national television. Opposition leader, Etienne Tshiskedi, went as far as berating Mobutu as "a human monster." After such insults and threats, Mobutu did all he could to scuttle the conference.

Similarly in Togo, delegate after delegate recounted in gory detail brutal-ities and torture meted out to dissidents—a badly maimed student activist was even wheeled into the conference hall—and the widespread corruption in the Eyadema administration. It was alleged that President Eyadema, unable to bear any further humiliation, left the conference hall in tears. Then "he sent in the army to close it down" (*The Economist*, 4 July 1998, 40).

Similarly, the mafia state in Africa will not reform itself. The incessant rhetoric and grandiloquent posturing are designed to dupe donors. The political will or commitment to reform is not there. Reform often is undertaken piecemeal and frequently interrupted or abandoned when conditions improve slightly. African governments throw up various impediments, arguing that economic reform will hurt the "poor"—read the elites. Even when implemented, the primary object is to save regimes and to regain control of economies slipping away from their grasp—not so much as to relinquish control or curb the voracious excesses of the state. It would be suicidal for the predatory state to reform itself as this would undermine the very patronage system that it uses to buy its political support. In fact, Musa Gendemeh, Sierra Leone's deputy agriculture minister, said exactly this on the BBC *Focus on Africa* program on 24 April 1990. As reported in *West Africa* (4-10 June 1990), "He won't give up his present privileged position for the sake of a multiparty system nor would one expect a policeman or soldier to give up his one bag of rice at the end of every month for the same. . . . He warned that anyone talking about another party would be committing treason . . . that ministers and MPs suspected of having something to do with the multiparty movement are now under surveillance . . . and that whenever there has been trouble in the country, his people, the Mende, have suffered the most and he warned them to be careful" (934).

Under these circumstances, various proposals can be recommended. The first is abolishing the state. As radical as this may sound, it is not without cultural precedent. It may be recalled from chapter 3 that there are still many indigenous African societies, such as the Ibo, the Kru, and the Somali, who traditionally have no centralized authority. They are called stateless or acephalous societies. The Somali have returned to the traditional system. However, the practicality of abolishing the state is doubtful, since the ruling elites would not consent to it.

The Confederacy Principle

A less radical proposal is the adoption of the confederacy principle. A confederation is a loose political structure in which the constituent states have a great deal of autonomy to manage their own affairs and even possess the right to secede. Hybrids of this system are consociational or associational and the Swiss canton system. The flexibility and autonomy inherent in this system made possible the incredible diversity (cultural, ethnic, linguistic, religious) that has become the hallmark of Africa today.

Most of Africa's indigenous polities were confederacies: Great Zimbabwe, the Mali empire, the Ghana empire, Ga kingdom and the Fante confederation.

The most restrictive form of polity is the unitary system, in which all power is centralized: the European or colonial model. Virtually all African nationalists after independence, as we saw in chapter 6, adopted the unitary, centralized system because it concentrated power in the hands of the state and, ultimately, in their own hands. But the unitary system has proven to be the most unsuitable model for governing a polyethnic African society. A case can be made for this system if the population is linguistically, culturally, and racially homogenous. But the collapse of Somalia, which is ethnically uniform, cautions against the unitary system and argues for some form of federalism. Consider the case of Tanzania.

In 1993 it became clear to Tanzanians that the forced union between Tanganyika and Zanzibar, crafted by ex-president Julius Nyerere in 1962, proved no longer workable. "The government has now agreed to introduce a federal system before April 1995" (*New African,* November 1993, 31). Nyerere called a press conference to warn against the abandonment of the unitary form of government, saying that the creation of a Tanganyikan state within the union would lead to its total collapse. He was ignored.

Bypass the Autocrats

The second proposal is to abandon efforts to reform the state and instead redirect them toward building the informal/indigenous sector where the bulk of the population lives. Most Africans are farmers, fishermen, artisans, bakers, traders, and the like; they are not factory workers or civil servants. The ruling elites should be bypassed and the marauding state chastened with a series of "containment measures": the establishment of an independent central bank and caps on money supply growth, income taxes, and corporate and sales tax rates. Governors of central banks may be rotated within a region to reduce undue pressures on the central bank. Furthermore, a prosperous and growing informal sector will absorb workers from the state sector. This could hasten the demise of the state sector or force the ruling elites to reform that sector.

The added advantage with this approach is that rejuvenation of the informal/indigenous sector may not cost very much. For the most part, it would entail the removal of offensive regulations and state controls and improvements of the existing infrastructure. For example, restrictions on foreign exchange transactions under $5,000 may be removed. Fear of capital flight prompted African government officials to impose foreign exchange controls, which they themselves repeatedly violate. But the controls have a far more pernicious effect on the rest of the population by killing off the informal and indigenous sectors.

African artisans have been particularly ingenious in breaking down imported European devices, such as cars and trucks, adapting their technology to deal with the products of modern mechanized industry, and producing their own commodities out of the scrap from these imports. In addition, they import simple items such as finished yarn, chemical dyes, rubber, spare parts, and other intermediate products to make their own creations. Since these items are not produced locally, they must be imported. Nor do these small items cost much, often less than $5,000.

Abena, a seamstress (dressmaker), may need only $1,200 to import finished yarn or $50 to import thread. Kwadwo, the owner of the *mutatu* (a passenger vehicle), may need $500 to buy new brakes for his vehicle. Florence, a baker, may need only $490 to import flour. Kofi, a native fisherman, may need $1,200 to import fishing net or an outboard motor. But because of strict foreign exchange controls, all these individuals are denied foreign exchange. The result is that their businesses grind to a halt. They lose their employment, and Abena ends up as a prostitute on the streets of Abidjan.

Second, build markets and link them with good roads. The nerve center of every indigenous African society was the market, where women always dominated the activity. Any government policy, such as institution of price controls, that has an adverse impact on market activity hits African women the hardest. A genuine middle class can be created in Africa if markets are developed.

Third, free trade and free movement of people should be permitted across Africa. This did occur in precolonial Africa. The continent was criss-crossed by an intricate web of free trade routes. Under colonialism, Africa was carved into various unviable political entities; after independence, African leaders rightly condemned the artificial boundaries. But today, those same leaders enforce those borders with uniformed bandits who extort money from innocent travelers.

For a lesson in free markets, African leaders would do well to visit Kodjoviakope in Togo. In the local Anlo language, Kodjoviakope literally means "Little Kodjo's village." It is situated between the

Ghanaian border town of Aflao (in the west), the Togolese capital, Lome (in the east), and the Bight of Benin in the south. As *West Africa* (26 March–1 April 1990) reported, "Kodjoviakope may not be well known or ancient a market as Freetown, Onitsha, Gao, Goree, Lagos or Accra, but currently it is the town most popular with business people of all types in the West African sub-region. Well traveled business men have variously dubbed the town as 'Africa's Florida' or 'Africa's Wall Street,' while local people call it 'Eyadema Liverpool Street Market' due to the vast number of goods and services traded in the town" (585).

Kodjoviakope has been successful because the state kept its hands off. Although hundreds of police are stationed in the town, together with other security personnel and the *douane* (customs) officials, to maintain peace and supervise immigration matters, traders are not harassed. As Amega Attati Kpoma, a Togolese businessman based in Ghana, told *West Africa,* "to do business in Kodjoviakope, all one has to do is to pay taxes regularly, avoid politics and respect our life-president, Papa Eyadema" (26 March–1 April 1990, 506). But would the ruling elites keep their grasping fingers to themselves?

A prosperous sector of the economy could invite envy or be perceived as a potential political threat. Perhaps another way of bypassing the thieving state is to establish private industrial zones by legislation. This is different from a free trade zone, where industrial inputs can be imported without duty or tariff, used in the manufacture of other products, which then can be exported—as has been the case with Mauritius. In private industrial zones, certain geographical areas of the country are delineated as places where economic activity can be pursued without government regulations and interference. Such an industrial zone could serve as a magnet for both foreign and domestic investment, create jobs, spur economic growth, and serve as a "demonstration model" for the hopelessly inefficient state sector. But then again, this idea would not fly with many African despots since it takes sections of the economy out of their control. This leads to yet another idea: tying the private industrial zone concept to an issue of paramount concern to African governments to achieve a greater "incentive effect." That idea is the free debt zone.

DEBT-FREE ZONE—A DIGRESSION

African governments lament that the debt overhang seriously impairs their ability to carry out reform. Strictly speaking, debt repayments impede efforts at development, not economic reform. The two are separate issues. Economic reform seeks to create the conditions necessary for development to take off. If a vehicle has broken down, fixing that vehicle ought to be a priority. Arguing that a new tire or lighter load would permit greater distances to be traveled makes little sense.

Nonetheless, crushing foreign debt is a problem in many African countries; debt servicing alone absorbs more than 40 percent of export earnings, leaving scant foreign exchange for the importation of capital goods, essential spare parts, and medical supplies. African governments have requested outright cancellation of their debts. Unfortunately, this option tends to reward past mismanagement and reckless spending. Insistence on full repayment, on the other hand, is not practical. Some of the foreign loans were used to establish inefficient state enterprises that have collapsed. In such cases, the "assets" cannot be "repossessed." Some of the loans were consumed—used to finance budget deficits—as in the case of Tanzania in the 1980s, where foreign funds were used to pay the salaries of government workers. In other cases, some of the foreign loan money was embezzled. In all these cases, little or nothing can be recovered and some debt relief may be necessary. However, partial cancellation opens up a whole new can of worms. Eligibility criteria are likely to be subjective and susceptible to political lobbying, chicanery, and favoritism. At their Toronto meeting in 1992, the Group-7 countries decided to write off half of the debts of the "poorest" African nations. Since then, Ghana and Zambia have been rewarded with partial debt cancellation for progress on economic and political reform. However, there is a better way to take care of the debt problem—create free debt zones.

In this scenario, a debtor African nation meets a consortium of creditor governments (Paris Club) and designates an area of its country— say 30 square miles—as a free industrial zone, in which companies from the creditor nation can operate freely for the next 20 years. Companies operating in this zone would enjoy certain benefits, such as zero profit tax, waivers on import, and custom duties. The management of this zone would be in the hands of the creditor governments, with observer status granted the debtor government to ensure compliance with domestic industrial regulations for, say, the protection of the environment and child labor. The zone may choose to establish its own judicial, security, electrical, or water supply systems, if domestic supplies are felt to be unreliable. It also may choose to set its own wages, provided these are not below the domestic level. Disputes with the domestic government shall be subject to international mediation. The zone shall not engage in political activity. The exact terms, of course, would be negotiated between the debtor nation and the creditors. Participation in such a zone would be open to the nationals of creditor governments and exiles of the African country. Once a final agreement has been reached, the country's entire foreign debt would be canceled.

Such an arrangement confers enormous benefits on both parties. For the creditor nation, say the United States or Britain, it opens up markets and investment opportunities. Foreign companies are guaranteed repatriation of profits and minimal government interference. The debtor nation, through this arrangement, may gain not only the cancellation of its debt but also more foreign investment, technology transfer, and employment opportunities for its citizens. Furthermore, the more efficient management of the debt-free zone would serve as a demonstration model for the government and the rest of the economy.

The debt-free zone also could serve as a "magnet." It could force an intransigent African government to match the incentives provided by the zone or face an exodus of domestic firms to it. Even more important, it could encourage the return of African exiles abroad. Most would like to return to their home countries and run their own private businesses but are wary of government assurances that their businesses would be safe. However, they may feel safe in a private industrial zone.

The World Bank, USAID and other donor agencies should encourage the establishment not only of debt-free zones but also of private industrial zones.

The Buy-Out Option

If none of these propositions are acceptable to African despots, as a last resort a buy-out option may be tried.[4] In a background paper on official

---

4. This author first made this proposal during an appearance on the Reverend Jesse Jackson's CNN TV program, *Both Sides,* on 4 August 1994. The program was to explore what to do in Nigeria. I suggested that, if General Abacha would not implement reform, "we should place $1 million dollars in a Swiss bank" to entice him out of the country ("safe passage" out). The Nigerian ambassador, who also appeared on the program, was visibly furious. Later one commentator who watched the program joked that what drew the ire of the ambassador was not the suggestion but rather the *amount* offered. In an article published in *African News Weekly* (31 March 1995), I subsequently raised this figure to $1 *billion.*

corruption, the secretariat of a U.N. conference said, "Some heads of state can be bribed for about $5 million. Five percent of $100 million may attract the serious attention of the head of state" (*The Washington Times,* 28 April 1995, A17).

Consider Nigeria's military rulers, who have committed heinous atrocities and adamantly refuse to implement reform. Diplomacy does not work with them. Military vandals are impervious to reason and diplomacy. Vindictiveness or retribution would not solve the problem. To punish or dislodge them from power may plunge Nigeria into a bloody civil war, which will destabilize the entire West African region. To save Nigeria, a buy-out may be the most viable option. These military thugs are thieves anyway; therefore, a bribe is the language they understand best.

A loan of $1 billion could be taken to buy out the military rulers. That loan would be added to Nigeria's $35 billion foreign debt. This would provide the military vagabonds a "safe passage out of the country" *à la* Haiti in 1994.[5] But before they leave the country, they must disband half—if not the entire—armed forces and install a transitional reformist government with some of its members drawn from neighboring African countries; that is, placed under an African trusteeship. For example, a transitional government in Sierra Leone would have eminent Ghanaians, Kenyans or Malawians serve on it for an interim period.

The buy-out option may be criticized as manifest moral turpitude—rewarding the thieves who have stolen the people's money. It makes a mockery of the concept of "accountability." Moreover, it may encourage other thieving military coconut-heads to seize or cling to power in the hope that they too might be bought out. But exceptional circumstances demand exceptional strategies. Let's look at the "economics" of it.

---

5. Lieutenant-General Raoul Cedras left Haiti on a U.S. military aircraft for Panama on 14 October 1993 with his family and fellow coup leader Brigadier Philippe Biamby. "In exchange for their agreement to leave Haiti peacefully, the U.S. government agreed to grant them access to their money, which had been frozen in U.S. bank accounts. Citing U.S. Treasury Department officials, *The New York Times* estimated that those accounts hold about $79 million. The U.S. government agreed to lease General Cedras' three homes in Haiti—two in the capital and a third on the beach—for between $5,000 and $12,000 a month" (*The Washington Times,* 15 October 1996, A11). Most people believe General Cedras and General Biamby stole the money from Haiti's state coffers, possibly including army pension funds.

The 1993 "Operation Rescue" in Somalia cost the international community over $3.5 billion, not to mention the cost of rebuilding crumbled infrastructure—roads, schools, telephone, government buildings. Total U.S. annual aid to sub-Saharan Africa in any year is less than $1 billion. In Rwanda, the humanitarian mission cost the international community over $400 million and feeding the Hutu refugees in Goma, Zaire, and Tanzania cost $1 million a day. Then the cost of rebuilding the country has to be factored in. Rebuilding Liberia would easily cost $5 billion. It is easy to destroy but extraordinarily difficult to repair the damage. It is mind-boggling how poor African countries engage in such wanton self-destructive acts.

Suppose back in 1990 a $50 million foreign loan was taken to buy out the regime of Siad Barre of Somalia, the Hutu-dominated regime of Juvenal Habryimana of Rwanda, or the regime of Samuel Doe of Liberia: imagine the savings not only in money but in the reduction of the loss of human lives. Would Nigerians be willing to incur an additional $1 billion foreign debt now or a hundred times more in the future to rebuild their country destroyed by civil war?

An Eminent Persons Group, made up of respected African statesmen or perhaps black Americans, with the backing of Western donors, may be charged with the task of negotiating the buy-out and setting up the transitional government. The buy-out idea is not without precedence in Africa, where coup leaders have been paid off to make way for civilian administrations.

In 1979 in Ghana, some members of the then ruling Armed Forces Revolutionary Council took bounty in U.S. dollars before leaving the political scene. But its leader Flight-Lieutenant Jerry Rawlings staged another coup in 1981. Similarly in 1995, the military leader of Sierra Leone was also paid a hefty amount before he agreed to step down to pave the way for an election, which was won by Ahmed Tejan Kabbah. But on 25 May 1997 Kabbah was overthrown by Major John Paul Koroma. "He demanded a ransom of $46 million from the international community before he would allow ousted President Kabbah to resume power. This demand was rejected outright" (*Free Press,* 27 June–3 July 1997, 12).

The buy-option did not work in Ghana and Sierra Leone because, in each case, it was not accompanied by at least a partial disbandment of the military—the primary source of the problem. It simply removed the coup leaders from the scene and left the military intact, which only encouraged other vagabonds.

HOW THE WEST CAN HELP AFRICAN REFORM

Far from being a seemingly hopeless continent, Africa may well be the next frontier for roaring democratic capitalism (Johns, 1996, 173). The West can help Africa, not through recolonization, but in several other ways. First of all, the West needs to "get tough" with African dictators. The United States in particular has been too soft on African despots, largely out of fear of antagonizing black Americans. Although it is understandable, the U.S. government must recognize that the regimes in Africa are brutal and barbarously vicious. As mentioned earlier, diplomacy does not work with them. In many cases, Western policies toward Africa amount to appeasement of these state terrorists. The record of the French is even more reprehensible, as they brazenly coddle African tyrants. As mentioned many times before, the solutions to Africa's crises lie in Africa itself. The vampire state and the leadership are the problems—not racism, Western imperialism, colonialism, or the alleged inferiority of the African people.

Second and as noted earlier, Western donors must always make a distinction between African leaders and the African people. The two are not necessarily synonymous since the leaders do not represent the people. In fact, in many countries it is even doubtful if the leaders can even be called "Africans," since they exhibit no sense of camaraderie with the people they are supposed to be serving. The expression, "The U.S. is helping Africans reform their economies," is very misleading. Who is being helped: the leaders or the people? This distinction was not made in a series of moves by the Clinton Administration to show concern for and grapple with the Africa's economic crisis.

The first attempt was a 27 June 1994 White House gathering "to raise the profile of Africa" and "express solidarity with its people." It turned out to be a public relations fluff with little substance. In attendance was a preponderance of apologists and representatives of failed African governments. Ten years earlier, a White House conference on the Soviet Union would have drawn its speakers and guests from the exiled Russian dissident community. There were no exiled African dissidents at the White House Conference on Africa.

This was followed by a visit to South Africa by Vice-President Al Gore in 1995. There were also high level visits by Warren Christopher, former Secretary of State in October 1996, and by First Lady Hillary Clinton in February 1997. Then on 15 March 1996, the United Nations launched a $25 billion Special Initiative for Africa to revive development on the African continent. The U.N. initiative subsequently dissolved into extinction and nothing much came out of the rest.

Earlier on 5 February 1996 President Clinton submitted to Congress a report that outlined a comprehensive trade and development policy for the countries of Africa. Its primary objective was "to work with the people and leaders of Africa in the pursuit of increased trade and investment." The policy framework was structured around five basic objectives: trade liberalization and promotion; investment liberalization and promotion; development of the private sector; infrastructure enhancement; and economic and regulatory reform.

However, this report drew a harsh denunciation from Washington Democrat Representative Jim McDermott. "Unfortunately, masquerading as a trade and development policy are an assortment of programs and initiatives that don't work well together, have no central focus, policy or direction—a compilation of programs and initiatives that are trapped in a Cold War and almost paternalistic approach to sub-Saharan Africa. A very good example of this disjointed approach is Vice President Gore's Bi-National Commission with South Africa," he said.[6]

A revised version was drawn up by U.S. Congressmen Phil Crane, Charles Rangel, and Jim McDermott, which tacitly recognized that the old donor-recipient approach had failed and attempted to sharpen focus and seek new direction. Said Jim McDermott: "We propose to move away from 'If you reform your economy we will give you development assistance' to a more dynamic response that says 'If you liberalize your trade, political and economic policies, we will expand our trade and investment relation with you'" (Congressional Testimony, 1 August 1996, 7).

---

6. Statement by Representative Jim McDermott before the Subcommittee on Trade Committee on Ways and Means, U.S. Trade Policy with Africa, 1 August 1996. His indictment of the Clinton's initiative was valid because I was invited to one session of Vice President Al Gore's Bi-National Commission at the White House on Dec 22, 1995. This was after the Vice-President had led a delegation of U.S. policymakers and businessmen to South Africa, to explore the possibilities of increased trade with South Africa. From the discussions, it became clear to me that the U.S. had no "Africa Policy." It focused most of its attention on South Africa and President Nelson Mandela and expected him to provide the leadership for the rest of Africa. Of course, Mandela's leadership had been *par excellence,* but he alone could not solve all of Africa's problems. South Africa had its own problems to attend to.

In June 1997 the Clinton Administration unveiled this as its new Africa initiative, encapsulated in the bi-partisan bill, "Growth and Investment Opportunity in Africa: The End of Dependency Act" (HR 4198). This sought "to create a transition path from development assistance to economic self-sufficiency for sub-Saharan African countries." The bill authorized a one time appropriation of $150 million for an equity fund and $500 million for a infrastructure fund beginning in 1998. These funds were to be used to mobilize private savings from developed economies for equity investment in Africa; stimulate the growth of securities markets in Africa; improve access to third party equity and management advice for Africa's small and medium-sized firms. The infrastructure funds were to help improve the operations of telecommunications, roads, railways and power plants in Africa. These improvements, it was hoped, would help attract U.S. investors to potentially profitable projects in Africa.

The other cornerstones of the initiative were: (1) U.S.–Africa Economic Forum (an annual high level discussion of trade and investment policies); (2) U.S.–Africa Free Trade Area (developing a plan to enter into one or more free trade agreements with sub-Saharan African countries by the year 2020); (3) a Textile Initiative (the lifting of World Trade Organization Textile and Clothing restrictions on imports from Africa until the aggregate value of such imports exceed $3.5 billion annually); and (4) granting the poorest African nations duty-free access to the U.S. market for 1,800 products.

To be eligible to participate in this program, an African country must show a "strong commitment to economic and political reform, market incentives and private sector growth and poverty reduction." (McDermott, Congressional Testimony, 1 August 1996, 9). President Clinton sought to sell this program to other donor countries at the June 1997 Group-7 Summit conference in Denver.

As the program itself acknowledged, a "strong commitment to economic and political reform" on the part of African leaders was required for the initiative to succeed in reducing African dependency on aid and expanding U.S. trade and investment. But as we saw earlier, this commitment has woefully been lacking in Africa—the "Babangida boogie," "Moi massamba," and so on.

The Clinton administration correctly recognized that handing over money to African reform laggards and acrobats had not stimulated much change. The pace of reform had been unimpressive. But it is unlikely that access to U.S. markets, as envisaged by the new initiative, would spark greater commitment to reform among African leaders. Their economies may collapse around them and their people in open rebellion against them. But they would be content as long as they occupied the presidency. In fact, President Clinton himself bemoaned this fact in his 5 February 1996 Report to Congress: "The responsibility rests with African countries to commit themselves to these objectives and to make policy choices that will enable them to achieve these objectives. Help from outside Africa cannot overcome lack of commitment or wrong choices by the governments of Africa" (U.S. Government Report, 1996, 3).

There is a better way to help place Africa on the fast-growth track. First, the administration should drop its French-like suffocating paternalism toward Africa and shed its obsession with a few "African success stories." It is not that there are no success stories in Africa. There are but the vast majority of African economies are faltering and these are the ones dragging the whole continent down and giving Africa a bad, negative image. It is understandable that the Administration may not want to offend the Congressional Black Caucus and African-American leaders by appearing too "negative" in focusing on the wanton carnage, famine, and destruction. But the excessive reliance on a few successful countries completely distorts the picture.

On 17 June 1997 the White House called another conference on Africa for President Clinton to announce his new policy toward Africa. Again, no exiled African dissident was invited. At that gathering, President Clinton painted an overly optimistic portrait of "a dynamic new Africa making dramatic strides toward democracy and prosperity" (*The Washington Post,* 18 June 1997, A18). Such a portrait is more apt to breed cynicism. There have been no such "dramatic strides," but rather "baby steps."

Second, the focus should be placed on the real causes of the Africa's economic decline, which is due to the absence of a few key institutions: an independent central bank, judiciary, media, and free enterprise—mechanisms for the peaceful resolution of conflicts and transfer of political power. As we saw earlier, the absence of these critical institutions has banished the rule of law; respect and security of persons and property; and social, political, and economic stability from much of Africa. As a result, corruption is rampant, commercial and personal property is arbitrarily seized by drunken soldiers, dissidents frequently "disappear," and senseless civil wars rage for years on end. Throw in a crumbling infrastructure and what you have is an environment that deters even African investors, so why would Americans want to invest in such a place? This environment cannot be cleaned up by the United States; only Africans themselves can do it. But the ruling vampire elites will not allow it.

Therefore, instead of persuading, cajoling, bribing or jaw-boning African autocrats to reform, the focus should be shifted. It would be expedient to work through a continental organization such as the Organization of African Unity. But that scandalous organization has yet to reform itself. This leaves one other alternative: To identify the internal (African) agents of reform and assist or empower them. After all, reform which is internally generated is far more sustainable and durable than that dictated externally.

A new Western policy toward Africa that would help the continent must be *inclusive*. African governments are not the only sources of good reformist ideas. Quite often, these ideas are to be found *outside* government. Therefore, Western policy toward Africa should also aim at assisting those groups outside government—civic groups, opposition political parties, African NGOs and individuals—who are seeking to advance intellectual, economic, and political liberty. In addition to the recommendations I have made elsewhere in Ayittey (1992), it would have the following elements briefly discussed earlier.[7]

The average person in the West takes the practical usefulness of radio for granted, without realizing its critical significance in civic empowerment in the Third World. In Africa, the radio is a political tool for the empowerment of the African masses. Says John Balzar, an American journalist: "To speak of radio in Africa is to discuss life and death. . . . Much of the rest of the world may be drowning in the flood of data from the Information Superhighway. But in Africa, for hundreds of millions of people, events over the next hill and beyond are known by just two means: word of mouth as carried by travelers and word of mouth as broadcast on radio. . . . On a continent that is crushingly poor, undereducated, rural and remote, only radio can truly be called the medium of the masses" (*The Washington Post*, 25 October 1995, A22).

---

7. In my earlier work I recommended that, in those African countries that agree to privatize state-owned enterprises, the media ought to be the first enterprise placed on the auction block, and that African governments should use their own local experts to draw up their own restructuring plans and present them to the donors for funding. Although the donors may accept or reject these plans, this approach establishes, African ownership of African problems.

This view was confirmed by ex-Senator Nancy Kasselbaum at an April 1996 hearing before the Senate Foreign Relations subcommittee on African affairs. She recalled that during her trip to Africa: "I was struck by the pervasive power of radio in Africa. From democratizing Mali to troubled Rwanda, radio holds immense power and possibilities" (*The Washington Times*, 25 April 1996, A16).

Although the number of nongovernmental radio stations has increased from 0 in 1983 to 137 in 27 countries in 1995, most stations are still state-controlled with governments justifying their control over the media as a means of enhancing national unity and development. In reality, however, the radio has served as a mouthpiece of the ruling party's propaganda. The powerful effect of propaganda radio was evidenced in Rwanda, where Hutu militiamen, the *interahamwe*—a government-sponsored group—broadcast hate messages against the Tutsis and whipped their Hutu kinsmen into a killing frenzy. "*Radio Milles Collines* was clearly one of the mouthpieces for the genocide," said Janet Fleishman of Human Rights Watch/Africa. "The killers, some of whom had a radio in one hand and a machete in the other, heeded the advice of *Radio Milles Collines* and slaughtered children as well as adults" (*The Washington Times*, 25 April 1996, A12). "Since the beginning of the war with [Rwandan Patriotic Front], this propaganda always said that the Tutsis were coming to attack the country. All day long on the radio, they said the Tutsis were coming to take power away from the Hutus," said Pierre-Claver Rwangabo, a Hutu moderate who joined the subsequent Tutsi-led government (*The Washington Post*, 18 April 1995, A17).

Consequently, those in power use the radio to perpetuate themselves and their views, blocking out dissenting or opposition views. For opposition politicians in Kenya and Nigeria to get their views to the masses, BBC and the Voice of America often serve as alternate outlets. Voice of America, for example, beams "83 hours a week of broadcasts to Africa in 7 languages, reaching more than 20 million listeners," said its director Geoffrey Cowan (*The Washington Times*, 25 April 1996, A14). As Jean-Louis Katambwe, a political reporter for the anti-Mobutu newspaper, *Umoja*, once complained bitterly: "The only power now for Mobutu is radio and television. He has reach into all the villages. One of the opposition's biggest failings may have been that it did not move quickly to wrest control of Zaire television. . . . [But] opposition leaders say they were prevented from doing so by the presence of Mobutu's troops" (T*he Washington Post*, 23 February 1993, A15).

The "Serbian Syndrome" should be a poignant lesson here. When Serbian president Slobodan Milosevic lost municipal elections to the opposition in November 1996, he canceled the results. Pro-democracy activists took to the streets, rallying more than 50,000 people for more than two weeks. But President Milosevic had one weapon—the state-controlled television. Said David Webster, chairman of the Trans Atlantic Dialogue on Broadcasting and the Information Society: "A recurrent image from the demonstrations against President Milosevic in Belgrade is that of a television set being thrown from a building and smashed on the ground. People do get tired of lies. Milosevic used Serbian state television to whip up nationalist hatred leading to the Bosnian tragedy, and he uses it now to keep himself in office and subdue the voices of the opposition. Serbia gives us the clearest example of the domination by the government of state television and its dangers . . . of drowning out of other voices" (*The Washington Post,* 15 December 1996, C7).

The establishment of a Radio Free Africa, similar to Radio Free Asia, would be of great help to the African people: "Radio Free Asia, the U.S. Government station that has been beaming uncensored news into China since September [1996], has so upset Beijing that Washington has kept the location of its transmitters a state secret. . . . Proponents of RFA insist it is not anti-Chinese, but aimed at all tyranny in Asia. But Congress created the radio station because of its disgust at the massacre of pro-democracy protesters at Tiananmen Square in June 1989" (*The Washington Times, 28* October 1996, A10).

There is great tyranny in Africa as well. Yet instead of expanding its broadcasts to Africa or helping break the state's stranglehold on radio, "the budget for U.S.-government-funded international broadcasting, including the [Voice of America] has been cut by 25 percent," Cowan said (*The Washington Times,* 25 April 1996, A14).

Johns (1996) makes a strong case for Radio Free Africa: "Such a project, by providing objective news and independent commentary by Africans and others, would expand informed public discourse throughout the African continent and ultimately could be the axe that enables Africans to smash the seemingly impenetrable wall of autocratic governance" (175).

Foreign aid, as noted earlier, is simply a concessional loan being contracted by an African government on behalf of its people. As such, representatives of the people should approve of loan agreements before they are entered into, and the use of the funds should be accounted for. A political party or organization cannot contract a foreign loan on behalf of the people in the same way that West Britain's Conservative Party or the Republican Party in the United States cannot accept a foreign loan in the name of their people.

Johns (1996) demands that "Washington should end all foreign aid to Africa that does not contribute to positive economic and political change. Many times, U.S. foreign aid is used by autocratic African regimes merely to strengthen their own political standing; it is especially urgent that this sort of assistance be ended immediately" (174).

In fact, in the following stipulations, there should be no Western aid to any African country:

• No aid should go to African countries in which a civil war rages. It makes no sense to provide aid for the construction of schools, bridges, and roads only to have them blown up by insurgents. In fact, the West should not provide any aid to repair *self-inflicted* damage. Negotiation is far superior to the military option.

   The West may help most in the resolution by insisting on an African solution. Of course, logistical support can be provided to support an African initiative but, the West should avoid sending troops, as the United States did in Somalia.

   Warring factions in Africa have signed truces and accords. But quite often they refuse to live by the agreement. Enforcement mechanisms and sanctions should be set in place to deal with recalcitrants. For example, neighboring countries should close their borders against a government that refuses to abide by an accord. If the present OAU cannot administer such sanctions, perhaps it should be disbanded and replaced with a new OAU— this time, formed only by democratic countries and called the Organization of Free African States (OFAS).

• No Western aid should be provided to an African country ruled by a military dictatorship or a one-party state system. African aid recipients should meet three tests: (1) The African government should be willing to pursue genuine free market reform, not the "voodoo" type of reform under which five state-owned enterprises are privatized and then eight new ones acquired simultaneously; (2) the country should be stable—democratic, with an independent judiciary and independent central bank, and where the rule of law prevails; and (3) the country should not spend more than 10 percent of its budget on the military and security forces. Today the military is simply out of control in Africa.

- No aid should be given to African countries transitioning to democracy unless the rules are transparent. The government in power cannot write or manipulate the rules of the transition, act as a referee, and participate in the elections on top. Doing so defies common sense. The rules must be written by an impartial body, not appointed by the government, and agreed to by all sides before any elections. South Africa's Convention for Democratic South Africa was a "African village meeting" concept to meet these tests. Furthermore, a transition period of more than two years should not be acceptable as countries such as Nigeria are in a "perpetual state of transition" to democratic rule. Nor should Western aid be given to "sham democracies" in Africa where fraudulent transition programs were put into place hastily to return the same despot to power: Angola, Cameroon, Equatorial Guinea, Ghana, Guinea, Guinea-Bissau, Côte d'Ivoire, Kenya, and Togo. All parties must accept the transition rules, certify the vote as "free and fair," and accept the results before Western governments recognize them.

- No Western aid should go to an African country whose government indemnifies itself from lapses in the use of funds. U.S. AID cannot preach "accountability" and allow African governments to exempt themselves from the same test. Recent cases occurred in Benin, Ghana, and The Gambia.

Consistency and "equal treatment" must be manifest. Donor countries cannot apply one standard to one African country and a different one to another country. Furthermore, the West needs to realize that it is Africans who ultimately bear the responsibility of saving their own countries. African reformers outside the state sector do exist who, despite suffering hardships and brutality, are doing their best to save their countries. The West needs to identify and support these reformers or agents of reform, as it did in South Africa and Eastern Europe—or at least not frustrate them. Recall this statement by Stephen Demming, director of the World Bank's Africa office, who said that "no project in South Africa would proceed unless all political parties consented, and one mission was called back to Washington after the ANC objected" (*The Wall Street Journal*, 6 October 1994, A15). Why wasn't the same rule applied in Ghana, Nigeria, or the rest of Africa?

Quite often, representatives of donor governments and institutions talk through their hats. They pontificate *ad nauseam* about "accountability," "middle class," "civil society," and "democracy"—as if these emerge out of thin air. They place the emphasis on the *outcome,* with little or no focus on the *processes* that achieve those desirable outcomes. They have watched silently as brutalities were heaped on civil society—the wellspring of reform and change and have done next to nothing to assist or fund the activities of indigenous African nongovernmental organizations or helped nurture civil society.

Rebuilding Civil Society

All experts agree that a civil society would put the brakes on tyrannical excesses of African regimes. Recall that for civil society to perform its watchdog role, as well as to instigate change, two key institutions are critical: freedom of expression and freedom of association. But since independence there has been a systematic strangulation of freedom of expression in Africa. The starting point was the accumulation of political power. Kwame Nkrumah of Ghana said it best with his famous aphorism: "Seek ye first the political kingdom . . . " Once acquired, political power was then used to subvert the constitution and banish the opposition. After decimating the opposition, the nationalists turned their attention to the press.

Very quickly, the state monopolized the information media and turned it into propaganda organ for the party elite. Anyone not in the government's party was necessarily a dissident, and any newspaper editor or journalist who published the slightest criticism of an insignificant government policy was branded a "contra" and jailed or killed, including journalists who for years had praised government measures. Even newspapers that have lavished praises on the government were closed for carrying an occasional critique (Ayittey, 1992, chapter 9).

After the collapse of communism in 1989, a brief gust of change swept across Africa. In a number of countries, long-standing autocrats were toppled. Free and independent newspapers sprouted and flourished but, by 1995, had begun to suffer a series of setbacks, as we saw in chapter 10. In a dramatic testimony before the House Africa and International Operations and Human Rights Sub-Committee in January 1996, Larry Diamond, a senior fellow at the Hoover Institution in California, made this observation:

Historically, Nigeria has had the most vibrant and pluralistic civil society in Africa (with the possible exception of South Africa). One of the most tragic consequences of military rule has been the decimation of and degradation of this sector as well. Interest groups, such as the labor movement, the professional associations, and women's organizations have been infiltrated, corrupted, and subverted by the authoritarian state. Those that would not bend have been relentlessly hounded and repressed. . . . The most independent publications have suffered prolonged closures and more subtle forms of state pressure, such as cutting off access to newsprint at affordable cost. Human rights groups have suffered constant surveillance, harassment, intimidation, and repeated arrest. Several leading human rights figures are now in jail. The decimation of civil society not only handicaps the campaign for a transition to democracy, it also weakens the infrastructure that could help to develop and sustain that democracy after transition. (*Congressional Records,* January 1996)

There has been no letup in the brutal clampdown of "dissident" activity. Beginning in 1994, Nigeria's military government closed three publishing houses—effectively shutting nearly 20 publications—for 14 months. Security agents also have arrested more than 40 journalists, detaining some for several days (*The Washington Post,* 7 April 1996, A18). The repression forced Nobel laureate Wole Soyinka to flee his own native Nigeria after instances such as the following: "Armed security forces descended on a book launching at Nkpolu Oraoorukwo Town Hall, firing tear gas at citizens and causing pandemonium. The object of their ire was the book, entitled *My Ordeal—A Prison Memoir of a Student Activist,* written by Christian Akani, Campaign for Democracy chairman in River State. It expresses the hardships of Nigeria and the treatment meted out to those who express displeasure with the country's policies. The security operatives who came to the launching claimed that the organizers did not obtain security clearance for such activities" (*African News Weekly,* 18 November 1994, 4).

The officers fired teargas into the crowd, which quickly scattered, and then seized copies of the book and arrested the author who was taken to an undisclosed location. Imagine. So when Shi'ite Muslims in Zaria (Nigeria) went on a demonstration in October 1996, "they carried coffins . . . in case security agents opened fire on them during the procession" (*African News Weekly,* 4-10 November 1996, 14).

The barbaric crackdown on political dissent and journalists has had an unintended effect of boosting urban crime. With the police going after political activists, Nigerian armed robbers have been having a field day, raiding one house after another with impunity. "No day passes without a robbery here or there. It is so common now as the police have focused their attention on just quelling political demonstrations to the detriment of curbing crime," said Lanre Olorunsogo, a tenant in Onike, a Lagos suburb (*African Observer*, 23 August–5 September 1994, 4). How can civil society emerge under these circumstances? But Africans are fighting back. In an irate comment, Charles Wereko-Bobby, a leading opposition figure in Ghana, demanded that, "the state-controlled media be dismantled because it has become an arm of the NDC Government propaganda machinery. The sooner we destroy the state media, the better for us all. . . . The state media is being used as mechanism to suppress opposing views. It is intertwined with Government. machinery" (*Free Press*, 11-17 August 1995, 12).

Establishing Freedom of Association and of Assembly

The other right vital for the sustenance of civil society—freedom of association—has progressively been squelched in postcolonial Africa. In many countries, gatherings of more than ten persons require official sanction or else they can be broken up by thugs or gun-toting zombies. In Cameroon, police disrupted a meeting of the opposition Union for Change on 19 August 1993 and arrested and detained the party's administrative secretary, François Evembe, over an article published on 9 August entitled "The Problem is the Man that Resides at Etoudi [government house]" (*Index on Censorship*, October 1993, 42).

In Nigeria, clearance must be obtained from a paranoid military government to hold even a seminar or conference, because such a gathering might pose a threat to state security. Consider these events as reported by *Index on Censorship* (March 1993, 38):

> On November 27, 1992, more than 250 police and state security forces disrupted a vigil for democracy in Lagos organized by the Civil Liberties Organization. Police subsequently visited vigil organizers Peter Eriose and Imogeo Ewhuba and threatened them with arrest if they continued their pro-democracy activities. Eriose went into hiding.

> On December 1, 1992, 500 security agents prevented members of the Campaign for Democracy (CD) from holding a meeting at the Nigeria Union of Journalists in Lagos. The same day, several people on a pro-

democracy march in Kano State were arrested, including Dr. Wada Abubakar, former deputy governor of Kano State, Onuana Ammani, former president of the Social Democratic Party, and Wada Waziri, a former union leader.

On December 2, 1992, police and security agents took over the senate chambers at the former National Assembly Complex where the Civil Liberties Organization was planning a seminar on "Women and Taxation in Nigeria." The seminar was rescheduled for 15 December, but previously granted permission was withdrawn the evening before and police refused participants entry to the premises.

On March 19, 1996, Government agents blocked the U.S. Ambassador, Walter Carrington, from a conference organized by the American Studies Association of Nigeria in the northern city of Kaduna. The organization often sponsors forums on a wide range of topics. Security agents turned Carrington and several embassy staffers away from the conference and then broke up the gathering (*The Washington Post,* 20 March 1996, A14). In September 1997, pro-democracy and human rights groups held a reception in honor of U.S. Ambassador Walter Carrington, who was leaving Nigeria. "Security agents broke down the gate at the house where the reception was being held. After entering the residence, they drew their guns and broke up the gathering" (*The Washington Post,* 3 October 1997, A9).

In many countries, the population at large also has been placed under surveillance by paramilitary organizations to suppress any signs of dissent or revolt. Young Pioneers spied on people in Malawi and Ghana under Nkrumah; *interahamwe* performed the job in Rwanda; and Committees for the Defense of the Revolution (CDRs) spied for Rawlings of Ghana. Their official purpose, of course, is to mobilize the youth for development.

On 7 July 1997 Kenyan opposition politicians and human rights activists organized protests to push the government of Daniel arap Moi, in power for 20 years, to reform electoral and other laws that are viewed as oppressive. The government's response was swift and ferocious. Riot police and elite paramilitary General Service Unit officers charged into the protest rallies, firing tear gas and live rounds. Eleven people were killed and dozens were injured.

Riot police even charged into Nairobi's All Saints Cathedral where about 100 people were praying. They lobbed a tear gas canister that landed near the altar and beat numerous parishioners bloody. "We were in the middle of the service when they broke in, fired tear gas into the house of God. This is Kenyan justice for you. Even in God's house they beat innocent protesters," said Reverend Peter Njoka (*The Washington Times,* 8 July 1997, A11). "These are the actions of fellows who are really primitive," said Mike Kibaki of the Democratic Party, whom police clubbed on the shoulders while he was in the cathedral.

Moi and ruling party leaders claim that the opposition parties seek to foment violence and are too disorganized and divided to rule the country effectively. "How can we tell the people what we are offering if we cannot meet," asked Kimani Kangethe, a political activist who helped organize the Nairobi protests. "Moi does not want to reason," Kangethe said (*The Washington Post,* 8 July 1997, A8).

On 11 May 1995 over 80,000 Ghanaians, exercising their constitutional right, marched through the principal streets of Accra, the capital, to protest the high cost of living. Article 21, Section 1(e), of Ghana's 1992 constitution states: "All persons shall have the right to freedom of assembly including freedom to take part in processions and demonstrations."

"We are protesting because we are hungry," said Kojo Dan, an accountant. "We are not against the Government. We are civil servants." But the government unleashed its paramilitary organ—the Association for the Defense of the Revolution, ACDR—whose members fired on the peaceful demonstrators, killing 4 and seriously injuring about 20 (*The Ghanaian Chronicle,* 17 May 1995, 3).

Even in Africa's supposedly "primitive and backward" society peaceful demonstrations were and are still allowed. Consider this case from Ghana where Nana Kwesi Tandoh IV, the acting *"Omanhene"* (king) of the Elmina Traditional Council, refused to celebrate a traditional festival known as *Bakutue.*

Members of the Elmina Youth Association on June 27 demonstrated peacefully through the principal streets of the town protesting against the non-celebration of the *Bakutue* festival. The Association strongly urged the Kingmakers to remove the acting *"Omanhene"* and replace him with "a more responsible and respectable regent to forestall any possible action which might make Elmina ungovernable."

Acting on the resolution presented by the Association, Dr. J. A. Mark Aaba, Chief spokesman of the Kingmakers, catalogued the chieftaincy sins of the deposed *"Omanhene,"* summoned all the Kingmakers on July 11, and read out the charges submitted by the Youth Association against Nana Kwesi Tandoh and asked him to respond.

Not satisfied with his answer, the Kingmakers unanimously decided and deposed the acting *"Omanhene."* The Kingmakers replaced the deposed chief with Nana Kojo Nguandoh III, the Adontenhene of the Elmina Traditional Council (*Akasanoma,* 11-17 August 1995, 17).

The other charges preferred against the destooled acting *"Omanhene"* included disrespect to traditional elders of Elmina, arrogance, incompetence, indiscipline, unilateral appointment and firing of directors and workers of the Elmina Salt Industry in violation of laid down rules and regulations, dissipation of funds and apathy to issues affecting the Elmina township. Note how the Youth Association (freedom of association) demonstrated (freedom of assembly) and petitioned the kingmakers to remove the chief. Charges were filed against the Chief, who was given an opportunity to respond or defend himself. The demonstrators were *not* arrested.

Establishing Accountability

"Accountability" is the gospel donor governments and the World Bank have been preaching to Africa. Of course, African governments must be held accountable. This is not new to Africa: Traditional African chiefs have been held accountable all the time. But who should demand accountability from modern African governments and through what channels? In its infinite wisdom, the World Bank finally recognized the role journalists could play in exacting accountability.

At the World Conference on Women in Beijing in 1994, Ishrait Husain, director of the bank's Poverty and Social Policy Department, called a press briefing with 20 journalists drawn from African countries where adjustment was under way. The purpose was "to just chat and answer questions" on World Bank operations, activities, and policies in Africa. At the press briefing, Husain argued that "Once governments adopted its [World Bank's] recipes, the onus was on the people and journalists to monitor their fiscal policies, budgetary allocations, and how they fulfil their commitments. 'You have to hold your governments accountable. If you don't take care of your own problems, who will do it for you?' he queried" (*African Observer,* 28 September–11 October 1995, 21).

Such self-serving pontification is nauseating. The *African Observer* slammed Husain's remark as "a public relations stunt designed to make

African journalists responsible for monitoring adjustment policies in their countries [and thus] had all the trappings of abdication" (21). There is more, however. How could he expect African journalists, who could not monitor their government's fiscal policies nor hold them accountable before structural adjustment programs to suddenly begin to do so after adopting SAP? And if the World Bank recognizes the importance of journalists, what assistance has it or Western agencies provided the private media in Africa to do this job?

More telling was the case of Ghana, where corruption has been rampant, evidenced by the sordid revelations in the 1993 Auditor-General's Report and at the Emile Short Commission (1995). High government officials had amassed great personal fortune and acquired huge mansions, complete with double swimming pools. Not one single kleptocrat was brought to book. Crusading editors and private newspapers took the government to task. But the World Bank, U.S. AID and donor agencies, which have been preaching accountability, watched silently as editors of such crusading newspapers as *The Ghanaian Chronicle* and *Free Press* were hounded, persecuted, and hauled into court to face criminal libel charges for exposing corruption in high places. In all this, the donor governments and agencies did nothing to assist editors and journalists under siege. So, how are they expected to hold governments "accountable?"

Then in September 1996 came this bombshell: "Rawlings' bloodthirsty Youth and Sports Minister, E. T. Mensah, has been speaking of bloodshed in this country [Ghana] in the event of the PNDC losing this year's elections. 'Let mothers warn their offspring, wives their husbands, for, there'll be killings when you fail to vote for the NDC into power,' he said. E. T. Mensah was speaking at an unprecedented all-night PNDC rally at Labadi" (Free Press, 6-12 September 1996, 1).

Of course, the donors saw no evil, heard no evil. In October 1996 U.S. AID held a two-day meeting with government officials at Akosombo. "Myron Golden, the Country Director of U.S. AID, expressed the hope that the relationship between Ghana and U.S. will grow to be a model for the rest of the developing world" (*African News Weekly*, 14-20 October 1996, 10).

It boggles the mind that the United States, a paragon of open and fair processes, would engage in a *closed* meeting at a secret location with a tyrannical regime that did not have the mandate to rule. *The Statesman* (June 18, 1995) warned:

We hope the international community, especially the Western diplomatic missions, are aware of the first steps to Kigali [Rwanda] that have been taken at Mankessim on 3 June 1995. They cannot, and must not, allow things to get out of hand before they fly in peacekeepers, water purification plants, tents and crisis management NGOs. It would then be too late. Rawlings is looking for an excuse to *strike,* and he is not short of blood-thirsty hounds to egg him on.

The Western missions must advise their governments and call Rawlings to order. After all, they built him up to what he is now and all his moves are dependent on the nod from the West. Rawlings is always taking a sidelong glance at the West and that is why the West cannot sit idly by while another African country slips into carnage and mayhem. (2)

CHAPTER 10

Epilogue and Conclusions

All symbols of military authority must be removed from our midst. Those arrogant photographs that desecrate public spaces, schools, hospitals, offices, even courts of justice. Street names, also, change them all. Remove them. Remove them by stealth, remove them openly, by cunning, remove them by bribery, remove them forcibly, remove them tactfully, use whatever method is appropriate, but remove them. I call on all who are resolved to play a role in our mutual liberation to participate in this exercise of psychological release, or mental cleansing and preparedness.
—Wole Soyinka (1996, 59).

One of the most urgent matters for Nigerians to address when they settle down to debate the National Question is the issue of collaboration by professionals and technocrats with corrupt and repressive regimes. We must devise effective sanctions against our lawyers and judges and doctors and university professors who debase their professions in their zealotry to serve as tyranny's errand-boys, thus contributing in large measure to the general decay of honesty and integrity in our national life.
—Chinua Achebe,
African News Weekly
(1 October 1993, 32).

It is imperative that the crusade against the corrupt but powerful few who turn state organs into their own little fiefdoms must be led by black professionals and intellectuals; in this very instance it must be blacks who must be seen to

campaign for clean and transparent conduct in public life.
—Jon Qwelane,
a black South African columnist for the
Johannesburg Star (24 May 1997, 10).

SUMMARY

Despite Africa's vast natural resources, its people remain in the deadly grip of poverty, squalor, and destitution while buffeted by environmental degradation and brutal tyranny. This book began as an inquiry into why Africa is disintegrating. Both external and internal causative factors were examined. Among the external factors are the legacies of colonialism, the lingering effects of the slave trade, Western imperialism, and a pernicious international economic system. The internal factors include bad leadership, corruption, economic mismanagement, political tyranny, senseless civil wars, military vandalism, exploitation and oppression of the peasant majority, denial of civil liberties, and capital flight, among others. While both external and internal factors have played some role, the preponderance of the internal factors was evident. In fact, a new generation of angry Africans subscribe to the internalist school of thought. They lay greater emphasis on the internal causes and therefore advocate internal (African) solutions.

The internal problems are highly interrelated. In particular, the political and economic systems in most African countries are fused. Consequently, what may appear to be a strictly "economic" problem may have political underpinnings. Corruption, for example, breeds inefficiency and waste and discourages foreign investment. But that problem cannot be eradicated effectively when the head of state himself is raiding the national treasury.

Agricultural production per capita has steadily fallen in the postcolonial period—an economic problem. However, price controls and misguided government policies alone are insufficient to explain the decline. In chapter 2 we emphasized that economic activity does not occur in a vacuum but in a development environment. We isolated some basic elements including security of persons, property rights, rule of law, and stability that must obtain in this environment. We argued that the development environment that prevails over much of Africa is inimical to productive effort. Elite bias against agriculture and Africa's interminable civil wars, for example, have done much to impede any agricultural revolution. But Africa's civil wars are really political conflicts. All the civil wars in Africa erupted as a result of a dispute over some aspect of the electoral process—or a struggle for power.

We asserted that virtually all the internal problems emanate from two deadly diseases: sultanism and statism. While acknowledging that the state or government has a role to play in the development process, the state, as it is conventionally understood, does not exist in Africa. Rather what exists in many African countries is a vampire state—a government hijacked by gangsters, con artists, and scrofulous bandits. This predatory African state has its own internal logic and ethics. Its driving motivation is self-perpetuation in power and self-aggrandizement. Poverty reduction and promotion of economic growth are the least among its priorities. It operates by extracting resources from the productive sections of the population (the peasant majority) and spends it in the urban areas and on the elites—a non-productive, parasitic class.

In country after country, the state has been captured or monopolized by one tiny group—an ethnic group, professional (soldiers), or a religious group—and the instruments of state power and government machinery have been used to advance the economic interests of the ruling group. All others are excluded. This politics of exclusion does not endure. It eventually leads to destructive competition, instability, civil strife, institutional break-down and ultimately to the implosion of the state.

In other words, the state vehicle that currently exists in many African countries cannot take Africans on the "development journey" into the twenty-first century. Fixing or junking the vehicle ought to be the first priority. For most African countries, discarding the state vehicle is beyond the realm of feasibility because of the cost and social disruption it would entail. Therefore, there is no other choice but to fix the vehicle. But where does one begin?

First, a good driver must have some operational understanding of how a vehicle operates or at least consult experts—"mechanics," or technicians. But most African despots have no idea about the condition of the state vehicle. Local experts (professors, editors, journalists, and writers) who point to problems are thrown in jail or tossed out of the vehicle. All advice is ignored. Obviously, the first place to start with reform is to establish intellectual freedom to permit the technicians to assess and discuss the condition of the vehicle.

Second, the incompetent and reckless driver must be let go. A new driver must be found who has some understanding of how the vehicle operates. This new driver can be chosen through elections (democratic reform). But note that merely changing the driver would not make much difference as far as the "development journey" is concerned. Without repairs, the vehicle can still land in a ditch with the new driver.

Before the vehicle is repaired, the next issue to consider is whether the vehicle should remain in the hands of the state or of the people. Privatization (economic reform) seeks to place the vehicle in the hands of the people or the private sector for the simple reason that it would be better taken care of. Evidence for this fact abounds in Africa. In West Africa some of the privately owned "mammy lorries," called *tro tros* in Ghana and *mutatus* in East Africa, that regularly ply the roads, have been in operation for the past 40 years. By contrast, brand-new buses ordered by African governments barely last six months. The ruling elites may raise pedantic, arcane, and ideological objections to privatization, but what workers and the people want is *reliable* transportation. To them, public transportation is unreliable whereas private transportation is reliable.

When the vehicle is finally in the hands of the private sector, then it can be fixed. Brakes must be checked and repaired. The electrical, cooling, transmission, and fuel systems must all be cleaned up (institutional reform). It may be argued that it is possible to have institutional reform without privatization. However, that is a daunting task, and the record on this is uninspiring. Few African leaders, both old and new, have proven themselves up to the task of cleaning up the rot in the state-owned corporations, banks, military, educational system, the judiciary, and others. Some government corporations, institutions, and operations must simply be sold off (privatized).

Regardless of how it is sliced, the state vehicle must be reformed (fixed). But the leadership loathes reform. Obsessed with remaining in the driver's seat, they manipulate, subvert the electoral process, and outmaneuver a fragmented opposition to stay in power. And Western donors compound the problem by handing over billions to them on their false promises of reform.

Various proposals on fixing the state vehicle were examined in chapter 9, ranging from abolishing the state to recolonization. However, we dismissed most of them as impractical. We concluded that reform must be internally generated; that is, it must come from within Africa itself. Only Africans can save Africa. An international conference entitled "Africa's Imperative Agenda," held in Nairobi in January 1995, emphasized this new philosophy. Conference participants expressed strong support for the following priority propositions:

- Africa's human and natural resources are more than sufficient to revive progress if a concerted, determined effort is launched within each society, and coordinated regionally.
- Such efforts will succeed only if Africans take full charge of them and formulate policies geared to meet national needs rather than win international approval.
- Participatory political structures and "good governance" are essential preconditions for effective policy making.
- Only Africa can reverse its decline.
- The criteria of success for economic policies must be the improved health and education of the population and increased employment and production. Therefore, the agricultural sector, which employs the vast majority of Africans, is central to economic revival.
- The role of political leadership and government action has been downplayed and private sector efforts stressed in international debate. (*Africa Recovery,* June 1995, 9)

But where would the impetus to reform come from? Certainly not from the leadership. The middle class could serve as a catalyst for reform, but it is too truncated. Besides, a large part of the middle class is made up of the same vampire elites that have monopolized the state. Civil society could play a key role, but it is too amorphous, not cohesive. Is there any hope for the twenty-first century? What does the future hold for Africa?

Professor Ali Mazrui predicted (in Kaplan, 1994) that France will withdraw from West Africa and become increasingly involved in the European affairs. Nigeria, a more natural hegemonic power, will fill France's West African sphere of influence. Nigeria's own boundaries then are likely to expand to incorporate the Republic of Niger, the Republic of Benin, and conceivably Cameroon. But Kaplan (1994) is less charitable: "The future could be more tumultuous, and bloodier, than Mazrui dares to say . . . even as Nigeria attempts to expand, it, too, is likely to split into several pieces." This is because prospects for a transition to civilian rule and democratization in Nigeria remain bleak (54).

A long entrenched military rule and the repressive apparatus of the state security service would be difficult to dismantle. The chasm between the northern Hausa-Fulani and the southern Yoruba and Ibo is growing wide. Religious cleavages between Muslim fundamentalism and evangelical Christian militancy have been on the ascendancy as well. Soyinka

(1996) is quite blunt: "In Sani Abacha's self-manifesting descry as the last Nigerian despot, we may be witnessing, alas, the end of Nigerian history" (16). Given that oil-rich Nigeria is a bellwether for the region— its population of roughly 100 million equals the populations of all the other West African states combined—a breakup of Nigeria could destabilize the entire region.

An even more disturbing political trend has appeared in West Africa region: the civilianization of military despots. In ten out of the 15 West African nations, former military dictators held fraudulent elections and returned themselves to power. This trend is particularly alarming in view of the recent experiences of Ethiopia, Liberia, Somalia, and Zaire. It has become almost like a rule of thumb: the removal of an entrenched military tyrant from power is always violent and unnecessarily destructive. And quite often, the tyrants take their countries down with them when they fall. The prognosis for the West African region does not look bright. Neither does that of the central African region.

The "Kabila effect" will send shock waves through the region, generating instability because the ruling vampire elites adamantly refuse to learn from the recent implosions on the continent. A few will be given the "Mobutu exit." But then again, the incoming "liberators," as Africans say, "would come and do the same thing." What about the Organization of African Unity, the continental organization? Can it do something to save the continent? Well, the less said about the OAU, the better.

The Useless OAU

The mandate of the Organization of African Unity (OAU) includes conflict resolution. But since its inception in 1964, the OAU has achieved the unenviable distinction of being the most useless organization on the African continent. It cannot even define "democracy." A den of unrepentant despots, the OAU is more noted for its glitzy annual jamborees, where rabid autocrats click champagne glasses to celebrate their longevity in office. They use the annual OAU summit to extort aid from the international community instead of taking the initiative to solve the continent's problems themselves.

The OAU was nowhere to be found when Somalia exploded in 1993 and during the 1994 Rwandan genocide against the Tutsis, the OAU was furiously doing the *watutsi* in Addis Ababa, Ethiopia. How did it respond when the United Nations requested African troops for peace-keeping duty in Rwanda? According to *The Washington Post* (8 May

1994), "No African nation offered troops. The Organization of African Unity (OAU) chief, Salim Salim, wrote [U.N. Secretary-General] Boutros-Ghali that the OAU does not want to take charge of raising a force, and he passed the burden back to the United Nations" (A5). But when it comes to finding troops to brutalize internal opposition members, African governments will find them with lightning alacrity.

In 1996 they congregated for an OAU summit in cash-strapped Cameroon. That summit carried a hefty price tag of $120 million that included the purchase of a fleet of brand new Mercedes Benzes to transport the visiting heads of state for three days. "Cameroon cannot afford to hold this summit at this time. Parents cannot send children to school. People are sick and cannot buy drugs," fumed Fru Ndi, leader of Cameroon's Social Democratic Front (*African Observer*, 7-15 July 1996, 3). University professors were still owed four months salary at the time.

When the war in eastern Zaire erupted in October 1996, the OAU was on vacation. Stung by criticism over its scurrilous inaction, it awoke from its stupor and roared into action. It convened two conferences in Nairobi of all places, under the watchful eye of President Daniel arap Moi, to discuss conflict resolution and power-sharing. Imagine. In power for 19 years and congenitally corrupt, Moi abhors sharing power and wages ethnic warfare against the Kikuyu and the Luo. After the failed Nairobi peace conferences, the OAU vowed to do better and summoned African leaders to another conference. This time in Lome, where another military despot and a clone of Mobutu, General Gnassingbe Eyadema, has been in power for 30 years! It was President Nelson Mandela of South Africa who stepped in to provide some saving grace to African leadership. He convened and presided over a series of meetings between Mobutu and Kabila. But Mandela alone cannot solve all of Africa's crises. So to whom then should Africans look up to?

The Remaining Font of Hope

Some African scholars place the onus on the people. Says Felix Oti, a Nigerian writer, "The military is not our problem, nor is ethnic distrust, neo-colonialism, or lack of seasoned leadership. They may have all contributed to magnify the core problem at one time or another, but the real problem is a lack of will among ordinary Nigerians to exert adequate revenge on any individual who betrays our trust and mandate of leadership. Until we recognize this fact and channel our energies toward eradicating complacency from our system, we will never escape our current mess" (*African News Weekly,* 14-29 October 1996, 22).

Ikenna Anokwute, a Nigerian journalist, echoed the same theme: "Careful observers of the Nigerian scene are asking why a country blessed and peopled with energetic and smart citizens must always be fooled by a few gangsters in uniform. Why have Nigerians cooperated in the murder of their nation?" (*African News Weekly,* 16-22 September 1996, 6).

Unfortunately, the African people are too traumatized to mount any effective challenge to brutal African dictators. Peasants, the majority of the population, are notoriously difficult to organize. Furthermore, the channels through which civil society can agitate for reform—protests, demonstrations, and strikes—have insidiously been blocked.

Africa's best hope lies with its intellectuals. They are a cohesive, educated group. It is this group that supplies the intellectual rationale to legitimize despotism and corruption. No military vandal will succeed in imposing his rule if judges do not swear in coup-makers; if the intellectuals do not serve under them; and if civil servants refuse to carry out their orders. If Africa is to be saved, the task rests on the shoulders of this elite group, especially the intellectuals—not the leaders. After all, the leaders emerge from this class; therefore, the primary target of any reform effort must be the elite class. It needs reeducation. But the tragedy here is that many of the intellectuals have sold out and the rest just talk, talk, and argue.

AFRICA'S INTELLECTUALS

The most painful and treacherous aspect of Africa's collapse was the willful and active collaboration by Africa's own intellectuals, many of whom were highly "educated" with Ph.Ds and who should have known better. Yet a multitude of them have been willing to sell off their principles and integrity and partake of the plunder and misrule, thereby prostituting themselves.

The Prostitutes

One such prostitute was Kokou Koffigoh, who joined President Gnassingbe Eyadema as Togo's Prime Minister in 1992. *New African* (January 1993) wrote that "the opposition thinks Koffigoh has sold out the gains of the Togo National Conference by not carrying out its decisions and by allowing President Eyadema to return to power" (19).

Another was Gwanda Chakuamba of Malawi, who was appointed the chairman of the "presidential council" by former Life-President Hastings Banda in 1993. As *The Economist* (20 November 1993) reported: "Chakuamba was an old Malawi Congress Party (MCP) and ex-minister, who was jailed in 1980 for sedition and released in July 1993. He then flirted briefly with the opposition United Democratic Front, but while Dr. Banda was in hospital suddenly emerged as secretary-general of ruling party and acting head of state" (47). Chakaumba's move was roundly denounced "as a betrayal to the opposition, who had tirelessly campaigned for his release following local and international pressure on the MCP government's poor human rights record. Reliable sources have reported that whilst he was in prison, Chakuamba was subjected to immersion in water and was chained hand-and-foot for months on end" (*African Business,* December 1993, 29). How could an educated man, whose basic human rights were viciously violated in detention, suddenly decide to join his oppressor?

When Captain Yahya Jammeh overthrew the democratically elected government of Sir Dawda Jawara on 24 July 1994, the only minister from the Jawara administration enticed to serve the military regime was the finance minister, Bakary Darbo, a very well respected economist— even in international circles. He was instrumental in getting the World Bank to resume aid to The Gambia. On 10 October 1994, he was fired by the military junta: He was no longer useful to them. Then on 15 November, he was accused of complicity in the 11 November abortive coup attempt. He fled to neighboring Senegal with his family.

Next to assume the finance ministry portfolio was Ousman Koro Ceesay. When he became no longer useful to the military junta, "they smashed his head with a baseball bat," said Captain Ebou Jallow, the number-two man in the ruling council who defected to the United States on 15 October (*The Washington Times,* 20 October 1995, A15).

Time and time again, despite repeated warnings, highly "educated" African intellectuals throw caution and common sense to the winds and jostle one another for the chance to hop into bed with military brutes. The allure of a luxury car, a diplomatic or ministerial post and a government mansion often proves too irresistible. So hordes of lecturers, professionals, lawyers, and doctors sell themselves off into prostitution and voluntary bondage to serve the dictates of military vagabonds with half their intelligence. And time and time again, after being raped, abused, and defiled, they are tossed out like rubbish—or worse. Yet more intellectual prostitutes stampede to take their places.

African countries that have imploded in recent years were all ruined by the military: Algeria, Burundi, Ethiopia, Liberia, Rwanda, Sierra Leone, Somalia, Sudan, Uganda, and Zaire, among others. In country after country in Africa, where military rule was entrenched, educational institutions (of the tertiary level—universities and colleges) have all decayed—starved of funds by the military. Although the official excuse is always lack of funds, the military predators always find the money to purchase shiny new pieces of bazookas for their thugs. The *real* reason: "It is not in the best interest of these military governments to educate their people," says Wale Deyemi, a doctoral student at the University of Lagos. "They do not want people to be able to challenge them" (*The Washington Post*, 6 October 1995, A30).

In Nigeria, the sciences have been hardest hit. Science teachers have been vanishing with such alarming frequency that Professor Peter Okebukola, the president of the National Science Teachers Association of Nigeria, lamented at the association's thirty-sixth annual conference at Maiduguri that "good science teachers are increasingly becoming an endangered species" (*African News Weekly*, 13 October 1995, 17).

In spite of all this evidence, some African intellectuals still vociferously *defend* military regimes while their own institutions—the very places where they taught or obtained their education—deteriorate right under their very noses. One would have thought that these professors and intellectuals would protect their own institutions, just as the soldiers jealously protect their barracks and keep them in top shape. But no! For small change, the intellectuals have been willing to help and supervise the destruction of their very own university system.

Another expendable intellectual prostitute was Abass Bundu of Sierra Leone—the former secretary-general of ECOWAS—though his fate was less horrible. When he was appointed by the 29-year-old illiterate Captain Valentine Strasser to be Sierra Leone's foreign minister in early 1995, he left home to grab the post in a cloud of dust. In August 1995 he was tossed into a garbage bin in a radio announcement. He claimed in a Voice of America radio interview that "he never applied to join the junta" (*African News Weekly*, 8 September 1995, 12).

"We just discovered that he's an opportunist and one cannot trust such people. So we kicked him out," said the spokesman of Strasser's National Provisional Ruling Council. "When we appointed Abass Bundu through a radio announcement, he didn't complain but when we fired him through another radio announcement, he wants to make noise" (*African Observer,* 8-21 August 1995, 5).

Another case was that of Sierra Leone's fearless human rights lawyer, Sulaiman Banja Tejan-Sie. He was a vociferous critic of the ruling NPRC over human rights abuses and was reported to have a personal dislike for the military. He was hailed on student campuses as a young radical barrister and was invited to student conventions, giving lectures on human rights and negative consequences of military rule. On several occasions he called for a national conference to prepare the way for civilian rule. Then suddenly in April 1995 he joined Sierra Leone's military-led government as secretary of state in the Department of Youth, Sport and Social Mobilization. His detractors never forgave him.

Then there was Paul Kamara of Sierra Leone—a fearless crusader for human rights and ardent advocate of democracy. He published and edited the widely respected *For Di People,* whose circulation exceeded 30,000 copies a week. In January 1996, he joined the military government of Brigadier-General Maada Bio—a decision that, by his own admission, "disappointed many people" (*New African,* May 1996, 14). On election night, 26 February, five men dressed in military fatigues with guns waited for him at his newspaper offices. When he left his office and got into his official four-wheel-drive car, the soldiers chased him and opened fire. "We've got the bastard at last," one of them shouted. But luckily, the "bastard" escaped death and was flown to London for treatment.

In Burkina Faso, Clement Oumarou Ouedraogo was not so lucky. He was the number-two man in the barbarous military dictatorship of Blaise Compaore. He later resigned and launched his own Burkina Labor Party. On 9 December 1992 he was killed "when unidentified attackers threw a grenade into his car as he was returning from a meeting of the opposition Coalition of Democratic Forces" (*West Africa,* 16-22 December 1991, 2116).

In neighboring Niger, when Lieutenant-Colonel Ibrahim Barre Mainassara seized power in the January 1996 coup, overthrowing the civilian regime of President Mahamane Ousmane, the first civilian to join the new military regime as prime minister was Boukary Adji, who was deputy governor at the Central Bank of West African States in Dakar (*The Washington Times,* 1 February 1996, A14). Do Africa's intellectuals learn?

In Nigeria Baba Gana Kingibe, a career diplomat, was the vice-presidential candidate of Moshood K. O. Abiola in the 12 June 1993 presidential elections. Abiola won the election fair and square, but the result was annulled by the military government of General Ibrahim Babangida. Baba Kingibe then accepted the post of foreign minister from that same military regime. Nor did he make a sound of protest or resign when his running mate, Abiola, was thrown into jail. Neither did Chief Tony Anenih, the chairman of the defunct Social Democratic Party, on whose ticket Abiola contested the 12 June election. In fact, Chief Anenih was part of a five-man delegation, sent by General Abacha to the United States in October 1995 to "educate and seek the support of Nigerians about the transition program." At a 22 October 1995 forum organized by the Schiller Institute in Washington, "Chief Anenih and Colonel (retired) Emeka O. Ojukwu took turns ripping apart the reputation of Abiola. . . . Anenih took pains to discredit Chief Abiola, whom he said was being presented by the Western media as the victimized President-elect. . . . Some of the Nigerians in the audience denounced the delegation as 'paid stooges' of Abacha" (*African News Weekly*, 3 November 1995, 3).

More pathetic was the case of Alex Ibru, the publisher of *The Guardian Group* of newspapers in Lagos who became the internal affairs minister. On 14 August 1994, his own newspaper was raided and shut down by the same military government under which he was serving. He did not protest or resign. After six months as interior minister, he too was tossed aside. In October 1995, his two newspapers, shut down by the military government for more than a year, were allowed to reopen after Ibru apologized to the authorities for any offensive reports they may have carried. Then on 2 February 1996, unidentified gunmen in a deep-blue Peugeot 504 trailed him and sprayed his car with machine-gun fire. The editor-in-chief, Femi Kusa, said that the car was bullet-ridden and Ibru was injured. He too was flown to Britain for treatment.

After the annulment of Nigeria's 12 June elections, General Babangida was eased aside by the military top brass. Ernest Shonekan became the 89-day interim civilian president until he too was removed by the current military despot, General Sani Abacha. On 19 September Shonekan accompanied Nigeria's foreign minister, Tom Ikimi, to London to deliver a "confidential message" to British Prime Minister John Major. Nigeria's military junta told Westminster that it would pardon the 40 convicted coup plotters if Britain would help with the rescheduling of Nigeria's $35 billion debt and support its transition program to democratic rule, its bid for a permanent seat on the U.N. Security Council, and its attempt to gain U.S. recognition of its effort to fight drug trafficking.

First of all, how could Ernest Shonekan act as an emissary for the same barbarous military regime that overthrew him? Not only that, he accepted an appointment from Abacha to a committee of experts to plan for "Vision 2010."[1] Second, who thought that 35 years after "independence" from British colonial rule, Nigeria's government would be holding its own citizens as hostages, demanding ransom from the former colonial power? It did not occur to any of the "educated" emissaries that their mission sank the concept of "independence from colonial rule" to new depths of depravity. Mercifully, the British refused to capitulate to these terrorist demands.

Dr. Tom Ikimi was the activist, who, in 1989, formed the Liberal Convention party to campaign for democracy in Nigeria. In June 1989 he launched a branch in the United Kingdom, where he made glorious speeches about participatory democracy and denouncing military regimes. In 1994 he became Nigeria's foreign minister under the military dictatorship of General Sani Abacha. He even appeared on *The MacNeil/ Lehrer NewsHour* on 3 August 1995 and strenuously defended the Nigerian military government's record on democratization, calling General Abacha "humane."

Vile opportunism, unflappable sycophancy, and trenchant collaboration of intellectuals allowed tyranny to become entrenched in Africa. Doe, Mengistu, Mobutu, and other military dictators legitimized and perpetuated their rule by buying off and co-opting Africa's academics for a pittance. And when the intellectuals fall out of favor, they are beaten up, tossed aside or worse. And yet more offer themselves up.

Punishing the Prostitutes

One poignant lesson that can be drawn from Africa's disastrous post-colonial record is the fact that sycophancy and collaboration seldom pay. Sycophants often delude themselves into thinking that, should their country blow, they would always escape to the West to enjoy their booty. But angry Africans have vowed to punish the traitors and intellectual collaborators. During the 11 May 1995 *"Kume Preko"* demonstrations

---

1. According to *African News Weekly* (7-13 October 1996), "Vision 2010 will focus on Nigeria's growth into the next century. Details of the plan are to be set out by a non-political committee which will sit for between 9 and 12 months, targeting gross domestic product, inflation, agriculture, industrialization, literacy, health and employment" (2).

in Ghana, the tires of some deputy ministers were deflated. "Escape now," the angry mob seemed to be saying. Kabena Kofi of Tema warned: "I would like to remind Messrs E.T. Mensah, Prof Awoonor, Obed Asamoah, Harry Sawyer and others, that if the unexpected happens as a result of their sycophancy, they and their families would be the first to bear the anger of Ghanaians" (*Free Press,* 10-16 April 1996, 2). In Nigeria, Zaire, and several African countries, the houses and cars of intellectual collaborators were burned down.

In Senegal, after President Diouf's ruling Socialist Party "won" a huge majority in parliamentary elections in February 1993, violence broke out amid charges of vote rigging. Babacar Seye, the vice president of Senegal's Constitutional Council, was killed. *African News Weekly* (4 June 1993) reported that: "Seye was found dead in his car, apparently the victim of an ambush. . . . According to the independent, *Sud Quotidien,* a group calling itself the 'People's Army' claimed responsibility for Seye's murder, the first political assassination in Senegal's history. . . . This is a warning for the other judges in the Constitutional Council, so they really respect the people's will, it quoted the anonymous caller as saying" (13). Seye's killer was never found.

In Sierra Leone, cashiered army Corporal Foday Sankoh, leader of the Revolutionary United Front, warned James Jonah, chairman of the Interim National Electoral Commission, in a two-way radio broadcast to leave the country. "'This is my country and I'm not going to quit,' said Jonah, who also claimed to have received several death threats from anonymous callers" (*African Observer,* 8-21 August 1995, 5). James Jonah was also chief adviser to head of state, Captain Valentine Strasser.

Elsewhere in Africa, civic groups and the private press are playing a key role in bringing these scoundrels to book. In August 1994 the Campaign for Democracy, an alliance of 52 human rights and political groups, urged the European Union to repatriate the men who annulled Nigeria's 1993 presidential election. Former military president Ibrahim Babangida and his deputy, Augustus Aikhomu, were both believed to be in Europe. "The popular opinion in Nigeria is that these elements must be tried for the untold hardship inflicted on the nation," the group said in a letter to the European Union. "We therefore, with a high sense of responsibility, request their expulsion from Europe where they are currently domiciled" (*African News Weekly,* 26 August 1994, 29).

"Over 80 percent of Rwanda's 700 judges and magistrates, many of them guilty themselves of the genocide, died or fled in the 1994 fighting" (*The Economist,* 23 March 1996, 37). Colonel Theoneste Bagosora of the late Juvenal Habyarimana's presidential guard, Marc Rugenera, former minister of finance, and many others fled into exile. The information minister, Eliezer Niyitegeka, who incited Hutus to kill Tutsis, fled to a refugee camp in Goma, Zaire. According to *The Washington Post* (19 February 1995), "Eliezer said in an interview in Zaire that he was so depressed that he was asking France for political asylum" (A46). Now *he* was depressed? At another squalid camp in Bukavu, Zaire, the former president, prime minister and cabinet ministers were holed up. Some settled in Cameroon, which refused political asylum to several Rwandan Hutu officials accused of having played a significant role in the genocide there in 1994. One of them was Ferdinand Nahimana, former director of the state information office and a founder of *Radio Mille Collines,* the Kigali radio station whose inflammatory broadcasts egged on Hutu soldiers and ethnic militia to kill Tutsis.[2] On 1 April 1996, Cameroon went further, rounding up eleven of the masterminds of the 1994 Rwanda genocide and throwing them into jail.

Outside Africa, various groups of African exiles also have vowed to work tirelessly to bring the collaborators to justice and block the granting of political asylum to these "useless idiots." After the Momoh regime was overthrown by Captain Strasser, the vice president, Dr. Abudulai Conteh, fled to Britain. Did he really escape? According to *West Africa* (31 August–6 September 1992): "Dr. Abudulai Conteh has been deported from Britain, following a failed attempt by his lawyers to convince the UK authorities that Conteh was a genuine refugee. The British High Court Judge, Mr. Simon Brown, agreed with the Home Office that Conteh should bear some responsibility for the corruption of the Momoh government which played a major role in bankrupting Sierra Leone" (1496).

U.S. courts now allow foreign victims of atrocities to sue the perpetrators. Ethiopian exiles in the United States have been taking Mengistu's henchmen—who fled to the United States—to court to

---

2. The others were Justin Mugenzi, president of the Liberal Party and former trade and industry ministry, Joseph Nzirorera, former interim president of the National Assembly and head of late president Juvenal Habyarimana's National Republican Movement for Democracy and Development party, and Pasteur Musabe, former director of Rwanda's National Bank. The decision to refuse them political asylum followed an intensive campaign by Cameroon's private press (*African News Weekly,* 5 May 1995, 3).

claim damages. In New York, Bawol Cabiri, a former Ghanaian diplomat, sued Baffour Assasie-Gyimah. As the *African Observer* (25 April–8 May 1996) wrote: "In a stunning decision, a U.S. judge has ruled that President Rawlings should surrender one of his henchmen to face trial in New York for atrocities he committed against humanity. U.S. Judge Allen G. Schwartz ruled April 18, 1996 that there is overwhelming evidence that Baffour Assasie-Gyimah, who is described in court papers as Deputy Chief of National Security, has committed outrageous human rights abuses and therefore should be brought to the U.S. immediately and tried under the Torture Victim Protection Act and Alien Tort Claim Act" (3).

Then there was Elsaphane Ntakirutimana, a Rwandan Hutu priest, who in April 1994 fled to take refuge in Mugonero Hospital and then participated in a daylong attack on 16 April in which hundreds of men, women, and children were killed. After Rwanda blew up, he fled to the United States. But Rwandan exiles in the United States were waiting for him. They fingered him to the FBI and on 27 September 1996 he was arrested in San Antonio, Texas, near the U.S.- Mexico border, which he was trying to cross.

The Crabs

African intellectuals abroad constitute the only group that can do much to bring the dictators to account and initiate efforts to bring reform to their home countries, just the Poles and the Jews helped their respective countries. For example, African intellectuals living in the United States have access to information, and the media (newspapers, radio, and television) and the freedom to expose corruption, tyranny, and economic mismanagement in Africa. But for the entire decade of the 1980s and much of the 1990s, one would be hard-pressed to name just 20 African intellectual activists who campaigned on the world stage for democratic and economic freedom in their respective countries. There are four reasons for this.

First, some have completely written off Africa. Ensconced in high-paying, benefits-rich jobs at the United Nations, the World Bank, and other international organizations, they wish Africa would go away. Not much can be expected from this "lost tribe" of African scholars, who pay more attention to their suits than events on the African continent.

Second, some African exiles fear that reprisals may be taken against their families at home, should they become outspoken critics of their country's regimes. While this risk is real, it can be removed through "adoption." Nigerian and Sudanese professors may adopt each other's country. The Nigerian would write about Sudan and the Sudanese about Nigeria. Since the Nigerian professor has no family in Sudan, there is little by way of reprisals that the el-Bashir regime in Sudan can take. Similarly, a Ghanaian may adopt Uganda and vice versa. Citizens of countries whose governments are pursuing the same repressive policies may adopt one another and write about them.

Third, some African intellectuals, especially the radical and leftist ones, are afflicted with intellectual astigmatism. They see only wrongdoing by whites (slave trade, colonial exploitation, and imperialist oppression). In their mind, black African leaders can do no wrong. Should a crisis occur, they offer all sorts of convoluted alibis for African leaders and look for a "racist conspiracy," even where none exists. Such African scholars are "intellectual failures," pure and simple.

Fourth, others engage in what may be called "negative competition." They are highly suspicious and jealous of other African scholars. They would rip apart the literary works of others, even though they have none to their credit. They may do so out of envy or the need to eliminate potential competitors. They may secretly desire a ministerial position at home, but since the number of these posts are limited, they believe they improve their chances by cutting down their rivals. Any African intellectual who shows some promise or wins some acclaim immediately becomes their target of ridicule and invective. As one wag quipped cynically: "We all have Ph.Ds—pull him down." In this way, they behave like "crabs in a barrel." As soon as one crab tries to get up and out, the rest pull him down. There is no sense of solidarity among them. They cannot cooperate because they do not trust one another. This explains why many African organizations or endeavors fail. Start an African organization and nobody wants to attend meetings or pay his dues. But say that a "president" will be chosen and 50 cockroaches will show up. When one is chosen, the rest will spend their time not helping the organization but undermining the president to prove they would have made a better one. Inevitably, the organization collapses from internal squabbles, backbiting, and personality feuds. African despots could not have hoped for a better situation.

Says a despondent Linus U. J. Thomas-Ogboji, a Nigerian scholar:

> It wounds the heart to contemplate the extent of damage done to the psyche and self-image of Nigerians by an endless succession of uniformed but uninformed thugs. In three decades of rapacious pillage, these semi-

illiterates have trashed the dignity of negritude more outrageously than three centuries of slavery ever did. Not long ago, George Ayittey was assailed by some Nigerian don Quixote for asking: In heaven's name, where are the Nigerian intellectuals? And CBS was vilified by Nigerian intellectuals for its exposé of the antics of a few vermin in Lagos. Now Randall Robinson and TransAfrica are giving voice to the growing perplexity among African-Americans: When will Nigerians get their act together? (*African News Weekly*, 26 May 1995, 6).

The level of trust among Africa's intellectuals has been so shamefully low that few Nigerian intellectuals can work together. They criticize military rule one day and join the Abacha regime the next. Even Nobel laureate Wole Soyinka knows that "several of his officers in his National Liberation Council of Nigeria would desert [the pro-democracy crusade] tomorrow for a lucrative government post," says *The Economist* (30 September 1995, 47)

Pro-Democracy Nigerian Groups in the U.S.

There are least 35 pro-democracy Nigerian organizations in the United States, but there is little coordination among them. Many of them are "419" (fake) organizations, sponsored and funded by Nigeria's military junta to counteract the "negative publicity" engendered by the activities of TransAfrica. According to Randall Echols, Chief Abiola's spokesman in the United States, Nigeria's military government spent $10 million in 1995 in a desperate public-relations effort to spruce up its battered international image. Paid ads were placed in major U.S. newspapers, denouncing the call for sanctions, and various Nigerian organizations staged pro-government demonstrations in the United States.

One such organization, the Coalition for Peaceful Democracy, led by Ben Igwe, marched on 22 September 1995 in front of the White House. Another organization, the Nigerian National Leadership Forum, held a conference on 12 August in Nashville with the lofty aim of tackling "Nigeria's problem." The coordinator of the conference was Professor David Muruako, president of the Organization of Nigerian Professionals (ONP), which was one of the Nigerian organizations that condemned TransAfrica's crusade in a paid advertisement in *The Washington Times*.

Now get this: There are two such organizations with exactly the same name (ONP) in exactly the same city (New Orleans). The other is headed by Professor Gibson Chigbu. The two were embroiled in an eight-year court battle to determine which should keep the name ONP. Imagine. While the vicious military regime in their home country was brutalizing the people, looting the treasury, and sipping champagne, these two organizations of highly educated Nigerian professionals were expending their energies and resources locked in combat over a name! O, the moon shines so brightly. . . .

On 11 November 1994, Professor David Muruako announced with much pompous fanfare in *African News Weekly* (11 November 1994, 2), the eleventh annual convention of the ONP from 11 to 13 November 1994. The convention theme was: "Nigeria in Crisis: ONP Finds a Solution." The eight-point solution suggested that, for the sake of peace and democratic transition in Nigeria:

General Abacha should stay to run the government as head of state.

Chief Abiola should be released from jail.

Striking workers should return to work.

The United States should lift its sanctions on Nigeria.

Gen. Abacha should form an implementation committee of three to include Chief Abiola.

Nigeria should ask/allow a superpower, the United States to sponsor the democratic transition.

General Abacha should give a date within one year to hand over power to civilians.

The committee of three should oversee the transfer of power and the establishment of (a) a constitutional conference; (b) political parties; and (c) to carry out the next series of elections.

Nine months later at Nashville, on 12 August the same Professor David Muruako insisted that Nigeria's greatest problem is tribalism. What happened to the ONP Solution?

In attendance at the Nashville conference were Nigeria's ambassador, Alhaji Zubair Kazaure, and other officials from the Nigerian Embassy. Ah, that explained a lot. In his keynote address, Ambassador

Kazaure asked the audience not to blame the problem of ethnicity on the present government but to blame the British colonialists. Naturally. "It is not fair to blame this present government or any Nigerian government for the problems of ethnicity in Nigeria," he added. In a sense, the ambassador was right but he should have blamed Nigeria's intellectuals and professionals, both at home and abroad, who have bastardized the campaign for change.

There was Dr. Edward C. Oparaoji, a professor at Howard University in Washington, D.C., and the chairman of the Nigerian Democracy Awareness Committee (NDAC). His organization was avowedly "prodemocracy" and vehemently opposed to the military regime of Genera Sani Abacha. It often held protests against Alhaji Kazaure in front of the Nigerian Embassy in Washington. The ambassador was recalled following international outrage over the brutal hanging of Ken Saro-Wiwa in November 1995. Alhaji Hassan Adamu was chosen as the replacement.

NDAC opposed the nomination, saying it was "illegal, fraudulent and must not be honored by the Clinton Administration" (*African News Weekly,* 22-28 April 1996, 3). The executive director of NDAC's research and development committee, Dr. Wole Alade, called the nomination "a big joke and an embarrassment to all Nigerians." But unbeknownst to NDAC members, their own president, Dr. Oparaoji, had quietly submitted his own name for consideration as the ambassador. So outraged were some members of NDAC that they formed a caretaker committee to replace the old leadership. "It ridicules our position. Who did he [Dr. Oparaoji] think he was going to report to, Abacha?" asked Philip Njowusi, a member of the caretaker committee (*The Washington Times,* 10 May 1996, A19).

African intellectuals abroad must clean up their act if they are to supply the necessary impetus to reform Africa. Toward this end, the following list of "commandments" or mandate for leadership into the twenty-first century is suggested.

INTELLECTUAL MANDATE FOR THE 21ST CENTURY

As we saw in chapter 5, many of Africa's institutions do not work because they have been perverted. Africans know of the rot in their professional organizations because some sycophantic members act unprofessionally and succumb easily to bribery and corruption. But instead of collectively expelling such scoundrels from their midst, they keep quiet, which helps nobody because the bad apples bring shame and disrepute to the entire profession. The professions in Africa whose images have been badly tarnished are the military, the civil service, and the university lecturers.

Reward and punishment is an ancient human behavior modification rule. Children or workers who are honest, diligent, and faithful are rewarded, while those who are lazy, unprincipled, and unreliable are punished. The rot in these professions has festered due to the simple fact that the sell-outs, disreputables, and scoundrels are never punished. Instead, they are welcomed back into the fold to continue the damage. This should change now. **NOW.**

Those intellectuals and professionals who knowingly and willingly participate in the rape, plunder and oppression of the people of Africa should be punished. *Ostracism* is the preferred punishment method. Those intellectuals who, with all their "education," cannot uphold high principles of probity, integrity, morality, and public duty should be expelled from professional associations—just as soldiers who flout strict military discipline can be discharged or court-marshaled.

One person alone cannot reform or fix all the systems. He may be proficient in the workings of one system but may lack the operational knowledge of other systems. In fact, the person who insists that only he can contribute to an African nation's progress by becoming the next president is least qualified for the job. Hundreds of people have contributed to the advancement of world civilization without being the presidents of their respective countries. An African intellectual who wants to make a contribution should work with others to reform an institution, a system, or a profession.

For each institution, system, or profession to work efficiently, it must have its own rules and regulations, which those who work in that system or institution must obey at all times. These rules are called a code of conduct: for example, the civil service code, the military code, the academic code, student code, and so on. In any school system, cheating is not tolerated, and any student caught cheating during exams could be expelled. Similarly in academia, plagiarism is not tolerated. A professor caught plagiarizing the work of other could be dismissed. Enforce these codes.

The purpose of the code is to establish professionalism or professional conduct. Any organization or institution that deals with the public at large must have a code that is nonpartisan (apolitical) and non-discriminatory. For example, a teacher passes a student, not because he is from his tribe but on the basis of merit. Similarly, a civil servant should report to work on time and process applications without bias or favor. If you work at the state broadcasting corporation, or state-owned newspaper, you give equal coverage to the opposition views too because you are a civil servant; as such, you must treat all Ghanaian citizens the same, whether they are in the government or in the opposition. Opposition people pay taxes too, damn it.

Disciplinary action must be taken against violations of the code for all to see. For example, in the teaching profession it is unethical and unacceptable for a teacher to have sexual relations with a student. The function of a teacher/lecturer is to impart knowledge and bring light where there is darkness, not to prey on students or add more darkness. An infraction of this code should result in the teacher's expulsion.

Therefore, the military, the civil service, the judiciary, the banking system, and the educational system must all be cleaned up. Here is what Major (retired) M. K. Sawyer wrote in *Free Press* (8-14 September 1995): "Real commandos do not go about beating, shooting and molesting their countrymen. They operate within the Armed Forces and not outside it. As part of the Armed Forces, they help protect their country against external aggression and not operate as the private army of their Head of state. What we have here is an institution whose inmates are trained as fake terrorists and are used as such by the powers that be against their own brothers and sisters." (2) Such commando or terrorist units must be disbanded by the military itself.

The other professions also must do the same. Any member of these professions who does not uphold professional integrity and ethics should be decertified or expelled. For example, a lawyer or judge who blatantly flouts the canons of law should be disbarred and expelled from the bar association. Similarly, any soldier who breaches the military code of discipline should be court-marshaled and discharged with dishonor.

The police department, civil service, media, and bar association must reform themselves and uphold professionalism. Civil servants should remain apolitical, showing no favors to any one political party. They are there to serve the people, who may belong to different parties. Civil servants who show favoritism to one party should be disciplined just as harshly as those openly support another.

Elsewhere, demand to see the code or constitution of your organization or profession and have it enforced. A University Teachers Association should define a Faculty Code of Ethics. Where none exists, demand to have one drawn up. Such codes should eschew tribalism and emphasize professionalism and merit. People in the army should be promoted not because they are Ashanti, Ewe, Kalenjin, or Hausa but solely because they have earned their promotion by merit and professional standards.

The house of chiefs also needs to be cleaned up. Chiefs should never involve themselves in national politics and desecrate that sacred institution of chieftaincy. A chief should realize that his subjects may belong to different political parties. Therefore, he should remain politically neutral. He should not be seen campaigning for any political party. Chiefs who violate this code should be destooled immediately.

In fact, the constitution of Ghana's Fourth Republic, for example, precluded them from the rough and tumble of partisan politics, so that chiefs, as fathers of their people, could maintain their honor, dignity, reverence, and the sanctity of the institution. As impartial players, chiefs are enjoined to treat all their people equally as their flock, no matter their political inclinations. While some chiefs strove to live by these tenets, many chiefs in Brong Ahafo turned themselves brazenly into party fanatics during the 1996 election campaign. Such sycophantic chiefs should be destooled at once.

Those in the opposition who preach democracy must practice it in their own organizations. Any politician who acts autocratically, as if the party belongs to him—and him alone—should be expelled at once! Nobody—absolutely nobody—has the God-ordained right to be the leader of a political party. The leader, or the presidential candidate, of a political party is chosen democratically—by the rank and file. Anyone who seeks to impose himself on the party should be thrown out immediately.

All professions, political parties, associations and groups must enjoin their members to uphold constitutional and democratic rule. Therefore, no member of any such group will serve an unconstitutional and illegal military regime. It should not be left to the individual to decide but debarred by collective action. Those who violate this injunction, such as judges who swear in coup leaders, should be decertified and expelled from the Bar Association. Similarly professors, civil servants, and medical doctors.

THE TEN COMMANDMENTS FOR AFRICAN INTELLECTUALS

1. *Never Forget Your Roots*
   Africa's traditions, institutions, and customs are integral part of your heritage. This heritage includes participatory democracy based on consensus, free village markets, free enterprise and free trade. You cannot reject this heritage and remain African.

2. *Seek Ye First the Economic Kingdom in the Private Sector*
    There is nothing wrong in wanting to be rich, but nobody
    became rich working for a wage/salary, unless he was prepared
    to steal or embezzle, like the African kleptocrats. But that does
    not pay in the long run. Earn your wealth in the private sector
    by actually producing something, even charcoal. If capital is a
    problem, do as the illiterates do by pooling savings as in the
    revolving credit schemes.

    The executive editor of *The Ghanaian Chronicle* called on
    graduating students of the Manifold Tutorial College in
    Kumasi "to be wary of the group of educated people who are
    sometimes referred to as 'intellectual collaborators.'" He said
    "these people give succor and cover to illiterate and semi-
    illiterate despots who adorn the continent of Africa. . . .
    education in itself does not confer respectability on an indi-
    vidual, it is rather the personal effort of the individual that
    counts. . . . since nobody [can] make money working forever
    for someone else, the graduates should develop an entrepre-
    neurial spirit and strike out on their own so that they can
    provide jobs for others" (*The Ghanaian Chronicle*, 2-4 Sep-
    tember 1996, 7).

3. *Privatize the Universities*
    Africa's universities should be privatized. They may be given
    a fixed annual government subvention and then allowed to
    raise their own revenue and manage their own affairs. This
    way, they can uphold academic freedom, which is currently
    not possible with the head of state, often a military imbecile,
    as the chancellor.

4. *Demand and Defend Freedom of Expression/Media*
    Recall that the first critical step in problem resolution is the
    exposure of the problem. Without freedom of expression this
    is nearly impossible. At a 6 November 1996 symposium,
    organized by the Pan African Writers Association in Accra, the
    president of the Senegal Writers Association, Mr. Alione
    Badara Beye, said that "African governments are responsible
    for the underdevelopment of African literature. Among the
    four main problems inhibiting the development of African
    literature is the expulsion of prominent African writers . . . the
    absence of African writers in international debates, absence of

integrative policies and lack of publishing infrastructure" (*The Ghanaian Chronicle,* 11-12 November 1996, 7). All African intellectuals must demand the right to free speech and defend the rights of others for the freedom to speak, publish and write. If you don't defend the right of others, who will defend you when your rights are taken away? Kweisi Mfume, President of NAACP said: "Free speech in a democratic society must be fought for whether we like what we hear or not, because one day someone will come to silence us, and then who will speak for us?" (The Washington Post, 16 January 1997, D2).

5. *Practice Intellectual Solidarity*
Respect and assist members of your own profession, regardless of differences of opinion. If one is under siege, all wherever they may be—in or out of government, in or out of the country—must go his or her aid. You may need group assistance yourself in the future. Extend this solidarity to other groups fighting the same cause. For example, when a coalition of civic groups, church leaders, students, and politicians marched through Nairobi on 7 June 1997 to demand constitutional reforms, police fired on and clubbed eleven people to death. But they kept up the pressure. The result? "The ruling Kenya African National Union party proposed the repeal or amendment of 11 controversial laws that an opposition-backed alliance demands should be repealed. 'They [the opposition] asked for constitutional reforms. We have not only agreed to these, but have also proposed that comprehensive reforms be examined,' said NEC member Nicholas Biwott, a government minister of state" (*The Washington Times,* 18 July 1997, A15). By contrast, when Nigeria's oil-workers went on strike in 1993 to protest the annulment of the presidential election results, no other group or profession joined them. Had the civil servants, professors, students, and even taxi-drivers joined them, the "Butcher of Abuja" would have long been history.

6. *Demand National Conferences*
When a national crisis erupts, demand that a national dialogue or conference be set up to resolve it, as is done in African villages. The national conference must be sovereign and its decisions binding on all parties, including the government.

No African intellectual should accept a national conference that is packed by government appointees, such as General Abacha's 1995 Constitutional Conference in Nigeria. Nor should any transition to democratic rule process be accepted that is manipulated and controlled by the government in power.

7. *Disband the Military or Cut It in Half*
   No African intellectual with an iota of intelligence and a modicum of Pan-Africanist spirit would support, much less serve, a barbarous military regime. Ever! All those African countries that imploded were ruined by the military.

8. *Practice Pan-Africanism*
   Pan-Africanism, originating from the belief that African countries share common problems, common solutions, and common destinies will remain a dream unless you learn more about African countries other than your own.

9. *Set Up a Rival OAU*
   The time has come for the useless OAU to be disbanded or for a rival body, the Organization of Free African States, to be set up. It should be made up of strictly democratic countries. OFAS can be set up under the aegis of President Nelson Mandela of South Africa.

10. *Selectively Repudiate Foreign Debt*
    Insist that foreign aid be given only to democratic African countries. Time and again, foreign loans are taken by corrupt, illegitimate and repressive African regimes without the approval of the people. And time and again, after the loans have been squandered, it is the brutalized and traumatized citizens who are asked to pay them back. This scandalous outrage must end. At the global marketplace, one is free to spend and invest one's money as one pleases. If one invests in a company that subsequently fails, one must be prepared to accept the loss. In the same vein, Western governments and donor agencies are free to spend and throw away their money in Africa as they wish. They may hand as much money as they wish to autocratic, brutally repressive African regimes. But they must be prepared to take the risks that come along with such a policy. They should not ask the African people to pay

for its folly. Loans contracted without the approval of the African people are not repayable.

The obvious wisdom in these injunctions was imported into Ghana's 1992 Constitution, which includes a clause stating that "the Government of Ghana cannot contract a foreign loan without the approval of parliament. Thus, parliamentary approval—if parliament is truly representative of the people—legitimizes the transaction or loan. But then the PNDC, like a typical African regime, tried to undermine that very constitutional check. In April 1996 the PNDC sought an exemption for "small foreign loans." Since the ruling PNDC held the overwhelming majority in parliament (the opposition boycotted the 1992 parliamentary elections), it rushed through parliament a huge number of such "small loans."

In this way Ghana's foreign debt mushroomed from $1 billion in 1981 to $5.4 billion in 1996. The World Bank bragged that it had provided Ghana with more than $2 billion in loans and credits. But when did the people of Ghana ask the World Bank or any foreign entity for a loan?

The maddening part of this blatant outrage is that the regime that preaches "accountability" and contracted huge loans on behalf of the people without their consent adamantly refuses to account for the loans. In fact, it indemnified itself by the inserting clauses 33, 34, and 36 into the constitution. Obviously, the people of Ghana should also indemnify themselves against illegitimate loans taken without their approval.

Even more outrageous was the case of Zaire (now Congo). When Mobutu Sese Seko fled Zaire in May 1997, he left behind a $9.6 billion national debt. Among those who trudged to Goma—the then temporary rebel capital—in April 1997 to see rebel leader Laurent Kabila were World Bank officials. They had gone to discuss with him repayment of Zaire's debt to the World Bank. Kabila should have told bank officials to take a hike. The money was loaned to Zaire, not the Democratic Republic of the Congo. Zaire is no more.

The people of Congo now have to start from scratch—32 years of their sovereign existence gone down the drain. Now they must be saddled with a debt from which they derived no benefit.

The looting of the country's resources by Mobutu was known around the world. Yet foreign creditors continued to loan him money, violating a cardinal free market principle: If you borrow from a loan shark, expect to be taken. Conversely, if you lend to a crook, expect to be taken.

While Zairians—among the poorest in the world—were struggling to meet their basic needs, Mobutu, who himself bragged to be among the richest—built mansions and hotels in France, Spain, South Africa, Morocco, Senegal, Togo, and Ivory Coast and stashed billions of dollars in the Swiss bank. During his 32 years in power, he ran Zaire like his personal fiefdom, without any regard whatsoever for the 45 million citizens of the country.

Switzerland announced that it would block any sale of a luxury villa owned by Mobutu near Lausanne and help recover some of Mobutu's loot. But how much of the Nazi stolen gold did the Swiss find? "Swiss banks are world champions in building empires for crooks and then protecting them behind smoke screens," said Jean Ziegler, a socialist member of parliament and longtime critic of Swiss banking secrecy (*The Washington Post*, 26 May 1997, A21).

Zaire's $9.6 billion national debt should be treated as Mobutu's personal debt. Foreign creditors should hold Mobutu personally liable and go after his assets. The Congolese did not benefit from those foreign loans. Neither did they give Mobutu any authorization to contract any foreign loan on their behalf.

What is being applied here is an international legal instrument known as the "doctrine of odious debts." Odious Debts is about a tax revolt. "The Third World's debts were accumulated without public knowledge and consent, with most people benefiting not one whit. Having paid once with their environment as the loans financed destructive development projects—among them hydro dams flooding rainforests and irrigation schemes destroying farmland—the Third World populace finds odious the proposition that it pays one more" (Adams, 1991, inside flap).

The doctrine was applied in 1923 when the Royal Bank of Canada sought to recover debt from a new government in Costa Rica. The new Costa Rican government successfully argued that the debt had been incurred by the former dictator, and not by the country's people. "If a despotic power incurs a debt not for the needs or interest of the state, but to strengthen its despotic regime, to repress the population that fights against it . . . this debt is odious to the population of the state," said the doctrine. "The creditors have committed a hostile act with regard to the people, they can't therefore expect that a nation freed from a despotic power assume the odious debts, which are the personal debts of that power," it added. (Adams, 1991, 23).

This principle was resurrected in South Africa, which is laboring under a debt of $71 billion; it is expected to reach $110 billion by the turn of the century. Millions of South Africans lacking basic services such as housing, decent schools, and hospitals toil daily to pay back the billions of dollars borrowed by former apartheid regimes to oppress them. When apartheid fell in 1994, it left behind a debt that is now the second largest component of South African annual expenditure after education. In the 1997/98 budget, debt service payments were projected at $8.8 billion. But the Alternative Information and Development Center (AIDC), a non-governmental organization based in Cape Town says South Africans should not shoulder the burden and be penalized for the debts of a system that oppressed them. In June 1997, AIDC launched a campaign against this odious debt. "Our targets will include international financiers such as the World Bank and the IMF," says Brian Ashley of AIDC, who plans to make a submission on South Africa's "odious debts" to the Truth and Reconciliation Commission. The TRC's Christelle TerreBlanche says the Commission is willing to listen to the AIDC submission (*African Observer*, 15-21 May 1997, 7)

It is important to keep in mind that it is not only Africans who are refusing to repay debts they find objectionable. The U.S. Congress has over the years refused to pay the United Nations a debt of over $1.3 billion in past dues and overdue assessments. It claimed it would not pay for an inefficient and bloated U.N. bureaucracy. Eventually legislation was passed in June 1997 that would pay the United Nations $819 million (about two-thirds of the debt) provided the world body meets congressional demands to cut budget and staff members and restrict its activities. The bill will not allow payment of these debts unless these congressional demands have been met by the United Nations.

A note of caution should be sounded here. However odious a debt may be, it should not be unilaterally repudiated by Africans, as the late General I. K. Acheampong, a former Ghanaian head of state did. That action resulted in the cancellation of all foreign credit to Ghana. Instead, the case should be taken to the World Court at The Hague or the Court for International Settlement in Geneva. After negotiations perhaps Ghanaians, Congolese, and South Africans may end up paying a third of their foreign debts.

Perhaps the threat of repudiating or renegotiating odious debts would force the World Bank, IMF, and other foreign creditors to become more careful and discerning in loaning money to corrupt and illegitimate African governments. Foreign aid is not free but a "soft loan," granted at concessionary rates (usually less than 5 percent) with a grace period and a long term to maturity. Everybody knows that much of this aid seldom reaches or benefits needy Africans. The billions of dollars poured into Burundi, Liberia, Rwanda, Sierra Leone, Somalia, Zaire and other African countries never helped their people—nor saved their countries

from destruction. Yet, foreign creditors continue to pump in more aid
and credits, knowing full well that much of it will be stolen and end up
in overseas bank accounts, while the rest will be used to buttress the
repressive capacity of the tyrant in power or extend a lifeline to his
incompetent regime. And then when the country finally implodes, a few
blankets and high-protein biscuits will be parachuted in to the refugees,
who will subsequently be asked to repay the loans. This is an outrage.

CAVEAT EMPTOR

Those who are driven by the market imperative must live by its
vicissitudes. Risk is an inevitable component of market activity and
international transactions. Manufactured products can be defective;
suppliers may fail to deliver on time; stock prices can collapse; debtors
can default; and so on. These market risks cannot be eliminated
completely—even by the government. Hence, the ancient expression
caveat emptor: Buyer beware.

If one borrows from a loan shark, one should expect to be taken.
Conversely, if one loans money to a crook, one should expect to be
swindled. If, in spite of all repeated warnings, one stupidly insists on
dealing with loan sharks and crooks, then one must take responsibility
for it. Therefore, those who *knowingly* dish out loans to criminal African
governments should be prepared to take the risk of loss, default, and
repudiation. They are at liberty to throw away their money in Africa but
should not expect the suffering African people to pay for their indiscre-
tion. Loans to illegitimate governments constitute illegitimate debt that
is not repayable under international law.

In the final analysis, however, foreign creditors alone are not Africa's
commanding problem. Rather it is the vampire elite–controlled state.

There will be hope for Africa if its intellectuals and professionals stop
their crab-like bickering, uphold probity and integrity, and follow some
of the ten commandments just enunciated. Perhaps it would be fitting
to end this book with a tribute to Jon Qwelane, a black South African
columnist, who has also been waging a fearless crusade against corruption
and the misuse of public office and funds by those in positions of trust:

> South Africa is this continent's last real chance to disprove the belief that
> once blacks come to power, everything goes down the tubes: thriving
> economies seize up, self-enrichment at the expense of the masses becomes
> the order, and wholesale corruption replaces orderly governance every-

where. If here in South Africa we fail to get it right and opt to go "the way of Africa north of the Limpopo, chances are that the survival of sub-Saharan Africa will be so greatly endangered that we could very well face anew the specter of colonialism. In that scenario there will then be two major differences between the new and old forms of colonialism. First, it could well be we ourselves pleading to be colonized and, second, this time no one will be in a hurry to colonise the continent. So black professionals must now stand up and be heard. (The Johannesburg Star, 24 May 1997, 10)

But then again, highly educated black professionals tend to see oppression and wrong-doing—only when perpetrated by whites and colonialists. Let the moon shine brightly—*in all places in Africa into the twenty-first century!*

LITERATURE CITED

GOVERNMENT PUBLICATIONS

A Comprehensive Trade and Development Policy for the Countries of Africa. Report Submitted by the President of the United States to the Congress: Washington, D.C., 5 February 1996.

African Socialism and its Application to Planning in Kenya, 1965. Nairobi: Government of Kenya Sessional Paper no. 10.

Effectiveness of Foreign Development Assistance (1997). Washington, D. C.: Congressional Budget Office.

Parliamentary Debates: Official Report, 1997. Fourth Series, Volume 14, No. 8. Wednesday, 29 January 1997. Accra: Graphic Corporation.

Report of the Commission of Enquiry into Trade Malpractices in Ghana, 1965. Accra: Government Printer (Abrahams Report).

The Role of Foreign Aid in Development, 1997. Washington, D.C.: United States Congress.

The Seven-Year Development Plan, 1963/64–1969-70. Accra: Government Printer, 1964.

Verbatim Report of the Commission of Enquiry into Irregularities and Malpractices in the Grant of Import Licences, 1967. Accra: Government Printer (Ollennu Report).

OTHER SOURCES

Achebe, Chinua (1985). *The Trouble with Nigeria.* Enugu, Nigeria: Fourth Dimension Publishing.

Adams, Patricia (1991). *Odious Debts.* Toronto, Canada: Earthscan.

Ahmad, Naseem (1970). *Deficit Financing, Inflation, and Capital Formation: The Ghanaian Experience, 1960-65.* Munich: Weltforum-Verlag GmbH.

Ake, Claude (1991a). "As Africa Democratises," *Africa Forum* 1, no. 2: 13-18.

——— (1991b). "How Politics Underdevelops Africa," in *The Challenge of African Economic Recovery and Development,* ed. Adebayo

Adedeji, Owodumi Teriba, and Patrick Bugembe. Portland, OR: Cass.

Amoah, G. Y. (1988). *Groundwork of Government for West Africa.* Illorin, Nigeria: Gbenle Press.

Andreski, Stanislav (1969). *The African Predicament.* New York: Atherton Press.

Arhin, Kwame (1985). *Traditional Rule in Ghana: Past and Present.* Accra: Sedco Publishing Limited.

Ayittey, George B. N. (1985). "A Double Standard in Black and White," *The Wall Street Journal,* 22 July 1985, A12.

——— (1987). "Economic Atrophy in Black Africa," *The Cato Journal* 7, no. 1, 195-222.

——— (1988). "African Peasants and the Market Economy," *Humane Studies Review* 5, no. 3: 1-4.

——— (1989). "The Political Economy of Reform in Africa," *Journal of Economic Growth* 3, no. 3: 4-17.

——— (1991). *Indigenous African Institutions.* Dobbs Ferry, NY: Transnational Publishers.

——— (1992). *Africa Betrayed.* New York: St. Martin's Press.

Bandow, Doug (1986). "The First World's Misbegotten Economic Legacy to the Third World," *Journal of Economic Growth* 1, no. 4: 17.

Bascom, William (1984). *The Yoruba of Southwestern Nigeria.* Prospect Heights, IL: Waveland Press.

Bates, Robert H. (1981). *Markets and States in Tropical Africa.* Berkeley: University of California Press.

——— (1987). *Essays on the Political Economy of Rural Africa.* Berkeley: University of California Press.

Bauer, Peter T. (1967). *West African Trade.* New York: Kelley.

———(1972). *Dissent on Development.* Cambridge, MA: Harvard University Press.

———(1984). *Reality and Rhetoric.* Cambridge, MA: Harvard University Press.

Bayart, Jean Francois (1994). *The State in Africa: The Politics of the Belly.* London: Longman.

Bell, Morag (1986). *Contemporary Africa.* New York: John Wiley & Sons.

Berg, Elliott (1964). "Socialism and Economic Development In Africa," *Quarterly Journal of Economics,* 2, no. 3: 549.

Berkeley, Bill (1996). "An Encore for Chaos," *The Atlantic Monthly*, February 1996, 30.

Biddlecome, Peter (1994). *French Lessons in Africa: Travels with My Briefcase through French Africa*. London: Abacus.

Biersteker, Thomas J. (1987). *Multinationals, The State, and Control of the Nigerian Economy*. Princeton, NJ: Princeton University Press.

Boahen, A. A. (1986). *Topics in West African History*. New York: Longman.

Boahen, A. A. and J. B. Webster (1970). *History of West Africa*. New York: Praeger.

Boamah-Wiafe, Daniel (1993). *Africa: The Land, People, and Cultural Institutions*. Omaha, NB: Wisdom Publications.

Bohannan, Paul (1964). *Africa and Africans*. New York: Natural History Press.

Bohannan, Paul and Laura Bohannan (1968). *Tiv Economy*. London: Longmans.

Bohannan, Paul, and George Dalton, eds. (1962). *Markets In Africa*. Evanston, IN: Northwestern University Press.

Busia, Kofi Abrefa. (1951). *The Position of The Chief In the Modern Political System of Ashanti*. London: Oxford University Press.

————(1967). *Africa in Search of Democracy*. New York: Praeger.

Caldwell, Don (1989). *South Africa: The New Revolution*. Saxonwold, South Africa: Free Market Foundation of Southern Africa.

Carlston, Kenneth S. (1968). *Social Theory and African Tribal Organization*. Urbana, IL: University of Chicago Press.

Casely Hayford, J. E. (1911). *Gold Coast Native Institutions*. Excerpted in Langley, ed. (1979).

Chazan, Naomi, Robert Mortimer, John Ravenhill, and Donald Rothchild (1992). *Politics and Society In Contemporary Africa*. Boulder, CO: Lynne Riener Publishers.

Chenery, H. B. and A. M. Strout (1966). "Foreign Assistance and Economic Development." *American Economic Review*, 679-733.

Christensen, James Boyd (1952). "The Role of Proverbs in Fante Culture." *Africa* 28, no. 3: 232-43

Cohen, Ronald (1970). "The Kingship in Bornu," in Crowder and Ikime, eds. (1970).

Colson, Elizabeth (1953). "Social Control and Vengeance in Plateau Tonga Society," *Africa* 23, no. 3: 199-211.

Colson, Elizabeth and M. Gluckman, eds. (1951). *Seven Tribes of British Central Africa.* London: Oxford University Press.

Coquery-Vidrovitch, C. (1976). "The Political Economy of the African Peasantry and Modes of Production," in Gutkind and Wallerstein (1976).

Crowder, Michael and Obaro Ikime, eds. (1970). *West African Chiefs.* New York: Africana Publishing Co.

Daaku, Kwame Y. (1971). "Trade and Trading Patterns of the Akan in the 17th and 18th Centuries," in Meillassoux, ed. (1971).

Davidson, Basil. (1967). *African Kingdoms.* Chicago, IL: Time-Life Books.

——— (1970). *The African Genius: An Introduction to African Cultural ad Social History.* Boston, MA: Atlantic Monthly Press.

——— (1987). *The Lost Cities of Africa.* Boston, MA: Little, Brown.

Decalo, Samuel (1976). *Coups and Army Rule in Africa: Studies in Military Style.* New Haven, CT: Yale University Press.

Diop, Cheikh Anta (1987). *Pre-colonial Black Africa.* Westport: Lawrence Hill & Company.

Dumont, René (1966). *False Start in Africa.* London: Deutsch Limited.

Dupire, Marguerite (1962). "Trade and Markets in the Economy of the Nomadic Fulani of Niger (Bororo)," in Bohannan and Dalton, eds. (1962).

Eberstadt, Nicholas (1988). *Foreign Aid and American Purpose.* Washington, D.C.: American Enterprise Institute.

Ellis, George W. (1914). *Negro Culture in West Africa.* New York: Neale Publishing Company.

Falola, Toyin (1985). "Nigeria's Indigenous Economy." in Olaniyan, ed. (1985).

Field, M. J. (1940). *Social Organization of the Ga People.* Accra: Government of the Gold Coast Printing Press.

Fieldhouse, D. K. (1986). *Black Africa, 1945-80.* London: Allen & Unwin.

Fitch, Bob, and Mary Oppenheimer (1966). *Ghana: End of an Illusion.* New York: Monthly Review Press.

Forde, Daryll, and Jones, G. I. (1950). *The Igbo and Ibibio-Speaking Peoples of South-Eastern Nigeria.* London: International African Institute.

Galli, Rosemary E., and Jocelyn Jones (1987). *Guinea-Bissau: Politics, Economics, and Society.* London: Frances Pinter Publishers.

Garlick, Peter (1971). *African Traders and Economic Development.* Oxford: Clarendon.

Gibbs, James L. Jr., ed. (1965). *Peoples of Africa.* New York: Holt, Rinehart and Winston.

Glazier, Jack (1985). *Land and the Uses of Tradition Among the Mbeere of Kenya.* Lanham, MD: University Press of America.

Gluckman, Max. (1959). *Custom and Conflict in Africa.* Oxford: Basil Blackwell.

―― (1965). *Politics, Law, and Ritual in Tribal Society.* Oxford: Basil Blackwell.

Gray, Robert F. (1962). "Economic Exchange in a Sonjo Village," in Bohannan and Dalton, eds. (1962).

Gulliver, P. H. (1962). "The Evolution of Arusha Trade," in Bohannan and Dalton, eds. (1962).

Gutkind, Peter and I. Wallerstein (1976). *The Political Economy of Contemporary Africa.* Newbury Park, CA: Sage Publications.

Hagen, E. E. (1962). *On the Theory of Social Change.* Homewood, IL: Dorsey Press.

Helleiner, Gerald K. (1986). *Africa and the International Monetary Fund.* Washington, D.C.: IMF.

Herbst, Jeffrey (1993). *The Politics of Reform in Ghana.* Los Angeles, CA: University of California Press.

Herskovits, M.J. and Harwitz, M. eds. (1964). *Economic Transition in Africa.* Evanston, IL: Northwestern University Press.

Hill, Polly (1958). "Pledging of Cocoa Farms," unpublished research paper, Achimota, Ghana.

―― (1971). *Rural Capitalism in West Africa.* Cambridge: Cambridge University Press.

―― (1987). *Development Economics on Trial.* Cambridge: Cambridge University Press.

Hirschman, Albert O. (1958). *The Strategy of Development.* New Haven, CT: Yale University Press.

――(1965). "Obstacles to Development: A Classification and a Quasi-Vanishing Act," *Economic Development and Cultural Change.* 385.

――(1980). *Essays in Trespassing: Economics to Politics and Beyond.* Cambridge: Cambridge University Press.

Hitchens, Christopher (1994). "Africa Without Pity," *Vanity Fair,* November: 43-52.

Hodder, B. W. (1962). "The Yoruba Rural Market," in Bohannan and Dalton, eds. (1962).

Holmes, Kim R., Bryan T. Johnson, and Melanie Kirkpatrick, (1997). *Index of Economic Freedom.* Washington, D.C.: The Heritage Foundation and Dow Jones & Company.

Howell, T. A. (1972). *Ghana and Nkrumah.* New York: Facts On File.

Iliffe, John (1987). *The African Poor.* New York: Cambridge University Press.

Isichei, Elizabeth (1977). *History of West Africa Since 1800.* New York: Africana Publishing Company.

Joe, Evelyne Kinang (1996). "How Minister Farrakhan Betrayed Africa," *The Free Africa Review,* 1, no. 1.

Johns, Michael (1996). "The African Challenge," in *Finding Our Roots, Facing Our Future.* ed. Kim Holmes. Lanham, MD: Madison Books.

Johnson, Paul (1993). "Colonialism's Back—and Not a Moment Too Soon," *New York Times Magazine,* 18 April.

Kaplan, Robert (1992). "Continental Drift," *The New Republic,* 28 December, 15.

——— (1994). "The Coming Anarchy," *The Atlantic Monthly,* February, 44-76.

Kenyatta, Jomo (1938). *Facing Mount Kenya.* London: Secker and Warburg.

Killick, Tony (1978). *Development Economics in Action: A Study of Economic Policies in Ghana.* London: Heinemann.

Kluckhorn, Richard. (1962). "The Konso Economy of Southern Ethiopia," in Bohannan and Dalton, eds. (1962).

Koyama, Digby Sqhelo (1980). *Customary Law in a Changing Society.* Cape Town, South Africa: Juta Publishing Co.

Krauss, Melvyn (1983). *Development without Aid: Growth, Poverty and Government.* New York: Columbia University Press.

Krumm, Kathie L. (1985). "The External Debt of Sub-Saharan Africa: Origins, Magnitude, and Implications for Action," World Bank Staff Working Papers, no. 741.

Lamb, David (1983). *The Africans.* New York: Random House.

Lancaster, Carol and John Williamson, ed. (1986). *African Debt and Financing.* Washington, D.C.: Institute for International Economics.

Langley, J. Ayo, ed. (1979). *Ideologies of Liberation in Black Africa, 1856-1970.* London: Rex Collins.

Leibenstein, Harvey (1957). *Economic Backwardness and Economic Growth.* New York: Harper & Row.

Leith, Clark J. (1974). *Foreign Trade Regimes and Economic Development: Ghana.* New York: Columbia University Press.

LeVine, R. A. (1962). "Wealth and Power in Gusiiland," in Bohannan and Dalton, eds. (1962).

LeVine, Victor (1975). *Political Corruption: The Ghana Case.* Stanford, CA: Hoover Institution Press.

Lewis, W. A. (1954). "Economic Development with Unlimited Supplies of Labor," *Manchester School of Economics.*

——— (1962). *Economic Problems of Development in Restless Nations: A Study of World Tensions and Development.* London: Allen & Unwin.

Libby, Ronald T. (1987). *The Politics of Economic Power in Southern Africa.* Princeton, NJ: Princeton University Press.

Lloyd, P. C., ed. (1964). *The New Elites of Tropical Africa.* London: Oxford University Press.

Lofchie, M. D., ed. (1971). *The State of the Nations: Constraints on Development in Independent Africa.* Berkeley: University of California Press.

Louw, Leon, and Frances Kendall (1987). *After Apartheid: The Solution.* Los Angeles: Institute for Contemporary Studies.

Luke, David Fashole (1995). "Building Indigenous Entrepreneurial Capacity: Trends and Issues," in *Development Management in Africa: Toward Dynamism, Empowerment and Entrepreneurship,* ed. Sadig Rasheed and David Fashole Luke. Boulder, CO: Westview Press.

Manning, Patrick (1988). *Francophone Sub-Saharan Africa, 1880-1985.* New York: Cambridge University Press.

Maren, Michael (1997). *The Road to Hell: The Ravaging Effects of Foreign Aid and International Charity.* New York: The Free Press.

Marshall, John (1973). "Hunting Among the Kalahari Bushmen," in Skinner (1973).

Martin, Phyllis M., and Patrick O'Meara, eds. (1986). *Africa.* Bloomington: Indiana University Press.

Matthews, Ronald (1966). *The African Powder-Keg.* London: Bodley Head.

Maylam, Paul. (1986). *A History of the African People of South Africa: From the Early Iron Age to the 1970s.* Cape Town: David Philip.

Mazrui, Ali (1986). *The Africans.* London: BBC Publications.

McCall, Daniel F. (1962). "The Koforidua Market," in Bohannan and Dalton, eds. (1962).

McDermott, Jim (1996). Statement by Jim McDermott before the Subcommittee on Trade Committee, Ways and Means, U.S. Trade Policy with Africa. Washington, D.C.: U.S. Congress, 1 August, 1996.

McKinnon, Ronald (1964), "Foreign Exchange Constraint in Economic Development and Efficient Aid Allocation," *Economic Journal.*

Meillassoux, Claude (1962). "Social and Economic Factors Affecting Markets in Guro Land," in Bohannan and Dalton, eds. (1962).

Meillassoux, Claude, ed. (1971). *The Development of Indigenous Trade and Markets in West Africa.* Oxford: Oxford University Press.

Mensah Sarbah, John. (1979). *Fanti Customary Laws, 1897.* Excerpted in Langley, (1979).

Michaels, Marguerite (1993). "Retreat From Africa," *Foreign Affairs.*

Miracle, Marvin P. (1962). "African Markets and Trade in the Copperbelt," in Bohannan and Dalton, eds. (1962).

—— (1971). "Capitalism, Capital Markets, and Competition in West African Trade," in Meillassoux, ed. (1971).

Morton, James (1994). *The Poverty of Nations: The Aid Dilemma at the Heart of Africa.* New York: I. B. Taurus Publishers.

Mussa-Nda, Mgumbu (1988). "A Greater Role for Local Development Strategies," *Regional Development Dialogue,* 9, no. 2: 1-11.

Mutharika, A. Peter (1995). "The Role of International Law in the 21st Century: An African Perspective," *Fordham International Law Journal,* 18, no. 5: 1706-19.

Newbury, Colin W. (1971). "Prices and Profitability in Early Nineteenth Century West African Trade," in Meillassoux, ed. (1971).

Nkrumah, Kwame (1957). *Ghana: An Autobiography.* London: Nelson.

——(1963). *Africa Must Unite.* New York: International Publishers.

——(1968). *Handbook of Revolutionary Warfare.* London: Panaf Publishers.

——(1969). *Dark Days in Ghana.* London: Panaf Publishers.

——(1973). *Revolutionary Path.* New York: International Publishers.

Nurkse, R. (1953). *Problems of Capital Formation in Under-Developed Countries.* New York: Oxford University Press.

Nyang'oro, Julius E. and Timothy Shaw, eds. (1992). *Beyond Structural Adjustment in Africa: The Political Economy of Sustainable and Democratic Development.* New York: Praeger.

Nye, Joseph S. (1967). "Corruption and Political Development: A Cost-Benefit Analysis." *American Political Science Review* 61, no. 2: 417-27.

Nyerere, Julius K. (1962). *Ujaama: The Basis of African Socialism.* Dar es Salaam: Government Printer.

——— (1966). *Freedom and Unity.* London: Oxford University Press.

Obasanjo, Olusengun (1988). *African Perspectives: Myth and Realities.* Washington, D.C.: Council on Foreign Relations.

Oguah, Benjamin Ewuku (1984). "African and Western Philosophy: A Study," in Wright (1984).

Olaniyan, Richard, ed. (1985). *Nigerian History and Culture.* London: Longman Group.

Olivier, N. J. J. (1969). "The Governmental Institutions of the Bantu Peoples of Southern Africa" in *Recueils de la Societies Jean Bodin XII.* Bruxelles: Fondation Universitaire de Belgique.

Pahl, Ronald (1995). "The Image of Africa in Our Classrooms," *Social Studies.*

Pickett, James, and Hans Singer (1990). *Towards Economic Recovery in Sub-Saharan Africa.* New York: Routledge.

Republic of Tanzania (1967). *The Arusha Declaration and TANU's Policy on Socialism and Self-Reliance.* Dar es Salaam: Government Printer.

Robinson, Ronald ed. (1971). *Developing the Third World: The Experience of the 1960s.* Cambridge: Cambridge University Press.

Rothstein, Robert (1977). *The Weak in the World of the Strong.* New York: Columbia University Press.

Ruddy, Frank (1991). "The Kindness of Strangers: How Foreign Aid Perpetuates Africa's Agony," *Foreign Service Journal.*

Sandbrook, Richard (1993). *The Politics of Africa's Stagnation.* New York: Cambridge University Press.

Schapera, I. (1953). *The Tswana.* London: International African Institute.

——— (1955). *A Handbook of Tswana Law and Custom.* London: Oxford University Press.

——— (1957). "The Sources of Law in Tswana Tribal Courts: Legislation and Precedent," *Journal of African Law* 1, no. 3: 150-162.

Schneider, Harold K. (1986). "Traditional African Economies," in Martin and O'Meara eds.

Skinner, Elliott P. (1961). "Intergenerational Conflict Among the Mossi: Father and Son," *Journal of Conflict Resolution* 5, no. 1: 55-60.

——— (1962). "Trade and Markets among the Mossi People," in Bohannan and Dalton, eds.

——— (1964). "West African Economic Systems," in Herskovits and Harwitz, eds. (1964).

——— (1973). *Peoples and Cultures of Africa.* New York: Doubleday/ Natural History Press.

Smith, Michael G. (1962). "Exchange and Marketing among the Hausa," in Bohannan and Dalton, eds. (1962).

Soyinka, Wole (1996). *The Open Sore of a Continent.* New York: Oxford University Press.

Steel, W. F. (1972). "Import-Substitution and Excess Capacity in Ghana," *Oxford University Papers.*

Tardits, Claudine, and Claude Tardits (1962). "Traditional Market Economy in South Dahomey" in Bohannan and Dalton (1962).

Taylor, D. R. Fraser, and Fiona Mackenzie (1992). *Development from Within: Survival in Rural Africa.* New York: Routledge.

Ungar, Sanford J. (1985). *Africa: The People and Politics of an Emerging Continent.* New York: Simon and Schuster.

Uphoff, Norman T. (1970). *Ghana's Experience in Using External Aid for Development.* Berkeley: University of California Press.

U.S. AID (1989). *Development and the National Interest: U.S. Economic Assistance into the 21st Century.* Washington, D.C.: Department of State.

Vansina, Jan (1962). "Trade and Markets Among the Kuba," in Bohannan and Dalton, eds. (1962).

——— (1975). *Kingdoms of the Savannah.* Madison: University of Wisconsin Press.

——— (1978). *The Children of Woot: A History of the Kuba.* Madison: University of Wisconsin Press.

Vaughan, James H. (1986). "Population and Social Organization," in Martin and O'Meara, eds. (1986).

Wanyande, Peter (1988). "Democracy and the One-Party State: The African Experience," in Walter O. Oyugi et al., eds., *Democratic Theory and Practice in Africa.* Portsmouth, NH: Heinemann.

Wherlin, Herbert (1973). "The Consequences of Corruption: The Ghanaian Experience," *Political Science Quarterly* 88: 71-85.

Wheetham, Edith, and Jean Currie eds. (1967). *Readings in Applied Economics of Africa.* Cambridge: Cambridge University Press.

Whitaker, Jennifer (1988). *How Can Africa Survive?* New York: Harper & Row.

White, E. Frances (1987). *Sierra Leone's Settler Women Traders.* Ann Arbor: University of Michigan Press.

Wickins, Peter (1981). *An Economic History of Africa.* Oxford: Oxford University Press.

Wilson, Peter J. (1967). "Tsimihety Kinship And Descent," *Africa* 37, no. 2: 133-153.

World Bank (1984). *Toward Sustained Development in Sub-Saharan Africa.* Washington, D.C.: World Bank.

——— (1986). *Financing Adjustment With Growth in Sub-Saharan Africa, 1986-90.* Washington, D.C.: World Bank.

——— (1989). *Sub-Saharan Africa: From Crisis to Self-Sustainable Growth.* Washington, D.C.: World Bank.

———. *World Development Report.* New York: Oxford University Press, annually.

——— (1995). *Ghana: Is Growth Sustainable?* Operations Evaluations Department. Report No. 99. Washington, D.C.: World Bank Publications.

World Bank/UNDP (1989). *African Economic and Financial Data.* Washington, D.C.: World Bank.

Wright, Richard A., ed. (1984). *African Philosophy: An Introduction.* Lanham: University Press of America.

Yelpaala, Kojo (1983). "Circular Arguments and Self-Fulfilling Definitions: 'Statelessness' and the Dagaaba," *History in Africa* 10: 349-385.

Yotopoulos Pan A. and Jeffrey B. Nugent (1976). *Economics of Development.* New York: Harper & Row.

Zinsmeister, Karl (1987). "East African Experiment: Kenyan Prosperity and Tanzanian Decline," *Journal of Economic Growth,* 2. no. 2: 28.

PERIODICALS

Africa Forum, a private quarterly magazine published in New York by Olusegun Obasanjo (ex-head of state of Nigeria).

African Guardian, a private monthly magazine published in Lagos, Nigeria.

Africa Insider, a monthly subscription newsletter published in Temple Heights, Maryland.

The African Letter, a private newspaper published weekly by Africans in Toronto, Canada.

African Mirror, a private monthly magazine published by Africans in Silver Spring, Maryland.

African News Weekly, a weekly newspaper published by Africans in Charlotte, North Carolina.

The African Observer, a private newspaper published bi-weekly by Africans in New York.

Africa Recovery, a quarterly publication of the United Nations Development Program (UNDP) on prospects of Africa's economic recovery.

Africa Report, a monthly magazine published by the African American Institute in New York.

African Voices, a quarterly newsletter published by the United States Agency for International Development in Washington, D.C.

Akasanoma, a weekly newspaper published in London, covering mainly Ghanaian political affairs.

The Atlantic Monthly, a private, monthly magazine published in Boston.

Business Week, a private magazine published weekly in the United States.

Christian Messenger, a private Presbyterian Church monthly, published in Accra, Ghana.

Daily Graphic, name changed to *People's Graphic,* a daily newspaper, published in Accra, Ghana, owned by the government of Ghana.

Daily Nation, a government-owned paper published in Nairobi, Kenya.

Daily News, is an independent daily published in Pretoria, South Africa.

Daily Sketch, a private daily published in Nigeria.

The Economist, a private weekly published in London.

Financial Times, a private weekly published in London.

Ghana Drum, a monthly newsletter published privately for the Ghanaian community in the Washington, D.C., metropolitan area.

The Ghanaian Times, a daily newspaper published in Accra, Ghana, owned by the government of Ghana.

The Independent, a private daily published in London.

Index on Censorship, a private monthly magazine published in London and dedicated to the defense of freedom of expression.

Insight, a private monthly magazine published in Washington, D.C.

International Health and Development, is a publication by the non-profit organization, Institute For International Health and Development in conjunction with The Catholic University of America. Both are based in Washington, DC.

The Johannesburg Star, is an independent daily published in Johannesburg, South Africa

Juluka, a monthly newsletter published in Bethesda, Maryland, for mostly white South African émigrés.

National Concord, a private daily published in Lagos, Nigeria.

New African, a private monthly published in London.

New African Yearbook, a sister publication of *New African*—an annual update of major events in each African country.

New Internationalist, a private monthly magazine published in London, Britain.

Newsweek, a private weekly magazine published in the United States.

The New York Times, a private daily published in New York.

The Nigerian Tribune, a private daily published in Lagos.

Punch, a private weekly published in Kumasi, Ghana.

South, a private monthly published in London.

Star Business Report, is a weekly supplement published by *The Johannesburg Star*.

The Wall Street Journal, private daily published in New York.

The Washington Post, a private daily published in Washington, DC; liberal.

The Washington Times, a private daily published in Washington, D.C.; conservative.

Time, private weekly magazine published in United States.

West Africa, a private weekly, published in London.

World Development Forum, a news bulletin by Hunger Project, a nonprofit organization based in San Francisco.

INDEX